EARLY PREDICTION AND
PREVENTION OF CHILD ABUSE
A HANDBOOK

WILEY SERIES

in

CHILD CARE AND PROTECTION

Series Editors

Kevin D. Browne
School of Psychology
The University of Birmingham, UK

Margaret A. Lynch
Newcomen Centre
Guy's Hospital, London, UK

The Child Care and Protection Series furthers the understanding of health, psychosocial and cultural factors that influence the development of the child. It also examines early interactions and the formation of relationships in and outside the family. This international series covers the psychological as well as the physical welfare of the child and considers protection from all forms of maltreatment.

The series is essential reading for all professionals concerned with the welfare and protection of children and their families. All books in the series have a practice orientation with referenced information from theory and research.

Other books in the series:

EARLY PREDICTION AND PREVENTION OF CHILD ABUSE
A HANDBOOK

Edited by

Kevin Browne
School of Psychology, University of Birmingham, UK

Helga Hanks
*Department of Clinical and Health Psychology, St James's
University Hospital, Leeds, UK*

Peter Stratton
School of Psychology, University of Leeds, UK

Catherine Hamilton
School of Psychology, University of Birmingham, UK

JOHN WILEY & SONS, LTD

Other Wiley Editorial Offices

John Wiley & Sons Inc., 111 River Street, Hoboken, NJ 07030, USA

Jossey-Bass, 989 Market Street, San Francisco, CA 94103-1741, USA

Wiley-VCH Verlag GmbH, Boschstr. 12, D-69469 Weinheim, Germany

John Wiley & Sons Australia Ltd, 33 Park Road, Milton, Queensland 4064, Australia

John Wiley & Sons (Asia) Pte Ltd, 2 Clementi Loop #02-01, Jin Xing Distripark, Singapore
129809

John Wiley & Sons Canada Ltd, 22 Worcester Road, Etobicoke, Ontario, Canada M9W 1L1

British Library Cataloguing in Publication Data

A catalogue record for this book is available from the British Library

ISBN   0-471-49122-5

Typeset in 10 / 12pt Palatino by TechBooks, New Delhi, India
Printed and bound in Great Britain by TJ International Ltd, Padstow, Cornwall
This book is printed on acid-free paper responsibly manufactured from sustainable forestry
in which at least two trees are planted for each one used for paper production.

CONTENTS

ABOUT THE EDITORS

Kevin Browne, BSc, MSc, MEd, PhD, MIBiol, AFBPS, is a Chartered Forensic Psychologist and Chartered Biologist. He is employed by the School of Psychology at the University of Birmingham, as Professor of Forensic and Family Psychology. He has been researching family violence and child maltreatment for over 22 years and has published extensively on these subjects. He co-edited the BASPCAN Wiley Journal *Child Abuse Review* between 1992 and 1999. His most recent book was entitled *Preventing Family Violence,* which was co-authored with Professor Martin Herbert and published by Wiley (1997). He is currently an Executive Councillor of the International Society for the Prevention of Child Abuse and Neglect (ISPCAN) and is Advisor/Consultant on Child Protection to the World Health Organization Regional Office for Europe.

Helga Hanks, BSc, MSc, DipPsych, AFBPsS, is a Chartered Clincial Psychologist and UKCP registered Psychotherapist and Family Therapist. She is a Consultant Clinical Psychologist and works in the Community Paediatric Department at St James's University Hospital in Leeds and is Clinical Director at the University of Leeds Family Therapy & Research Centre (LFTRC). She is also an Honorary Senior Lecturer in the School of Psychology. Over the past 20 years, her work with families and children who are failing to thrive or who have been sexually abused has become internationally known. She has taught and trained on these subjects in many countries around the world and was also involved in founding the Expert Witness Group (EWG), which developed guidelines for expert witnesses in child-abuse cases. She has published and researched widely with eminent paediatricians, her most recent book being *Child Abuse and Neglect,* 2nd edition, co-authored with Chris Hobbs and Jane Wynne (1999), published by Churchill Livingstone.

Peter Stratton, BSc, PhD, Dip Psychotherapy, is a Chartered Psychologist and Fellow of the British Psychological Society. He is a UKCP accredited family therapist and supervisor, and Full (professional) member of the Market Research Society. He is Senior Lecturer in Developmental Psychology and Family Therapy at Leeds University, and Director of the Leeds Family Therapy and Research Centre (LFTRC), which houses four training courses leading to an MSc in systemic family therapy. He is also Managing Director of The Psychology Business Ltd, a research agency providing rigorous qualitative research to business/industry that provides information on family decision processes. Since 1990, he has been editor of *Human Systems: The Journal of Systemic Consultation and Management* and was joint-editor of *Journal of Reproductive and Infant Psychology* between 1982 and 1990. His most recent book is *Attributions in Action*, co-authored with Munton, Silvester and Hanks (1999), published by Wiley.

Catherine Hamilton, BSc, PhD, is a Chartered Forensic Psychologist and Lecturer in Applied Psychology at the School of Psychology, University of Birmingham, where she acts as Course Tutor for the Diploma/Masters in Applied Social Learning Theory and Counselling. Previously, she worked for Birmingham Social Services Department undertaking care proceeding assessments and working in a residential unit for families where child maltreatment has occurred or is suspected. Catherine has published a number of papers and book chapters related to recurrent child maltreatment, domestic violence, and the link between child maltreatment and offending behaviour. She is currently on the committee of the West Midlands branch of the British Association for the Study and Prevention of Child Abuse and Neglect (BASPCAN) and is a member of the British Association of Behavioural and Cognitive Psychotherapies (BABCP).

Contributors

Dr Tony Beech   School of Psychology, University of Birmingham, Birmingham B15 2TT, UK

Professor Jay Belsky   Director, Institute for the study of children, families and social issues, Birkbeck College, University of London, 7 Bedford Square, London WC1B 3RA, UK

Dr Arnon Bentovim   Department of Psychological Medicine, The Hospital for Sick Children, 34 Gt Ormond Street Hospital, London WC1N 3JH, UK

Dr Lucy Berliner   Sexual Assault Center, Harborview Medical Center, 1401 East Jefferson, 4th Floor, Seattle WA 98122, USA

Dr Michelle Bosquet   Institute of Child Development, University of Minnesota, 51 East River Road, Minneapolis, MN 55455, USA

Professor Kevin Browne   School of Psychology, University of Birmingham, Edgbaston, Birmingham B15 2TT, UK

Dr Roger Bullock   Department of Health, Dartington Research Centre, Warren House, Dartington, Devon TQ9 6EG, UK

Dr Warren Cann   Victorian Parenting Centre 230 Rae St North Fitzroy Vic 3068, Australia

Dr Alissa Chung   North Shore Family Psychiatry, 1601 Sherman Avenue, Suite 230, Evanston IL 602014, USA

Dr Susan Creighton   NSPCC, 42 Curtain Road, London EC2A 3NH, UK

Dr Pat Crittenden   The Family Relations Institute, 9481 SW 147 St, Miami, Florida FL 33176 USA

Dr Deborah Daro   The Chapin Hall Center for Children, University of Chicago, 1313 E 60th St, Chicago IL 60637, USA

Dr Louise Dixon   School of Psychology, University of Birmingham, Edgbaston, Birmingham B15 2TT, UK

Dr Sylvia Duncan Baker and Duncan Family Consultancy, Ashwood Centre, Stonemason's Court, Cemetery Pales, Brookwood, Woking, Surrey, GU 24 OBL, UK

Dr John Eckenrode Department of Human Development and Family Studies, Cornell University, Ithaca, New York, USA

Professor Byron Egeland Institute of Child Development, University of Minnesota, 51 East River Road, Minneapolis MN 55455, USA

Dr Louise Falshaw Offending Behaviour Unit, HM Prison Service, Abell House, John Islip Street, London SW1P 4LH, UK

Dr Dawn Fisher Llanarth Court Psychiatric Hospital, Llanarth, Raglan Gwent NP5 2YD, UK

Dr Caroline Friendship Offending Behaviour Unit, HM Prison Service, Abell House, John Islip Street, London SW1P 4LH, UK

Dr Danya Glaser Department of Psychological Medicine, Great Ormond Street Hospital for Sick Children and Institute of Child Health, Great Ormond Street, London WC1N 3JH, UK

Dr David Gough Social Science Research Unit, Institute of Education, London University, 18 Woburn Square, London WC1H 0NR, UK

Dr Catherine Hamilton School of Psychology, University of Birmingham, Edgbaston, Birmingham B15 2TT, UK

Dr Helga Hanks Department of Clinical & Health Psychology, Ashley Wing Extension St James's University Hospital Leeds LS9 7TF, UK

Dr Charles Henderson Department of Human Development and Family Studies, Cornell University, Ithaca, New York, USA

Professor Martin Herbert Department of Clinical Psychology, University of Exeter, Church Lane, Heavitree, Exeter EX2 5SH, UK

Dr Chris Hobbs Department of Community Paediatrics, St James's University Hospital, Beckett Street Leeds LS9 7TF, UK

Professor Dorota Iwaniec Department of Social Work, The Queen's University of Belfast, 7 Lennoxvale, Belfast BT9 5BY, UK

Professor Richard Krugman Dean Health Science Center, School of Medicine, University of Colorado, 4200 East 69th Avenue, Box C290, Denver, CO 80262, USA

Dr Michael Little Department of Health Dartington Research Centre, Warren House, Dartington, Devon TQ9 6EG, UK and Chapin Hall Center for Children, University of Chicago, 1313 E 60th St Chicago, IL 60637, USA

Dr Margaret A. Lynch Newcomen Centre, Guy's, King's and St Thomas School of Medicine, St Thomas Street, London SE1 9RT, UK

Prof David Olds Director, School of Medicine, Prevention Research Center for Family and Child Health, University of Colorado Health Sciences Center, 1825 Marion St, Denver, CO 80218, USA

Dr Vivien Prior   Behavioural Sciences Unit, Institute of Child Health and Great Ormond Street Hospital, 30 Guildford Street, London WC1N 1EH, UK

Dr Peter Reder   Child and Family Consultation Centre, West London Mental Health Trust, 1 Wolverton Gardens, London W6 7DQ, UK

Prof Matthew Sanders   Director, Parenting and Family Support Centre, School of Psychology, The University of Queensland, Brisbane, Old 4029, Australia

Mrs Alice Sluckin   Department of Psychology, Family Violence Research Group, University of Leicester, Leicester LE1 7RH, UK

Dr Peter Stratton   Director, Leeds Family Therapy and Research Centre, School of Psychology, University of Leeds, Leeds LS2 9JT, UK

Dr David Thornton   Sandridge Secure Treatment Center, PO Box 700, Mauston WI 53948, USA

Dr Jane Wynne   Department of Community Paediatrics, Belmont House, 3/5 Belmont Grove, Leeds General Infirmary, Leeds LS2 9NP, UK

FOREWORD

The modern era in the study of child abuse and neglect is slightly over 40 years old. During this time, professionals of many disciplines throughout the world have worked long and hard to elucidate answers to critical questions for the field. Earliest among these was how to make the diagnosis of a battered child, how best to intervene to keep the child's family from continuing the practice, and how to prevent the abuse from happening in the first place. In my own view, much of the progress made in addressing the problem of physical abuse and neglect occurred within the first two decades of work in the field, and many of the problems faced by the child protection systems in developed countries can be associated with the rediscovery of sexual abuse of children over the last 20 years. Our societies have had a huge tolerance for the physical abuse of children without invoking criminal sanction, but have a zero tolerance for the sexual abuse of children. This dichotomous approach has greatly complicated the task for child welfare professionals who have attempted to intervene and treat abusive and neglectful families. It is hard to be therapeutic while a law enforcement colleague is reading the subject his or her "right to remain silent". Nevertheless, we have learned a great deal about the recognition of both physical and sexual abuse of children, a fair amount about how to treat them and something about violent and sexual offenders—their motivation and their control. Most impressively, we have had significant success in the realm of prevention of several forms of child maltreatment.

The child protection systems in the Commonwealth nations and the United States of America have a lot in common, and are also quite different. Reporting of suspected abuse is not mandatory in the UK; it is in Australia and the USA. Most systems seem to have been overwhelmed by the challenges of dealing with more cases than can be handled comfortably, and all systems have struggled with the extraordinary challenges posed by accurately recognizing abused and neglected children, prosecuting their abusers and sorting out how to assure the child's safety if the perpetrator is a member of the family (particularly if the criminal prosecution fails).

This book is a wonderful compilation of chapters written by internationally known authors from a variety of disciplines. Most have been working in the field for quite some time and have a great deal of clinical experience. The theme is prevention—primary, secondary and tertiary prevention. Further, the editors have done a nice job of summarizing and introducing each of the four sections of the book. All those who work in the field of child maltreatment all over the world will benefit from a careful reading of this book. It will help us in our practice and with our policy development no matter where in the world we may be.

Richard D. Krugman, MD
Professor of Pediatrics and Dean
University of Colorado School of Medicine
Denver, Colorado, USA

Editors' Preface

Kevin Browne, Helga Hanks, Peter Stratton and
Catherine Hamilton

This Handbook arose out of the necessity and wish to update and build on the comprehensive review of research and practice commissioned in *Early Prediction and Prevention of Child Abuse and Neglect* (Browne et al., 1988). The original volume, published 14 years ago, successfully brought together experts from various disciplines to share their knowledge and experience on best practices to prevent child maltreatment before it occurs. However, it was recognised that primary prevention (universal services aimed at the whole population) and secondary prevention (targeting services to those most at risk) are not possible in every case. Hence, the last Section of the original volume also discussed tertiary prevention (intervention following maltreatment). Given how successful this formula was to researchers and practitioners alike, it was felt to be important to repeat the process and discuss the advances in understanding, predicting and preventing child maltreatment over the past decade. It is not the intention to repeat the information published in the original volume, which is still being widely used, but rather to expand and modernise the information available. Therefore, this Handbook presents the most progressive approaches to the early prediction and prevention of child abuse and neglect by the most experienced professionals in the field of child protection, many of whom readers will recognise from their earlier contributions.

Section I (on "Prevalence and Prediction") provides some evidence that the prevalence of child maltreatment has marginally decreased over the past decade for those countries which have collected regular data and provided child protection services on the basis of this information (e.g., USA, UK). However, similar trends have not been observed for fatal child abuse and neglect (child homicide and manslaughter). This may be related to the fact that most deaths from child maltreatment occur to children in infancy, before it can be easily predicted and child protection services can intervene effectively (See Reder & Duncan, Chapter 2). As a result, a more holistic approach towards violence to children has been proposed. In England and Wales, this is consistent with the implementation of the new

Framework for Assessment of Children in Need and their Families (Department of Health et al, 2000). The limitation of this approach to predicting and preventing child abuse and neglect relates to the fact that the framework is seen as primarily aimed at social work assessments, undertaken once a family has become a concern.

On an international level, the World Health Organization (1998, 1999) recommends that health professionals take a public health approach to early child maltreatment. This regards child protection as a component of primary care services for child health and development that begins with good perinatal care and the promotion of emotional bonds. Nevertheless, best practice for prediction and prevention involves multi-disciplinary teamwork between health professionals, social workers, police, teachers and many others, as exemplified in *Working Together to Safeguard Children* (Department of Health, 1999). Indeed, a multi-sector public health approach is consistent with the ecological model of child health and development first proposed by Bronfenbrenner (1979) more than two decades ago.

In practice, prevention is best organised into a tiered system of child protection where: firstly, every family receives some support; secondly, those families with risk factors receive targeted services as well as universal support; thirdly, those families where a parent/caregiver has been identified as maltreating a child receive specialist services, for both victim and perpetrator, in addition to the targeted and universal support they may already have access to.

Governments do have the ultimate responsibility for developing and enhancing services for children and families through changes in policy, planning and resource allocation. Professionals at "the sharp end" are only able to carry out programmes to protect children if governments acknowledge and act upon their responsibility for optimal child protection, health and development. Many countries have proposed that a single government department and minister be responsible for children's services. For example, both Scotland and Wales have appointed a "Minister for Children". However in some countries, for example England, there are still many departments (ie: Home Office, Justice, Education, Health and Social Services) who all deal with a particular aspect of children's needs. This limits the co-ordination of services.

Early prevention involves changing families, community institutions and society so that maltreatment of children is both unacceptable and unlikely, and offering intensive support from pregnancy and birth to those families most at risk. Advances in primary and secondary prevention are the focus of Section II. It is in this area that Bronfenbrenner's (1979) ecological model of the influences on child development has most direct relevance. Figure 1 is an adaptation of the Model, outlining the macro, exo and micro contexts in which child protection takes place (see Figure 1). The widest macro context draws attention to global economic, political and military strategies that impinge on children and their families. The suffering of refugee children and children caught up in war zones and civil armed conflict is a clear demonstration of the need to take a world-wide perspective on the prevention of child maltreatment but is beyond the scope of this current volume. Within the more micro contexts described in this book, the damage of dysfunctional parenting for the children's health and development is recognised. Nevertheless, it is also acknowledged that the parent/caregiver's capacity to meet the needs of their child is partly a consequence of the social and environmental contexts in which the family lives. Such considerations demonstrate that a greater responsibility of care for children *is* required at all levels (Stratton, 1988). Primary and secondary prevention means more than just interventions to control parents by statutory health, social and law enforcement services.

It has been argued that the economic burden of child maltreatment more than justifies financial investment into services that prevent violence to children (National Commission of Enquiry in the Prevention of Child Abuse, 1996). Of course, this is not to mention the immense human cost to children psychologically and physically, which is sometimes forgotten in the auditing process. Nevertheless the cost-effectiveness of preventative strategies, such as positive parenting programmes, differ when they are applied universally to all (primary prevention) or targeted to those most in need (secondary prevention). There is a myth that universal services are more expensive and less effective. However, advances in the last decade have shown that this is not necessarily the case (see Browne & Herbert, 1997). Targeted services are only effective if families can be correctly predicted and identified as in need and at risk. Research and clinical practice evidence have shown that targeting the right families is by no means straightforward (see Browne, 1995; Hamilton & Browne, Chapter 3). There is a need for re-focusing intervention to be more proactive rather than reactive. To some extent this involves putting evidence-based research into practice and incorporating this principle into social and health policies on child protection. The contributions to Section II show that we have made considerable "advances in primary and secondary prevention". While not under-estimating the need for more sound research and clinically based knowledge, the capability to provide successful universal interventions and cost-effective targeted services is now apparent.

Perhaps one of the most significant advances over the past decade has been in "Helping children and families affected by child abuse", the focus of Section III. The traumatic impact of child abuse and neglect has now been well documented (e.g., Briere, 1992; Bentovim, 1992), whilst the recent documentation of the extent of neurological atrophy in maltreated infants is both disturbing and illuminating (Glaser & Balbernie, 2001). Hence, help for the family must begin early in the child's life and cover emotional, as well as sexual and physical, safety. It is now recognised that intergenerational continuity of dysfunctional parenting is common (see Crittenden, Chapter 7 and Egeland et al, Chapter 13), although it is not always expressed in physically or sexually violent ways. Therefore the major advantage of therapeutic support for children and their families is breaking the cycle of dysfunctional parenting and potential violence. Despite a lack of provision and long waiting-lists that limit the number of maltreated children who can receive support (Prior et al., 1997), all victims are likely to benefit from therapeutic intervention to help alleviate their traumatic consequences. For those most at risk, it reduces the chances of repeat abuse by the same perpetrator or revictimisation by different perpetrators through empowerment and promoting resilience among victimised children (Hamilton & Browne, 1998). One of the most important outcomes of appropriate interventions for children is that it may reduce the possibility of antisocial acts upon others.

An example of the way that societal assumptions geared to adult concerns can make tertiary prevention more difficult arises when treating families where a child is failing to thrive without organic cause. Western nations have become rightly concerned by the fact that too many children and adults are obese. However, in

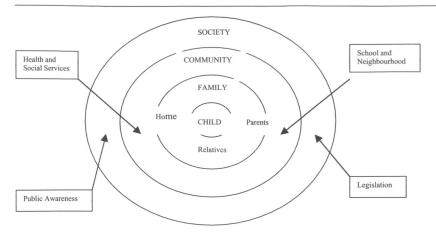

FIGURE 1 Ecological model of Child Protection, adaption from Bronfenbrenner, 1979

the effort to overcome this problem it seems to have forgotten that there are many children who are failing to thrive. Attitudes, beliefs and, at times, obsession in modern society aspire to thinness and a culture has grown up around the belief that thin is beautiful. For young parents this is a powerful pressure to adhere to restricted diets which are adequate for adults but do not suit the needs of growing infants and children. Children who are failing to thrive non-organically, need high calorie foods and love. Since the problem stretches across the social scale, parents need education and support to help their children to achieve their optimal growth and emotional capacity. The consequences for children with non-organic failure to thrive are considerable physically, developmentally and psychologically (Iwaniec, 1995; Hobbs et al., 1999). The chapters in Section III of this book deal with parenting issues and intergenerational transmission of all forms of abuse and describe a great number of programmes which, backed up by sound theoretical assumptions and research, might help to give children and parents a chance to make things better. Even if these interventions have a limited effect in this generation, there is the hope that they will have a cumulative effect to prevent abuse in the next.

The unique addition to this book on early prediction and prevention of child abuse is Section IV on "Working with Offenders". This reflects the growing emphasis on therapeutic programmes for violent and/or sexual offenders that recognise the need to prevent child maltreatment at the source. Typically, this deals with interventions offered to adult perpetrators in order to prevent re-offending against children. However, it is also important to recognise that at least a third of offenders begin to engage in antisocial behaviour against other children in adolescence or even earlier and that one factor in the development of offending behaviour may be earlier victimisation (Elliott et al., 1995). Hence, treatment programmes for juvenile sexual offenders have recently been developed and interventions with violent young people more firmly established (Calder et al., 2001). As a general principle, all victims and all offenders require intervention.

However, despite the advances since the late 1980's, there is still no consistent approach to child protection at a national or international level. Despite the UN Convention on the Rights of the Child (UN, 1989), which all countries with the exception of the USA have signed and ratified, few countries have implemented clear policies and effective child protection programmes, in line with Article 19. Most countries could still benefit from firstly, state funded universal health and social services for children and their families, and secondly, the parallel development of public awareness, legal reform and services for the protection of children and the treatment of offenders. While there has been much progress since 1988, there is also evidence of avoidance and retreat with reductions in both investigations and resources in some places.

What is required for the future of child protection are international guidelines that elaborate on Article 19 of the Convention of the Rights of the Child, which calls upon states to develop services to help families protect their children from harm. However, international concern for children is not sufficient to prevent child abuse and neglect. The responsibility for prevention cannot rest with child protection services alone, it must become a responsibility for all individuals from all sections of society, worldwide.

REFERENCES

Bentovim, A. (1992) *Trauma Organised Systems*. London: Karnac Books.

Briere, J.N. (1992) *Child Abuse Trauma*. Newbury Park: Sage Publications.

Bronfenbrenner, U. (1979) *The Ecology of Human Development*. Cambridge, MA: Harvard University Press.

Browne, K.D. (1995) Preventing Child Maltreatment through Community Nursing. *Journal of Advanced Nursing*, **21** (1) 57–63.

Browne, K.D. and Herbert, M. (1997) *Preventing Family Violence*. Chichester: Wiley.

Calder M.C. with Hanks, H., Epps K., Print, B., Morrison T. & Henniker J. (2001) *Juveniles and Children who Sexually Abuse: Framework for Assessment* (2nd ed.) Lyme Regis: Russell House Publishing.

Department of Health (1999) *Working Together to Safeguard Children*. London: The Stationery Office.

Department of Health, Department of Education and Employment and the Home Office (2000). *Framework for the Assessment of Children in Need and their Families.* London: The Stationery Office.

Elliott, M., Browne, K. and Kilcoyne, J. (1995) Child Sexual Abuse Prevention: What Offenders Tell Us. *Child Abuse and Neglect*, **19** (5) 579–594.

Glaser D. and Balbernie R. (2001) Early Experience, Attachment and the Brain. In *Fragile Handle with Care–Protecting Babies from Harm*, eds Gordon & Harran. London: NSPCC.

Hamilton, C.E. and Browne, K.D. (1998) The Repeat Victimisation of Children: Should the Concept be Revised? *Aggression and Violent Behavior*, **3** (1) 47–60.

Hobbs, C., Hanks, H. and Wynne, J. (1999) '*Child Abuse and Neglect: A Clinicians Handbook*' Iwaniec D. (1995). *The emotionally abused and neglected child*. Chichester: Wiley.

National Commission of Enquiry in the Prevention of Child Abuse (1996) *Childhood Matters*, Vols 1 & 2. London: NSPCC.

Prior, V., Glaser, D. & Lynch, M.A. (1997) Responding to Child Sexual Abuse: The Criminal Justice System. *Child Abuse Review*, **6**: 128–140.

Stratton, P. (1988) Understanding and treating child abuse in the family context. In K. Browne, C. Davies, & P. Stratton (Eds.) *Early Prediction And Prevention Of Child Abuse*, pp 193–202. Chichester: Wiley.

United Nations (1989) '*Convention on the Rights of the Child*' United Nations: New York.

World Health Organization (1998) First Meeting on Strategies for Child Protection. Padua, Italy, 29–31 October 1998. Copenhagen: WHO Regional Office for Europe.

World Health Organization (1999) *Report of the consultation on child abuse prevention. WHO, Geneva, 29–31 March 1999*. Geneva: WHO.

Section I

PREVALENCE AND PREDICTION

EDITOR'S INTRODUCTION

Kevin Browne

The prevention of child abuse and neglect can occur only with the parrallel development of public awareness, legal reform and refocused health and social services. Where these three areas of activity have developed in a co-ordinated way, the Countries concerned have seen significant advances in child protection over the past decade.

The most recent figures available on the number of new reports (incidence) of child sexual abuse in the USA shows that, from 1992 to 1998, substantiated cases of child sexual abuse decreased by nearly a third (Jones and Finkelhor 2001). When a number of influencing factors were taken into account the authors concluded that this had been a real effect, possibly as a result of the developments in child protection legislation and systems. By comparison, slight reductions have been observed for physical abuse and none for fatal abuse in the USA, during the same time period.

Sue Creighton takes up the theme of recognising changes in incidence and prevalence in Chapter 1. She observes that the development of child protection services in the UK and Australia has also led to a slowing down in the number of reports for child maltreatment in the 1990's compared to the previous decade. The fact that this trend has not been evident for fatal child abuse is an important indicator that there is a need for early intervention with high-risk families. Indeed, it has been known for some time that infants are most at risk of head injury and serious assault. This harm often leads to fatalities in children under two years.

Indeed, it is alarming that despite the significant developments in child protection systems over the past decade, Browne and Lynch (1995) report that approximately two children die per week in the UK (50 per million) as a result of child abuse and neglect. In the vast majority of cases (80%), this is perpetrated by their parents. The difficulties in predicting fatal abuse are discussed by Peter Reder and Sylvia Duncan in Chapter 2. They identify the importance of the perinatal period for recognising and predicting fatal child abuse. This is in line with the approach of the World Health Organization (1998) which regards child maltreatment and violence in the family as a significant public health problem, where good perinatal care promotes parental bonding to the child and is seen as an inoculation against abuse, neglect and abandonment.

The theme of public health is developed further by Catherine Hamilton and Kevin Browne in Chapter 3 entitled "Predicting Physical Maltreatment". They justify investment into the prediction and prevention of violence in the family, before child maltreatment begins. This is on the basis of the economic cost of child protection and related matters once child abuse and neglect is recognised. They claim that predicting and targeting families for services before maltreatment occurs is best carried out within the broader context of child welfare, families and communities. Using a public health approach, child protection is seen as just one of many important developmental needs of the child. The assessment of the parent's capacity to meet the child's needs and the impact of social and environmental factors (e.g. poverty) on parenting are the main components of screening families. The objective of screening is to promote positive parenting and enhance parental capacity to meet the needs of the child prior to a breakdown in the parent–child relationship. Evidence is provided for the success of this approach, which has shown an effect 15 years after community-based visits to the child's home (Kitzman et al, 1997).

The focus on the parent–child relationship is further elaborated in Chapter 4 by Danya Glaser and Vivian Prior in discussing the prediction of emotional abuse and neglect. They provide a detailed description on what is meant by emotional abuse and neglect and how accurately the phenomenon can be predicted in practice. Of course, a parent's emotional abuse and neglect of a child may not be deliberate or direct. Sometimes it may be the consequences of work stress, anxiety and depression, alcohol and drug abuse where the parent is not cognitively available to the child (see Browne & Herbert, 1997). Nevertheless the most dramatic form of emotional abuse is the child witnessing domestic violence between the parents, which is often associated with the indirect causes outlined above.

Approaches to the prediction of child sexual abuse and its association with other forms of child maltreatment is the topic of Chapter 5, the last in Section I. Clinical approaches for paediatricians and other health professionals to recognise and assess signs of sexual abuse, associated physical abuse, neglect and failure to thrive are clearly identified with sometimes disturbing illustrations. The authors are well known for their pragmatic clinical approach to predicting and preventing all forms of child maltreatment (see Hobbs et al., 1999).

Overall the contents of Section I demonstrate the changes observed in incidence and prevalence over the past decade. These changes may be due to advances made in the prediction and recognition of child maltreatment. Nevertheless there is still room for improvement in the co-ordination of health and social services, especially for the early prevention of fatal child abuse and neglect. The inter-relationship between mental health, domestic violence and child maltreatment is yet to be fully appreciated in multi-agency work. Child protection incorporated into mainstream services for children and families is seen as the way ahead.

Browne, K.D. and Herbert, M. (1997) *Preventing Family Violence*. Chichester: Wiley.
Browne, K.D. and Lynch, M.A. (1995) The nature and extent of child homicide and fatal abuse, *Child Abuse Review* 4:309–315.

Jones, L. and Finkelhor, D (2001) The decline in child sexual abuse cases *OJJDP Juvenile Justice Bulletin* no. NCJ 18471. Washington DC: US Department of Justice Office of Juvenile Justice and Delinquency Prevention.

Kitzman, H., Olds, D., Henderson, C., Hanks, C., Cole, R., Tatelbaum, R., McConnochie, K., Sidora, K., Luckey, D., Shaver, D., Engelhardt, K., James, D. and Bernard, K. (1997) Effect of prenatal and infancy home visitation by nurses on pregnancy outcomes, childhood injuries, and repeated childbearing: A randomized controlled trial. *Journal of the American Medical Association (JAMA)*, **278** (8): 644–680.

Hobbs, C.J., Hanks, H.G.I. and Wynne, J.M. (1999) *Child Abuse and Neglect: a Clinician's Handbook.* 2nd ed, London: Churchill Livingstone.

World Health Organization. (1998). First Meeting on Strategies for Child Protection. Padua, Italy 29–31 October 1998. Copenhagen: WHO Regional Office for Europe.

1

RECOGNISING CHANGES IN INCIDENCE AND PREVALENCE

Susan J. Creighton
NSPCC, London, UK

INTRODUCTION

One of the most regular questions child protection professionals get asked by the public and the media is "Is child abuse greater now than it was 10, 20, 50 years ago?" In the mid 1970's, when official child protection management systems were introduced in the UK and the USA, the answer would have been "We don't know, we have no comparative data." Some 25 years later we are able to offer some *cautious* comparisons. This chapter examines the changes in incidence and prevalence of child abuse, but is also concerned with outlining the cautions involved in recognising such changes. Recognising changes in the incidence and prevalence of a phenomenon requires us to have a clear idea of what that phenomenon consists of. In the case of child abuse that idea is continually evolving.

Child abuse can be, and is often, likened to an iceberg with a number of levels.

Level 1 Those children who are reported to the police as having been chronically abused or neglected

Level 2 Those children who are reported to child protection agencies and agreed as being in need of protection i.e. registered

Level 3 Those children who are reported to child protection agencies by other professionals such as doctors and health personnel and by the general public

Level 4 Abused and neglected children who are recognised as such by neighbours or relatives but are not brought to the attention of a professional agency

Level 5 Children who have not been recognised as abused or neglected by anyone

Actual and estimated numbers can be provided for levels 1 to 3.

Early Prediction and Prevention of Child Abuse: A Handbook.
Edited by Kevin Browne, Helga Hanks, Peter Stratton and Catherine Hamilton. © 2002 John Wiley & Sons, Ltd.

Level 1 During the year 1 April 1998 to 31 March 1999 there were 2300 reported offences of "cruelty to or neglect of children" and 1293 of "gross indecency with a child under the age of 14" in England and Wales (Home Office, 2000).

Level 2 There were 30 100 children's names added to child protection registers during the year in England (Department of Health, 1999) and 2516 in Wales (National Assembly for Wales, 1999).

Level 3 On the basis of research conducted on the registration process (Department of Health, 1995) an estimated 213 000 children would have been reported to child protection agencies during the year.

There are no estimates for the numbers of children in levels 4 and 5. The assumption underlying the iceberg analogy is that the numbers of children in levels 4 and 5 the "undiscovered" child abuse, are larger than those which have been "discovered" and responded to.

The regular education campaigns directed towards informing the public about the problem of child abuse, and the public concern generated, may have undermined this assumption. Behaviours which were previously judged as acceptable may now be re-designated as abuse by both victims and perpetrators. The bottom level of the child abuse iceberg may be declining and pushing up into higher levels. More of the iceberg may now be visible above the water than below it. Recognising changes in the incidence and prevalence of child abuse over the years requires us to clarify a number of concepts. These include: incidence, prevalence, child abuse and change.

DEFINITIONS

Incidence

The incidence of child abuse is the number of new cases occurring to a defined population of children in a specified period. In the UK the defined population is children under the age of 18 and the specified period is a year.

Prevalence

The prevalence of child abuse is the percentage of children who are abused during childhood or some similar specified time period.

Child Abuse

Child abuse, or child maltreatment, is broken down into its different types especially when looking at incidence or prevalence. These are physical injury, sexual abuse, emotional or psychological abuse, and neglect. The precise definition of each is important when establishing numbers of children affected, as evidenced by Kelly et al.'s (1991) survey of the prevalence of sexual abuse among students.

When using the definition "any event/interaction that the young person reported as unwanted/abusive before they were 18" a prevalence figure of 59% for women and 27% for men was obtained. When the definition was narrowed to "those cases involving some form of penetration or coerced/forced masturbation where the abuser was at least 5 years older" the prevalence figure fell to 4% for women and 2% for men.

The definitions currently used in England and Wales for children placed on child protection registers are:

- *Physical Abuse*   may involve hitting, shaking, throwing, poisoning, burning or scalding, drowning, suffocating, or otherwise causing physical harm to a child. Physical harm may also be caused when a parent or carer feigns the symptoms of, or deliberately causes ill health to a child whom they are looking after. This situation is commonly described using terms such as factitious illness by proxy or Munchausen syndrome by proxy.
- *Emotional Abuse*   is the persistent emotional ill-treatment of a child such as to cause severe and persistent adverse effects on the child's emotional develop-ment. It may involve conveying to children that they are worthless or unloved, inadequate, or valued only insofar as they meet the needs of another person. It may feature age or developmentally inappropriate expectations being imposed on children. It may involve causing children frequently to feel frightened or in danger, or the exploitation or corruption of children. Some level of emotional abuse is involved in all types of ill-treatment of a child, though it may occur alone.
- *Sexual Abuse*   involves forcing or enticing a child or young person to take part in sexual activities, whether or not the child is aware of what is happening. The activities may involve physical contact, including penetrative (e.g. rape or bug-gery) or non-penetrative acts. They may include non-contact activities, such as involving children in looking at, or in the production of, pornographic mate-rial or watching sexual activities, or encouraging children to behave in sexually inappropriate ways.
- *Neglect*   is the persistent failure to meet a child's basic physical and/or psycho-logical needs, likely to result in the serious impairment of the child's health or development. It may involve a parent or carer failing to provide adequate food, shelter and clothing, failing to protect a child from physical harm or danger, or the failure to ensure access to appropriate medical care or treatment. It may also include neglect of, or unresponsiveness to, a child's basic emotional needs.

[Source: Working Together to Safeguard Children, 1999]

Change

The concept of change in the incidence or prevalence of child abuse incorporates two elements. The first is what is *recognised* as child abuse, and the second is what is *included* in the official incidence or prevalence figures.

Kempe (1978) outlined the six stages in recognising and addressing the problem of child abuse. From the stage 1 denial that it exists outside a small minority of deviant families, recognition progresses through more widespread physical abuse, neglect, emotional abuse and sexual abuse to stage 6, that of guaranteeing each child that he or she is truly wanted and provided for. The impact of a number of sensational cases, the media interest in the problem and a succession of public education campaigns has led to most developed countries both recognising and responding to all the different types of child abuse. Few, if any, countries would claim to have reached stage 6.

Whilst life-threatening parental behaviours have long been recognised as abusive, there have been changes in the recognition of other behaviours as potentially abusive. Child abuse is a culturally defined phenomenon. We live in a culture which values individual rights and freedoms. These rights have been exercised in the developed countries in controlling fertility to the extent that the birth rate has been dropping to below replacement level. The numbers and proportion of children in the population have been declining. Aligned to this the growth of the post-industrial society has led to a need for a more highly educated and skilled workforce. Training children for this role takes more time, thus increasing the period of their dependency on their parents. Declining family size and increased parental investment in individual children lead to more behaviours used in child rearing becoming unacceptable to the majority. In a recent nationally representative survey of the child rearing experiences of adults aged 18–45 (Creighton & Russell, 1995) some 35% said they had been hit with an implement as a child. Only 7% felt that it was acceptable to do this to a child now.

Changes in what is *included* in official incidence or prevalence figures can be illustrated by the English experience of registering child abuse. Unlike in the USA the management of child abuse in England has followed Kempe's stages more closely. When inter-disciplinary child protection management systems were introduced in England in 1974/1975 registers were "non-accidental injury" registers. They included the names of all the children in the area who had been reported as physically injured in a manner thought to be non-accidental. In 1980, following a number of high profile cases where children had died of neglect, the registers were expanded into "child abuse" registers. These included the names of children in the area who were judged to have been physically abused, neglected or emotionally abused. Children who had been sexually abused were not included in the criteria for registration in the 1980 circular. They were added to the register criteria in 1988 when the registers became "child protection registers". Hence if you were to compare the number of children registered in England in 1975 with that in 1995 you would not be comparing like with like. Additional types of abuse were registered and included in the official figures over the period.

There were other changes in what was included in the official data: these were the age range of the children and the reporting-registration/substantiation procedure.

Age Ranges   Most incidence data uses the specified period of a year but the defined population for child abuse in England has also changed over the years. In the early 1970's it was confined to children under the age of four years old. It rose to children under the age of 16 in 1974 when the first official guidance was issued by the DHSS (DHSS, 1974). In 1980 when the second DHSS guidance (DHSS, 1980) was issued, the defined population rose to children under the age of 17, and in 1988 to 18, when *Working Together* (DHSS, 1988) was published. If you were unaware of these underlying changes in the way the defined population for child abuse has expanded, the increasing numbers of new cases brought about by this expanded population would be misleading. In order to compare incidence data over years the use of rates per 1000, 10 000 or 100 000 of the underlying child population is recommended.

Reporting-Registration/substantiation   This refers to the difference between Level 2 and Level 3 numbers. In England and Wales, the USA and Australia, reported cases of child abuse go through a number of investigations which leads to the majority being filtered out of the system. The remaining cases are then said to be "registered" (England and Wales), or "substantiated" (USA and Australia). Research has shown [Gibbons et al., (1995); Giovannoni, (1989); Eckenrode et al., (1988)] that certain types of cases are more likely to be filtered out of the system than others. The type of abuse reported, the age and sex of the child concerned and the source of the report have all been shown to affect the registration/substantiation rate. What is clear from the research is that unregistered and unsubstantiated cases include some where maltreatment was found. Child protection services are provided to those children and their families who remain in the system to the extent of being registered or substantiated. Given the finite nature of the available services, the criteria for inclusion into those services is constantly being adjusted.

Any changes seen in the incidence and prevalence of child abuse over the years need to be interpreted against this background of the changes in recognition of the phenomenon, reporting of it and inclusion into the "official" data.

CHANGES IN INCIDENCE OF "OFFICIAL" CASES

This section deals with the data on the officially reported, registered, substantiated, validated cases in the USA, the UK, the Netherlands and Australia. The USA, the UK and the Netherlands all introduced management systems for recording cases of child abuse in the mid-1970's. National child protection data started to be collected in Australia at the beginning of the 1990's. The systems used in the different countries varied considerably so each country's data will be presented separately, with a brief descriptive background.

The United States of America

In 1974 the Child Abuse Prevention and Treatment Act was signed into law. It provided a mandate to establish a National Center on Child Abuse and Neglect. The Center was given the responsibility for conducting a national incidence study of child abuse and neglect. A standard reporting form was devised and the individual states and territories were persuaded to complete a form on each case and return it to the national registry. States which had already set up systems of their own were asked to provide cumulative data to the registry. The form included all types of child abuse. There were specific physical injuries such as skull fractures and cuts, bruises, welts, neglect, emotional abuse and neglect, and sexual abuse. The first report (American Humane Association, 1978) on the national data collection

TABLE 1.1 Changes in incidence of "official" cases of child abuse in the USA

Year	Number of Reports	Number of Children	Rate/1000 Child Population	% Substantiated	Breakdown of Cases*
1976	357 533	–	–	47	Neglect 58% Abuse only 26.5% Abuse & Neglect 15%
1982	929 310	1.4 million	20.08	–	Neglect 62% Physical 24% Emotional 10% Sexual 7% Other 9%
1986	–	–	32.8	40	Neglect 55% Physical 28% Sexual 17% Emotional 9% Other 4%
1989	2.4 million	–	–	45	Neglect 53% Physical 28% Sexual 19% Emotional 9% Other 4%
1992	2.9 million	–	45.0	40	Neglect 45% Physical 27% Sexual 17% Emotional 7% Other 8%
1994	2 million	2.9 million	43.0	–	Neglect 53% Physical 26% Sexual 14% Emotional 5%
1998	2.8 million	2.97 million	–	32	Neglect 53.5% Physical 23% Sexual 11.5% Emotional 6% Multiple 25%

* *Cases do not necessarily add to 100% in some years*
Source: American Humane Association (1978, 1984); American Association for Protecting Children (1988); Daro & Mitchel (1990); McCurdy & Daro (1993); US Department of Health and Human Services (1996a, 2000)

was produced for the year 1976 when 28 states were fully participating and a further 22 provided cumulative data. The report provided a detailed breakdown of the characteristics of the reported children, their families, the type of abuse and the variations between the different states. Over the years the emphasis of the reported data has changed to concentrate more on those cases which were substantiated (validated in earlier years) by the Child Protective Services (CPS). Table 1.1 shows the changes in some of the key data over the years.

In 1987 Schene wrote that there had been a 188% increase in reports over the decade 1976 to 1985 and Table 1.1 demonstrates that increase continued but at a slower rate. By 1998 reports had increased to over 2.8 million but the number of substantiated cases had declined to "903,000 victims of maltreatment nation-wide. The 1998 rate of victimization was 12.9 per 1,000 children" (US Department of Health and Human Services, 2000). This was the lowest rate recorded for a decade.

The type of abuse that has shown the greatest decline in the 1990's has been cases of child sexual abuse. Between 1992 and 1998 substantiated cases of child sexual abuse showed a 31% decrease. The decline was not restricted to substantiated cases alone as reported cases showed a similar 26% decline.

Table 1.1 shows that the majority of the reported cases of child maltreatment throughout the entire period concerned child victims of neglect. Some 58% of the reports in 1976 were cases of neglect and a further 15% combined abuse and neglect. By 1998 over half (53.5%) of the child victims suffered neglect whilst 25% were victims of more than one type of maltreatment. Jones and Finkelhor (2001) have suggested that the dramatic decline in child sexual abuse cases may be due to a decrease in the actual incidence, a change in reporting behaviour, and/or policy and program changes within the child protective services. Further research is needed for a better understanding and to ensure that children are best protected.

The United Kingdom

As was described earlier in this chapter, registers of non-accidental injury to children were established in each local authority area in England in 1975, following the 1974 DHSS circular. These were to include the names of all the children in the area who were assessed by a multi-disciplinary team as having been non-accidentally injured or thought to be at serious risk of non-accidental injury. Wales adopted the same system as did Northern Ireland. Scotland, which has an independent legal system, established a slightly different system. The child population of England is far larger than that of the other constituent countries of the UK, with a proportionally larger number of registrations for child abuse. Table 1.2 shows the latest number of registrations for the different countries.

For the purposes of looking at changes in incidence over the years it is clearer to look at the data for England alone. Prior to 1988, data on the numbers of children registered in each local authority was not collated nationally. The largest source of child abuse statistics was that collected by the NSPCC, from the registers it managed for a number of local authorities between 1974 and 1990. The child population covered by these register areas included some 10% of the child population of England and the areas covered both rural and urban communities. From this

TABLE 1.2 Registrations for child abuse in the UK

Country	Number of Registrations	Year Ending	Rate/1000 child population
England	29 300	31 March 2000	2.6
Northern Ireland	1093	31 March 1999	2.6
Scotland	1919	31 March 1998	1.9
Wales	2516	31 March 1999	3.7

Registration, Injury, Sexual Abuse & Grave Concern Rates by Year (rate per 1000)

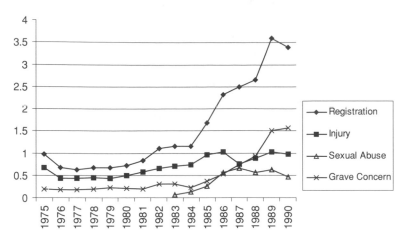

FIGURE 1.1 Registration, Injury, Sexual Abuse & Grave Concern Rates by Year (1975–1990) Reproduced from *Child Abuse Trends in England and Wales 1988–1990 and an overview from* 1973–1990 Susan J. Creighton (1992) by permission of NSPCC.

10% sample national estimates could be derived and Figure 1.1 shows the rate of new registrations per 1000 child population aged less than 15 over the period 1975 to 1990. The figure also shows the rates for the physically injured, "grave concern or at risk" and sexually abused cases.

The figure shows a massive increase in registration rates between 1984 and 1989.

The later increase, between 1988 and 1989, can be attributed to the change from "child abuse" to "child protection" registers and a corresponding increase in registrations in the "grave concern" category. The earlier increase, between 1984 and 1986, coincided with a massive increase in public awareness, following a number of individual tragic child abuse deaths and television programmes on child sexual abuse. The registration rate for new cases of sexual abuse increased most between 1985 and 1986 and reached a peak in 1987. The 1987 Cleveland Inquiry (Butler-Sloss, 1988) into the management of child sexual abuse in Cleveland was partly in response to the public perception that child protection professionals were being over-intrusive in family life. How much this public backlash was responsible for the decline in sexual abuse registrations after 1987 is not known.

The Department of Health has been collating the register figures for all the local authority areas in England since 1988.

Figure 1.2 shows the number of new registrations added to child protection registers in England from 1 April 1987 to 31 March 2000.

The rate of registration per 1000 children aged less than 18 rose from 2.1 for the year ended 31 March 1989 to 2.6 for the year ended 31 March 1991. The Department of Health introduced changes in the criteria for registration in October 1991 which led to a considerable drop in the number of children on child protection registers and those added in the next year. By 31 March 1992 the rate of new registrations during the year had fallen to 2.3 per 1000 children aged less than 18. Since then it

Number of Registrations

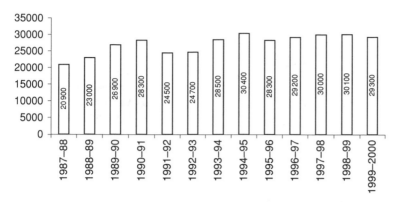

FIGURE 1.2 New registrations added to child protection registers in England 1988–2000.
Source: Department of Health (1988–2000) Children and Young People on Child Protection
Registers Year ending 31 March. England.

increased to 2.7 during the year ended 31 March 1995 and has fluctuated between
2.5 and 2.7 since then.

The changes in criteria for registration, introduced in October 1991, means
that you cannot compare the different types of abuse registered before and after
1991. The changes involved abolishing the "grave concern" as a separate register
category. By 31 March 1991 the percentage of children placed on child protection
registers in this category had risen to 50%. The changed register criteria incorporated the "grave concern" cases into the different types of abuse so that children who
had been physically abused or were thought to be at serious risk of physical abuse
were placed in the physical injury category. The changes had the effect of making
the child protection professionals involved in the case clarify their thinking from a
more general anxiety that a child was at risk from abuse to "what type of abuse" was
the child at risk of. It also led to the significant decrease in registrations discussed
earlier.

Figure 1.3 shows the breakdown of new registrations by the different register
categories for the years ending 31 March 1993 to 2000 when the new criteria were
fully operational.

The figure shows how the percentage of new registrations categorised as neglect
has increased over the period, as have those for emotional abuse. The abuse profile
of registered cases is now much more similar to that for the USA, though at a
considerably reduced rate.

The Netherlands

The Netherlands has a system of "confidential doctors" to whom concerned individuals can report cases of child abuse. Many reports are incomplete, or too short,
or even unreliable, necessitating further enquiry. Every report to the confidential
doctors has to be verified before it is accepted for further help. The confidential
doctor system started officially in 1974 and included all types of abuse.

Percentage of New Registrations

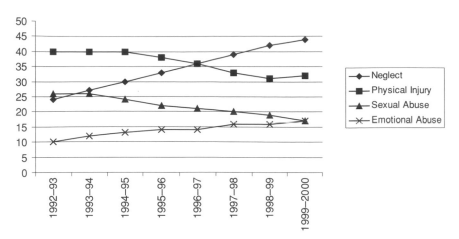

FIGURE **1.3** New registrations by different register categories 1992–2000 (England)
Source: Department of Health (1992–2000) Children and Young People on Child Protection
Registers Year ending 31 March. England.

Pieterse and Van Urk (1989) looked at the data on the changes in verified reports
between 1974 and 1983. The incidence per thousand children had increased from
0.19 in 1974 to 0.71 in 1983. The increase in reports was mainly among the older
children (the over-12-year-olds) and the types of abuse reported changed over the
decade. In 1974, the majority (64%) of the cases were of physical abuse. By 1983,
this had changed to half of them being emotional abuse/neglect. Sexual abuse was
hardly recognised in 1974 but accounted for over 7% of the verified cases in 1983.
No change was found in the identity of the perpetrators or the social conditions of
the families.

Australia

The community services department in each State or Territory is responsible for
child protection in their area. Children who are thought to have been abused or neglected, or whose parents cannot provide adequate care or protection, are referred
to these services. Whilst there are different legislation and policies in each State,
the protection processes are broadly similar across jurisdictions. The Australian
Institute of Health and Welfare has been responsible for collecting national child
protection data since the early 1990's (Johnstone, 2000).

Reports to community services departments which relate to child protection are
classified as notifications. A proportion of these notifications are investigated further to make an assessment of the degree of harm to the child and the notification is
either "substantiated" or "not substantiated". The Australian Institute has national
data on the number of child protection investigations and substantiations for the
years from 1990–91 to 1998–99, and on the number of notifications for the years
1995–96 to 1998–99.

Number of Notifications

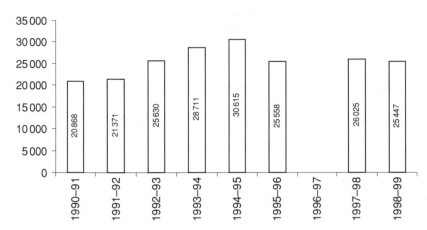

FIGURE **1.4**   Substantiated child protection notifications (Australia) 1990–91 to 1998–99
Note: 1996–97 figures not available.
Source: Johnstone (2000)

The substantiated cases in Australia are most similar to those in the USA and the registered cases in the UK. Figure 1.4 shows the number of substantiated cases from 1990–91 to 1998–99.

The figure shows that substantiations increased to a peak in 1994–95 and then decreased. The number of notifications has increased steadily from 1995–96 to 1998–99, reflecting the influence of child protection policies, legislation and guidance on "official" child protection data.

The Australian data shows a different breakdown to that of the USA and UK in the types of abuse substantiated (Australian Institute of Health and Welfare, 1998). In the year 1996–97 the largest category was physical abuse with some 32% of cases, followed by neglect with 29%. This was followed by emotional abuse (25.5%) and sexual abuse with 13% of the cases.

The data on the incidence of "official" cases of child abuse and neglect from the different countries show a number of similarities and some differences. The similarities lie in the rapid increase in reported and substantiated cases in the early years of the child protection systems, followed by a levelling off, and even decline in some countries, during the last five years. These are the cases which have priority in the allocation of scarce resources and services. Given the continued increase in reports and notifications, the incidence of "official" cases would seem to reflect the availability of resources rather than the underlying levels of child abuse and neglect.

CHANGES IN INCIDENCE OF "SEMI-OFFICIAL" CASES

This is an attempt to look at changes in incidence of child abuse down to Level 3, that below the "officially" recognised cases. The data comes from the three National

TABLE 1.3 Comparison of the three National Incidence
Studies (USA)

Year	No of Children	Rate/1000	Physical Abuse Rate
1980	625 100	9.8	3.1
1986	1 000 000	14.8	4.3
1993	1 553 800	23.1	5.7

Incidence Surveys (NIS1, NIS2 and NIS3), commissioned by the US Department of Health in 1980, 1986 and 1993 (US Department of Health and Human Services, 1988, 1996b; Sedlak, 1990).

The surveys included all cases of child abuse and neglect recognised and reported by both the community professionals concerned with the child protection system (CPS), and also non-CPS agencies (such as schools and hospitals). These latter agencies had been briefed to act as "sentinels" for cases which came to light during the study period. The cases had to meet the study's definitions of child maltreatment which had been designed to be clear, objective and to involve demonstrable harm to the child. For example the definition of physical abuse specified that the child must be under 18 years of age at the time of the abuse, have suffered demonstrable harm at the hands of a parent or adult caretaker (over 18), and that the abusive behaviour must have been non-accidental and avoidable.

The three surveys showed an increasing number of cases being recognised as fulfilling the study's definitions of child maltreatment. Table 1.3 shows the increases in some of the key data.

Cases of neglect (educational, physical and emotional) exceeded cases of abuse in all three surveys but the increase in cases of maltreatment between 1980 and 1986 was largely in cases of abuse. The incidence of both abuse and neglect had more than doubled from NIS1 to NIS3. The increases were from those agencies not usually involved in the investigation of child maltreatment cases (schools, hospitals, mental health agencies). As the numbers in each survey increased the percentage of cases which had been investigated by the Child Protective Services decreased.

CHANGES IN INCIDENCE OF PHYSICALLY ABUSIVE BEHAVIOUR

Changes in recognition of the incidence of child abuse at Level 4, that below any official, semi-official or professional involvement, are shown in the data from the Family Violence Research Program at the University of New Hampshire (Straus, 1979; Straus & Gelles, 1986; Straus et al., 1998). The programme has conducted three nationally representative surveys of American families to ascertain the levels of physical violence used within them. The surveys have examined violence between spouses, between siblings and by parents to children. Concentrating on physically abusive behaviour by parents towards children, severe violence was ascertained when a parent acknowledged that they, or their spouse, had "hit with an object, punched, bitten, kicked, beaten up or used a knife or gun" on their child in the last year. The surveys were conducted in 1975, 1985 and 1995. The first two surveys looked at behaviour towards children aged between three and 17 years living at home. Recognising that the under three-year-olds are the most vulnerable to child abuse the 1995 survey included a nationally representative sample of children under the age of 18 years.

The incidence rates for severe violence by parents towards their children fell from 140 per 1000 in 1975 to 107 per 1000 in 1985 and 49 per 1000 in 1995. Although these rates show a significant decrease over the decades, in contrast to the increase shown in the National Incidence Surveys, the actual numbers are much greater. The 1995 Family Violence rate of 49 per 1000 US children, is over eight times the 1993 NIS3 rate of 5.7 per 1000 for physical abuse. On the basis of the 1985 Family Violence Survey and the official reporting rate for that year, Schene (1987) estimated that only one physically abused child in seven was reported.

PREVALENCE STUDIES OF CHILD MALTREATMENT

Child sexual abuse has been the type of maltreatment examined in most prevalence studies. Possible reasons for this may include media interest, the lack of external signs, and the average age of the victims. In the UK the only nationally representative surveys of child abuse prior to 1994 were those conducted for use on TV programmes. These included the 1984 MORI poll (Baker & Duncan, 1985), conducted for a Channel 4 documentary on child sexual abuse and the 1987 BBC Childwatch Survey conducted for Esther Rantzen's programme.

Sexual abuse presents fewer external signs than physical abuse and neglect and the average age of the victim is higher. Sexual abuse has been recorded in infants and toddlers but the majority of cases have been in children aged 10 or more (Creighton, 1992). Memories of events prior to the age of three, when a large proportion of physical abuse and neglect takes place, is hazy, making adult recall less reliable.

There have been a few surveys which have looked at the prevalence of other types of maltreatment in addition to sexual abuse. The 1987 BBC Childwatch Survey asked adults about their childhood experiences of all types of abuse. Unfortunately, the only data they published from this survey was a brief press release on the prevalence of childhood sexual abuse. McMillan et al. (1997) looked at the prevalence of child physical and sexual abuse in Ontario in Canada, as did Creighton and Russell (1995) in England, Scotland and Wales. The growing recognition of the long term damage caused by emotional abuse and neglect led the NSPCC to commission a national survey of all types of child maltreatment in the UK (Cawson et al., 2000).

Methodological Considerations

When looking at changes in the prevalence of various types of child abuse there are a number of important methodological limitations to consider. Chief among these are:

- definition
- sample
- measurement instruments

DEFINITION

Pilkington and Kremer (1995), reviewing the major empirical studies on the prevalence of child sexual abuse, suggested that the "myriad of definitions of child sexual abuse" (p. 84) contributed to the variance in reported prevalence rates. The majority of the studies they reviewed used definitions that incorporated both contact (including touching of breasts and genitals to forced vaginal/anal intercourse) and non-contact (exhibitionism, viewing of pornography) abuse. The different prevalence rates associated with different definitions can be illustrated by two surveys.

The first, by Siegal et al. (1987), used the question: "In your lifetime, has anyone ever tried to pressure or force you to have sexual contact? By sexual contact, I mean their touching your sexual parts, or sexual intercourse."

They then established, for those respondents who answered yes to the question, whether they had been under 16 years old at the time. They found that 5.3% (3.8% men, 6.8% women) had experienced pressured sexual contact before the age of 16, one of the lowest figures among the prevalence studies.

The second study was the MORI survey (Baker & Duncan, 1985) who used the definition: "A child (anyone under 16 years) is sexually abused when another person, who is sexually mature, involves the child in any activity which the other person expects to lead to their sexual arousal. This might involve intercourse, touching, exposure of the sexual organs, showing pornographic material or talking about sexual things in an erotic way."

This definition included both contact and non-contact sexual abuse and did not necessarily involve force or pressure. They found a prevalence rate of 10% (8% men, 12% women). However, if their data is re-analysed to exclude the non-contact cases, their figures become very similar to the Siegal et al. study.

If we are to look at possible changes in prevalence of child sexual abuse over the years or in different countries, it is very important that similar, if not identical, definitions are used.

SAMPLE

Early prevalence studies tended to use "captive samples" such as GP patients (Nash & West, 1985), social science students (Finkelhor, 1979) or clinic patients (Benward & Densen-Gerber, 1975). Whilst these studies provided useful insights into the problem, they were limited due to the biased nature of the sample. Community samples, though more representative of the general population, can also be subject to bias. Prevalence surveys which use volunteer samples (e.g. readers of a particular teen magazine or viewers of a TV programme) are inevitably self-selecting. In order to be able to generalise to the general population, it is necessary to interview random samples of that population. It is preferable to use a nationally random sample as the result of a random sample in one area (e.g. Russell, 1983) may not generalise to other areas.

MEASUREMENT INSTRUMENTS

The way potential respondents are approached, the type and wording of the questions they are asked, the order of those questions and the sensitivity of them can all affect a respondent's co-operation and answers. Pilkington and Kremer (1995) state: "The literature clearly suggests that the preferred method must involve direct face-to-face interview of the client by a trained interviewer using a standard format which contains a series of questions to elicit abuse histories." (p. 94)

Recently, the use of computers in surveys has helped respondents to answer sensitive questions (Turner et al., 1998). Computer assisted personal interviewing (CAPI) has now largely replaced the paper questionnaires used in previous social surveys. The self-completion questionnaire which was formerly used for the most personal parts of an interview has been replaced by computer assisted self-interviewing (CASI). The interviewer is able to demonstrate to the respondent that any answer they key into the computer is completely confidential.

CHILD MALTREATMENT IN THE UNITED KINGDOM

This report (Cawson et al., 2000) is a study of the prevalence of child abuse and neglect in the United Kingdom commissioned by the NSPCC. It is the first national random probability survey of all types of abuse and neglect experienced by young people in the UK using CAPI and CASI technology.

The survey was carried out between September 1998 and February 1999 by BMRB on behalf of the NSPCC. They interviewed 2869 young adults aged 18–24 years, who had spent the majority of their childhood in the United Kingdom. This age group was chosen as their experience of childhood was sufficiently recent for their recall to be relatively accurate. The questionnaire was introduced as being about childhood experiences and the questions started with broad aspects of care and gradually moved to more sensitive ones. There were no definitions of abuse or neglect but respondents were asked if they had experienced specific behaviours. These had been chosen to be comparable to previous studies.

The prevalence figures obtained were as follows:

- Serious physical abuse (violence used regularly over the years, or which had caused physical injury or frequently led to physical effects): 7%
- Serious absence of physical care (acts which carried a high risk of injury or long-term harmful effects): 6%.
- Serious absence of supervision (staying home overnight without adult supervision under the age of 10, or allowed out overnight without parents knowing their whereabouts under the age of 14 years): 5%
- Serious emotional maltreatment (a score of 7 or more on experience of at least four of the dimensions; control and domination (psychological and/or physical), humiliation, withdrawal, antipathy, terrorising and proxy attacks): 6%
- Sexually abused (contact and non-contact) (against wishes or aged 12 and under): 16%
- Sexually abused (contact) (against wishes or aged 12 and under): 11%

The Child Maltreatment survey provides a benchmark against which future changes in the prevalence of child abuse and neglect can be measured.

CHANGES IN THE PREVALENCE OF CHILD SEXUAL ABUSE

The number of studies looking at the prevalence of physical abuse, neglect or emotional abuse are too few and too recent to provide data on possible changes. Prevalence studies of child sexual abuse go back to Kinsey in the 1940's, (Kinsey et al., 1953). In spite of the wide variation in reported figures and the methodological difficulties outlined earlier, there have been attempts to look at the changes over the decades. Feldman et al. (1991) reviewed 20 prevalence studies, including the Kinsey report. Applying pre-determined criteria for definitions of child sexual abuse, measurement tools and research design, they came up with three strong studies: Kinsey et al.'s, in the 1940's, one in 1984 (Badgley et al.) and 1987 (Siegal et al.). All three produced prevalence figures for girls younger than 14 years of age having sexual contact with an adult male at least five years older, of between 10% and 12%. Given that the underlying prevalence of child sexual abuse seems not to have changed between the 1940's and the 1980's, the increase in reported cases is probably due to changes in legislation and public awareness.

CONCLUSIONS AND FUTURE CHANGES

This chapter has shown how changes in incidence and prevalence data on child maltreatment reflect the growing professional and public awareness of the problem. Official and semi-official reported cases have shown considerable increases over the period from the 1970's to the late 1980's, with a slowing down in the last decade. The changes in the data have also demonstrated how substantiated/verified/registered cases (i.e. those to whom child protection services are provided) are constrained by the resources available. Whilst reported incidence figures for maltreatment have increased, the prevalence data for child sexual abuse seems not to have changed. The prevalence figures are still considerably higher than those cases which have been recognised and reported. Both sets of data provide child protection professionals with baselines against which to mount public education, preventive and treatment services for all maltreated children.

REFERENCES

American Association for Protecting Children (1988). Highlights of Official Child Neglect and Abuse Reporting 1986.

American Humane Association (1978). National Analyses of Official Child Neglect and Abuse Reporting.

American Humane Association (1984). Highlights of Official Child Neglect and Abuse Reporting 1982.

Australian Institute of Health and Welfare (1998). *Child Protection Australia 1996–97*. Child Welfare Series No 21. Canberra.

Badgley, R.F., Allard, H.A., McCormick, N. et al. (1984). *Sexual Offences Against Children*. Volume 1. Report of the Committee on Sexual Offences Against Children and Youths. Ottawa, Canada: Minister of Supply and Services.

Baker, A.W. and Duncan, S.P. (1985). Child sexual abuse: a study of prevalence in Great Britain. *Child Abuse and Neglect* **9**: 453–467.

Benward, J. and Densen-Gerber, J. (1975). Incest as a causative factor in anti-social behaviour. *Contemporary Drug Problems* **5**: 323–340.

Butler-Sloss, E. (Chairman) (1988). *The Report of the Inquiry into Child Abuse in Cleveland 1987.* London: HMSO.

Cawson, P., Wattam, C., Brooker, S. and Kelly, G. (2000). *Child Maltreatment in the United Kingdom. A study of the prevalence of child abuse and neglect.* London: NSPCC.

Creighton, S.J. (1992). *Child Abuse Trends in England and Wales 1988–1990 and an Overview from 1973–1990.* London: NSPCC.

Creighton, S.J. and Russell, N. (1995). *Voices from Childhood. A survey of childhood experiences and attitudes to child rearing among adults in the United Kingdom.* London: NSPCC.

Daro, D. and Mitchel, L. (1990). *Current Trends in Child Abuse Reporting and Fatalities: The Results of the 1989 Annual Fifty State Survey.* Working Paper No. 808. Chicago: National Center on Child Abuse Prevention Research.

Department of Health, Home Office and Department for Education and Employment (1999). *Working Together to Safeguard Children.* London: The Stationery Office.

Department of Health and Social Security (1974). Non-accidental injury to children, LASSL (74) 13.

Department of Health and Social Security (1980). Child Abuse: central register systems, LASSL (80) 4: HN (80) 20.

Department of Health (1995). *Child Protection: Messages from Research.* London: HMSO.

Department of Health (1999). *Children and Young People on Child Protection Registers Year ending 31 March 1999 England.* London: Government Statistical Service.

Eckenrode, J., Munsch, J., Powers, J. and Doris, J. (1988). The nature and substantiation of official sexual abuse reports. *Child Abuse and Neglect* **12**(3): 311–319.

Feldman, W., Feldman, E., Goodman, J.T., McGrath, P.J., Pless, R.P., Corsini, L. and Bennett, S. (1991). Is childhood sexual abuse really increasing in prevalence? An analysis of the evidence. *Pediatrics* **88**(1): 29–33.

Finkelhor, D. (1979). *Sexually Victimized Children.* New York: Free Press.

Gibbons, J., Conroy, S. and Bell, C. (1995). *Operating the Child Protection System: A Study of Child Protection Practices in English Local Authorities.* London: HMSO.

Giovannoni, J. (1989). Substantiated and unsubstantiated reports of child maltreatment. *Children and Youth Services Review II:* 299–318.

Home Office (2000). *Criminal Statistics 1999.* Cm 5001. London. The Stationery Office.

Johnstone, H. (2000). The national child protection data collection – what does 10 years worth of data tell us? Paper presented at the 7th Australian Institute of Family Studies Conference. Sydney, 24–26 July 2000.

Jones, L. and Finkelhor, D. (2001). The Decline in Child Sexual Abuse Cases *Juvenile Justice Bulletin.* January 2001. U.S. Department of Justice.

Kelly, L., Regan, L. and Burton, S. (1991). *An Exploratory Study of the Prevalence of Sexual Abuse in a Sample of 16–21 Year Olds.* Child Abuse Studies Unit. London: PNL.

Kempe, C.H., (1978). Recent developments in the field of child abuse. *Child Abuse and Neglect* **2**(4): 261–267.

Kinsey, A.C., Pomeroy, W.B., Martin, C.E. and Gebhard, P.H. (1953). *Sexual Behaviour in the Human Female.* Philadelphia, Pennsylvania: W.B. Saunders.

McCurdy, K. and Daro, D. (1993). *Current Trends in Child Abuse Reporting and Fatalities: The Results of the 1992 Annual Fifty State Survey.* National Center on Child Abuse Research, Working Paper No. 808. Chicago: NCPCA.

McMillan, H.L., Fleming, J.E., Trocme, N., Boyle, M.H., Wong, M., Racine, Y.A., Beardslee, W.R. and Offord, D.R. (1997). Prevalence of child physical and sexual abuse in the community. *Journal of the American Medical Association* **278**(2): 131–135.

Nash, C.L. and West, D.J. (1985). Sexual molestation of young girls. In D.J. West (ed.): *Sexual Victimisation.* Aldershot: Gower.

National Assembly for Wales (1999). Local Authority Child Protection Registers: Wales 1999. Government Statistical Service.

Pieterse, J.J. and Van Urk, H. (1989). Maltreatment of children in the Netherlands: an update after ten years. *Child Abuse and Neglect* **13**: 263–269.

Pilkington, B. and Kremer, J. (1995). A review of the epidemiological research on child sexual abuse: community and college student samples. *Child Abuse Review* 4(2): 84–98.

Russell, D.E.H. (1983). The incidence and prevalence of intrafamilial and extrafamilial sexual abuse of female children. *Child Abuse and Neglect* 7: 133–146.

Schene, P. (1987). Is child abuse decreasing? Commentary on Gelles and Straus paper. *Journal of Interpersonal Violence* 2: 225–227.

Sedlak, A.J. (1990). *Technical Amendment to the Study Findings: National Incidence and Prevalence of Child Abuse and Neglect: 1988.* Westat, Inc.

Siegal, J.M., Sorenson, S.B., Golding, J.M., Burnam, M.A. and Stein, J.A. (1987). The prevalence of childhood sexual assault: the Los Angeles epidemiologic catchment area project. *American Journal of Epidemiology* 126: 1141–1153.

Straus, M.A. (1979). Family patterns and child abuse in a nationally representative American sample. *Child Abuse and Neglect* 3(1): 213–225.

Straus, M.A. and Gelles, R.J. (1986). Societal change and change in family violence from 1975 to 1985 as revealed by two national surveys. *Journal of Marriage and Family* 48: 465–479.

Straus, M.A., Hamby, S.L., Finkelhor, D., Moore, D.W. and Runyan, D. (1998). Identification of child maltreatment with the parent–child conflict tactics scales: development and psychometric data for a national sample of American parents. *Child Abuse and Neglect* 22(4): 249–270.

Turner, C.F., Ku, L., Rogers, S.M., Lindberg, L.D., Pleck, J.H. and Sonenstein, F.L. (1998). Adolescent sexual behavior, drug use, and violence: increased reporting with computer survey technology. *Science* 280 (5365): 867–873.

US Department of Health and Human Services (1988). *Study Findings. Study of national incidence and prevalence of child abuse and neglect.* National Center on Child Abuse and Neglect, Washington DC.

US Department of Health and Human Services (1996a). *Child Maltreatment 1994: Reports from the States to the National Center on Child Abuse and Neglect,* Washington DC.

US Department of Health and Human Services (1996b). *The Third National Incidence Study of child abuse and neglect (NIS-3).* National Center on Child Abuse and Neglect, Washington DC.

US Department of Health and Human Services (2000). *Child Maltreatment 1998: Reports from the States to the National Center on Child Abuse and Neglect,* Washington DC.

2

PREDICTING FATAL CHILD ABUSE AND NEGLECT

Peter Reder

West London Mental Health Trust, UK

Sylvia Duncan

Baker & Duncan Family Consultancy, Woking, Surrey, UK

The report of the public inquiry into the death of four-year-old Jasmine Beckford (Inquiry Report, 1985) pronounced authoritatively that her death was both "predictable and preventable" and went on to censure specific practitioners for their failure to protect her. At the time, few challenged the presumed wisdom that fatal child abuse can be predicted by front line professionals (Parton & Parton, 1989; Dingwall, 1989). Since then, acknowledgement of the difficulties of predicting child abuse in general (e.g. Browne & Saqi, 1989; Browne & Herbert, 1997) has drawn attention once again to the question whether it is possible to anticipate the ultimate tragedy of a child death.

In this chapter we shall review current knowledge about fatal child abuse in order to consider whether claims for predictability have reasonable credence. We shall discuss the difficulties in forecasting such a rare and complex event and consider the attempts that have been made to identify characteristics unique to fatally abusing families. We shall then refer to two studies that we have conducted into such cases, which have offered additional pointers towards prediction.

DIFFICULTIES IN PREDICTING FATAL ABUSE

Nature of Abusive Scenarios

The first difficulty of predicting fatal abuse is that the origins of child maltreatment are multi-determined. It is generally agreed that incidents of child abuse of any severity are not merely caused by dysfunctional parents but are interactional

Early Prediction and Prevention of Child Abuse: A Handbook.
Edited by Kevin Browne, Helga Hanks, Peter Stratton and Catherine Hamilton. © 2002 John Wiley & Sons, Ltd.

events, occurring at moments of heightened stress in the lives of adults who suffer from unresolved conflicts and who are caring for vulnerable children (e.g. Schmitt & Krugman, 1992). Therefore, any attempt to predict fatal abuse must consider abusive scenarios and the interplay between parent, child and circumstance and not focus exclusively on attributes of individuals.

Furthermore, it is likely that circumstances differ between various forms of fatal maltreatment and, in order to be practically valid, predictive procedures should be able to distinguish between the various scenarios. These include: abandonment of a baby at birth following a denied pregnancy; killing a baby during postnatal psychosis; the sudden shaking of an infant by its caretaker in a fit of overwhelming frustration; a murderous assault on a child by a deluded parent; induced fatal illness; smothering disguised as Sudden Infant Death Syndrome (SIDS); and relentless neglect of an older child.

Gelles (1991) has also warned that mild physical punishment, severe abuse and child homicide may be distinct behaviours rather than continuities on the same spectrum of phenomena. Indeed, there are no clear parameters for deciding what constitutes "child abuse" and we have discussed elsewhere (Reder et al., 1993a) that it is a social construction, open to different interpretations. Many epidemiological researchers use the term "child homicide" generically.

Needles in Haystacks

The occurrence of fatal child abuse in the general population is not accurately known and a significant under-reporting is widely acknowledged (McClain et al., 1993; Ewigman et al., 1993). Nonetheless, it is undoubtedly a rare event. Creighton & Gallagher (1988) have estimated that some 198 child deaths per annum in the United Kingdom are directly caused by, or contributed to by, abuse or neglect, while Wilczynski (1997a) suggested a higher figure of 308 for England and Wales. An approximate rate for the UK can be inferred from these estimates that perhaps 200 to 300 children die annually, out of a population of 11 million children (Department of Health, 1995) i.e. 2 to 3 per 100 000 children.

Estimates for the USA vary between 2000 and 5000 deaths per year (US Advisory Board on Child Abuse & Neglect, 1995). McClain et al. (1993) proposed that as many as 11.6 per 100 000 children under four years of age die in the USA from abuse or neglect, although Levine (1996) considers that 4 per 100 000 is more realistic.

Physical abuse is the commonest cause of death, but a substantial number of neglect fatalities also occur, perhaps as many as 40% of abuse related deaths (Alfaro, 1988; Margolin, 1990; Levine et al., 1994).

These figures must be set against the number of children known to child protection agencies. A series of studies, which were summarised by the Department of Health (1995), traced children through the child protection system and gave the following approximations. Of 11 million children in England, some 160 000 (1.5%) are referred each year to social services for investigation of maltreatment allegations. Forty four per cent of the referrals are for suspected physical abuse and 25% for possible neglect, meaning, therefore, that approximately 1% of all children are referred annually with these particular concerns. Of the 160 000 children who are referred, around 24 500 (15.3%) have names newly entered onto a Child Protection Register, implying that a child protection plan is considered necessary. If 200–300 children die annually as the result of abuse, this is approximately 0.002% of all children, 0.15% of all referred children and around 1% of all newly registered children.

"Unknown" Families

The third complexity is that the majority of maltreatment deaths occur in families not previously known to child protection agencies. Although Sabotta & Davis (1992) quoted evidence that 45–55% of fatally abused children had previously been reported to child protection services, other reported figures tend to be lower. According to Alfaro (1988) and Levine et al. (1994), only about one third of cases in the USA had previous contact and Anderson et al. (1983) and Showers et al. (1985) suggested that it is only one quarter. Out of 14 fatal abuse cases known to one children's hospital (Hicks & Gaughan,1995), six families (43%) had had prior protective service involvement but the previous concerns had been about a sibling in four of them. Margolin's report (1990) that 39% of neglect fatalities in Iowa had any previous involvement with child protection services is salutary, since neglect is likely to be a more prolonged form of abuse than physical maltreatment and could be expected to come to the awareness of a range of professionals.

In the UK, Scott (1973) found that 28% of fathers or father substitutes convicted of killing a child in his care were already being visited by social agencies on account of child abuse, while Creighton (1989) reported that the names of 25% of children whose deaths were notified to the NSPCC between 1983 and 1987 were previously known to protective services. Wilczynski (1997a; b) reviewed 48 cases referred to the Director of Public Prosecutions: there had been previous contact with professionals about physical abuse in only 21% of cases, but 11 of 17 surviving siblings had suffered neglect, physical or emotional abuse or suspicious prior injuries.

Levels of Prediction/Prevention

Fourthly, it is necessary to recognise the distinctions between prediction/prevention at the primary, secondary and tertiary levels. Primary prevention aims to prevent a problem before it starts and, for fatal child abuse, this would require us to identify potentially infanticidal parents in the general population. Secondary prevention focuses on certain selected families identified as more at risk. Measures at the tertiary level attempt to minimise the consequences of the problem in those families already known to be demonstrating it: in other words, predicting which parents already known to child protection services because of child maltreatment are the ones who will fatally abuse.

In practice, most attention has been focused at the tertiary level because of social and professional concern about children dying who were already known to child protection agencies. We have therefore condensed our discussion of primary and secondary prediction in order to concentrate on the tertiary level issues.

PREDICTION AT THE PRIMARY AND SECONDARY LEVELS

Awareness about Child Care Issues

What is apparent from case studies of abusive deaths is that, although only a minority of the families were previously known to statutory agencies, many more had had recent contact with other professionals at the time of the fatality. Bennie and Sclare (1969) reported that 5 of 10 physically abusing parents had seen a doctor immediately prior to the assault, including to complain about the child's behaviour and to seek help in management. In a review of the literature on filicide (the killing of children by parents), Resnick (1969) found that 40% of the parents had seen a psychiatrist or physician shortly before the crime. d'Orban (1979) interviewed 89 women charged with killing or attempting to murder their child and found that 47 (42%) were in contact with their general practitioner, a psychiatrist, social worker or health visitor at the time of the offence. Korbin (1989) interviewed nine women imprisoned for the fatal abuse or neglect of a child: three had either contacted a paediatrician or another family member a few days before the child's death, including expressing concerns about the child's safety. In Wilczynski's study (1997a; b), 44% of the suspects had seen a medical practitioner (GP, psychiatrist or paediatrician) prior to the offence and 40% had seen a social worker: the commonest reason for professional contact had been about a parent's mental health.

All this points to the importance of professionals considering the welfare of the children of adults who present to them. This was illustrated in a report by Mogielnicki et al. (1977), who discussed three parents attending a casualty department with chest pain, limb weakness, headache or visual blurring. Psychiatric interviews with the parents revealed that they harboured fears of being violent to their child or were actually inflicting harm on the child.

There have been occasional reports about mothers who presented to psychiatrists with overt obsessional fears of harming their child (Anthony & Kreitman, 1970; Button & Reivich, 1972). The mothers were successfully treated with psychotherapy and none acted upon their murderous thoughts. However, the authors make no reference to child protective measures during the treatment, which we would consider to be essential.

Awareness in the Perinatal Period

One finding common to all studies concerns the very young age of children killed. The majority of abuse fatalities are to children in the first year of life, although the heightened risk does continue into the second year (e.g. Schloesser et al., 1992; Hegar et al., 1994; Durfee & Tilton-Durfee, 1995; US Advisory Board on Child Abuse and Neglect, 1995). This suggests that many of the mothers and children will recently have been seen by obstetric, postnatal or infant health services and that opportunities exist for preventive work around the perinatal period.

Children who are "unwanted" in some way are among those at risk of maltreatment generally (Altemeier et al., 1984; Murphy et al., 1985) and of fatal abuse or neglect (Resnick, 1970; d'Orban, 1979; Oliver, 1983). Clues to this in the perinatal period include the mother considering termination of the pregnancy, failing to present for antenatal care, wanting the baby to be adopted but changing her mind at the last moment, or carrying a baby conceived as the result of incestuous abuse.

A significant sub-group of cases concerns mothers who do not acknowledge that they are pregnant and fail to present for any antenatal care. The baby is born in secret and is abandoned to die or is actively killed (Brozovsky & Falit, 1971; Finnegan et al., 1982; Saunders, 1989; Green & Manohar, 1990; Fitzpatrick, 1995), although a few babies survive (Wilkins, 1985; Cherland & Matthews, 1989). Marks & Kumar (1993) found Home Office records for England and Wales of 45 neonaticides (children killed within 24 hours of birth) between 1982 and 1988—an average of some 7 per year, being 21% of all known infant homicides. There were Scottish Office records of six confirmed neonaticides between 1978 and 1993 (Marks & Kumar, 1996). In Queensland, Australia, Wilkey et al. (1982) found 11 such cases over a 10 year period from a population of two million, out of a total of 49 child killings from all causes.

Accounts of such cases usually report therapeutic work with the mothers some time after the baby's death. The nature of the problem—in which the mother denies the pregnancy and ignores antenatal care, while relatives remain unaware of the mother's state—means that professionals rarely have the opportunity to intervene before the infant is killed. However, Bonnet (1993) had the opportunity to interview a number of such mothers when they eventually acknowledged the pregnancy or soon after delivery and uncovered denied violent fantasies towards the infants: she recommended that planned adoption at birth could prevent neonaticide.

PREDICTION AT THE TERTIARY LEVEL

Here we are concerned with the possibility of predicting which abused children already known to statutory agencies will be killed by their caretakers. A few retrospective studies have indicated the number of abused children who are killed. Wilkey et al. (1982) gave a figure from Brisbane of 1–2% and Showers et al. (1985) reported that four deaths occurred in a group of 776 cases (0.5%) reported to the Children's Hospital in Columbus, Ohio. The American Association for Protecting Children (1986) estimated fewer than 1% but added that 11% suffer life-threatening, disabling or disfiguring injuries.

Hollander (1986a) and Sabotta & Davis (1992) concluded that child homicide is preceded by physical abuse at rates greater than that found generally. According to Hollander, if a child has been returned home following physical abuse: "there should be no hesitation or delay in recommending a second removal of the child if physical abuse is noted, because physical abuse precedes a large percentage of child homicides" (1986b, p. 90).

However, this advice is not specific enough, since reabuse rates are generally reported to be high. Herrenkohl et al. (1979) found that, among families in which physical abuse had occurred, 54% showed repeat incidents in up to 10 years of follow-up (the figure was 44% for gross neglect). Alexander et al. (1990) gave a recidivism rate for all child abuse in Iowa as one third, with a similar figure emerging from Browne's follow-up study in North Carolina (1986). Murphy et al. (1992)

followed up maltreated children who had been restored to parental custody by the Boston Juvenile Court for two years and found that almost one third of them had a subsequent official report of mistreatment. In half of these cases, the reabuse was so serious that the case had to return to court. Wood (1997) found lower repeat rates in El Paso in a two year follow up of validated child abuse/neglect cases: new allegations of physical abuse had occurred in 16% of cases (9% were substantiated) and of neglect in 13% (5% were substantiated). In the UK, Corby (1987) studied families receiving casework following physical abuse and neglect and found a recurrence rate of 28%.

From an epidemiological perspective, then, there is insufficient guidance in the literature to help us predict fatal abuse from among a group of known abusive families. We therefore turn to trying to identify predictive factors from specific cases.

High-Risk Check Lists

Greenland (1987) reviewed child abuse fatalities from different countries and constructed a high risk check list from observed similarities between the cases. Factors relevant to the parents were said to be:

- previously abused/neglected as a child
- a history of abusive/neglectful parenting
- a history of criminally assaultive and/or suicidal behaviour
- single, separated or living with a partner who is not the child's biological parent
- poor, unemployed or received inadequate education
- abuses alcohol and/or drugs
- pregnant or in the post-partum period or has a chronic illness

Factors concerning the child were:

- previously abused/neglected
- premature, low birth weight, birth defect, chronic illness or developmental lag
- prolonged separation from the mother
- adopted, fostered or a step-child
- currently underweight; cries frequently or difficult to comfort
- difficulties in feeding or elimination

According to Greenland, an infant who has suffered a serious non-accidental injury remains at "high risk" if more than half of the factors are positive. Although Greenland admitted that his check list needed to be tested in everyday practice, it so impressed the authors of the Jasmine Beckford Inquiry Report (1985) that it lent weight to the panel's belief that prediction of fatal abuse is possible.

However, on closer examination, there is little in this check list which appears to be specific to fatal abuse, as opposed to non-fatal physical maltreatment, so as to act as a tertiary level guide to front-line professionals. For example, Browne has worked for some time with colleagues to refine primary preventive measures by which health visitors can screen the general population for risk of child maltreatment (Browne & Saqi, 1988; Browne & Herbert, 1997). Significantly predictive factors have included: parental history of family violence; single or separated parent; unemployment; history of mental illness; drug or alcohol addiction; and parent abused or neglected as a child. The only item not on Greenland's list was "parent indifferent, intolerant or over-anxious towards child".

Of the few attempts to compare fatal and non-fatal cases, Husain & Daniel (1984) compared filicidal and abusive mothers referred by courts for psychiatric assessment and concluded that the risk of fatality as a complication of child abuse increases significantly when mental illness is present in the mother. However, Alfaro (1988) collated the findings from nine studies in the USA and found that the only features which statistically distinguished between fatal and non-fatal cases were: child very young; child health problems; young mother; male caretaker's history of criminality and drug use. Wilczynski (1995) also concluded that very few factors appear to be more or less frequent among filicidal cases.

Although Greenland's list does offer a framework for assessments, it exemplifies the problem with risk check lists for the prediction of fatal abuse, which have been summarised by Wilczynski (1997a):

- they are better at distinguishing between groups rather than individuals
- they are over-inclusive and generate a high number of false positives
- they are insufficiently sensitive and generate a high number of false negatives, especially since the problem is rare
- they are based on imprecise studies, with inconsistent definitions of abuse, no control groups and unrepresentative samples
- there is poor predictive clustering of factors and they do not adequately discriminate between non-fatal and fatal cases
- there has been little attention to buffering factors
- prior professional contact with the families has not usually focused on maltreatment

Recognising the Risk of Serial Filicide

Resnick (1970), Wilkins (1985) and McGrath (1992) believed that repetition of infanticide was very rare indeed. However, it is now recognised that a small number of parents, predominantly mothers, kill successive children in ways that can go undetected. The children may be smothered and, in the absence of diagnostic post-mortem evidence, the death is recorded as Sudden Infant Death Syndrome (SIDS) (Emery, 1985; 1986; Meadow, 1990; d'Orban, 1990; Hobbs et al., 1995; Hobbs & Wynne, 1996). Others are slowly poisoned or the parents induce symptoms such as fits and bring the child to paediatricians with illnesses that defy diagnostic efforts—so called Munchausen syndrome-by-proxy cases (Meadow, 1982; 1984). It is only if the physician becomes suspicious and investigates the circumstances further that it becomes apparent that the child was killed (Southall et al., 1987; Southall et al., 1997) and that previous siblings had also died in mysterious or suspicious circumstances, although their death had also been recorded at the time as SIDS.

There is increasing awareness that some abuse-related infant deaths are misdiagnosed as SIDS and that, if the cause of death had been more accurately determined, the risk of a similar fate to later siblings might have been recognised (Emery, 1985). Meadow (1984) discussed 32 children whose parents presented them with factitious epilepsy: they had had a total of 33 siblings, seven of whom had died suddenly and unexpectedly in infancy. Meadow (1990) later described 27 children whose death from suffocation was confirmed following recurrent symptoms of apnoea, cyanosis or seizures. Between them, they had had 33 siblings, 18 of whom had died suddenly in early life, often following similar episodes, and most had been diagnosed as SIDS. In 128 cases of Munchausen syndrome-by-proxy notified to a central register, 83 of the families had contained siblings, of whom 18 had previously died, five with a diagnosis of SIDS (McClure et al., 1996). Southall et al. (1997) detailed abuse to 39 children by their parents confirmed through covert video surveillance after they had been admitted to hospital with episodes of loss of consciousness, cyanosis or apnoea. These 39 children had had 41 siblings, 12 of whom had died unexpectedly and a diagnosis of SIDS had been given to 11 of them. Four parents ultimately admitted suffocating eight of these 12 siblings and a ninth was found to have died from deliberate salt poisoning.

Bacon (1997) has therefore advised that post-mortem pathologists should be more experienced at recognising the subtle signs of child abuse and should also be provided with the social history of the child who has died so that they could consider a wider range of causes of death. The model in Leeds, by which the deaths of all children between seven days and two years of age receive a detailed inquiry, has revealed previously unrecognised abuse-related deaths and a number of SIDS misdiagnoses (Hobbs et al., 1995). Similar experiences are reported from Child Death Review Teams in the United States (Durfee & Tilton-Durfee, 1995; US Advisory Board on Child Abuse & Neglect, 1995) and in Australia (New South Wales Child Protection Council, 1995). As a result, we have recommended in a report to the Department of Health (Duncan & Reder, 1997) the establishment of local and regional standing committees to review all child deaths in order to reduce the likelihood of missed abuse cases and to act as a preventive measure for siblings.

PREDICTIVE INFERENCES FROM TWO FATAL CHILD ABUSE STUDIES

We have conducted two studies into cases of fatal abuse. One concerned child deaths that had been the subject of public inquiry because the families were already known to statutory agencies (the "Beyond Blame" study, Reder et al., 1993a; b) and the second looked at all child abuse deaths reported to the Department of Health over a one year period (the "Lost Innocents" study, Duncan & Reder, 1997; Reder & Duncan, 1997; 1999).

The "Beyond Blame" Study

In 1987, we set out to review all available public inquiries into child abuse deaths to determine whether further practice lessons were possible. Our approach with each case was to draw up a genogram of the family and compile a detailed chronology of the events as they had unfolded. We tried to make sense of each case within a systemic framework and, as we read through the chronology, we would pause repeatedly to hypothesise why the family or professionals had behaved in the ways that they had. We then looked for patterns across the 35 cases studied and were able to to identify common themes in the family relationships, in the families' interactions with members of their professional networks, and in the relationships between professionals in the networks (Reder et al., 1993a; b). Some of the patterns we described appeared to have predictive potential, although the selected nature of the cases and the retrospective status of our study warrants caution when translating them into everyday practice.

CLOSURE

Some families attempted to withdraw from contact with the outside world and particularly from monitoring professionals. The parents did not keep scheduled appointments and social workers or health visitors repeatedly failed to gain entry to the home. The child/ren stopped attending school or nursery school and were not taken to appointments at health clinics. Neighbours no longer saw the child/ren playing around the home and, occasionally, the curtains of the home remained tightly drawn. We have referred to this as "closure".

Closure was evident in a majority of the 35 cases and usually occurred in intermittent cycles. By piecing together the chronology of events and medical evidence of the timing of the physical injuries to the child, it was evident that the episodes of closure coincided with periods of escalating abuse. An episode of closure also tended to lead up to the death of the child but this 'terminal closure' was no different in character from previous phases of intermittent closure. We inferred, therefore, that all periods of closure by families known to professionals because of a history of abuse should be considered an indicator of heightened risk to the child under surveillance that may prove fatal (Reder & Duncan, 1995; 1996).

A few other authors have also noted this phenomenon, including Oliver (1988), who termed it "avoidance behaviour". Greenland (1987) conducted an international study of fatal abuse cases and observed that "failure to gain access to a previously abused child should be regarded as one of the most critical danger signals" (pp 167–8). Despite this, he did not include the factor in his proposal for a high risk check list. Armstrong & Wood (1991) reviewed nine infant deaths known to a children's hospital in Brisbane and found that: "In all cases parents were avoidant of home visits and failed to attend appointments at other centres." (p. 595) However, this issue was not commented upon further in their final recommendations.

COVERT WARNINGS

A number of the families had approached professionals and communicated what was, in retrospect, a disguised admission that abuse was critically escalating. The warning nature of these incidents only emerged in reviewing each case, when it was apparent that they had been followed a few days later by the child's death.

In three families, the warning took the form of a request for their child to go into care, while another mother asked a hospital to admit her child to investigate his 'tendency to fall'. The week before another child sustained near fatal injuries, his foster mother stopped the health visitor in the street and asked her what medical conditions caused bruising, because she was being accused of beating her child. In the weeks preceding another child's death, her foster mother repeatedly told the child minder and general practitioner about her own severe headaches.

Other authors have made similar observations. Bennie and Sclare (1969) reported that five of 10 physically abusing parents had seen a doctor immediately preceding the assault, including to complain about the child's behaviour and to seek help in management. Korbin (1989) interviewed nine women imprisoned for abuse and neglect of a child who had subsequently died. Three had either contacted a paediatrician or another family member a few days before the child died, including expressing concerns about the child's safety.

Ounsted and Lynch (1976) referred to "open warnings", which are more explicit evidence of maltreatment offered by some parents prior to a violent attack, including taking the child to a doctor and displaying bleeding or bruising. An example cited by Lynch and Roberts (1982) was of a mother who, two weeks prior to a severe assault, had shown her general practitioner minor bruising that she had caused to the buttocks of her 10-week-old infant in a "feeding battle". The covert warnings that we have identified differ somewhat from these open warnings, being more masked and requiring the professional to translate the presentation into risk of severe child abuse.

Clearly, a vast number of parents ask social workers to take their child into care or complain to physicians about their child and it is only in retrospect that we have been able to claim that such parental behaviour was a covert warning of impending fatal abuse. However, these observations do point to the need for increased vigilance and suspiciousness by professionals. As with closure, in the context of a known history of child abuse by the parents, professionals should be aware that requests for care or displaced health inquiries about the child may signal escalating abuse that could prove fatal to a vulnerable child.

The "Lost Innocents" Study

We were interested to follow up our first study with a more representative group of cases and were supported by a grant from the Department of Health to study a series of "Part 8" Reviews. These are local case reviews, undertaken in accordance with procedures detailed in Part 8 of *Working Together* (Home Office et al., 1991), into deaths or serious harm to a child when maltreatment is confirmed or suspected. Each report is submitted to the Department of Health.

We looked at case reports for the year to March 1994, using the same approach as in the "Beyond Blame" study, and concluded that there had been 51 notifications to the Department that year of deaths either confirmed or suspicious of being caused by abuse. Patterns emerged across the cases which may have predictive potential, although the same caveat as before is necessary in interpreting these findings.

ADULT MENTAL HEALTH PROBLEMS

Fourteen of the 35 confirmed perpetrators of the fatal abuse (40%) had been currently suffering from an active mental health problem, which was substance misuse in seven cases. Similar associations have been found by Falkov (1996) and Wilczynski (1997a). In cases where the parent suffered from a paranoid psychosis, the child was at serious risk when incorporated into their parent's delusional thinking or hallucinations. Another feature common to these cases was that professionals' assessments tended to become preoccupied with whether the parent did or did not have a diagnosable psychiatric disorder at the expense of assessing the risk to the child. When the conclusion was reached that no psychiatric illness was present at that time, despite the history of violent threats to others and irrational behaviour, then the risk to the child from the parent's behaviour was not assessed as a separate issue and the possibility of preventing a fatal assault was missed. We have described this as "assessment paralysis".

COVERT AND OVERT WARNINGS

Additional examples of covert warnings emerged from this study. They included: a mother who told her neighbour and her father that professionals might have been suspicious that she had hit her child; an alcoholic father who demanded to speak to his GP, a child psychologist and a psychiatrist in the 24 hours before he killed two of his children; a mother who suddenly telephoned her midwife to insist that she stopped breast feeding the day before she strangled her baby; and a mother who commented to the social worker that her sister was continually hitting her child just six days before she smothered her own infant. There were also numerous instances of overt warnings, such as psychotic parents threatening to kill their child, or mothers' confessions to health visitors that they were smacking their child because of incessant crying and that they were at the end of their tether. The inference is that overt warnings should be taken seriously and that practitioners should be sensitive to the masked message that may be contained in apparently innocuous remarks.

REPETITION OF FILICIDE

Three of the 35 "Beyond Blame" cases involved parents who had killed or nearly killed a previous child and, of the 35 certain abuse fatalities in our "Lost Innocents" study, there were five confirmations or strong suspicions that the perpetrator had previously killed another child, either of their own or whilst childminding.

The significance of SIDS misdiagnoses for later siblings is underlined by two deaths which we reviewed during these projects. In both instances, misdiagnosis of a previous child's death meant that primary care professionals were visiting the family to try to prevent recurrence of SIDS. They had no reason to consider that there was a risk of fatal abuse with the next child and, as a result, were less sensitive than they might otherwise have been to evidence that the child was being mistreated.

A Possible Model of Risk

One interactional theme did arise from our studies that may have merits in predicting risk of severe harm or possible fatalities.

It was very apparent that the parents who killed the children usually came themselves from depriving, rejecting, hostile or abusive backgrounds, leaving them with what we have termed "unresolved care and control conflicts". Care conflicts might show in later life as excessive reliance on others and fear of being left by them, or recurrent separations and reunifications between partners, unwillingness to receive antenatal care in readiness for a dependent baby, or intolerance of the child's dependency needs when born. Control conflicts were enacted through violence, low frustration tolerance, attempts to assert power over others or intolerance of others perceived as being controlling (such as a baby when crying for attention). Constellations of these conflictual interactions appeared in the majority of the cases we reviewed.

We also inferred that episodes of severe abuse to a child often coincided with crises in the caretaker's relationships with their social context (such as their partner) or with the child. In particular, the crises could be understood as additional stresses to already conflictual care or control relationships. Examples included parents who felt acutely rejected by, or who had actually been abandoned by, their partner or their family of origin. Serious escalation in abusing couples' arguments, especially when accompanied by increasing alcohol or drug abuse, also appeared to be dangerous because of the implied threat of abandonment and violent loss of control. A newborn baby, or progressively more assertive toddler, could also be understood as stressing precarious care and/or control conflicts in the parent. We also found evidence that precipitants of fatal assaults included a child's inconsolable crying, or a baby's soiling a freshly changed nappy or inability to control their bladder or bowels whilst being bathed. Again, we understood that these events were probably experienced by the parents as a final exacerbation of their already stressed care or control conflicts.

While we are not able to suggest that this model is reliably predictive of the risk of severe or fatal child abuse, we do believe that it has merits as a framework within which to conduct assessments. If the caretakers are known to have experienced abuse and rejection in childhood, their history of relationships with others suggests residues of unresolved care or control conflicts including maltreatment of a child of their own, then episodes of crisis could be considered as especially risky to that child.

CONCLUSIONS

Most commentators have reached the conclusion that it is not possible to predict accurately whether a parent will kill their child. According to the US Advisory Board on Child Abuse and Neglect (1995): "Research suggests that the same kinds of high risk family situations are producing both fatally and seriously injured children . . . If true, prevention efforts directed at the larger group of families with the potential to seriously injure their children will encompass the smaller group of families at risk for fatalities. With the right approach, we also may be able to prevent so-called 'serial' fatal abuse and neglect by parents who have already lost one child but remain undetected by the system because the death was diagnosed as accidental or natural..." (p. 128)

Wilczynski (1997a) also reported that: "identifying a potential child-killer from a caseload of at-risk parents is a very difficult task. Indeed, there is general agreement that the only effective way to prevent child fatalities is to improve service provision to the entire at-risk population..." (p. 197) Alfaro (1988) concluded that: "the demand for accurate prediction is unrealistic in view of the nature of the fatality phenomenon and problems in predicting human behaviour in general." (p. 257) while Levine et al. (1994) believed that: "... the difference between a fatal and non-fatal injury may be a matter of chance. The conditions triggering severe injury or fatality are probably highly similar." (p. 456) and: "No risk measure is so closely predictive of actual harm that it could be used to justify drastic legal intervention into families..." (p. 465)

If our predictive capacities are meagre, is it appropriate to focus research or practice resources on the very rare fatal child abuse event? This is partially a moral issue, since one measure of a society's concern for its citizens is its willingness to focus on childhood and on children's suffering. Another dimension is the estimate offered by Baladerian (quoted by the US Advisory Board on Child Abuse and Neglect, 1995) that at least 10 times as many children survive abuse as die from it and are left permanently and severely disabled. In the UK, Buchanan & Oliver (1977) found that the brain damage of at least 3%, and possibly up to 11%, of children residing in subnormality hospitals had been directly caused by violent abuse or neglect.

The question has been raised whether preoccupation with predicting and preventing fatalities has inappropriately skewed practitioners' efforts. Gibbons et al. (1995) noted during their follow-up study of abused children that: "The unstated fear behind the [child protection] procedures may be that another child will be killed. Yet this is a comparatively rare event that can probably never be successfully predicted... The ever-present fear of serious or fatal injury to a child may explain why the social workers in this study concentrated on surveillance and monitoring to ensure children's physical safety. They appeared to pay less attention to warning signs of distorted socio-emotional development and low achievement." (p. 176) The Department of Health (1995) went on to encourage local authorities to review the balance of their work between statutory investigation and family support. The sad irony is that the social workers censured by the Jasmine Beckford inquiry had been focusing their endeavours on supporting the parents.

While we would endorse the need to monitor and review continually the focus of practitioners' work, our two studies have led us to the firm conclusion that assessment deficiencies can be found in many fatal abuse cases. While we acknowledge that caution is needed when translating retrospective findings into prospective strategies, it is our contention that the lessons which can be learned from fatal abuse cases are relevant to child maltreatment in general, of all degrees of severity.

It seems unrealistic to expect that all child deaths at the hands of their caretakers can be predicted and prevented. Unfortunately, abuse fatalities will continue to occur. However, it is apparent that there are different pathways leading to fatal abuse which epidemiological research does not satisfactorily distinguish. Clinical case studies, on the other hand, have the potential to alert professionals to constellations of factors which, taken together, could enhance prediction of serious maltreatment or fatal abuse. A greater understanding of seriously abusive scenarios might help reduce the number of such tragedies.

REFERENCES

Alexander, R., Crabbe, L., Sato, Y., Smith, W. & Bennett, T. (1990) Serial abuse in children who are shaken. *American Journal of Disease of Children*, **144**, 58–60.

Alfaro, J. (1988) What can we learn from child abuse fatalities? In: D. Besharov (ed.) *Protecting Children from Abuse and Neglect: Policy and Practice*. Springfield, Ill.: Charles C. Thomas.

Altemeier, W.A., O'Connor, S., Vietze, P., Sandler, H. & Sherrod, K. (1984) Prediction of child abuse: a prospective study of feasibility. *Child Abuse and Neglect*, **8**, 393–400.

American Association for Protecting Children (1986) *Highlights of Official Child Neglect and Abuse Reporting: 1984*. Denver, Col: American Humane Association.

Anderson, R., Ambrosino, R., Valentine, D. & Lauderdale, M. (1983) Child deaths attributed to abuse and neglect: an empirical study. *Child and Youth Services Review*, **5**, 75–89.

Anthony, E.J. & Kreitman, N. (1970) Murderous obsessions in mothers toward their children. In: E.J. Anthony & T. Benedek (eds) *Parenthood: Its Psychology and Psychopathology*. Boston: Little, Brown & Co.

Armstrong, K.L. & Wood, D. (1991) Can infant death from child abuse be prevented? *The Medical Journal of Australia*, **155**, 593–596.

Bacon, C.J. (1997) Cot death after CESDI. *Archives of Disease in Childhood*, **76**, 171–173.

Bennie, E.H. & Sclare, A.B. (1969) The battered child syndrome. *American Journal of Psychiatry*, **125**, 147–151.

Bonnet, C. (1993) Adoption at birth: prevention against abandonment or neonaticide. *Child Abuse and Neglect*, **17**, 501–513.

Browne, D.H. (1986) The role of stress in the commission of subsequent acts of child abuse and neglect. *Journal of Family Violence*, **1**, 289–297.

Browne, K. & Herbert, M. (1997) *Preventing Family Violence*. Chichester: John Wiley.

Browne, K.D. & Saqi, S. (1988) Approaches to screening families high risk for child abuse. In: K. Browne, C. Davis & P. Stratton (eds) *Early Prediction and Prevention of Child Abuse*. Chichester: John Wiley.

Brozovsky, M. & Falit, H. (1971) Neonaticide: clinical and psychodynamic considerations. *Journal of the American Academy of Child Psychiatry*, **10**, 673–683.

Buchanan, A. & Oliver, J.E. (1977) Abuse and neglect as a cause of mental retardation: a study of 140 children admitted to subnormality hospitals in Wiltshire. *British Journal of Psychiatry*, **131**, 458–467.

Button, J.H. & Reivich, R.S. (1972) Obsessions of infanticide: a review of 42 cases. *Archives of General Psychiatry*, **27**, 235–240.

Cherland, E. & Matthews, P.C. (1989) Attempted murder of a newborn: a case history. *Canadian Journal of Psychiatry*, **34**, 337–339.

Corby, B. (1987) *Working with Child Abuse: Social Work Practice and the Child Abuse System*. Milton Keynes: Open University Press.

Creighton, S.J. (1989) *Child Abuse Trends in England and Wales 1983–1987*. London: NSPCC

Creighton, S.J. & Gallagher, B. (1988) *Child Abuse Deaths. Information Briefing No. 5*. London: NSPCC.

Department of Health (1995) *Child Protection: Messages from Research*. London: HMSO.

Dingwall, R. (1989) Some problems about predicting child abuse and neglect. In: O. Stevenson (ed.) *Child Abuse: Public Policy and Professional Practice*. Hemel Hempstead: Harvester Wheatsheaf.

d'Orban, P.T. (1979) Women who kill their children. *British Journal of Psychiatry*, **134**, 560–571.

d'Orban, P. (1990) A commentary on consecutive filicide. Review of J. Egginton's 'From Cradle to Grave'. *Journal of Forensic Psychiatry*, **1**, 259–265.

Duncan, S. & Reder, P. (1997) *Study of Working Together "Part 8" Reports. The Review Process: Retrospect and Prospect*. Report to the Department of Health. London: HMSO

Durfee, M. & Tilton-Durfee, D. (1995) Multi-agency child death review teams: experiences in the United States. *Child Abuse Review*, **4**, 377–381.

Emery, J.L. (1985) Infanticide, filicide, and cot death. *Archives of Disease in Childhood*, **60**, 505–507.

Emery, J.L. (1986) Families in which two or more cot deaths have occurred. *Lancet*, i, 313–315.

Ewigman, B., Kivlahan, C. & Land, G. (1993) The Missouri child fatality study: underreporting of maltreatment fatalities among children younger than five years of age, 1983 through 1986. *Pediatrics*, **91**, 330–337.

Falkov, A. (1996) *Study of Working Together "Part 8" Reports. Fatal Child Abuse and Parental Psychiatric Disorder: An Analysis of 100 Area Child Protection Committee Case Reviews Conducted under the terms of Part 8 of Working Together under the Children Act 1989*. London: Department of Health.

Finnegan, P., McKinstry, E. & Robinson, G.E. (1982) Denial of pregnancy and childbirth. *Canadian Journal of Psychiatry*, **27**, 672–674.

Fitzpatrick, G. (1995) Assessing treatability. In: P. Reder & C. Lucey (eds) *Assessment of Parenting: Psychiatric and Psychological Contributions*. London: Routledge.

Gelles, R.J. (1991) Physical violence, child abuse, and child homicide: a continuum of violence, or distinct behaviours. *Human Nature*, **2**, 59–72.

Gibbons, J., Gallagher, B., Bell, C. & Gordon, D. (1995) *Development after Physical Abuse in Early Childhood: A Follow-up Study of Children on Protection Registers*. London: HMSO.

Green, C.M. & Manohar, S.V. (1990) Neonaticide and hysterical denial of pregnancy. *British Journal of Psychiatry*, **156**, 121–123.

Greenland, C. (1987) *Preventing CAN Deaths: An International Study of Deaths Due to Child Abuse and Neglect*. London: Tavistock.

Hegar, R.L., Zuravin, S.J. & Orme, J.G. (1994) Factors predicting severity of physical child abuse injury: a review of the literature. *Journal of Interpersonal Violence*, **9**, 170–183.

Herrenkohl, R.C., Herrenkohl, E.C., Egolf, B. & Seech, M. (1979) The repetition of child abuse: how frequently does it occur? *Child Abuse and Neglect*, **3**, 67–72.

Hicks, R.A. & Gaughan, (1995) Understanding fatal child abuse. *Child Abuse and Neglect*, **19**, 855–863.

Hobbs, C.J. & Wynne, J.M. (1996) Child abuse and sudden infant death. *Child Abuse Review*, **5**, 155–169.

Hobbs, C.J., Wynne, J.M. & Gelletlie, R. (1995) Leeds inquiry into infant deaths: the importance of abuse and neglect in sudden infant death. *Child Abuse Review*, **4**, 329–339.

Hollander, N. (1986a) Physical abuse as a predictor of child homicide. *Texas Medicine*, **82**, 21–23.

Hollander, N. (1986b) Homicides of abused children prematurely returned home. *Forensic Science International*, **30**, 85–91.

Home Office, Department of Health, Department of Education and Science, and Welsh Office (1991) *Working Together under the Children Act 1989: A Guide to Arrangements for Inter-Agency Co-operation for the Protection of Children from Abuse*. London: HMSO.

Husain, A. & Daniel, A. (1984) A comparative study of filicidal and abusive mothers. *Canadian Journal of Psychiatry*, **29**, 596–598.

Inquiry Report (1985) *A Child in Trust: The Report of the Panel of Inquiry into the Circumstances Surrounding the Death of Jasmine Beckford*. London Borough of Brent.

Korbin, J.E. (1989) Fatal maltreatment by mothers: a proposed framework. *Child Abuse and Neglect*, **13**, 481–489.

Levine, M. (1996) Letter. *Child Abuse and Neglect*, **20**, 643–4.

Levine, M., Freeman, J. & Compaan, C. (1994) Maltreatment-related fatalities: issues of policy and prevention. *Law & Policy*, **16**, 449–471.

Lynch, M.A., & Roberts, J. (1982) *Consequences of Child Abuse*. London: Academic Press.

Margolin, L. (1990) Fatal child neglect. *Child Welfare*, **69**, 309–319.

Marks, M.N. & Kumar, R. (1993) Infanticide in England and Wales. *Medicine, Science, and the Law*, **33**, 329–339.

Marks, M.N. & Kumar, R. (1996) Infanticide in Scotland. *Medicine, Science, and the Law*, **36**, 299–305.

McClain, P., Sacks, J. & Frohlke, R. (1993) Estimates of fatal child abuse and neglect, United States, 1979 through 1988. *Pediatrics*, **91**, 338–343.

McClure, R.J., Davis, P.M., Meadow, S.R. & Sibert, J.R. (1996) Epidemiology of Munchausen syndrome by proxy, non-accidental poisoning, and accidental suffocation. *Archives of Disease in Childhood*, **75**, 57–61.

McGrath, P. (1992) Maternal filicide in Broadmoor Hospital 1919–69. *Journal of Forensic Psychiatry*, **3**, 271–297.

Meadow, R. (1982) Munchausen syndrome by proxy. *Archives of Disease in Childhood*, **57**, 92–98.

Meadow, R. (1984) Fictitious epilepsy. *Lancet*, ii, 25–28.

Meadow, R. (1990) Suffocation, recurrent apnea, and sudden infant death. *Journal of Pediatrics*, **117**, 351–357.

Mogielnicki, R.P., Mogielnicki, N.P., Chandler, J.E., & Weissberg, M.P. (1977). Impending child abuse: psychosomatic symptoms in adults as a clue. *Journal of the American Medical Association*, **237**, 1109–1111.

Murphy, S., Orkow, B. & Nicola, R.M. (1985) Prenatal prediction of child abuse and neglect: a prospective study. *Child Abuse and Neglect*, **9**, 225–235.

Murphy, J.M., Bishop, S.J., Jellinek, M.S., Quinn, D. & Poitrast, F.G. (1992) What happens after the care and protection petition? Reabuse in a court sample. *Child Abuse and Neglect*, **16**, 485–493.

New South Wales Child Protection Council (1995) *Preventing Child Homicide: A Report from the New South Wales Child Protection Council's Child Death Review Committee*.

Oliver, J.E. (1983) Dead children from problem families in N E Wiltshire. *British Medical Journal*, **286**, 115–117.

Oliver, J.E. (1988) Successive generations of child maltreatment: the children. *British Journal of Psychiatry*, **153**, 543–553.

Ounsted, C., & Lynch, M.A. (1976). Family pathology as seen in England. In R.E. Helfer & C.H. Kempe (eds) *Child Abuse and Neglect: The Family and the Community*. Cambridge, Mass: Ballinger.

Parton, C. & Parton, N. (1989) Child protection, the law and dangerousness. In: O. Stevenson (ed.) *Child Abuse: Public Policy and Professional Practice*. Hemel Hempstead: Harvester Wheatsheaf.

Reder, P. & Duncan, S. (1995) Closure, covert warnings, and escalating child abuse. *Child Abuse and Neglect*, **19**, 1517–1521.

Reder, P. & Duncan, S. (1996) Letter (reply to Murray Levine). *Child Abuse and Neglect*, **20**, 644–645.

Reder, P. & Duncan, S. (1997) *Study of Working Together "Part 8" Reports: Practice Implications from a Review of Cases*. Report to the Department of Health. London: HMSO.

Reder, P. & Duncan, S. (1999) *Lost Innocents: A Follow-up Study of Fatal Child Abuse*. London: Routledge.

Reder, P., Duncan, S. & Gray, M. (1993a) *Beyond Blame: Child Abuse Tragedies Revisited*. London: Routledge.

Reder, P., Duncan, S. & Gray, M. (1993b) A new look at child abuse tragedies. *Child Abuse Review*, **2**, 89–100.

Resnick, P.J. (1969) Child murder by parents: a psychiatric review of filicide. *American Journal of Psychiatry*, **126**, 325–334.

Resnick (1970) Murder of the newborn: a psychiatric review of neonaticide. *American Journal of Psychiatry*, **126**, 1414–1420.

Sabotta, E.E. & Davis, R.L. (1992) Fatality after report to a child abuse registry in Washington State, 1973–1986. *Child Abuse and Neglect*, **16**, 627–635.

Saunders, E. (1989) Neonaticides following "secret" pregnancies: seven case reports. *Public Health Reports*, **104**, 368–372.

Schloesser, P., Pierpoint, J. & Poertner, J. (1992) Active surveillance of child abuse fatalities. *Child Abuse and Neglect*, **16**, 3–10.

Schmitt, B.D. & Krugman, R.D. (1992) Abuse and neglect of children. In: R.E. Behrman (ed.) *Nelson Textbook of Pediatrics*, 14th Edn. Philadelphia: Saunders.

Scott, P.D. (1973) Fatal battered baby cases. *Medicine, Science and the Law*, **13**, 197–206.

Showers, J., Apolo, J., Thomas, J. & Beavers, S. (1985) Fatal child abuse: a two-decade review. *Pediatric Emergency Care*, **1**, 66–70.

Southall, D.P., Stebbens, V.A., Rees, S.V., Lang, M.H., Warner, J.O. & Shinebourne, E.A. (1987) Apnoeic episodes induced by smothering: two cases identified by covert video surveillance. *British Medical Journal*, **294**, 1637–1641.

Southall, D.P., Plunkett, M.C.B., Banks, M.W., Falkov, A.F. & Samuels, M.P. (1997) Covert video recordings of life-threatening child abuse: lessons for child protection. *Pediatrics*, **100**, 735–760.

US Advisory Board on Child Abuse and Neglect (1995) *A Nation's Shame: Fatal Child Abuse and Neglect in the United States*. Washington: US Advisory Board on Child Abuse and Neglect.

Wilczynski, A. (1995) Risk factors for parental child homicide: results of an English study. *Current Issues in Criminal Justice*, **7**, 193–222.

Wilczynski, A. (1997a) *Child Homicide*. London: Greenwich Medical Media.

Wilczynski, A. (1997b) Prior agency contact and physical abuse in cases of child homicide. *British Journal of Social Work*, **27**, 241–253.

Wilkey, I, Pearn, J., Petrie, G. & Nixon, J. (1982) Neonaticide, infanticide and child homicide. *Medicine, Science and the Law*, **22**, 31–34.

Wilkins, A.J. (1985) Attempted infanticide. *British Journal of Psychiatry*, **146**, 206–208.

Wood, J.M. (1997) Risk predictors for re-abuse or re-neglect in a predominantly Hispanic population. *Child Abuse and Neglect*, **21**, 379–389.

3

PREDICTING PHYSICAL MALTREATMENT

Catherine Hamilton
Kevin Browne
School of Psychology, University of Birmingham, UK

INTRODUCTION

Physical abuse and neglect are the most commonly recognised forms of child maltreatment, as exemplified by data from prevalence and incidence studies (see Chapter 1). Using England as an example, during the past 12 years the Department of Health has assessed the number of children and young persons on child protection registers in England each year, based on annual statistical returns from 150 local government authorities. From the most recent statistics for England (Department of Health, 2000a), 14 600 girls and 15 400 boys in England were considered to require protection from maltreatment on 31 March 2000 together with 300 unborn children. In total, 28 in 10 000 children under 18 years were on child protection registers for actual or likely abuse and/or neglect. Of these, 29% were registered for physical abuse, 46% for physical neglect, 18% for sexual abuse and 18% for emotional abuse. Nearly one in ten of these children are registered for more than one type of abuse (11%) and nearly one in four (23%) of them were "children in public care". A similar situation is seen in other countries.

Services for these children are rarely offered until they have been placed on the register and there has been some recognition that maltreatment has or will occur. This approach produces a whole catalogue of financial consequences for local authorities and society in general. For example, the World Health Organization (WHO, 1999) have identified the following financial costs:

- medical care for victims (including long term disabilities)
- mental health and substance abuse programmes for victims or offenders
- criminal justice system expenditure on prosecution and treatment of offenders

Early Prediction and Prevention of Child Abuse: A Handbook.
Edited by Kevin Browne, Helga Hanks, Peter Stratton and Catherine Hamilton. © 2002 John Wiley & Sons, Ltd.

- legal costs for public child care and the rehabilitation of family breakdown
- social welfare costs for social work provision and the prevention of delinquency
- costs to the educational system in providing specialist educational provision for victims who are developmentally delayed or underperform at school

In the UK, the total economic cost for child protection per annum has been estimated at 735 million pounds (the National Commission into the Prevention of Child Abuse, 1996). In comparison, the total economic cost per annum in the USA has been estimated as 12 410 million dollars (WHO, 1999). Therefore, there has been increasing discussion about what services can be delivered in order to prevent the maltreatment of children and minimise the cost of child protection to society.

One area of debate has been the ethical issues raised by the process of assessment and service delivery, especially where the intention is to screen for indicators of children "in need". Clearly, account must be taken of parents' understanding of the function of family-based assessments. Under the rubric of partnership in child protection (Department of Health, 1995a) parents should be invited to share information with the professional and take an active role in the completion and interpretation of any assessment. It needs to be made clear to the parents that the presence of a high number of risk factors for adverse outcome identifies them as a *"family in priority"* for support and services. Negative labels such as *"high risk family"* should never be used.

The most recent information given to child protection professionals to assist their decision-making process is the new Department of Health "Framework for Assessment of Children in Need and their Families", commonly referred to as the "Lilac Book" (Department of Health et al., 2000b). However, the framework guidelines are primarily aimed at social workers to encourage them to take a more holistic approach to family assessment and consider the wider environment and its influence on family functioning. Specifically, three family components are assessed (see Figure 3.1):

- assessment of the developmental needs of the child
- assessment of the parents' capacity to meet the child's needs
- assessment of the social and environmental factors that impinge upon the parents' capacity to meet the child's needs

This latest Department of Health initiative is welcome in that it broadens a narrow view of child protection to include broader issues such as child welfare and development. Nevertheless, it can be argued that this more holistic assessment of the family arrives too late, as social workers will only be involved once a child has been suspected of significant harm. A public health approach would dictate that this form of assessment be carried out on all newborns during the first year of the child's life. Although any community professional could be involved in this process, in the UK such a preventative approach would be the responsibility of primary health care teams and community nurse home visitors in particular. It is unfortunate that social workers are so overwhelmed with reactive child protection work that there is little opportunity or resources for them to be used, perhaps more effectively, in a proactive and preventative way (as many social workers would

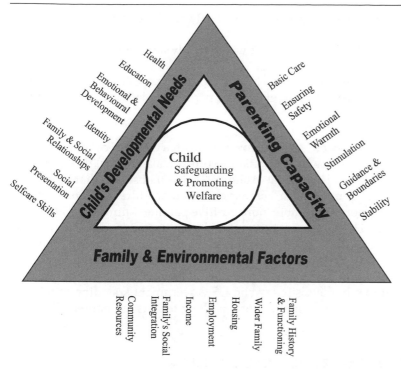

FIGURE 3.1 Framework for the Assessment of Children in Need and their Families (Department of Health et al, 2000b)

prefer). The causes of family violence are now better understood, so that preventative social work is both possible and desirable.

PUBLIC HEALTH PERSPECTIVE

A number of researchers have put forward models of child and family abuse (Browne, 1988; Frude, 1980; Gelles, 1997) which emphasise the multi-modal causes of maltreatment. Most importantly, there is now recognition that dysfunctional family relationships and a poor parent–child interaction can both contribute to and maintain child abuse and neglect (Burrell et al., 1994; Crittenden, 1985; Wolfe, 1991). In turn, there is the potential for good family relationships and parent–child interactions to act as protective factors and provide some resilience to social and environmental stress impinging on the family (Browne & Herbert, 1997). These realisations have led to the development of a public health approach to child protection. This may be defined as follows:

- Child abuse and neglect is considered within the broader context of child welfare, families and communities.
- Children's developmental needs are assessed in general rather than specifically in relation to child protection.

- The parent's capacity to respond appropriately to their child(ren)'s needs is evaluated.
- Consideration is paid to the impact of wider family and environmental factors on the capacity to parent.
- Child protection is integrated within health and social services to families, while promoting positive parenting and enhancing parental capacity to meet the needs of children.

Therefore, attention has been directed towards primary and secondary prevention methods, aimed at the whole population (universal services) or a high-risk group (targeted services) respectively. Wolfe (1991; 1993) observes that there have been promising developments in early interventions that address parental competency and family support to promote more positive parental knowledge, attitudes, skills and behaviour. He claims that personalised programmes such as home visits over a period of one to three years stand out as the most successful interventions in achieving desired outcomes in terms of fewer child injuries, emergency room visits and reports to protective agencies. Indeed, Olds and his colleagues (1993; 1994) have shown that home visits save on US Government spending in relation to disadvantaged families both in the short and long term (see Chapter 10).

THE IMPORTANCE OF EARLY INTERVENTION

During 2000, the highest rates of registration were found for physical abuse and neglect in very young children under one year of age (71 per 10 000). The likelihood of being on the Child Protection Register then decreases with age, with 69% of children on registers aged under 10 years. Boys and girls were equally represented in all age groups (Department of Health, 2000a). Given the number of children on Child Protection Registers under the age of 10 years with the highest risk group aged under one year, the majority of abused children cannot be expected to be proactive in preventing their own abuse. While helplines are excellent for teenagers, they do not prevent the maltreatment of younger children (Browne & Griffiths, 1988). Furthermore, many children will be abused before they have the opportunity of being exposed to school based prevention programmes. The most telling indicator that there is a need for early prevention is the level of fatal abuse and serious injury in the UK (see Chapter 2). Home Office figures show that two children a week die as a result of non-accidental injury and a further two children per week become disabled for life due to the injuries they have suffered (see Browne & Lynch, 1995). Notably, 75% of child fatalities registered on NSPCC Child Abuse Registers between 1983 and 1987 were not known to social services prior to the death (Creighton, 1995). Therefore, health professionals involved with families from the time of birth must be proactive rather than reactive in the protection of children.

The above highlights the importance of early intervention involving both universal and targeted services and the essential role of home visits carried out by community nurses in the first five years of a child's life. Using methods to target families who are high risk for child maltreatment, community nurses can place parents and children in priority for services before significant harm occurs.

TARGETING FAMILIES IN NEED

The protection of children by targeting scarce resources is a "risk strategy". The aim of the risk strategy is to give special attention to those in the greatest need of help in parenting before physical or psychological damage to the child occurs. This approach has developed because primary prevention services for all children, although preferable, may be unrealistic in economic terms. For example, since 1995 universal health promotion programmes (incorporating child health surveillance and home visits) have continued to be reduced by a number of health authorities and NHS trusts. As a result, there has been a reduction in both health visiting and the school health services (Browne & Lynch, 1998).

Thus, secondary prevention is considered to be a more realistic alternative and methods have been developed to target interventions at those families identified as most at risk of harming their children. Community nurses are now asked to prioritise their home visits and only visit those families in "high priority" for services, that is those most in need of help. Methods for identifying these families over the last two decades have included checklists and interview schedules for predicting high risk families prior to the onset of child maltreatment (Browne et al., 2000; Browne & Saqi, 1988a; Finkelhor, 1980; Magura & Moses, 1986; Monaghan et al., 1986).

SCREENING EFFECTIVENESS

With the practical application of risk factor checklists, especially to large birth cohorts, difficulties can arise through high numbers of false positives (children classed as high risk but not maltreated) and misses (children identified as low risk who are maltreated). Establishing this information with regard to child protection risk assessment is essential but rarely carried out (e.g., Department of Health et al., 2000b). This has important implications, both for the child and for appropriate use of resources. Failing to identify a child at risk of maltreatment will mean that no intervention is provided and the child remains unprotected from harm, whilst incorrectly classifying a child as high risk may lead to unnecessary interventions (sometimes resulting in harm), "labelling" and poor allocation of resources. Table 3.1 highlights the possible outcomes in decisions to separate a child or not, taken from Dalgleish (pers. comm.).

Leventhal (1988) stated that there are two main questions to ask about a means of identifying high risk groups. First, how many of the high risk group are subsequently maltreated (positive predictive accuracy) and second, of the maltreated group how many had originally been identified as high risk (sensitivity). He concludes that the best approach is to devise a checklist that maximises both the positive predictive accuracy and the sensitivity. A balance is required between using: (1) narrow threshold criteria (e.g., a higher number of risk factors present) to obtain high positive predictive accuracy but which may lead to a lot of missed cases; and (2) wide threshold criteria (i.e., a lower number of risk factors present) that correctly identify a greater number of cases but will also lead to a greater number of false alarms.

The relatively low prevalence of child abuse and neglect in the population as a whole, combined with even the most optimistic estimates of screening

TABLE 3.1   Consequences of decisions in child protection work (Dalgleish, pers. comm.)

	Should have taken action Should have said **"YES"**	Should NOT have taken action Should have said **"NO"**

Actual decision
YES Separate child
	Hit
	breaks cycle
	child feels safe
	child's "burden" lifted
	child develops protective
	    behaviours
	placement disruption,
	    anger hurt
		False Alarm
		child is abused by system
		child experiences trauma and
		    stress
		child is separated from family
		    (inappropriately)
		mistrust of "do-gooders"
		powerlessness feeling

Actual decision **NO** Do not separate child	**Miss** child is reabused child does not feel safe child does not develop trust child becomes dysfunctional child dies	**Correct No** no placement disruption family relationships remain intact child's network remains intact

effectiveness implies that a screening programme would yield large numbers of false positives. Indeed, this has been shown to be the case by Browne and Saqi (1988a) who evaluated a typical health visitor "checklist" of risk factors, completed on just one occasion. The checklist detection rate of 82% compared to 12% false alarms suggested that for every 10 000 births screened it would be necessary to distinguish between 33 true risk cases and 1 195 false alarms. This has been perceived by some as an argument against the use of any screening tools (e.g., Howitt, 1992). Nevertheless, Leventhal (1988) provides evidence from longitudinal cohort studies that suggests prediction is feasible, but concludes that improvements in the assessment of families are necessary, including the development and use of a standardised assessment of the parent–child relationship. Therefore, this research could indicate the requirement of a "second" screening procedure based on parent–child interaction and behavioural indicators, such as attachment, parental sensitivity and expectations (Browne & Saqi, 1988b; Leventhal, 1988; Morton & Browne, 1998).

ATTACHMENT PATTERNS IN THE HOME ENVIRONMENT

A considerable amount of research has been carried out on infant attachment patterns to parents (see Cassidy & Shaver, 1999). However, there have been relatively fewer studies of infant attachment patterns and their pathology in the home environment compared to clinical settings/strange situations. Home-based studies are essential for reliable and valid assessments by community health professionals. In the UK, an unpublished study by one of the authors estimated the infant attachment patterns derived from brief separation and reunion of the infant and mother in the home environment (see Table 3.2). Abused infants showed the highest number of insecure attachments (82%), in comparison to high risk infants (31%) and lower risk infants (28%), as determined by risk factors associated with physical maltreatment (see Table 3.3).

TABLE 3.2 Attachment patterns derived from brief separation and reunion of infant and mother in the home environment (Browne; unpublished)

Pattern	Ainsworth Category	Abused infants (n = 23) %	High risk (n = 42) %	Lower risk (n = 46) %
Avoidant	A_1A_2	52	21.5	17
Independent	B_1B_2	9	50	48
Dependent	B_3B_4	9	19	24
Ambivalent	C_1C_2	30	9.5	11
Total number of insecure attachments		**82%**	**31%**	**28%**

FACTORS ASSOCIATED WITH PHYSICAL MALTREATMENT AND ITS RE-REFERRAL

Table 3.3 presents a number of risk factors for physical abuse and neglect to children under five years (taken from Browne & Herbert, 1997). This considers the prevalence of these factors in both abusing and non-abusing families, as well as the percentage of families with a particular characteristic that are likely to go on to

TABLE 3.3 Relative importance of screening characteristics for child abuse as determined by discriminate function analysis (in percentages), from Browne and Herbert (1997; p. 120)

Checklist characteristics n = Parents with a child under 5 (baseline)	Abusing Families % (n = 106)	Non-abusing families % (n = 14.146)	Conditional probability* % 0.7
History of family violence	30.2	1.6	12.4
Parent indifferent, intolerant or over-anxious towards child	31.1	3.1	7.0
Single or separated parent	48.1	6.9	5.0
Socio-economic problems such as unemployment	70.8	12.9	3.9
History of mental illness, drug or alcohol addiction	34.9	4.8	5.2
Parent abused or neglected as a child	19.8	1.8	7.6
Infant premature, low birth weight	21.7	6.9	2.3
Infant separated from mother for more than 24 hours post delivery	12.3	3.2	2.8
Mother less than 21 years old at time of birth	29.2	7.7	2.8
Step-parent or cohabitee present	27.4	6.2	3.2
Less than 18 months between birth of children	16.0	7.5	1.6
Infant mentally or physically disabled	2.8	1.1	1.9

* Conditional probability refers to the percentage of families with a particular characteristic that go on to abuse and/or neglect their newborn in the first five years of life

maltreat their child in the first five years of life. It can be seen that environmental/ socio-economic factors (e.g., unemployment), parental factors and child factors are all represented, with higher rates of each characteristic present in the abusing families as compared to the non-abusing. The factor with the highest probability of and association with future maltreatment is a history of family violence. This is consistent with a large literature on the link between child abuse and spouse abuse (e.g., see Browne & Hamilton, 1999). However, this checklist may be criticised as only relevant to infants given the sample on which it was evaluated. For example, it may have less relevance to sexual abuse and some forms of emotional abuse and neglect, which may be experienced by older children.

In terms of assessing risk factors associated specifically with child maltreatment for all ages, Table 3.4 presents the factors associated with a referral to police child protection units in an English police force in 1994 (Hamilton, 1998). Each maltreatment type has been included for comparison. For example, those risk factors associated with a referral for physical maltreatment included a prior referral for the child, a small number of child related factors (e.g., child with behavioural problems), with the majority of associated characteristics relating to the child's family (e.g., criminality, drug or alcohol misuse, spouse abuse).

It has been claimed by Browne and Hamilton (1997) that abuse is a process and not an event. Therefore it is important to consider indicators of recurrent maltreatment. These are most easily established by studying the characteristics of re-referral. Consideration of risk factors associated with re-referral following an index referral for physical abuse demonstrated similar risk factors with an overall accuracy of 84.2% (sensitivity = 81.5%, specificity = 85.7%, positive predictive accuracy = 75.9%). These risk factors for re-referral (from Hamilton, 1998) are:

- family spouse abuse
- child has behavioural problems
- family member with a drug problem
- family member with an alcohol problem
- family member with learning difficulties
- previous referral for the child
- family member with criminal record
- perpetrator not an acquaintance or stranger
- child self-harming
- child has at least one sibling

The factors predictive of re-referral following sexual or physical abuse were found by Hamilton (1998) to be related to family or child factors, whilst for neglect the predictive factors were mainly service related (e.g., social services, continued intervention). Re-referral following physical abuse was predicted by factors relating to difficulties with family members and family perpetrators, with less emphasis on child features. These included family drug and alcohol misuse, spouse abuse, family criminality and a member of the family with learning difficulties.

Another limitation of risk factor checklists is the lack of recognition of the interrelationships and correlations between each risk factor, with some patterns of combination being much more dangerous than others. The links between child abuse and spouse abuse are well documented, but less weight has been placed

Table 3.4   Variables significantly correlated with child maltreatment at any age at an index referral (Hamilton, 1998)

Sexual abuse	Gender, prior referrals for the child, prior referrals for the family, mother in the family home, child in care, child showing criminal behaviour, child with behavioural problems, child abusing alcohol or drugs, child with learning difficulties and age above or below 10 years at index referral.
Physical abuse	Prior referral for the child, child has at least one sibling, family criminality, family member with drug problem, family member with alcohol problem, family spouse abuse, family member with learning difficulties, child with behavioural problems, child self-harming and acquaintance perpetrator at index referral.
Neglect	Prior referrals for the child, prior referrals for the family, Child Protection Register status, social services continued involvement, Child Protection Conference called, child with severe medical problems, perpetrator not previously known to the police and perpetrator involved in a No Further Action prior referral.
Emotional abuse	Child Protection Conference called, child with severe medical problems, child self-harming and child with learning difficulties.
Mixed abuse	Child Protection Register status, police decision on index referral still pending, social services continued involvement, Child Protection Conference called, step-father in the family home, family member with drug problem, family member self-harming or has self-harmed, child with severe medical problems, perpetrator not previously to the police and severity of maltreatment classed as known "concern".

on the role of substance addictions in child maltreatment (Steinmetz, 1987). It is well recognised though that being under the influence of alcohol or drugs is frequently cited as an explanation for abusive behaviour (Gelles, 1997; Lickey & Gordon, 1991). In addition, substance misuse can potentially increase risk through a number of ways. Many battered women blame their own victimisation on their partner's drinking (Gelles, 1997; Dobash et al., 2000) or even become alcoholic themselves (Sedlack, 1988; Stark & Flitcraft, 1988). Furthermore, child behavioural problems have been linked both to growing up in a violent household and one in which a parent is a substance misuser (Frude 1991; Jaffe et al., 1990; Orford, 1987).

Clearly predictive models can identify some children at risk of both initial maltreatment and re-referral following physical maltreatment. However, as discussed above, without consideration of protective factors (such as secure attachments and positive parenting), there is a tendency for potential cases to be missed and for there to be a significant number of false alarms. This emphasises the necessity of a second form of assessment based on the parent–child relationship to increase accuracy. While screening for child protection remains less than perfect, the means of intervention must be positive in nature (e.g., nursery placements). In this way, families gain benefits from the assessment, rather than merely negative connotations such as being the subject of a child protection conference. This ideology has been put into practice with the Child Assessment Rating Evaluation (Browne et al., 2000).

THE CARE PROGRAMME

In keeping with recommendations for practice (Hall, 1995) and the Children Act 1989, a Child Assessment Rating and Evaluation (CARE) Screening Programme was introduced into the Southend Community Care Services for the identification of "need" in all families with newborns in that area for three years (Browne et al., 2000). This is achieved in partnership with parents.

The CARE programme is designed for community-based primary health care professionals to:

- offer a child- and family-centred assessment of need that covers the child's first year of life, rather than being a one-off judgement
- offer an objective assessment of parenting capacity and family difficulties as a basis for referrals and joint work with other agencies
- offer, for the first time, the means for parents to identify their own situation and perceptions of parenting
- offer reliable behavioural indicators (such as parental sensitivity and infant to parent attachment) to distinguish between priority families and the remainder of the population

The purpose of the programme is to assess risk factors, as well as parental perceptions, attributions and sensitivity over four visits (see Table 3.5). The development of the child's attachment behaviours is also monitored, as a potential protective factor (see Table 3.6). The objective is for this screening information to be routinely used as an insert in parent-held records.

Following the four home visits during the first year, the community nurse is required to indicate the plan for the years up to five years of age when their involvement traditionally ceases. There are two options, "routine surveillance" where the community nurse is reactive to the family's requests and needs and "prolonged active management" where the community nurse is proactive and continues to make regular visits to the family either because the child is in "need" or is of "concern". All children on the Child Protection Register would fall into the latter category. Either at this time or at any during the first twelve months, referrals can be made to other agencies for additional support. These include home visiting services (e.g., postnatal depression, infant sleep), voluntary groups (e.g., mother and toddler, counselling), health services (e.g., pediatricians, psychologists) and social services (e.g., nursery placements, family support). In some instances, child protection procedures may have to be implemented.

However, formalised screening programmes based on objective criteria require research to establish their reliability and validity in the home environment, as well as a feasibility study.

Evaluation

A pilot study has already been carried out on all families with newborns (1583 families) in the Southend Health Care District to establish the feasibility of the above procedure to everyday health visiting practice. This feasibility study was considered a success because the CARE programme gained the full co-operation

TABLE 3.5   Risk factors and behavioural indicators recorded during home visits (from Browne et al., 2000)

A. Risk factors recorded	Assessed at:
Demographic data (e.g. occupation, marital status)	1st visit (4–6 weeks)
Index of Need	
birth complications/separation from baby due to ill health	1st visit (4–6 weeks)
mother or father under 21	and
mother/father not biological parent	4th visit (9–12 mths)
twins/less than 18 months between children	
child with physical/mental disabilities in family	
either parent feels isolated	
serious financial problems	
mental illness/depression in parental history	
parent(s) drug/alcohol problems	
parent(s) physically or sexually abused as a child	
infant characteristics (illness, prematurity, birthweight)	
single parent	
adult in house with violent history/tendencies	
parent(s) have indifferent feelings towards baby	
Changes in family circumstances	
(e.g., marital status/partner/occupation)	3rd visit (6–8 mths)
B. Behavioural indicators recorded	**Assessed at all visits:**
(frequency of behaviours recorded: rarely, occasionally, frequently)	
Attributions & perceptions:	
frequency of positive statements by parents about their	1st visit (4–6 weeks)
infant and to their infant	2nd visit (3–5 mths)
frequency of realistic perceptions by parents	3rd visit (6–8 mths)
about their infant's behaviour	4th visit (9–12 mths)
Quality of parenting:	
the frequency of sensitive, supportive/cooperative,	1st visit (4–6 weeks)
accessible and accepting behaviour by the parent	2nd visit (3–5 mths)
to the infant	3rd visit (6–8 mths)
	4th visit (9–12 mths)

Reproduced by permission from the National Youth Advisory Service publication; Reprecenting Children.

of nearly all health visitors and their clients (parents). In addition, responses from a questionnaire to parents in the CARE programme confirmed they were highly satisfied with the health visiting (community nursing) service.

From a validity perspective, 3.7% of families in this district were identified as a *"family in priority"*, 30.2% were rated with a low index of need (*low priority*) and 66.1% were of no concern in relation to the needs of the newborn and their family. It was also found that positive parenting occurred in the vast majority (97%) of families. As postulated, the minority of parents (3%) with unrealistic expectations and fewer positive attributions were significantly more likely to be a "family in priority". This confirmed that the methods were reliable and behavioural characteristics may be of predictive value. The success of the referrals based on the identification of "families in priority" with children in need was followed up and the multi-agency referral process was observed to run smoothly due to the contracts that were in place before the programme started (Browne et al., 2000).

TABLE 3.6 Assessment criteria for the development of attachment to primary caregiver (from Browne et al., 2000)

A. Infant attachment behaviours observed *(frequency of behaviours recorded: rarely, occasionally, frequently)*	Assessed at:
Smiles at caregiver Quietens when picked up by caregiver Responds to caregiver's voice Eye contact and scans caregiver's face Settles in caregiver's arms	1st visit (4–6 weeks)

Turns head to follow caregiver's movements
Responds to caregiver's voice with pleasure
Imitates speaking to caregiver by moving lips
  in response
Shows preference for being held by caregiver
  by settling and quieting
	2nd visit (3–5 mths)

Shows preference for a primary caregiver
Demonstrates some distress when left by
  primary caregiver
Confident to explore: crawls away from
  and turns round to look at primary caregiver
Relaxed and comforted when held by primary caregiver
	3rd visit (6–8 mths)

B. Classification of infant attachment style *Classify by allocating to category:*	4th visit (9–12 mths)

Avoidant (Insecure): Tends not to seek interaction
  with caregiver and does not become
  distressed when separated from caregiver.
  On reunion, often resists physical contact	

Independent (Secure): Often seeks interaction but
  not especially physical contact, rarely
  distressed at separation, reunion characterised
  by smiling and reaching out	

Dependent (Secure): Actively seeks physical contact and
  interacts with caregiver, on reunion
  with caregiver smiles and reaches out	

Ambivalent (Insecure): Low levels of play, lack of
  interaction and obvious anxiety
  with strangers with intense distress
  at separation. On reunion, may
  continue to cry. Mixes contact
  seeking behaviour with active resistance
  to caregivers approaches	

Represented by permission from the National Youth Advisory Service publication; Representing Children.

CONCLUSION

The importance of providing an objective technique for the prediction of physical abuse and neglect cannot be understated. For many years research has demonstrated a number of potentially negative outcomes for victims of child maltreatment. These include psychological dysfunction, eating disorders, conduct disorders, poorly learned parenting skills, poor relationships with significant others and offending behaviour (Bagley et al., 1984; Briere & Runtz, 1986; Fromuth, 1986; Perez & Widom, 1994; Widom & Ames, 1994).

More recent literature has begun to address the issue of recurrent maltreatment for children and the implications this has for long-term outcomes (Fryer & Miyoshi, 1994; Hamilton & Browne, 1998; 1999; Hamilton, Falshaw & Browne, 2002; DePanfilis & Zuravin, 1998). Not least of these is the increased risk of further victimisation in adulthood (Gidycz et al., 1993; Himelein, 1995; Mayall & Gold, 1995). Moeller et al. (1993) reported that 5.3% of women with no history of abuse were the victims of adult physical abuse compared to 9.4% of those who had experienced one type of maltreatment in childhood, 28.9% who had experienced two types and 32.4% who had experienced three types.

The invaluable advantage of providing services to ameliorate risk factors before abuse and neglect occurs is that this facilitates protection against both initial victimisation and later revictimisation. Fifteen years ago, it was claimed that approximately one-third of sexually abused children had been previously physically abused (Finkelhor & Baron, 1986) and some of the risk factors associated with physical abuse and neglect are common to the prediction of sexual abuse. There are also commonalities with other conditions such as Sudden Infant Death Syndrome (SIDS) and Munchausen by Proxy (Meadow, 1990; Southall, 1987).

Thus, early identification of child need, parenting capacity and family difficulties are essential to the protection of children and there is no doubt that this must involve home visitation programmes to provide effective prevention that intervenes before maltreatment begins.

REFERENCES

Bagley, C., Wood, M. and Young, L. (1994). Victim to abuser: mental health and behavioural sequels of child sexual abuse in a community survey of young adult males. *Child Abuse and Neglect*, **18**(8), 683–697.

Briere, J. and Runtz, M. (1986). Suicidal thoughts and behaviour in former sexual abuse victims. *Canadian Journal of Behavioural Sciences*, **18**, 414–423.

Browne, K.D. (1988). The nature of child abuse and neglect. In K. Browne, C. Davies, and P. Stratton (Eds). *Early Prediction and Prevention of Child Abuse*. Chichester: Wiley, 15–30.

Browne, K.D. and Griffiths, P. (1988). Can telephone help lines prevent child abuse? *Changes*, **16**(4), 120–122.

Browne, K.D. and Hamilton, C.E. (1997). The repeat and revictimisation of children: possible influences on recollections for trauma. In D. Read and S. Lindsay (Eds.), *Recollections of Trauma*. New York: Plenum Press.

Browne, K.D. and Hamilton, C.E. (1999). Police recognition of the links between spouse abuse and child abuse. *Child Maltreatment*, **4**(2), 136–147.

Browne, K.D., Hamilton, C.E., Heggarty, J. and Blissett, J. (2000). Identifying need and protecting children through community nursing home visits. *Representing Children*, **13**(2), 111–123.

Browne, K.D. and Herbert, M. (1997). *Preventing of Family Violence*. Chichester: Wiley.

Browne, K.D. and Lynch, M.A. (1995). The nature and extent of child homicide and fatal abuse. *Child Abuse Review*, **4**(5), 309–316.

Browne, K.D. and Lynch, M.A. (1998). Community interventions for child protection and government Policy. *Child Abuse Review*, 7(1), 1–5.

Browne, K.D. and Saqi, S. (1988a). Approaches to screening families high-risk for child abuse. In K.D. Browne, C. Davies and P. Stratton (Eds). *Early Prediction and Prevention of Child Abuse*. Chichester: Wiley, 57–86.

Browne, K.D. and Saqi, S. (1988b). Mother-infant interactions and attachment in physically abusing families. *Journal of Reproduction and Infant Psychology*, **6**, 163–82.

Burrell, B., Thompson B. and Sexton D. (1994). Predicting child abuse potential across family types. *Child Abuse and Neglect*, **18**(12), 1039–1049.

Cassidy, J. and Shaver, P.R. (1999). *Handbook of Attachment: Theory, research and clinical applications*. New York: The Guildford Press.

Creighton, S. (1995). Fatal child abuse: is prevention possible? *Child Abuse Review*, **4**(5): 318–328.

Crittenden, P.M. (1985). Maltreated infants: vulnerability and resilience. *Journal of Child Psychology and Psychiatry*, **26**, 85–96.

Dalgleish, L. (pers. comm.). Risk assessment and decision making in child protection. Paper taken from chapters in the book, *Risk and Decision in Child Protection*. Chichester: Wiley (manuscript in preparation).

DePanfilis, D. and Zuravin, S.J. (1998). Rates, patterns and frequency of child maltreatment recurrences among families known to CPS. *Child Maltreatment*, **3**(1), 27–42.

Department of Health (1995a). *The Challenge of Partnership in Child Protection: Practice Guide*. London: HMSO.

Department of Health (1995b). *Child Protection: Messages From Research*. London: HMSO.

Department of Health (1999). *Working Together to Safeguard Children*. London: HMSO.

Department of Health (2000a). Children and Young People on Child Protection Registers Year Ending 31st March 2000, England (Personal Social Services and Local Authority Statistics). London: Government Statistical Service.

Department of Health, Department of Education and Employment and the Home Office (2000b). *Framework for the Assessment of Children in Need and their Families*. London: HMSO

Dobash, R.E., Dobash, R.P., Cavanagh, K. and Lewis, R. (2000). *Changing Violent Men*. Thousand Oaks, CA: Sage.

Finkelhor, D. (1980). Risk factors in the sexual victimization of children. *Child Abuse and Neglect*, **4**, 265–273.

Finkelhor, D. and Baron, L. (1986). Risk factors for sexual abuse. *Journal of Interpersonal Violence*, **1**, 19–28.

Fromuth, M.E. (1986). The relationship of childhood sexual abuse with later psychological and sexual adjustment in a sample of college women. *Child Abuse and Neglect*, **10**, 5–15.

Frude, N. (1980). 'Child abuse as aggression'. In N. Frude (Ed.), *Psychological Approaches to Child Abuse*. London: Batsford Academic.

Frude, N. (1991). *Understanding Family Problems: A psychological approach*. Chichester: Wiley.

Fryer, G.E. and Miyoshi, T.J. (1994). A survival analysis of the revictimization of children: the case of Colorado. *Child Abuse and Neglect*, **18**(12), 1063–1071.

Gelles, R.J. (1997). *Intimate Violence in Families* (3rd edn.). Thousand Oaks, CA: Sage.

Gidycz, C.A., Coble, C.N., Latham, L. and Layman, M.J. (1993). Sexual assault experience in adulthood and prior victimization experiences: a prospective analysis. *Psychology of Women Quarterly*, **17**(2), 151–168.

Hall, D.M.B. (1995). *Health for All Children* (3rd edn.). London: HMSO.

Hamilton, C.E. (1998). *The repeat victimisation of children*. Unpublished thesis, University of Birmingham.

Hamilton, C.E. and Browne, K.D. (1998). The repeat victimization of children: should the concept be revised? *Aggression and Violent Behaviour*, **3**(1), 47–60.

Hamilton, C.E. and Browne, K.D. (1999). Recurrent maltreatment during childhood: a survey of referrals to police child protection units in England. *Child Maltreatment*, **4**(4), 275–286.

Hamilton, C.E., Falshaw, L. and Browne, K.D. (2002). The link between recurrent maltreatment and offending behaviour. *International Journal of Offender Therapy and Comparative Criminology*, **46**(1), 75–94.

Himelein, M.J. (1995). Risk factors for sexual victimization in dating. *Psychology of Women Quarterly*, **19**, 31–48.

Howitt, D. (1992). *Child Abuse Errors: When Good Intentions Go Wrong*. Hemel Hempstead: Harvester Wheatsheaf.

Jaffe, P.G., Wolfe, D.A. and Wilson, S.K. (1990). *Children of Battered Women*. Beverley Hills, CA: Sage.

Leventhal, J. (1988). Can child maltreatment be predicted during the perinatal period: evidence from longitudinal cohort studies. *Journal of Reproductive and Infant Psychology*, **6**, 139–61.

Lickey, M.E. and Gordon, B. (1991). *Drugs and Mental Illness*. New York: WH Freeman.

Magura, M. and Moses, B.S. (1986). *Outcome measures for child welfare services*. Washington, DC: Child Welfare League of America.

Mayall, A. and Gold, S.R. (1995). Definitional issues and mediating variables in revictimization of women sexually abused as children. *Journal of Interpersonal Violence*, **10**(1), 26–42.

Moeller, T., Bachmann, G. and Moeller, J. (1993). The combined effects of physical, sexual, and emotional abuse during childhood: Long-term health consequences for women. *Child Abuse and Neglect*, **17**, 623–640.

Monaghan, S.M., Gilmore, R.J., Muir, R.C., Clarkson, J.E., Crooks, T.J., and Egan, T.G. (1986). Prenatal screening for risk of major parenting problems: further results from the Queen Mary Maternity Hospital Child Care Unit. *Child Abuse and Neglect*, **10**, 369–375.

Morton, N. and Browne, K.D. (1998). Theory and observation of attachment and its relation to child maltreatment: a review. *Child Abuse and Neglect*, **22**(11): 1093–1104.

National Commission of Enquiry into the Prevention of Child Abuse (1996). *Childhood Matters*, Vols 1 & 2. London: NSPCC.

Olds, D.L., Henderson, C.R. and Kitzman, H. (1994). Does prenatal and infancy nurse home visitation have enduring effects on the qualities of parental care giving and child health at 25 to 50 months of life. *Pediatrics*, **93**(1): 89–98.

Olds, D.L., Henderson, C.R., Phelps, C., Kitzman, H. and Hanks, C. (1993). Effect of prenatal and infancy nurse home visitation on government spending. *Medical Care*, **31**(2): 155–174.

Orford, J. (1987). Alcohol problems and the family. In T. Heller, M. Gott and C. Jeffrey (Eds.), *Drug Use and Misuse: A Reader*. Chichester: Wiley, 76–82.

Perez, C.M. and Widom, C.S. (1994). Childhood victimisation and long-term intellectual and academic outcomes. *Child Abuse and Neglect*, **18**(8), 617–633.

Sedlack, A.J. (1988). Prevention of wife abuse. In V.B. Hasselt, R.L. Morrison, A.S. Bellack and M. Hersen (Eds.), *Handbook of Family Violence*. New York: Plenum.

Southall, D.P., Stebbens, V.A., Rees, S.V., Lang, M.H., Warner, J.O. and Shybourne, E.A. (1987). Apneic episodes induced by smothering: two cases identified by covert video surveillance. *BMJ*, **294**, 1637–1641.

Stark, E. and Flitcraft, A. (1988). Violence among intimates: An epidemiological review. In V.B. Hasselt, R.L. Morrison, A.S. Bellack and M. Hersen (Eds.), *Handbook of Family Violence*. New York: Plenum.

Steinmetz, S.K. (1987). Family violence: past, present and future. In M.B. Sussman and S.K. Steinmetz (Eds.), *Handbook of the Marriage and the Family*. New York: Plenum Press.

World Health Organization (1999). *Report of the consultation on child abuse prevention*. WHO, Geneva, 29–31 March 1999. Geneva: WHO.

Widom, C.S. and Ames, M.A. (1994). Criminal consequences of childhood sexual victimisation. Child Abuse & Neglect, **18**(4), 303–318.

Wolfe, D. (1991). *Preventing Physical and Emotional Abuse of Children*. New York: Guildford Press.

Wolfe, D. (1993). Child abuse prevention: blending research and practice. *Child Abuse Review*, **2**(2): 153–165.

4

PREDICTING EMOTIONAL ABUSE AND NEGLECT

Danya Glaser

Great Ormond Street Hospital, London, UK

Vivien Prior

Institute of Child Health, London, UK

The quality of a prediction is governed by the degree of confidence with which it is made. In this respect, the study of emotional abuse and neglect is fraught with difficulty. The subject matter involves complex human relationships which are not amenable, ethically or pragmatically, to the usual manipulations of scientific enquiry and particularly prospective longitudinal studies. Nevertheless, theoretical considerations, research to date and clinical experience allow us to suggest the likely important components in the prediction equation as applied to emotional abuse and neglect, and put forward directions for future practice.

While the focus in this chapter is on the relationship between the primary caregiver(s) and the child, this relationship is obviously nested within the family which is, in turn, significantly influenced by the social environment in which the family is located (Fortin & Chamberland, 1995).

WHAT IS EMOTIONAL ABUSE AND NEGLECT?

Beyond the physical injury which can result from the various forms of child abuse and neglect, most of the sequelae of all forms of abuse and neglect affect the child's psychological, emotional and behavioural development. It may indeed be the attendant emotional abuse and neglect which are the mediators of the harm caused by other forms of child abuse and neglect (Hart et al., 1996; McGee et al., 1997). Emotional abuse and neglect also exist independently of other forms of abuse and neglect. While, for instance, physical neglect is often accompanied by

Early Prediction and Prevention of Child Abuse: A Handbook.
Edited by Kevin Browne, Helga Hanks, Peter Stratton and Catherine Hamilton. © 2002 John Wiley & Sons, Ltd.

psychological neglect, the converse is not always the case (Egeland & Erickson, 1987).

Since it is generally believed that emotional abuse and neglect are difficult to define and recognise, it is necessary to discuss these issues first. A summary definition is provided in *Working Together to Safeguard Children* (Department of Health, 1999), split between Emotional Abuse, and Neglect. There are various aspects which distinguish this form of maltreatment from other forms of child abuse and neglect.

Emotional abuse refers to a relationship between the abuser and the child rather than to an event or a series of repeated events occurring within the carer–child relationship. Physical abuse and sexual abuse are single, or more commonly, repeated events. The child can usually remember some temporal or associated physical circumstance of significant abuse events.

In emotional abuse and neglect, the interactions of concern pervade or characterise the relationship. The interactions are actually or potentially harmful. Emotional abuse includes omission as well as commission and the full term is therefore emotional abuse and neglect. (The term maltreatment includes both abuse and neglect.) Emotional abuse and neglect require no physical contact between abuser and child.

Significant Harm is the threshold criterion used in the Children Act 1989, to activate child protection procedures, both at the level of social services and the courts. It distinguishes between ill-treatment (omission and commission) by the abuser and impairment of the child's health and development (the damage sustained by the child). There is no requirement to prove parental or the abuser's intent to harm the child, in order to satisfy the threshold.

In emotional abuse and neglect, for definitional purposes it is more useful to refer to ill-treatment than to focus on the harm to the child (McGee & Wolfe, 1991). This is so for two reasons. Firstly, the difficulties shown by children who have been psychologically maltreated are both numerous and not specific to emotional abuse and neglect. It is not therefore appropriate to recognise the emotional abuse or neglect by the child's impairment, since it could also be accounted for by other factors. Secondly, if the definition depended on the evidence of harm to the child, this would preclude the possibility of prevention or early intervention. In emotional abuse and neglect, the ill-treatment can be conceptualised as five categories of harmful interactions between the parent and the child (Glaser, 2002), each capturing the violation of an essential aspect of a child's needs and rights.

Categories of Ill-Treatment

I EMOTIONAL UNAVAILABILITY, UNRESPONSIVENESS AND NEGLECT

In category I, the primary carer(s) are usually preoccupied with their own particular difficulties such as mental ill health (including postnatal depression) and substance abuse, and are unable rather than unwilling to respond to the child's emotional needs. If the child is perceived as not deserving parental attention, then this category still applies but is secondary to category II.

II NEGATIVE ATTRIBUTIONS AND MISATTRIBUTIONS TO THE CHILD

This includes hostility towards, and denigration and rejection of a child, who is perceived as deserving these.

Some children grow to believe in and act out the negative attributions placed upon them.

III DEVELOPMENTALLY INAPPROPRIATE OR INCONSISTENT INTERACTIONS WITH THE CHILD

This category includes the following:

- expectations of the child beyond her/his developmental capabilities
- over-protection and limitation of exploration and learning
- exposure to confusing or traumatic events and interactions

This category contains a number of different interactions including exposure to domestic violence and parental (para)suicide. This category is often found in association with categories I and II. When found as the primary category, the parents lack knowledge of appropriate caregiving practices and child development, often because of their own childhood experiences.

IV FAILURE TO RECOGNISE OR ACKNOWLEDGE THE CHILD'S INDIVIDUALITY AND PSYCHOLOGICAL BOUNDARY

- using the child for the fulfilment of the parent's psychological needs
- inability to distinguish between the child's reality and the adult's beliefs and wishes

This form of abuse is also not infrequently found in the context of custody and contact disputes within parents' divorce proceedings.

Fabricated or induced illness is a variant of this category.

V FAILING TO PROMOTE THE CHILD'S SOCIAL ADAPTATION

- promoting mis-socialisation (including corrupting)
- psychological neglect (failure to provide adequate cognitive stimulation and/or opportunities for experiential learning)

This category includes involving children in criminal activities.

Child Impairments

The timing, extent and nature of the manifest signs of impairment in the child vary, according to the child's age and possible protective factors. For some children, explicit signs of impairment will lag some way behind the ill-treatment, while for others, signs of impairment may never be manifest. The difficulty is that it is often not possible at an early stage to predict factors leading to the resilience of the child. For this reason, prediction and possible early prevention must focus on ill-treatment. The Children Act 1989 is helpful here in that it stipulates that a finding of actual or *likely* significant harm can be made as a result of ill-treatment and/*or* impairment, attributable to the care given or likely to be given. The combination of the term "likely" and the word "or" provides professionals with the opportunity to intervene on the basis of ill-treatment alone. It is not necessary, at least within the terms of the Children Act, to wait for actual impairment.

This does not address the separate issue of whether ill-treatment per se is *ever* acceptable, regardless of its consequences.

FACTORS ASSOCIATED WITH EMOTIONAL ABUSE AND NEGLECT

From empirical and clinical work, certain factors have been found to be associated with emotional abuse and neglect. They are: parental or adult factors; physical abuse and physical neglect; and certain impairments of the child's health and development.

Parental or Adult Factors

As a first principle, it will be taken that responsibility for ensuring that the relationship between the parent and the child is non-abusive or neglectful lies with the parent. This is not to deny that children can be temperamentally difficult, provocative or, in some cases, have physical or psychological conditions which cause stress for the parent and challenge their ability to cope. Nor is this to be unsympathetic to parents or to blame them. It is an attempt to understand, as from understanding flows appropriate action. Children are, by definition, dependent and therefore vulnerable, and developing rapidly. In the parent–child relationship, responsibility lies primarily and ultimately with the parent. If the parent is unable to cope, a responsible action is to seek help. If the parent, for whatever reason, is unable to seek help, the responsibility lies with others to intervene on behalf of both the child and the parent. In any event, children are not responsible for abuse inflicted upon them. Winnicott (1982) coined the phrase "goodenough" mother, in which he described the maternal capacity to meet the child's emotional needs. The goodenough parent has to be goodenough for any particular child, whatever their attributes.

Four sorts of parents can be distinguished:

- adults with clearly defined harmful attributes
- troubled adults who do not have clearly defined attributes
- coping adults who become vulnerable parents
- adults who are not recognised as troubled

ADULTS WITH CLEARLY DEFINED HARMFUL ATTRIBUTES

Three particular forms of difficulty have been found to be associated with emotional abuse and neglect: mental ill-health, domestic violence and drug and alcohol abuse (Cleaver et al., 1999). In one study (Glaser & Prior, 1997), the parents of 69% of children recognised as emotionally abused or neglected showed these difficulties, either singly or in combination: 38% mental ill-health, 28% domestic violence and 21% drug and alcohol abuse.

A further group of adults are those who present with somatisation disorder or Munchausen syndrome. These are adults who perceive and express their psychological conflicts and difficulties through bodily symptoms and who seek resolution through the physical treatment of these symptoms. An extreme variant of this is Munchausen syndrome in which the person repeatedly presents to doctors and hospitals with false reports, and self-induced symptoms and signs, seeking medical treatment. Some mothers do so in pregnancy by falsely reporting premature labour or falsifying bleeding (Jureidini, 1993). There is an association between these adult presentations and falsification of illness in their children, or factitious disorder by proxy (Eminson & Postlethwaite, 2000).

TROUBLED ADULTS WHO DO NOT HAVE CLEARLY DEFINED ATTRIBUTES

Some adults are recognised as troubled, but their difficulties do not fall into one of the specific forms listed above. Some of these adults might be thought to be suffering from a personality disorder, and others may not have been recognised as falling within any named diagnostic disorder. It is likely that these troubled adults have unresolved feelings and issues related to their own past experiences which may have included childhood abuse and/or neglect.

COPING ADULTS WHO BECOME VULNERABLE PARENTS

There are some adults whose vulnerability is only expressed in their role as parents. One expression of this occurs when partner or marital disharmony sets in, especially when this leads to divorce or dissolution of the partner relationship (Johnston & Campbell, 1988).

Adults with recognised learning difficulties in the learning disability range and very young parents are likely to encounter significant difficulties in the parenting of their children, which may amount to emotional abuse and neglect in categories I & III.

Children may have particular attributes which present the parent with specific difficulties in their interactions with the child. The child's difficulties range from disfigurement to temperamental difficulties.

Some adults function adequately as parents until a traumatic event occurs which disturbs or disrupts the parent–child relationship. This includes a traumatic pregnancy or birth, or an unexpected or traumatic loss.

ADULTS WHO ARE NOT RECOGNISED AS TROUBLED OR VULNERABLE

There are some adults who would not, in their own right, be recognised as troubled and this only becomes recognised in their difficulties as parents or when their children become symptomatic. These adults, too, may have unresolved issues from a troubled past. Many of these adults are professionals, or belong to the middle or upper social classes, who are far less likely to have become known to helping agencies, specifically social services.

Other Forms of Child Abuse and Neglect

Different forms of child abuse and neglect frequently co-exist (Briere & Runtz, 1988; Ney et al., 1994). In particular, emotional abuse and neglect or psychological maltreatment, measured separately, are found in a majority of children who have been physically abused and neglected (Claussen & Crittenden, 1991). In a study of children on child protection registers under the sole categories of Physical Abuse, and Neglect, 81% respectively were reported by their social workers to be suffering emotional abuse (Glaser et al., 2001).

Certain Impairments of the Child's Health and Development

The difficulties which have been found in children who have been emotionally abused, or neglected children, may be grouped into different domains of functioning:

Emotional state   Within this domain, children may be unhappy, show low self-esteem, experience fear, anxiety and distress and may suffer from post-traumatic stress disorder following witnessing of domestic violence.

Behaviour   Behavioural difficulties include oppositional behaviour, attention-seeking or assuming age-inappropriate responsibility.

Developmenta/educational attainment   While younger children may show developmental delay, older children often underachieve educationally, some through irregular school attendance.

Peer and social relationships   Social interaction may be impaired because of aggression or because of social withdrawal and isolation.

Physical state Children may present as physically neglected or unkempt, may show growth failure, encoproesis or complain of pains and other physical symptoms not based on physical illness.

THE MEANING OF PREDICTION

The meaning of prediction can be understood in a number of ways. There is the prediction that if something exists, something else will follow; this could be termed *prospective* prediction. There is the prediction that if something exists, something else exists with it (co-exists); this could be termed *concurrent* prediction. There is the prediction that if something exists, something else preceded it; this could be termed *retrospective* prediction. Thus, prediction can provide more than a forecast for the future; it can link the present with the future, the present with the present and the present with the past. Prospective prediction allows for secondary prevention of the problem. Concurrent prediction is the root to identification of the problem. Retrospective prediction, which might appear to be an idiosyncratic use of the term prediction, could equally be called an explanation. However, whether driven by theory, as in the prediction that the "big bang" preceded an expanding universe, or by probability based on experience, it is possible to predict, with varying degrees of confidence, that something previously occurred. For example, it is possible to predict with a high degree of probability that a person who is serving a jail sentence has previously committed a crime.

It is necessary to mention the role of risk factors in the context of prediction. While prospective prediction must rest on the presence of risk factors, individual risk factors will vary in the power of their predictiveness. All the prospective predictors mentioned here are risk factors. There are few quantitative data about the predictive strength of these risk factors. It should be recognised that, in themselves, parental factors do not describe the abuse or ill-treatment, but rather form risk factors or the context within which the abuse or neglect occur. Particular risk factors do not, however, consistently predict specific forms of ill-treatment.

A MODEL FOR PREDICTING EMOTIONAL ABUSE AND NEGLECT

We now propose to apply these three forms of prediction to emotional abuse and neglect. A model can be constructed linking different forms of prediction with factors associated with emotional abuse and neglect, as follows:

Forms of prediction	Factors associated with emotional abuse and neglect
Prospective prediction *(prevention)*	Parental or adult factors
Concurrent prediction *(identification)*	Concurrent abuse and neglect
Retrospective prediction *(explanation)*	Child impairments

HOW ACCURATELY CAN WE PREDICT EMOTIONAL ABUSE AND NEGLECT FROM THIS MODEL?

Prospective Predictors of Emotional Abuse and Neglect

PARENTAL OR ADULT FACTORS

It is known that a high proportion of emotional abuse and neglect exists in the presence of parental mental ill-health and alcohol and drug abuse. The converse, namely the proportion of children living with parents experiencing these difficulties and who suffer emotional abuse or neglect, is not known. The available data do, however, indicate that parental mental ill-health and substance abuse are risk factors for emotional abuse and neglect, although the magnitude of the risk is not currently known. Children living with a mentally ill or substance abusing parent may of course be protected and adequately nurtured by a second, well carer. Mental ill-health and alcohol or drug dependence in single carers therefore must be seen as serious risk factors for emotional abuse and neglect and, without considerable external support for the child, can be considered as highly predictive.

Any one form of parental difficulty can be associated with different categories of emotionally abusive ill-treatment. For instance, drug and alcohol abuse may lead to emotional unavailability of the parent (category I). The child or children may be faced with developmentally inappropriate responsibilities which actively interfere with their own development, such as looking after younger siblings or caring for the parent (category III). Additionally, there are several ways of failing to promote the child's social adaptation (category V). Children may not attend school regularly either because the parent fails to ensure school attendance or because of the child's excessive domestic responsibilities. Children may feel compromised in their peer relationships because of the stigma which follows having a parent who abuses drugs or alcohol (Coleman & Cassell, 1995). Exposure to active drug intake, especially intravenous use, provides the child with inappropriate models of behaviour. Due to the variety of forms of maltreatment associated with drug and alcohol abuse, the children show a range of difficulties (Christensen, 1995). These include fear of losing the substance-abusing parent due to the effect of the drug or alcohol, fear of not being loved and fear of being stigmatised. In the face of chronic parental substance abuse, children develop more or less adaptive coping strategies.

Postnatal depression is an important aspect within this group (Murray, 1997). The mothers tend to be negative, emotionally unavailable or unresponsive to the infant's communications and affective state, or out of synchrony and consequently intrusive with the infant, who becomes more aroused and distressed.

Postnatal depression has been found repeatedly to be associated with harmful sequelae for the child. Infants are particularly susceptible to these effects between six and 18 months of age (Dawson et al., 1994). Enduring changes have been found in their behaviour and emotional state, including social withdrawal, negativity and distress. Reduced cognitive verbal abilities in the pre-school years of boys whose mothers had been depressed before the boys were 18 months old (Sinclair & Murray, 1998) have also been found. It is the effect on the mother–child interaction which leads to the difficulties in the children, rather than the depression per se. Postnatal depression is therefore not absolutely predictive of emotional neglect, but sufficiently important to warrant early intervention.

Children whose parents have a violent relationship are very likely to be aware of it, and those children who have witnessed it, experience it as traumatic (Somer & Braunstein, 1999). Domestic violence is therefore a risk factor strongly predictive of emotional abuse or neglect.

For adults who are not recognised as troubled or vulnerable parents, prediction is theoretically possible providing the difficulty or vulnerability is recognised. Again, the presence or absence of another carer who is able to nurture the child is crucial. Although the prevalence of the emotional abuse of children whose parents are in the process of parting has not been quantified, suffice it to say that the number of cases coming to court as private proceedings under the Children Act 1989 is four times as great as the number of public law care cases. What we do not know is what proportion of dissolving parental relationships end up in these private law proceedings.

Prediction in the case of adults who are not recognised as troubled is probably impossible.

Onset of ill-treatment in the presence of parental attributes

Bearing in mind that parental attributes are risk factors for, rather than descriptors of, ill-treatment (harmful parent–child interactions), the question arises about the timing of the onset of the ill-treatment in the presence of parental attributes. Since parental substance abuse and domestic violence are usually chronic and often progressive, it is difficult to identify the point at which the deterioration in the parent–child relationship or exposure of the child reaches the threshold for emotional abuse or neglect.

Parental mental ill-health is somewhat different. The illness may have a gradual or sudden onset, and may be episodic. The onset of the ill-treatment may therefore be gradual or abrupt.

Concurrent Predictors

PHYSICAL ABUSE AND PHYSICAL NEGLECT

The presence of physical abuse and physical neglect has been shown to concurrently predict emotional abuse or neglect in a high proportion of cases. This is an important means of identifying emotional abuse and neglect. Families in which physical abuse and physical neglect are found are frequently socially disadvantaged and therefore more likely to have come to the attention of social services than families in whom there is solely psychological maltreatment. It is important to note that emotional abuse and neglect also exist independently of other forms of abuse and neglect. Until recently it has, however, been less frequently recognised and named as such by child protective services when occurring on its own.

In sexual abuse, the abuser is not usually the primary or sole primary care-giver of the child. Beyond the psychological damage caused by the sexual abuse, emotional abuse would emanate from the relationship between the non sexually-abusing caregiver(s) and the child.

ALERTING SIGNS IN FACTITIOUS DISORDER BY PROXY

There are a number of alerting signs to identification of factitious disorder by proxy. The alerting signs are:

- reported symptoms which are disproportionate to, unrelated to, or not explained by the child's medical condition, if any
- reporting of new symptoms on resolution of previous problems
- physical examination which does not support reported symptoms
- results of investigations which do not explain symptoms or signs
- inexplicably poor response to prescribed therapy
- escalation of complexity of therapy
- reported symptoms not observed by anyone other than the mother
- signs or reported symptoms not present when the parent is absent, or when the child is continuously observed
- child's daily life (e.g. school attendance, diet) impaired, disproportionately or inappropriately, in relation to any known medical condition

These alerting signs should not be considered as proof of the condition. Each calls for a search for the others, and requires the exclusion, by a paediatrician, of the possibility that the child's illness is being falsely presented or falsified.

Retrospective Predictors

CERTAIN IMPAIRMENTS OF THE CHILD'S HEALTH AND DEVELOPMENT

The difficulties which children who have been psychologically maltreated show are both numerous and not specific to emotional abuse and neglect. It is not therefore safe to predict that emotional abuse or neglect has occurred from knowledge of child impairment, since it could also be accounted for by other factors.

In summary, prediction of emotional abuse and neglect is limited. Clearly recognised parental difficulties or particular child vulnerabilities can be recognised as risk factors. In certain circumstances, for example children living with a sole mentally ill or substance dependent carer, or children living with domestic violence, the risk of emotional abuse or neglect is high. However, in the absence of clearly recognised parental difficulties, prospective prediction is very difficult. In a high proportion of cases, physical abuse and physical neglect concurrently predict emotional abuse and neglect. It may, however, exist on its own. Lastly, emotional abuse and neglect are a cogent but not sole explanation for certain child impairments.

APPLYING PREDICTION TO PRACTICE

Prospective Prediction

Adults with clearly recognised difficulties are usually known to adult services, including adult mental health services, substance misuse services and the police, who may not even be aware of the fact that the adult is also a parent. From the child's point of view, in order to prevent or halt emotional abuse or neglect there is an imperative to treat the parental attribute or difficulties (Christensen, 1997). Because in practice emotional abuse and neglect may already be occurring at the time the adult risk factors are recognised, any professional who comes into contact with a troubled parent needs to ensure that enquiries are made about the well-being of any child in their care and specifically about emotional abuse and neglect. Such professionals include GPs, health visitors, pre-school and school staff.

Concurrent Prediction

In the light of the strong association between physical abuse and neglect, and emotional abuse and neglect there is a need to search specifically for emotional ill-treatment, when physical abuse and/or neglect are found. The reason for this is that there has been relatively little success in the treatment of emotional abuse and this has been attributed in part to the lack of specificity in treatment offered to mal-treating families as a generic group (Brassard & Hardy, 1997). The new *Framework for the Assessment of Children in Need and their Families in England* (DoH, 2000) may utilise the concurrent prediction of emotional abuse and neglect.

Retrospective Prediction

The known association between child impairments and emotional abuse and ne-glect calls for a search for emotional abuse and neglect in the absence of a very clear alternative explanation for the child's difficulties. This explanation will help relieve the child from the burden of self-blame, indicate a direction for treatment, and also enable protection of the child from still ongoing abuse.

THE RELATIONSHIP BETWEEN PREDICTION AND PREVENTION

The point of prospective prediction is to prevent actual damage to the child. In prevention terms, concurrent, let alone retrospective predictions are therefore not helpful. As can be seen from the above, prospective predictions are imperfect for prevention, although the model we have presented suggests a way forward. How-ever, there is considerable evidence that, currently, emotional abuse which is al-ready ongoing is unrecognised and unnamed. This is important because early recognition may be a substitute for actual prevention, and significant harm may thus be avoided. One of the protective factors ameliorating the impact of emotional abuse and neglect (and other forms of child abuse and neglect) is brief duration of the harmful parent–child interaction.

PREVENTING EMOTIONAL ABUSE AND NEGLECT—RECOGNITION OF ILL-TREATMENT

A distinctive feature of emotional abuse and neglect, which it shares with physical neglect, is that the ill-treatment is readily observable. The issue for recognition is not whether there is unseen or secret abuse, but rather whether what is observed is described and named as ill-treatment. In practice, this step is often omitted. In research carried out by the authors, it was found that in 22% of cases of children on child protection registers under the category of emotional abuse, no form of ill-treatment was explicitly stated to explain the category of registration. In nearly all these cases, however, the presence of parental attributes (parental mental ill-health, alcohol/drug abuse and/or domestic violence), either singly or in combination, was reported (Glaser et al., 2001).

Obstacles to Recognition of Ill-Treatment

There are several reasons for the difficulties in recognising emotional abuse and neglect:

- There is at times confounding of ill-treatment and impairment, and uncertainty about whether the term emotional abuse should be applied to the ill-treatment or the impairment of the child's functioning.
- There have been questions about how harmful interactions which are observed and described should be understood and classified within the overall concept of emotional abuse and neglect.
- There is a further difficulty for individual professionals in deciding whether the threshold for significant harm has been reached. The forum for this decision is a multidisciplinary child protection conference.
- The term "abuse" is often considered to be pejorative, particularly where there is no clear intent to harm the child, although the interaction is clearly harmful to the child.
- There is greater difficulty in recognising emotional abuse and neglect in the absence of very clear adverse parental attributes, or other forms of child abuse or neglect, i.e. emotional abuse and neglect in isolation.

Obstacles to Effective Protection of the Child

Even when emotional abuse and neglect are recognised and named, there is concern about the acceptance of the threshold by the courts. Moreover, in emotional abuse and neglect the "abuser" is almost invariably the primary carer and attachment figure for the child. In two-parent families, either both parents contribute to the abuse or the other parent is unable to offer effective protection. Therefore, if protection requires separation of the child from the abusive situation, this is invariably at the cost of interrupting an attachment bond. Questions arise about whether the cure is worse than the problem.

Consequences—Delay and Lack of Protection

The obstacles to recognition lead to delay during which the child continues to be emotionally abused or neglected. The likely consequence is that by the time of eventual recognition, the child will be older and very troubled, the emotional abuse will be entrenched and the potential for change will be slight. This was found, for example, in a study of children registered under the category of emotional abuse. These children had been known to social services between eight months and 14 years, with a mean of four years, before registration. The mode age at registration was nine years and 34% of these children were placed permanently away from their original primary carers (Glaser et al., 2001).

There is a further consequence to the delay in recognition. While the child continues to remain unprotected, there is a temptation and indeed practice to begin to describe and "diagnose" the child's disorders without fully explaining and dealing with the antecedent circumstances of the emotional abuse or neglect.

CONCLUSIONS

Prediction and early recognition are both necessary for the effective protection of children from emotional abuse and neglect. This chapter has offered a classification to assist in recognition of ill-treatment and a model for predicting emotional abuse and neglect. There remains a professional perception that it is difficult to protect children when there is ill-treatment in the absence of actual impairment. The immediate challenge, however, is to recognise early ill-treatment and to thereby protect those children whose impairment is already evident or imminent.

REFERENCES

Brassard, M., & Hardy, D. (1997). Psychological maltreatment. In M. Helfer, R. Kempe & R. Krugman (Eds.), *The battered child*. Chicago: University of Chicago Press.

Briere, J., & Runtz. (1988). Multivariate correlates of childhood psychological and physical maltreatment among university women. *Child Abuse and Neglect*, **12**, 331–341.

Christensen, E. (1995). Families in distress, the development of children growing up with alcohol and violence. *Arctic Medical Research*, **54**, Suppl. 1, I 53–59.

Christensen, E. (1997). Aspects of a preventive approach to support children of alcoholics. *Child Abuse Review*, **6**, 24–34.

Claussen, A., & Crittenden, P. (1991). Physical and psychological maltreatment: Relations among types of maltreatment. *Child Abuse and Neglect*, **15**, 5–18.

Cleaver, H., Unell, I., & Aldgate, J. (1999). *Children's needs – parenting capacity: the impact of parental mental illness, problem alcohol and drug use, and domestic violence on children's development*. London: The Stationery Office.

Coleman, R., & Cassell, D. (1995). Parents who misuse drugs and alcohol. In P. Reder & C. Lucey (Eds.), *Assessment of parenting: psychiatric and psychological contributions* (pp. 183–193). London: Routledge.

Dawson, G., Hessl, D., & Frey, K. (1994). Social influences on early developing biological and behavioral systems related to risk for affective disorder. *Development and Psychopathology*, **6**, 759–779.

Department of Health. (1999). *Working together to safeguard children.* London: The Stationery Office.

Department of Health. (2000). *The new framework for the assessment of children in need and their families in England.* London: The Stationery Office.

Egeland, B., & Erickson, M. (1987). Psychologically unavailable caregiving. In M. Brassard, B. Germain, & S. Hart (Eds.), *Psychological maltreatment of children and youth* (pp. 110–120). Elmsford, NY: Pergamon.

Eminson, M., & Postlethwaite, R. (Eds.). (2000). *Munchausen syndrome by proxy abuse: a practical approach.* Oxford: Butterworth-Heinemann.

Fortin, A., & Chamberland, C. (1995). Preventing the psychological maltreatment of children. *Journal of Interpersonal Violence*, **10**, 275–295.

Glaser, D. (2002). Emotional abuse and neglect (psychological maltreatment): a conceptual framework. *Child Abuse and Neglect*, **26**, July, in press.

Glaser, D., & Prior, V. (1997). Is the term Child Protection applicable to emotional abuse? *Child Abuse Review*, **6**, 315–329.

Glaser, D., Prior, V., & Lynch, M.A. (2001). *Emotional abuse and emotional neglect: antecedents, operational definitions and consequences.* York: BASPCAN.

Hart, S, Brassard, M., & Karlson, H. (1996). Psychological maltreatment. In L. Berliner, J. Briere, J. Bulkley, C. Jenny & T. Reid (Eds.), *The APSCA handbook on child abuse and neglect* (pp. 72–89). London: Sage Publications.

Johnston, J., & Campbell, L. (1988). *Impasses of divorce: dynamics and resolution of family conflict.* New York: The Free Press.

Jureidini, J. (1993). Obstetric factitious disorder and Munchausen syndrome by proxy. *Journal of Nervous and Mental Disease*, **181**, 135–137.

McGee, R. & Wolfe, D. (1991). Psychological maltreatment: towards an operational definition. *Development & Psychopathology*, **3**, 3–18.

McGee, R., Wolfe, D., & Wilson, S. (1997). Multiple maltreatment experiences and adolescent behavior problems: Adolescents' perspectives. *Development & Psychopathology*, **9**, 131–149.

Murray, L. (1997). Postpartum depression and child development. *Psychological Medicine*, **27**, 253–260.

Ney, P., Fung, T., & Wickett, A. (1994). The worst combinations of child abuse and neglect. *Child Abuse and Neglect*, **18**, 705–714.

Sinclair, D., & Murray, L. (1998). The effect of postnatal depression on children's adjustment to school. *British Journal of Psychiatry*, **172**, 58–63.

Somer, E., & Braunstein, A. (1999). Are children exposed to interparental violence being psychologically maltreated? *Aggression and Violent Behavior*, **4**, 449–456.

Winnicott, D. (1982). Ego distortion in terms of true and false self. In *The maturational processes and the facilitating environment* (pp. 145–146). London: Hogarth Press.

5

PREDICTING SEXUAL CHILD ABUSE AND NEGLECT

Chris Hobbs
Jane Wynne
University of Leeds, UK

The understanding of child sexual abuse (CSA) has progressed considerably since the first edition of this book (Browne et al., 1988). Another decade has seen elaboration, expansion and extension of knowledge in many countries which already had systems in place to investigate and manage abuse. These countries had developed typically and followed the sequence described by Kempe. Developing countries and those without child protection procedures have professionals who can recognise well the "abuse" but have the difficult task of managing the sequel to diagnosis. Examples of these include the protective placement of children in penal institutions in close proximity to perpetrators in Sri Lanka and the death penalty for all child rapists in the Philippines.

There has been a keen, continuing interest in research into CSA from the early 1970s in the USA. In the UK work followed some 10–15 years later.

Clinical assessment of CSA was assumed able to give an instant opinion: "sexual abuse yes or no". This was what the police and child protection agencies wanted to know. General practitioners employed as part-time police surgeons worked with the police. There was remarkably little in the paediatric literature to assist paediatricians and a paucity of advice from the Department of Health. It is noteworthy that there was no guidance for doctors until after the Cleveland Inquiry. Initially interest in CSA was almost overwhelming and the press and media appeared constructive in their interest.

The 1980s saw the beginnings of clinical practice develop. From society's viewpoint the debate moved from denial of the problem to a limited acceptance and in the last few years back again toward denial. In the UK procedures have developed which have sometimes inhibited understanding and inquiry. Doubt about what is clinically reliable has eroded confidence. In the last decade the lack of an

Early Prediction and Prevention of Child Abuse: A Handbook.
Edited by Kevin Browne, Helga Hanks, Peter Stratton and Catherine Hamilton. © 2002 John Wiley & Sons, Ltd.

agreed evidence-based practice may have left more children without intervention (some would say has avoided unwarranted intervention).

In the USA where statistics have been more assiduously collected than in the UK, there is evidence of a shrinking problem (Finkelhor, 2001). A reduction in reported cases over the past decade must be set against the substantial rise in cases in the preceding twenty years. What is happening? Some commentators have suggested this may be the natural progression of all that has gone before. "Our efforts at prevention, incarceration of offenders, public education may now be paying off" (Finkelhor, 2001). Those involved on the front line tell a different tale. Of hard fought struggles against societal disbelief, of failures of the health, social and legal systems to support children, of indifference, of inadequate, absent or threatened funding, of silenced children and families.

Alternative explanations for children's distress have become institutionalised. For example the widespread provision of medication for attention deficit hyperactivity disorder has contributed undoubtedly in some cases to disguising trauma as the cause of a child's distress.

Adult revulsion to child abuse means that children are less likely to be thought of as "abused", but rather they are "in need". Failure of the child protection system has overtaken parental failure as our prime concern (Department of Health 1995a). Numbers of children on child protection registers is falling (Department of Health, 1995; 2000). Families are now trusted, treated and made partners. The bogeyman remains the paedophile living on the estate. Public care has been shown to be dangerous but currently there is no evidence of falling use. (Hobbs et al., 1999, Wynne 2001). It remains a reality for many children, which cannot be avoided. Where does child sexual abuse fit into this jigsaw?

Is it in?

- "Safe or Stranger" abuse
- Abuse of children with disability
- Abuse by children
- Institutional abuse
- Abuse in the context of ". . . materially poor, emotionally deprived, poorly educated, unemployable, adults who have mental health problems and were multiply abused as children, continuing abuse as adult in families where there is inter-generational abuse
- Sex rings—as in:
    "Leeds rings" (Wild & Wynne, 1986)
    organized paedophile rings+/− pornography
    abducted children from poor countries
    sex tourism

Anywhere except in educated, middle class families "like us"—what right have professionals to cause upset and children do tell lies.

WHAT IS CHILD SEXUAL ABUSE?

There is little doubt that child sexual abuse has been encountered wherever sought in all human societies. (Moghal et al., 1995; Finkelhor, 1994; La Fontaine, 1990) It is unclear whether it confers evolutionary advantage to individuals or the species or whether there are comparable animal models. Human aggression can be understood in terms of defence e.g. of territory, space, possessions or person but sexual abuse of sexually immature individuals sometimes including infants and toddlers is not easily understood. Human sexuality has extensive expression. Much is non-procreational. There are many perversions. Deviant sexuality includes destructive sexual drives and the abuse of children. The sexual abuser (or "perpetrator") frequently develops this pattern of behaviour in childhood or adolescence and it is assumed that the roots are to be found in the perpetrator's childhood. Many perpetrators were themselves sexually abused as children but not in every case. What also appears to be true is that most abused children do not themselves become perpetrators. However from our own experience and clinical practice, generational patterns of child sexual abuse are commonly encountered.

Definition

Child Sexual Abuse is defined as the involvement of children and adolescents in activities which they do not comprehend or are unable to give informed consent to and that violate the social taboos of family roles (Schechter & Roberge, 1976)

PHYSICAL ABUSE OF YOUNG CHILDREN

When "the battered baby syndrome" was described and named in 1962 (Kempe et al., 1962), the doors opened to reveal a previously hidden problem. Physical abuse occurs to children of all ages with the youngest more vulnerable, likely to die or suffer permanent physical harm. The clinical features are well described and best illustrated by a few brief case histories.

CASE HISTORY 1

A nine-month-old male infant was brought to hospital not moving one arm. Mother said she put the baby on the bed to dry him after giving him a bath and he rolled off it onto the floor. She said he whimpered a little but didn't cry. She brought him to hospital after he wouldn't use his arm properly. A displaced spiral humeral fracture was diagnosed with no bruising or other injury. The junior doctor accepted this history but the consultant paediatrician said it was probably abuse.

CASE HISTORY 2

An 18-month-old girl was brought to hospital with extensive bruising to one side of the face after allegedly falling against the kitchen wall. The staff were alerted to the possibility of abuse having found linear bruises which involved the cheek and ear. When a senior doctor was called the cohabiting new boyfriend became aggressive and insisted on taking the child home against the wishes of the hospital staff. The health visitor was called but she was not let into the house and social services were notified. Before they were able to find the parents the child was returned moribund, shocked and was found to have sustained extensive liver fracture, lower right-sided rib fractures and internal bleeding. After resuscitation in the intensive care unit further examination revealed extensive labial fusion which made catheterisation difficult and a grossly abnormal anus indicating abusive anal penetration.

The child was discharged to her extended family where she failed to thrive and sustained an inadequately explained arm fracture suspicious of non-accidental injury. She was removed to a foster home where she made much better progress.

CASE HISTORY 3

A four-month-old boy was rushed to hospital with a history suggesting a brief convulsion. He was observed to have faint bruising around his eye and a superficial laceration on one cheek where his mother said she caught him with her ring. She explained that she had been winding him over her shoulder when his head had banged on the wall behind her causing the bruising. The infant looked pale and shocked and was immediately x-rayed and CT scanned. The scan was reported to be normal and no skull fracture was found. The infant was admitted to the ward where he remained irritable and unwell for three or four days. Careful examination by an opthalmologist identified a number of retinal haemorrhages in each eye and this prompted a further head scan with MRI. On this scan subdural haemorrhages were clearly seen overlying the surface of the brain. A case conference was held and care proceedings initiated in the children's court. An interim care order was made and opposed by the parents. The infant was discharged to foster care. He made a full recovery. The diagnosis was of non-accidental shaking injury and the court made a care order to the local authority. Eventually he was returned to his parents' care. Shortly afterwards he sustained at the age of 12 months a fracture of his arm from a fall in the home from a toy he was sitting on. The injury was investigated but considered to be accidental.

CASE HISTORY 4

A 15-month-old boy was said to have climbed into a bath of hot water whilst his mother briefly left the bathroom to get some clothes. On her return she found him in the crawling position in the bath. He was brought to hospital straight away. Symmetrical immersion scalds to both arms extended circumferentially about four inches above the wrist with clear line of demarcation from non-scalded skin, below the elbow (Figure 5.4, Plate I), with no splash marks. Re-enactment of the scene at the child's home revealed a water temperature of 57°C when four inches of water had been run from the hot tap alone indicating immersion for several seconds. The child was aggressive and had nightmares for many months after the incident. His mother was convicted of the assault.

Common Injuries Which Occur in Physical Abuse

- bruises—head and neck, ears, face, eyes, trunk, buttocks, limbs from slaps, punches, pinches, kicks, bites, implements, grips, strangulation

- lacerations, scratches—from nails, teeth, implements, ligatures
- burns and scalds—from immersion, thrown, poured liquids, cigarettes, matches and lighters, irons, fires, caustic chemicals, friction e.g. dragged on carpet
- fractures—from pulling, twisting, squeezing, hitting, head, limbs and trunk
- brain injury—from shaking or banging head, asphyxiating or suffocating
- abdominal injury—from blows, kicks, stamping, standing on abdomen

Diagnostic Features in the History

- repeated injury in time and space
- inadequate, vague, inconsistent or absent explanation
- unusual or inappropriate response to injury in carer or child e.g. lack of pain, delay in presentation
- changes in history, several explanations
- unusual manner in parents (e.g. defensive, aggressive, evasive, anxious, unconcerned)
- evidence of other abuse including non-organic failure to thrive, neglect, sexual abuse
- other evidence of violence in the home e.g. spouse abuse, criminal record for violence, Schedule 1 offender present

Jigsaw Approach (Hobbs et al., 1999)

- build a picture from collected information
- ask other professionals who have had contact
- ask family members about previous injuries/concerns
- search of hospital and GP records
- undertake a full medical assessment, including as appropriate skeletal x-rays, head scans, full ophthalmic examination, assessment of growth and development, look for sexual abuse, do genital and anal examination, talk to child
- ask police if any records of domestic violence or criminal records for violence in family members
- identify poor attachment, signs of neglect including failure to thrive (check parent held record, health visitors records), lack of health care, immunisation status
- explore parental perceptions about child
- consider trigger factors e.g. difficult crying infant, handicap, acute stress
- look at all the siblings including paediatric assessment
- assess the family—what are the strengths and weaknesses?
- share relevant information at a strategy meeting and case conference

EPIDEMIOLOGY OF SEXUAL ABUSE

This has been the subject of various studies in many countries (Finkelhor, 1994). The scientific basis of these studies has been developed and reviewed (Peters et al., 1986).

FIGURE 5.1 12-month-old infant with an unexplained burn to the buttock. The mother consulted several professionals angrily denying that this was a burn and saying it was a nappy rash.

FIGURE 5.2 12-month-old infant with fracture of lower end of shaft of femur. History that he had been jumping up and down in his cot. Later found sitting in cot with bleeding mouth. Old torn frenulum, old bite mark and bruising to right arm noted. Infant was failing to thrive.

FIGURE 5.3 Infant of 6 months with diffuse bruising of the lower abdomen with tracking down to scrotum and the base of penis. Injury caused by blunt force applied to lower abdomen, probably a kick. Unexplained bruise over right maxilla. N.B. this child had Von Willebrand's disease which is not associated with an increased frequency of bruising but characteristically after operation the wound continues to ooze. This child had no bruising in foster care.

FIGURE 5.4 Boy aged 18 months with forced immersion scald of arm. See Case History 4 p. 74 for details of history.

FIGURE 5.5 3-month-old infant severely failing to thrive was presented to accident and emergency department with a history that mother noticed a sore bottom when she removed the baby's nappy. No further history obtainable. Clearly demarcated dip scald of buttocks present.

FIGURE 5.6 Reflex anal dilatation in a girl of 5 years who was sexually abused over a 2–3 year period by her father. Parents separated and child spent weekends with father. When concerns of abuse arose from recurrent genital soreness and presence of anal signs, contact was ordered by court to be supervised by paternal grandparents. Continuing signs after contact and disclosure to child psychotherapist led to court stopping all contact with father and grandparents who failed to protect. Signs healed after contact stopped.

FIGURE 5.7 Rape and buggery in a 5-year-old girl who refused to give any history. Long history of concerns about her 10-year-old brother who had suffered unusual burns and was thought to have been sexually abused and to have abused other children. Note the gaping anus, vulval bruising, dilated hymenal opening, disrupted hymen and torn posterior fourchette.

PLATE I **77**

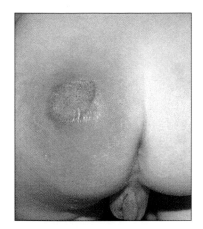

FIGURE 5.1

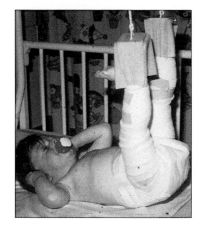

FIGURE 5.2

FIGURE 5.3

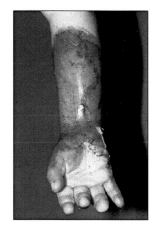

FIGURE 5.4

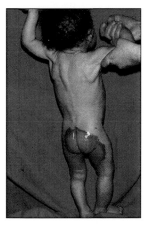

FIGURE 5.5

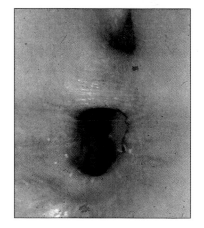

FIGURE 5.6

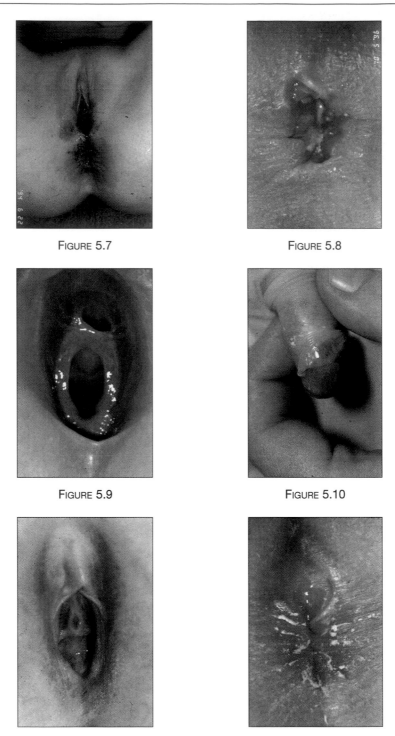

FIGURE 5.7

FIGURE 5.8

FIGURE 5.9

FIGURE 5.10

FIGURE 5.11

FIGURE 5.12

PLATE II   **79**

FIGURE 5.8   6-month-old baby with a severely disrupted anus. The child was taken to hospital by the mother who thought her baby's bottom looked unusual. There had been a previous similar problem a month before which was undiagnosed. Infant was admitted and referral made surgically by paediatric team. Surgeon said "not surgical" and one week later infant referred to child protection paediatric team at another hospital. The anus falls open with little apparent "tone". There is a substantial deep anterior fissure. Rectal mucosa is seen centrally through the dilated sphincter. These findings indicate forceful penetration probably by a penis. When the police asked the parents for an explanation, the mother said the infant had been constipated and she had sought to relieve the child by inserting a finger into the anus. The findings are not consistent with this. There was no prosecution but the child was protected away from the family. Rape and buggery of infants as young as this is occasionally encountered although there are many more cases referred after the second birthday. One infant became shocked from blood loss after vaginal penetration produced a substantial laceration. The father's explanation of a finger slipping during bathing was not accepted and he was convicted.

FIGURE 5.9   9-year-old girl who presented with a history of recurrent genital soreness without explanation. 3-year history of urinary tract symptoms and abdominal pain. Said she had a secret she could not disclose. The doctors had to make her better because mummy couldn't. Mother later disclosed that there were two relatives who had a history of sexually abusing children but did not have contact with this child. The genitalia show a dilated urethra, annualer hymen with a square shaped notch in the hymen at 6 o'clock. The introitus is generally reddened. Penetration of the urethra has been described in adults and this may be the explanation for the dialatation seen here. Persistent notches in this position of the hymen are unusual and support a diagnosis of traumatic penetration.

FIGURE 5.10   Burn of the glans penis of a 3-year-old boy. The parents' only attempt to explain this very unusual injury was that he must have stood too close to a radiator whilst passing urine. The burn, which is clearly circumscribed, requires retraction of the foreskin to visualise. Genital injuries in boys are common in sexual abuse. Accidental injuries to the penis occur from entrapment in zips but only very rarely from toilet seats. Bruising, burns and deep incised wounds are typical of abusive injury. The histories are often unbelievable as in this case. There were other features in the jigsaw of abuse in this case and the child was eventually removed into foster care.

FIGURE 5.11   Genitalia of a 9-year-old girl who had a long history which strongly suggests sexual abuse. At 3 years of age she developed perianal warts (human papilloma virus infection). How she acquired this sexually transmitted infection was not investigated. At the age of 5 she was taken to hospital having bled briskly from a vaginal injury which was said to have occurred when she fell astride a chair back. She required suturing of a laceration of the posterior vaginal wall under a general anaesthetic by a gynaecologist. Following this she developed soiling which gradually became worse. She was unable to cope with her schoolwork. The genitalia show reddened skin, a gaping vagina, with only remnants of hymen posteriorly. An old scar is present on the posterior vaginal wall between the hymenal remnants. The posterior vaginal wall looks smooth. The fourchette is friable. These findings are diagnostic of repeated vaginal penetration which the child confirmed in later disclosures.

FIGURE 5.12   6-month-old infant who has an anterior (6 o'clock) anal fissure. This was discovered during a child protection paediatric medical examination for concerns, which had been raised after a previous child had died under suspicious circumstances. Anal fissures may occur in constipation after the passage of a hard stool. However this fissure is wide, extensive and took many weeks to heal. Such fissures are more often the result of penetrative trauma. It extends out of the anal canal and across the perineal skin toward the genital area. Fissures are uncommon in children. It is usual to inquire of a history of constipation, bleeding or pain, none of which were present in this case. The conclusion in this case was that abuse was likely.

In the UK CSA has been found to occur more often outside the family (Kelly et al., 1991) and to involve perpetrators of both sexes with a heavy male predominance. The research of this UK student sample found that one in two young women and one in four young men had experienced sexual abuse as children—before age 18 years. The definition was broadly defined to included exposure or "flashing". It is important to state what is included within a definition of CSA as this has a major effect on the prevalence figure. Most cases were unreported to authority but many children told a friend or other close person (Kelly et al., 1991).

It is not known how often predatory paedophiles are responsible for the abuse revealed in this and other studies. It may be that certain high profile individuals receive disproportionately greater publicity in professional and public circles. Experience in Leeds has determined that in schools the activities of paedophile teachers went unchecked for many years. In one case, an inquiry determined that a well-respected teacher had married several pupils over his career with few fellow members of staff aware of this. In another case several attempts to stop a deputy head teacher's abusing behaviour were aborted by an agency system of self inquiry. Clinical experience (a more accurate measure than retrospective prevalence data) indicates that the abuse involves children of all ages but with many under the age of five years (Hobbs & Wynne, 1987) and with some infants involved. As stated in the Inquiry report (Butler-Sloss 1987) at Cleveland, boys as well as girls are involved. It is clear that children from all social classes are involved (including children of some of the most powerful and influential members of society). Although our clinical sample is inevitably heavily weighted toward the poorer end of the social spectrum from which most abuse and neglect we see comes, we have encountered other social classes.

The National Commission of Inquiry into the Prevention of Child Abuse which reported in the UK in 1996 estimated that 100 000 children were "exposed to potentially harmful sexual experiences" every year (National Commission, 1996). This gives an estimated frequency very different from the figure derived from the only incidence study from Northern Ireland in 1987 (Department of Health, 1995a). The figure was 0.9 per 1000 for established case (0.34 for boys, 1.49 for girls).

A more recent prevalence study (Cawson et al., 2000) of 2869 young adults age 16–24 years (1235 men and 1634 women) used a different definition. Abuse was defined as no consent or consent when the age difference between victim and perpetrator was five years or more and the individual aged 12 years or less. They found that the prevalence of CSA was 1% by parents/carers (mostly physical contact); 3% by other relatives (2% contact, 1% non-contact); 11% by other known people (8% physical contact, 3% non-contact); 4% by strangers or person just met (2% of each type); and 7% suffered indecent exposure with more than a third by a stranger. Most abuse except indecent exposure involved repeated incidents. A significant number experienced sexual acts by non-relatives or by age peers, including boy or girlfriends, friends of brothers or sisters and fellow pupils or students.

Many studies now agree that a quarter to a third of all reported abuse is committed by perpetrators under 18 years.(Finkelhor, 1979; Hobbs and Wynne, 1987). The majority of perpetrators reported are male but women also abuse more often than is generally believed.

Changes in Epidemiology—US and UK Experience

Leventhal asked, "Has there been a change in the epidemiology of sexual abuse of children during the 20th century?" (Leventhal, 1988). The current debate in the USA is centred on changes in reported cases. Finkelhor noted that after a 15-year increase in reporting of sexual abuse to a peak in 1992 of 149 800 cases that the number of cases of sexual abuse has declined each year with a low of 103 600 in 1998 (a decline of 31% over a six-year period). Although other forms of maltreatment have declined, the decrease in sexual abuse has been more marked (Finkelhor, 2001).

Finkelhor questioned whether this represents a real decline in incidence or whether fewer cases are being reported and substantiated and therefore increasing numbers of victims left unprotected. There are no regional patterns evident in the USA with the decline being across all the states.

IN THE UK

On 1 March 1995 (Department of Health, 1995b) in England there were 34 954 children on child protection registers, 26% as the result of sexual abuse. Scotland, Wales and Northern Ireland accounted for a further 5792 children registered with 12% to 21% sexually abused. On 31 March 2000 (Department of Health, 2000) there were 30 300 children on the child protection registers in England. The registered categories (by percentage) of total is shown in Table 5.1.

Therefore there has been a 40% reduction in the number of sexually abused children on the child protection register in England over the five-year period from 1995 to 2000 suggesting a decline of similar magnitude to the US pattern.

Pre- and Post-Cleveland Changes

In the UK Cleveland was the single most important event in the history of CSA. Many articles and books have been written (Richardson & Bacon, 1991). In Leeds practice before Cleveland was reported for 1985 and 1986. A total of 337 children of all ages were described including diagnosis, social and legal intervention and early outcome (Hobbs & Wynne, 1987). Levels of prosecution, legal protection and multi-agency agreement have shown a decline since Cleveland, which was followed by extensive new legal statute and procedure which some feel made the protection of children more difficult (Speight & Wynne, 2000). In Leeds children diagnosed

TABLE 5.1 Categories on child protection registers in England (DoH, 2000)

neglect	46%
physical abuse	29%
emotional abuse	18%
sexual abuse	18%
categories not recommended	1%

by the same doctors before and after Cleveland were studied (Frothingham et al., 1993). The results revealed that whilst cases continued to be referred and diagnosed as before, the proportion registered at case conference fell from 86% to 75%, cases reaching legal protection from 36% to 24% and those with successful criminal prosecution from 17% to 5%. A new type of case emerged—the medically diagnosed non-disclosing child (36% of all cases) who was left at risk of further abuse because the evidence was deemed insufficient to protect the child. Prior to Cleveland this child would have been removed to a safe environment with less family contact which gave the opportunity to disclose. In effect the parents' voices have become louder than the silenced children's. This has continued and is reflected in fewer children sexually abused on child protection registers.

EFFECTS OF CHILD SEXUAL ABUSE

The short and long term effects of sexual abuse have been the subject of substantial study. There are few studies of medically diagnosed groups where the predominance of cases was of intrafamilial abuse. The Leeds group undertook a study based on a 1989 cohort of sexually abused children diagnosed by paediatricians (Frothingham et al., 1993). Children aged seven years or less were studied using school health records (Frothingham et al., 2000). High levels of morbidity were found in children eight years after sexual abuse was diagnosed. Social, educational and health morbidity left many children substantially disadvantaged compared to a control group: 24% had educational problems including 16% with a statement of special educational need; others had adverse behaviours (60%) including aggressive (22%) and sexualised (19%), chronic health problems including soiling (10%) and wetting (20%), abnormal growth patterns (18%) and involvement of mental health services (32%); 35% experienced further abuse after original diagnosis; 25% had spent time in care or had been adopted and 30% had a surname change. The group experienced significantly more moves of home and school than controls.

CLINICAL ASSESSMENT OF THE SEXUALLY ABUSED CHILD

- jigsaw
- interviews
- medical or paediatric assessment
- sharing information
- constructing a picture

TABLE 5.2   The "jigsaw" in the diagnosis of child sexual abuse

History from parent	History from child	Any disclosure
Physical symptoms	Child's behaviour	Bruises/injuries
Physical examination	Sexually transmitted infection	Forensic investigations
Police inquiry	Social work assessment	Siblings

Information is shared by all the agencies at a strategy meeting. Following an investigation a case conference is held except where it is felt that the abuse has stopped, the child is protected and no further child protection plan is needed. This most often occurs where the abuse has taken place outside the family or extended family.

Paediatric Assessment (Hobbs et al., 1999)

This term is preferred to medical examination because of the emphasis on whole child assessment rather than the examination of his or her genitalia/anus. Some time is spent in dispelling myths which have long endured in the minds of carers and referrers. The paediatrician brings knowledge and understanding of children and child development to this assessment.

The aims of the assessment are:

1. to assess any injury
2. to determine if abuse has occurred and its nature
3. to collect any forensic evidence (includes proper documentation of "physical signs" associated with abuse)
4. to start and assist the process of (psychological) healing
5. to arrange referral/treatment for any consequences of the abuse (e.g. sexually transmitted disease, pregnancy, psychological trauma)

Sources of information in the assessment:

1. parents' history of child including concerns and problems, what the child has told them and their own history
2. other significant adult history
3. the child's statements including any disclosure of abuse
4. previous medical contacts
5. child's health
6. any specific complaints:
   - Psychosomatic and behavioural complaints including abdominal pain and headaches, anorexia and eating disorders, constipation, soiling and encopresis (passing stools into socially inappropriate places), day or night wetting, and behavioural indicators. The latter include sexualised behaviour (excessive or indiscriminate masturbation, preoccupation with genitals, seeking to engage others in differentiated sexual behaviour, sexual aggression, prostitution, extreme sexual inhibition in teenager) and most of the range of behaviours seen in child psychiatry practice including anxiety symptoms, school failure, psychotic symptoms and apparent mental deterioration
   - Physical complaints—vaginal or anal pain, soreness, bleeding or discharge. Sexually transmitted disease, pregnancy, vaginal foreign body, genital or anal injury, urinary symptoms—dysuria.

CASE HISTORY 5

The mother of a five-year-old girl became worried when she found her common law husband (putative father of her child) with an erection whilst showering with the child. After confronting him he denied any wrongdoing saying that he had become emotional. The child developed abdominal pain and had occasional discomfort on passing urine. Eventually the cohabitation ended but he insisted on seeing the child at his new home. In desperation the mother moved abroad to avoid his persistent demands. Six months later when the mother was talking about returning, the child disclosed genital touching and intracrural (penis between thighs) intercourse and made detailed drawings indicating she did not wish to see her father. A medical examination found subtle external genital changes of skin thickening, labial fusion and scarring consistent with the child's statement.

CASE HISTORY 6

A four-year-old girl was referred to a child psychiatrist because the parents complained that she persistently pulled out her hair. A paediatrician was asked to see her. Her parents also said she slept badly, intermittently wet the bed and was badly behaved. Past history revealed previous concerns by another family living in the street that the father had inappropriately touched their child. At another time concern was raised by the mother that the father had attempted to smother the child. After case conferences, registration and supervision the child had been de-registered but never paediatrically assessed.

The paediatrician found a severely denuded scalp with many broken and missing hairs and genital signs indicating vaginal penetration. The child was removed to a foster home. Disclosure followed months later of sexual abuse by both parents and one set of grandparents. The child gradually stopped pulling her hair out and it re-grew.

CASE HISTORY 7

A 10-month-old twin was brought to the casualty department with a boggy swelling of the scalp which they had noticed the day before. A skull x-ray revealed a linear parietal skull fracture. The parents said they had no idea how this injury had occurred and asked if it was "a medical problem". Both twins were underweight (height 50th centile, weight 2–9th centile). There were no other injuries found and a skeletal survey was normal. A six-year-old sibling was brought for examination and preferred a stranger to be present rather than either parent. There were genital signs indicating vaginal penetration. She disclosed sexual abuse by her father to her foster parent. The skull fracture remained unexplained.

CASE HISTORY 8

A three-year-old child from a respectable family living in a comfortable area was referred by their general practitioner with a deep labial laceration. Her mother gave a history that the girl had complained to her grandmother whilst being pushed around a supermarket sitting in a trolley, that her "tuppence" was hurting. Her mother inspected her genitalia in a nearby toilet and found no bruising or bleeding and clean knickers. A few hours later her mother put some cream on and told her husband when he returned from work later in the day. When her mother asked what had happened the child said, "I fell over at nursery."

The following day the mother spoke with the nursery, who had no knowledge of any problem and took her to the general practitioner who confirmed a deep 1–2 cm laceration of the external labia majora. When she saw the paediatrician she refused to say what had happened but cooperated with the examination. Later the father said that whilst caring for the child the previous evening whilst his wife was at work, he had found her in her mother's bedroom with a needle in her hand. Sexual abuse was suspected but not confirmed.

CASE HISTORY 9

Two girls aged two and three years developed green vaginal discharges simultaneously. Their mother took them to their general practitioner who took swabs and sent them to the pathology laboratory. The swabs were reported to have grown gonococcus from both children and on receiving the reports a paediatrician was contacted. The children were seen with their mother and the diagnosis of gonococcal vulvitis confirmed. When the paediatrician told the mother that he believed that the girls had been sexually abused she abruptly rushed out of the room to telephone the father leaving the children with the doctor. One of the girls immediately told the doctor that "daddy put a knife in my tuppence". The children were removed into care and the adults in the family all tested negative for gonorrhoea. Further disclosures of sexual abuse involving both parents followed.

NEGLECT

Neglect is insidious.

Working Together (Department of Health, 1999) defines neglect: "...the persistent failure to meet a child's basic physical and/or psychological needs, likely to result in the serious impairment of the child's health or development. It may involve a parent or carer failing to provide adequate food, shelter and clothing, failing to protect the child from physical harm or danger, or the failure to ensure access to appropriate medical care or treatment. It may also include neglect of, or unresponsiveness to, a child's basic emotional needs.

Children at risk include:

• children with a disability—physical and sensory, learning problems
• children who have parents with disability—learning, physical, sensory psychiatric disorder
• children who live in conditions of severe social disadvantage
• children in large families with poor networks of support and poverty

A paediatrician may assist in the multi-agency assessment by looking at the child in some detail:

TABLE 5.3   The "jigsaw" in the diagnosis of neglect

Denial of problems by parents (may have learning problems)	History from child—bullied, no friends, aggressive	"Attention seeking" Concern by nursery, school of standard of care
Physical symptoms e.g. pain from dental caries	Poor physical condition—dirty, thin hair, nappy rash	Growth—stunted/fail to reach potential height
Development delayed e.g. language, social skills	Poor compliance with treatment e.g. asthma	Increased risk of accidents: RTA, fire, crowning
Supportive network i.e. with family and friends—little effect as share similar problems	Poverty with poor housing, diet, parents with poor health (physical and mental), little education	Large number of involved professionals—health visitor, school nurse, social worker, home care, housing, GP, paediatrician etc.

The general characteristics of neglect are a long history of intercurrent illness, accidents (in the home and on road/canal), ingestions, repeated hospital admissions, and medical, educational and social neglect.

Documentation of the effects of neglect:

- on the physical appearance of the child
- on growth
- on development
- on emotional and behavioural history—and observation in clinic

Physical Appearance

- dirty clothes and, body, hair matted or thin, dirty nails, odour, dental caries, chronic infestation (head lice)
- examination may reveal chronic nappy rash, infected sores (especially in skin folds), untreated squint, perforated eardrums, thin limbs, wasted buttocks, protuberant abdomen, cold injury (red, swollen extremities)
- growth pattern is often of a long term suboptimal pattern and assessment includes
  - measurement of the child's height, weight, mid-upper arm circumference, head circumference
  - recording the measurements and plotting on standardised growth charts
  - finding any previous measurements to assess growth rate
  - looking for signs of physical and/or sexual abuse
  - development may be globally delayed
  - motor skills may be immature and the child is clumsy
  - language is characteristically delayed
  - social skills have not been acquired

Behaviour in the clinic may be quiet and apathetic (more usual in infancy) or range to the restless, flitting pre-schooler who is distractible, seeks attention and has frequent tantrums. Play is immature and lacks imagination, being typically more destructive than showing attention and perseverance to the task.

Information should be sought from the carers and nursery staff and others involved in the child's care.

N.B. the severely neglected child may be clumsy, have a neglected squint, little language and few pencil skills, may have immature peer and adult relationships, visual and auditory attention may be poorly developed, distractible, over-active/apathetic, and nursery/school attendance may be poor. Social skills like eating with implements, toileting, dressing and nose-blowing may not have been taught.

- Medical surveillance—immunization, developmental checks, hearing and vision assessments: fails to attend
- Medical appointments—asthma, convulsions missed: poor compliance with appointments and therapy

The paediatrician should work closely with the primary care team, social services department and nursery, to minimise the consequences but also to form an opinion as to whether the parenting is "good enough".

NON-ORGANIC FAILURE TO THRIVE (NOFT)

NOFT is the failure of an infant or child to achieve his expected growth in the absence of an organic disorder. He may also fail to achieve his full potential in other parameters of development. Documentation of failure to thrive requires serial measurement of height, weight, mid-upper arm circumference and head circumference. The measurements must be plotted on appropriate growth charts. Physical examination should exclude organic causes of failure to thrive. Signs will depend on the disorder.
In NOFT:

- the child may appear well cared for or have a neglected appearance
- associated signs include wasting, protuberant abdomen, thin hair, signs of neglect
- behaviours observed include apathy, attention-seeking, over-activity and flitting from toy to toy
- development is variably delayed with language and social skills most affected

The interpretation of growth charts in NOFT: (Hobbs et al., 1999) there are several patterns including:

- falling centiles
- parallel poor centiles
- markedly discrepant height and weight centiles
- discrepant family pattern
- retrospective rise
- saw-tooth—erratic, fluctuating pattern

The differential diagnosis of failure to thrive:

TABLE 5.4   Mid-upper arm circumference (MUAC)—where child is 12–60 months

Child older than 12 months and MUAC less than 14 cm	Likely to be significantly malnourished—warrants referral to a paediatrian
MUAC is 14–15 cm	If older i.e. 4–5 years, likely to be malnourished, refer to paediatrician. Younger child—monitor carefully and assess in detail
MUAC is greater than 15 cm	Nutrition is likely to be adequate
MUAC at school entry, 5–6 years, 16–17 cm	Likely to be adequately nourished

- adequate intake with poor weight gain—malabsorption e.g. celiac disease
- inadequate intake due to swallowing difficulty—cerebral palsy
- poor appetite—renal failure

The selection of laboratory investigations to elucidate the aetiology of the observed failure-to-thrive depends upon the clinical assessment and the majority will require a haemoglobin check or no tests at all. The observation of improved growth as a consequence of an increased food intake renders further laboratory tests unnecessary.

CONCLUSION

The various forms of abuse have been well described. Some of the major forms are summarised in this chapter from a paediatric point of view. Undoubtedly child abuse is common and a major source of morbidity in childhood with consequences reaching forward into adulthood and persisting for the remainder of the individual's life. Much abuse remains undiscovered or undisclosed. The current increased awareness, knowledge and expectations have not been met by the necessary resources with which to tackle these difficult problems. After abuse is recognised, case management in many situations is too complex, costly and controversial. This has led to a retreat from child protection and a search for other solutions (for example family support, prevention of abuse, tackling poverty and other social issues considered to be related). The continuing level of preventable child death from abuse remains an incontrovertible reminder of the limited effectiveness of current interventions and of the need for continued societal and professional commitment to this important social issue.

REFERENCES

Butler-Sloss E, 1988. *Report of the Inquiry into Child Abuse in Cleveland 1987.* HMSO, London.
Cawson P, Wattam C, Brooker S, Kelly G, 2000. *Child Maltreatment in the United Kingdom. A study of the prevalence of child abuse and neglect.* NSPCC, London.
Department of Health, 1995a. Messages from Research. *Studies in Child Protection.* HMSO, London.
National Commission, 1996. *Childhood Matters – Report of the National Commission of Inquiry into the Prevention of Child Abuse* Volume 1. The Stationery Office, London.

Department of Health, 1999. *Children and young people on the child protection registers year ended 31st March 1999*. HMSO, London.

Department of Health, 1995b. *Children and young people on the child protection registers year ended 31st March 1995*. HMSO, London.

Department of Health, 2000. *Children and young people on the child protection registers year ended 31st March 2000*. HMSO, London.

Department of Health, 1999. *Working Together under the Children Act*. HMSO, London.

Finkelhor D, 1979. *Sexually Victimized Children*. Free Press, New York.

Finkelhor D, 1994. The international epidemiology of child sexual abuse. *Child Abuse and Neglect* **18**: (5) 409–417.

Finkelhor D, Conference presentation, San Diego 2001.

Frothingham TE, Barnett R, Hobbs CJ, Wynne JM, 1993. Child sexual abuse in Leeds before and after Cleveland. *Child Abuse Review* **2**: 23–34.

Frothingham TE, Hobbs CJ, Wynne JM, Yee L, Goyal A, Wadsworth DJ, 2000. Follow up study eight years after the diagnosis of sexual abuse. *Archives of Disease in Childhood*, **83**: 132–134.

Hobbs CJ, Wynne JM, 1987. Child sexual abuse—an increasing rate of diagnosis. *Lancet* ii: 837–841.

Hanks HGI, Hobbs CJ, Wynne JM, 1988. Early signs and recognition of sexual abuse in the pre-school child. In: Browne K, Davies C, Stratton P (eds) *Early Prediction and Prevention of Child Abuse*. Wiley, Chichester.

Hobbs G, Hobbs CJ, Wynne JM, 1999. Abuse of children in foster and residential care. *Child Abuse and Neglect* **23** (12): 1239–1252.

Hobbs CJ, Hanks HGI, Wynne JM, 1999. *Child Abuse and Neglect. A Clinician's Handbook* 2nd ed. Churchill Livingstone, London.

Kelly L, Regan L, Burton S, 1991. *An Exploratory Study of the Prevalence of Sexual Abuse in a Sample of 16–21 Year Olds*. University of North London.

Kempe CH, Silverman FN, Steele BF, Droegmueller W, Silver HK 1962. The battered child syndrome. *JAMA* **181**: 17–24.

La Fontaine J, 1990. *Child Sexual Abuse*. Polity Press, Cambridge, England.

Leventhal J, 1988. Have there been any changes in the epidemiology of sexual abuse of children during the 20th century? *Pediatrics* **83**: 766–773.

Moghal NE, Nota IK, Hobbs CJ, 1995. A study of sexual abuse in an Asian community. *Archives of Disease in Childhood* **72**: 346–347.

Peters SD, Wyatt GE, Finkelhor D, 1986. Prevalence, Chapter 1 in *A Sourcebook on Child Sexual Abuse*. Sage, London, pp 15–59.

The Research Team, Queen's University, Belfast: Child Sexual Abuse in Northern Ireland: A Research Study of Incidence quoted in Messages from Research: Studies in Child Protection. London 1995 HMSO.

Richardson S, Bacon H, 1991. *Child Sexual Abuse: Whose Problem? Reflections from Cleveland*. Venture Press, Birmingham.

Schechter M, Roberge L, 1976. Child sexual abuse. In: Helfer R, Kempe C (eds) *Child abuse and neglect: the family and the community*. Ballinger, Cambridge, Mass.

Speight N, Wynne JM, 2000. Is the Children Act failing severely abused and neglected children? *Archives of Disease in Childhood* **82**: 192–6.

Wild NJ, Wynne JM, 1986. Child sex rings. *British Medical Journal* **293**: 183–185.

Wynne JM, 2001. Children: whose problem? – an editorial. *Child Health Care and Development* **27** (5): 383–388.

Section II

PRIMARY AND SECONDARY PREVENTION

EDITOR'S INTRODUCTION

Peter Stratton

Abuse distorts the whole operation of our society and needs to be tackled and reduced as far as possible at the level of our societal systems. This section deals with large-scale attempts to influence the ways that we as a society understand and react to maltreatment of children. We may hope to achieve primary prevention by changing the whole way that our societies regard and treat children and there is some evidence in the chapters that follow that this is an achievable goal. But there is also good evidence for secondary prevention with resources directed towards those groupings of people who are most likely to abuse or to be abused.

There can be no doubt that primary prevention is needed. The high levels of abuse, and the continuing resistance to recognising it, indicate that we have a whole cultural pattern which fails to generate the basic necessary care for many of our children. But because societal change is a long and difficult process we have an immediate need to intervene at more specific levels. The process has to be one of mobilising those societal and personal values which can be used to protect children and we do have concepts of parenting that can be strengthened and supported in ways that will reduce the risks of abuse. This is the approach that is emphasised in this section.

First we need to understand why abuse is so common. Belsky and Stratton take us beyond the simple linear assumption that a deficiency in the parent causes them to abuse their child. Drawing on Bronfenbrenner's ecological theory they develop an account of the transactional processes by which parent and child adapt to each other's behaviour, and to their broader contexts. Each level of context is shown to be relevant and the etiology of abuse emerges as a complex product of processes at many different levels. However, while this complexity precludes simple answers it does indicate that there are many levels at which intervention can by applied. Following this overview of etiology, Pat Crittenden applies her immense experience of parent–child functioning to examine the direct causes and consequences of mal-treatment. Her dynamic-maturational model of the strategies that individuals use to organise self-protective and reproductive behaviour leads to the conclusion that it is danger and lack of comfort that lead to fragmentation of mental functioning and of relationships. An implication is that prevention and treatment should be focused on integration—of information, of psychological functions, and of families and their relationships.

Both chapters offer insights into the ways that abused children may become abusing parents. However, it is realistic to see abuse as the far segment of a con-tinuum of mistreatment of children, at a cut-off determined by the mores and legal definitions of society at any time. The current focus of research on parents with a history of abuse overlooks the possibility that many other styles of parenting (authoritarian, coercive, modelling successful aggression, psychologically absent, non-verbal) may not be classified as abusive but may create developmental pro-cesses from which emerge a new generation of parents who abuse. The parent education programmes reviewed here undertake prevention by tackling support-ive action for parents and their value may be underestimated if outcomes are only evaluated in terms of reductions in registerable abuse.

Deborah Daro starts from an analysis of the requirements of parenting and de-duces the requirements for effective programmes of parental education. She then reviews the different types of parent education programmes, whether direct or through the media. The chapter is consistent with the conclusions from Chapter 6 on the need for multiple strategies but also the requirement for quality in these pro-grammes. It becomes clear that we must draw on the full range of modern media if we are to achieve the levels of prevention that we need. The chapter concludes with the implications for policy planning for community support. Matthew Sanders and Warren Cann follow with a critical review of parenting interventions and a detailed report of Sanders' imaginative Australian programme. This is a tiered provision starting so broadly that his level 1 is effectively primary prevention. Subsequent levels move towards secondary prevention by progressively targeting parents at greater risk. The triple P approach targets coercive and harmful parenting and aims to reduce a wide range of maltreatment within whole communities by enhancing parenting practices. As well as the extensive use of varied media, a strength of the approach is in recognising that parents have different needs and receptivity, and that a cost-effective programme will capitalise on the fact that simple limited interventions are often all that is needed.

David Olds, Charles Henderson and John Eckenrode review the extensive series of preventative programmes that Olds and his associates have conducted over many years. The importance of this chapter is not only in showing that these pro-grammes had significant effects, but also the careful research to find out just what is effective, with whom, in what ways and why. They have a strong specific recom-mendation of using existing professional skills of the trusted profession of nurses. Another important finding is that the programme did not reduce domestic vio-lence and that where this was present the programme of maternal support was relatively ineffective. Again it is recommended that programmes be targeted at those at greater risk, for example where the mother is low-income, unmarried and had external locus of control. Finally, David Gough examines another aspect of prevention in a review of how statutory intervention works, compared with ideas of how it should work. He points to the difficulties, but also the advantages, posed by very broad definitions used in all aspects of child protection from "case work" through "abuse" itself. In a concrete application of the ecological conclusions of Chapter 6 he shows how state provision is focussed on intervening in families, whereas it needs to be operated in relation to fostering communities that support children.

Primary and secondary prevention are urgent priorities for our societies. Despite the magnitude of the task, the lessons of this section are positive. We are beginning to get a realistic understanding of the ecology of abuse and its transmission across generations. In parallel we have a variety of effective programmes that are reaching substantial numbers of families. The benefits to society of progressively integrating our developing understanding of child maltreatment with large-scale implementation are immeasurable. If we can envisage a process of more and more children growing up secure, often happy, and valuing themselves and others, our investment will be magnified through successive generations of families. And very concretely, the need for emergency action to protect children from their parents will slowly reduce.

6

AN ECOLOGICAL ANALYSIS OF THE ETIOLOGY OF CHILD MALTREATMENT

Jay Belsky

Birkbeck College, University of London, UK

Peter Stratton

University of Leeds, UK

The first step in the prevention of child abuse is to understand why it occurs. Preventative action can be wasted if effort is directed to the wrong targets. This chapter considers the etiology of child maltreatment and the wide range of causal agents that have been invoked to explain why children may be physically abused or neglected. Such factors may be historical (e.g., societal attitudes toward family privacy) or contemporaneous (e.g., poverty); cultural (e.g., disciplining children) or situational (e.g., crying episode); characteristics of parents (e.g., impulse control) or their children (e.g., difficult temperament). Past reviewers have often concentrated on a single type of cause but it is well appreciated today that no model based on simple linear causality will be adequate.

Largely due to the seminal contribution of Bronfenbrenner (1979), child maltreatment is now widely recognised to be multiply determined by a variety of factors operating via transactional processes at various levels of analysis (i.e., immediate situational through life-course history to historical-evolutionary) in the broad ecology of parent–child relations. Moreover, it is well appreciated that what determines whether child maltreatment will take place is the balance of stressors and supports (Belsky, 1980; 1993; Belsky & Vondra, 1989). When stressors (of a variety of kinds: parent, child, social conditions) outweigh supports (also of a variety of kinds), or when potentiating factors are not balanced by compensatory ones, the probability of child maltreatment increases. In other words, as this chapter concludes, it is not

Early Prediction and Prevention of Child Abuse: A Handbook.
Edited by Kevin Browne, Helga Hanks, Peter Stratton and Catherine Hamilton. © 2002 John Wiley & Sons, Ltd.

just that there is no single cause of child maltreatment, but nor are there necessary or sufficient causes. All too sadly, there are many pathways to child abuse and neglect.

There is a fundamental problem in using research findings to unravel the etiology of abuse. This problem pertains to virtually all etiologic research, namely, the strategy of comparing groups on one variable or factor at a time. If one takes seriously the notion that child maltreatment is multiply determined and arises as the result of transactional processes involving parent, child and the family, community, cultural and even evolutionary context in which they are embedded, then it must be recognised that what etiological studies seek to identify are contributing rather than determining agents. From this perspective, then, failure to discern a significant group difference does not imply, nor should it be interpreted to mean, that factor X or Y or Z is not important in the etiology of child maltreatment. Rather it might mean—if the sample, measures, and research design are sound— that the effect of the factor in question is not discernible when examined in isolation. The fact that effects work "synergistically" in this way may account for much of the inconsistency in research findings reviewed below and in more detail by Belsky (1993).

One reason why risk factors may compound is that the kinds of adaptation elicited from a parent or a child by one aspect of a potentially abusive environment may create greater vulnerability to a second factor when present. By the time the child and their parents are adapting to several deleterious factors they may have patterns of coping and of interaction that make abuse highly likely. An example of such synergistic effects is provided by Belsky (1988) reporting a classification of attachment in relation to three potentially negative factors: parental personality, child temperament and social context (marriage, neighbourhood). When one negative factor was present the proportion of children securely attached reduced from 92% to 87%; with two factors the proportion dropped to 37%; and with all three factors negative only 17% were securely attached. Researching variables in isolation has other consequences. It leads to thinking in terms of linear cause–effect sequences, and this in turn raises concerns about blaming whoever is responsible for that cause. A solution is to consider that each event calls forth an adaptation and that each behaviour is an outcome of previous adaptations. Each factor considered below can be thought of not as building some kind of deficiency into the child or the parent, but as demanding adaptations. The ways in which adaptations may either create and maintain conditions for abuse or alternatively reduce risk are considered in detail elsewhere (Hanks & Stratton, 2002; Stratton & Hanks, 1991).

This chapter applies a developmental-ecological perspective to the question of the etiology of physical child abuse and neglect by organising the material around a variety of "contexts of maltreatment". We start with the "developmental context", focussing attention on the role of parent and child factors in the etiological equation, including the issue of intergenerational transmission. The "immediate interactional context" of child abuse and neglect is examined next, focussing attention on what is known generally about the parenting of caregivers identified as physically abusive or neglectful. Because of the ecological nature of this analysis, attention is turned in the subsequent section to the "broader context" of maltreatment, with attention paid, in three separate subsections, to the community, cultural and evolutionary context of child abuse and neglect. Finally a summary of the state of our knowledge is provided and implications for prevention are considered.

THE DEVELOPMENTAL CONTEXT: CONTRIBUTIONS BY PARENT AND CHILD

The Role of Parental Characteristics

Consideration of parental factors that might contribute to child maltreatment has focussed attention on the childhood histories of abusive and neglecting parents, their personalities and their psychological resources.

DEVELOPMENTAL HISTORY AND INTERGENERATIONAL TRANSMISSION

Two of the clinicians at the forefront of inquiry into the etiology and sequelae of child maltreatment observed that "the most constant fact (concerning child abusers) is that parents themselves were nearly always abused or battered or neglected as children (Fontana, 1973; p. 74) and that "we see an unbroken line in the repetition of parental abuse from childhood into the adult years" (Steele, 1976; p. 15). Although there is substantial evidence linking the perpetration of child abuse and neglect with a childhood history of victimisation (e.g. Crouch et al., 2001; Whipple & Webster-Stratton, 1991), most scholars are all too aware of the inherent limitations of the available data base.

Kaufman and Zigler (1987) noted that among better-designed studies using standardised self-report measures (e.g., written questionnaires, structured interviews) and reasonably-selected comparison groups, consistent differences emerge in the developmental histories of index and control samples; they estimated the rate of intergenerational transmission to be 30% (plus or minus 5%), given a range in rates between 7% (Gil, 1973) and 70% (Egeland & Jacobvitz, 1984) chronicled in the literature. Thus *only* about one-third of individuals who were abused or neglected will maltreat their own children. What is most disconcerting about the Kaufman and Zigler (1987; 1989) analysis, which is widely cited in the literature, is the failure to take into consideration the ages of the children. For example, in discussing the results of Hunter and Kilstrom's (1979) prospective follow-up of at-risk and comparison mothers *one year* after the birth of a child, Kaufman and Zigler (1989, p. 132) describe a parent whose child has not been identified as maltreated as one of the 81% who "broke the cycle of abuse". Such a conclusion ignores the fact that those who are said to have broken the cycle have many more years to care for the study child, to say nothing of other children (including those not yet born). Egeland, Bosquet and Levy (Chapter 13) report that extending the monitoring of abuse until the child was six raised the incidence to 45% in their data, and conclude that intergenerational transmission has been underestimated.

While the number of previously abused adults who break the cycle may be over-estimated, so too are there limitations in data that lead some to conclude that "the majority of abusive parents were not abused in their own childhoods" (Widom, 1989, p. 8). It must be acknowledged that retrospective reports of childhood experience can not only be inaccurate because of over-reporting of maltreatment, but because of under-reporting as well. As clinicians and attachment researchers point out, painful experiences in childhood are often excluded (unconsciously) from memory (Bowlby, 1980). Thus, it remains all too conceivable that certain individuals who report no history of maltreatment simply cannot recollect, or bear to report, their troubled childhoods. This is not to argue that every mistreated child grows up to be a maltreating parent, or even that only individuals with histories of maltreatment will mistreat their own offspring (though this is an hypothesis that needs serious testing by means of skilled clinical interviews). As Kaufman and Zigler (1987. p. 190) themselves note, even though "being maltreated puts one at risk for becoming abusive . . . the path between these points is far from direct or inevitable."

One of the major strengths of attachment theory as a tool for understanding the etiology of child maltreatment is that it provides a theoretical basis for the conditions under which, and the mechanisms by which, child maltreatment is *not* transmitted across generations (Belsky & Pensky, 1988). In two separate, prospective studies of at-risk mothers followed from the post-partum period, it was found that parents with histories of maltreatment who did not maltreat their own children (during the study period) had more extensive social supports, had experienced a nonabusive and supportive close relationship with one parent while growing up, or were more openly angry and better able to give a detailed coherent account of their earlier abuse than were repeaters (Hunter et al., 1978; Egeland, et al., 1987). Additionally, Egeland et al. (1987) found that involvement with a supportive spouse or boyfriend or a positive experience in therapy characterised the nonabusing parents with at-risk developmental histories. The role of attachments in the etiology of abuse is extensively reviewed by Crittenden (Chapter 7) and Egeland et al. (Chapter 13). Their analyses show clearly how children adapt to abuse with internal working models of relationships which are likely to be problematic if carried through to their own parenthood. But they also indicate the conditions in which the working models are likely to be modified in ways that will break the intergenerational cycle of abuse.

PERSONALITY

Early theorising about the etiology of child maltreatment was often based on the assumption that abuse and neglect were the result of mental illness or that a distinct psychological syndrome or disorder characterised perpetrators (Melnick & Hurley, 1969; Steele & Pollack, 1968). While this rather comforting belief is no longer promoted, there is little agreement over the possible role of the personality or psychological attributes of maltreating parents. Whereas any number of studies reveal an association between low self esteem (measured in a variety of ways) and child maltreatment (Baumrind, 1995), this anticipated relation is not always discerned (Lawson & Hays, 1989) and the possibility that abusing one's child could reduce a parent's self esteem is rarely considered. Similarly, many studies demonstrate a variety of negative emotional states such as depression, anxiety and irritability among parents who abuse (Eth, 1996; Putallaz, et al. 1998; Whipple & Webster-Stratton, 1991), as well as that when such states manifest themselves as stable personality traits, that parenting is less sensitive and more negative, critical, intrusive, and overcontrolling (for review, see Belsky & Barends, 2002). There is evidence that depression (without regard to maltreatment) is associated with intrusive, hostile and rejecting care, as well as detached and unresponsive parenting (for review, see Gelfand & Teti, 1990), but in general the causal routes between parental state, abuse, and the wider aspects of family ecology reviewed in this chapter remain unclear.

The Role of Child Factors

AGE

Physical abuse and neglect that comes to the attention of community authorities (and thereby to researchers) has consistently been found to vary with the age of the child. Younger children appear more likely to experience maltreatment for a variety of reasons. One is that physical force is more often used against them (Straus & Stewart, 1999). Another is that they spend more time with their caregivers and are more physically and psychologically dependent upon them. A third reason is that they are simply more susceptible to injury, given their physical vulnerability. The fact that young children have more difficulty regulating their emotions than older children may also increase the chances that they evoke hostile care from their parents. Toddlers may be especially vulnerable as their self-assertive and sometimes defiant efforts to function autonomously (while often being clinging and dependent as well) may be misinterpreted, or simply be too difficult to cope with, when parents are under stress (Ammerman & Patz, 1996).

PHYSICAL HEALTH

Early clinical reports that maltreatment was more likely in the case of premature and low birth weight infants drew attention not only to the health of the child as an etiological factor, but to the role of the child more generally (e.g., Klein & Stern, 1971). Brown et al. (1998) report an association of abuse with pregnancy/birth problems but not with low birth weight. The linkage between prematurity and maltreatment seemed particularly plausible in light of evidence that such infants are often physically unattractive and emit disturbing, high-pitched, arrhythmic and thus potentially abuse-eliciting cries (Frodi, 1981). Although several studies have documented an association between prematurity and child maltreatment, including some prospective investigations (Hunter et al., 1978), others have not (see Belsky, 1993 for a review).

Such inconsistency in the literature should once again not be read to imply that such factors do not play a role in the etiology of physical child abuse and neglect. Not only is it the case that a careful, prospective study found that health difficulties preceded the occurrence of maltreatment, but the issue of synergistic processes applies to combinations of child and parent factors. Raine et al. (1994) showed in a large Danish sample that it was when birth complications were combined with parental rejection that there was a substantial increase in violent crimes when the children were 18 years old.

BEHAVIOUR

A bi-directional perspective on the parent–child relationship suggests that children's own behaviour may function to elicit or maintain child maltreatment. Their adaptations to the abusive environment may involve withdrawal or aggression, and combine a desperate need for contact with an absence of prosocial behaviour (Eth, 1996; Putallaz, 1998). However it is also the case that abusive parents report more problem behaviour on the part of their children than more "objective" observers (Whipple & Webster-Stratton, 1991), so their problematic behaviour could be exaggerated.

Nevertheless, although it seems plausible that parents play a larger role in the etiologic equation than do children, there is no disputing the fact that children inadvertently contribute, too. Parents less able to manage negative emotion, who feel badly about themselves, perhaps because of their own troubled childhoods, seem most at risk of mistreating their offspring. From the vantage of the transactional-contextual perspective adopted here, such an outcome seems most likely to occur when age, health and behavioural aspects of children conspire to make some more of a challenge to rear than others. But the quality of health and behaviour are already affected by the previous treatment the child has received. We therefore need to extend the transactional perspective to take account of the cycles of adaptation that both parents and children are operating. It is useful to conceptualise the cycles by which abuse induces consequences which affect the future probability of abuse, as processes of "transactional adaptation" (Stratton, 1977; 2002). An analysis of underfeeding and of sexual abuse (Stratton & Hanks, 1991) showed how child characteristics could contribute to cycles of adaptation that in some cases help instigate maltreatment, in other cases to merely maintain it.

THE IMMEDIATE CONTEXT: PARENTING AND PARENT–CHILD INTERACTION

Since child maltreatment is defined by the problematic quality of parenting, there is every reason to expect that maltreating and non-maltreating parents care for and interact with their children differently. What is difficult to determine is whether the findings generated reflect proximal causes of child abuse and neglect, and thus deserve to be considered as part of the etiological equation or whether, instead, they are the very phenomena to be explained. That is, is it not tautological to discover that maltreating and comparison parents care for their offspring differently?

The study of parent–child interaction is the one arena of inquiry concerning the etiology of maltreatment where sufficient effort has been made to consider abusive and neglectful parents separately. Studies of neglectful parents paint a disturbing picture of parental functioning. In the case of infants, Crittenden (1981) observed, not surprisingly, that neglectful mothers were unresponsive in that they tended neither to initiate interaction nor to respond to the child's initiatives. Studies of older children also highlight low rates of social interaction (Burgess & Conger, 1978) and prosocial behaviour (Bousha & Twentyman, 1984) on the part of neglectful parents.

There is a pervasive negative tone to interactions between abusive parents and their children. Repeatedly it has been found that physically abusive parents are less supportive and direct fewer positive behaviours (e.g., instructing, joining play, talking to child, praising) toward their children (Burgess & Conger, 1978; Bousha & Twentyman, 1984); are less responsive to child initiations (Kavanagh et al., 1988); and express less positive affection toward the child (Brown et al., 1998) than comparison parents. An important extension of these findings is that physically abusive mothers are in turn highly likely to be suffering violence from their partners (Coohey and Braun, 1997).

In light of these findings with respect to parenting in general, it is no surprise to learn that the actual disciplinary practices of abusive and nonabusive parents are quite different. Abusive parents are more likely to rely on physical punishment and negative acts as control (Gelles & Cornell, 1997) and less likely to use reasoning and inductive strategies (Trickett & Kuczynski, 1986). Notable, too, is that physically abusive parents are less likely than other parents to vary their discipline in response to different kinds of child misbehaviour (Trickett & Kuczynski, 1986).

That abusive parents are less positive in their parenting in general and more punitive in their discipline in particular is consistent with the previously discussed personality data concerning negative affectivity (depression, anxiety, hostility) and emotional reactivity. What often happens in the abusive event is that an aggressive act of physical punishment, which may have a functional goal of influencing child behaviour, gets out of control instead of being self-limiting.

Why does the instrumentally-aggressive behaviour that many parents dispense—physical punishment—turn into irritable and uncontrolled aggression that defines physical abuse in some families? According to Vasta (1982) it is the very arousal or negative reactivity that seems to characterise the psychological make-up of abusive parents that turns "what begins as an act of physical discipline" . . . into "an act of interpersonal violence" (p. 135). In other words, abuse appears to emerge in the immediate context of parent–child interaction when a parent with a predisposition toward anxiety, depression and hostility becomes irritated with a child, attempts to physically and instrumentally control the child, but becomes so aroused as to lose control of him/herself and overdoes what was initially intended to be an act of discipline. It is not difficult to imagine how this process could be very much shaped by a childhood history of mistreatment and exacerbated by features of the victimised child and by the adaptations the child is making to this form of parenting.

THE BROADER CONTEXT

Up to this point we have concentrated on the intra-familial context of child maltreatment and have shown, as Azar et al. (1998) have also concluded, that models based on simple linear cause cannot account for the findings. However a transactional-ecological approach demands a wider perspective. In this final, substantive section, attention is turned to the broader context in which physical child abuse and neglect take place and in which individual life courses and daily interactions between parents and children are embedded. More specifically, we consider first the community context of child maltreatment, and then cultural factors. Finally, we place the phenomenon of child maltreatment in a long-history, evolutionary context.

Community and Social Support

There is substantial evidence linking social isolation and limited social ties with elevated risk of child abuse and neglect. Garbarino and Sherman (1980) compared two neighbourhoods matched for social class and found that families in the one with the higher maltreatment rate had less extensive social networks. Coohey and Braun (1997) have shown that it is the emotional support, rather than the practical help that appears to protect against abuse.

Other investigations reveal that maltreating parents have smaller peer networks (Polansky et al., 1985); have less contact with (Zuravin & Greif, 1989), and receive less help from their family of origin and other relatives (Polansky et al., 1981); and are socially isolated (Whipple & Webster-Stratton, 1991). The relationships that abusive parents do have are more negative than those of nonabusive parents (Corse et al., 1990). When considered together, such findings are consistent with the cross-cultural record which indicates that isolated mothers with little periodic relief or assistance are most likely to be harsh or rejecting (Korbin, 1991). Causal direction is difficult to determine in this area but some insight is provided by a recent study (Crouch et al., 2001). While childhood abuse was a strong predictor that an adult would abuse, if they perceived that they had received support following their abuse, they were more likely to see themselves as receiving current support, and this significantly reduced the risk that they would abuse.

Despite evidence and argument that the social isolation repeatedly found to be associated with physical child abuse and neglect is, at least in part, a creation (real *and* imagined) of the parent's own making, it would be a mistake not to acknowledge the objective reality of community contexts and the roles they play in the etiological equation. Garbarino and Kostelny (1992) documented this rather convincingly by comparing in terms of their "community climates" socioeconomically similar neighbourhoods in Chicago that varied dramatically in rates of maltreatment. The truly high-risk areas were characterised by social disorganisation and lack of social coherence, whereas the socioeconomically-matched neighbourhoods in which maltreatment was less likely showed evidence of a stronger social fabric.

The Societal/Cultural Context

What transpires within the life course of an individual, within the family, and within communities is a function, at least in part, of the broader cultural context in which people, households and neighbourhoods are embedded (Bronfenbrenner, 1979). Central to an ecological perspective on child maltreatment is the assumption that societal willingness to tolerate high levels of violence sets the stage for the occurrence of family violence, one form of which is physical child abuse (Belsky, 1980; Gelles & Cornell, 1997).

The widespread use of physical punishment as a means of controlling children in societies such as Britain and America (Straus & Stewart, 1999) differs dramatically from that found in other nations. Perhaps most noteworthy is Sweden where a law was passed two decades ago banning corporal punishment (Ziegart, 1983). The fact is that in cultures in which physical punishment is rare, child abuse in quite unusual (Japan, China, Tahiti, Arapesh in New Guinea: Zigler & Hall, 1989). Also implicated in a broad-scale cultural analysis of the etiology of child maltreatment is society's general attitude toward children. Particularly important may be the belief that children are property to be handled as parents choose (Garbarino, 1977).

Despite the fact that advances are being made in the fight for children's rights, it is doubtful that maltreatment can be eliminated so long as parents rear their offspring in a society in which violence is rampant, corporal punishment is condoned as a child-rearing technique, and parenthood itself is construed in terms of ownership. It is likely, moreover, that contemporary cultural developments, such as denigration of the role of child care provider (as indicated by the low status of teachers, the poor pay of child care workers, and the widespread exodus of parents from the primary caregiving role) and the feminisation of poverty (which results in 20% of America's children living in poverty), work against efforts to prevent child maltreatment. Such forces not only devalue the role of caring (well) for children, but place children in contexts that all-too-many parents will find overtaxes their coping capacity, thereby resulting in child abuse or neglect.

In sum, then, although most child maltreatment takes place in the family and thus "behind closed doors", this immediate and even developmental context of maltreatment itself needs to be contextualised. Cultural attitudes, values and practices, as well as the economic circumstances of a society and its cultural history, play an important role in the etiology of child maltreatment. Even though they are not in any sense an immediate or proximate cause of child abuse and neglect, they create a fertile soil in which these disturbing practices can grow and even flourish.

The Evolutionary Context of Child Maltreatment

Child abuse and neglect offer an apparent anomaly in terms of evolutionary theory. Why would a parent damage, maybe kill, the child who will carry their genes into the next generation? An answer to such questions may be helpful both in overcoming the resistance that still exists to recognising child abuse; and in helping preventative measures to be targeted at the more fundamental causes of abuse rather than incidental correlates.

Across the animal kingdom, the mistreatment of progeny is so widespread that it would seem to be as much a part of the "natural" condition as is sensitive, solicitous parental behaviour. Young animals are especially likely to be attacked by their parents if they are defective or in some way different. The explanation offered by evolutionary biology is that interests of parent and offspring are not always consistent (Daly & Wilson, 1980; 1981).

Modern evolutionary theory, then, with its emphasis on the reproductive interests of individuals rather than groups or species, shows why *the capacity for* child maltreatment could have developed within the human species, despite seeming so contrary to the best interests of the parent. Under conditions in which the provision of sensitive and responsive care adds nothing to the reproductive fitness of parents—and more likely, actually undermines it—abuse and/or neglect should become more likely (Daly & Wilson, 1980; 1981). Central to this theoretical perspective are the following notions: (1) that parental behaviour has evolved during the course of human evolution in the service of biological, i.e., reproductive, goals; (2) that in certain circumstances child abuse and neglect may actually enhance reproductive fitness—or at least would have done in the environment of evolutionary adaptation; and (3) that abuse is most likely when contextual conditions accentuate the biological conflict of interest between parent and child (Burgess & Draper, 1989).

There are grounds for claiming that the circumstances that evolutionary theorists claim are "favourable" to the occurrence of physical abuse and/or neglect are consistent with those found in (often sociologically driven) research on the determinants of abuse. According to Burgess and Draper (1989) circumstances which demarcate the instability, unpredictability or unavailability of resources needed for sustaining and reproducing life would be high on the list. Consistent with this evolutionary view—but by no means proving it—is the highly replicated finding that poverty and low income are related to both child abuse and neglect, as are unemployment and limited parental education (Whipple & Webster-Stratton, 1991; Olds and others in this Handbook).

When resources are scarce, neglecting some children may enable the parent to invest more effectively in others—ones who presumably have more reproductive potential (see earlier discussion of child age and health)—thereby enhancing the parent's (but not the neglected child's) reproductive fitness. Physical abuse may itself be a means of combating the demands of children whose requests for resources challenge the parent's view of the optimal allocation of limited assets—psychological and material. Thus, by physically abusing the child the parent may be seeking to prevent the child from coercing them to allocate resources in a way that are more in the child's best interest than in the parent's. In this way they may promote the reproductive prospects of their other offspring or even of offspring not yet conceived.

An evolutionary perspective would also predict that family structure would relate to the probability of child maltreatment. Factors such as the spacing of pregnancies, age of parents and number of children have the potential to overload the parental resources needed to sustain their investment in all of their children. Thus, it is not surprising to find that unplanned pregnancies and larger family size are related to abuse (Zuravin, 1991). These fertility-maltreatment relations remain, it should be noted, even when controls for socio-economic status are implemented (Zuravin, 1991).

Zuravin (1988) argues that the fertility-maltreatment relation is a function of younger, poorer mothers having more children, closely spaced, so that (1) limited material and emotional resources are divided into smaller and smaller parcels; (2) there is less likelihood of single-parent mothers marrying or remarrying and thus getting financial and emotional support from a spouse; and (3) it decreases the probability that others will be available to assist with (all) the children. Collectively, these processes generate more stress than the parent can cope with, thereby resulting in abuse and/or neglect that may, in fact, be regarded as reproductively strategic (though not necessarily consciously chosen) when viewed from an evolutionary perspective.

In addition to predicting that physical abuse and neglect should occur disproportionately when economic resources are limited, unstable or over-extended, a sociobiological perspective also draws attention to family structural factors denoting biological relatedness. Specifically, it predicts that stepchildren should be more likely to be physically abused and/or neglected (Daly & Wilson, 1980; 1981; Gelles & Harrop, 1991).This prediction derives from the straightforward observation that stepchildren share none of the step-parent's genes and thus cannot *directly* enhance the reproductive fitness of a step-parent; and from the theoretical inference that resources (economic and emotional) devoted to such a child may interfere with the reproductive prospects of the step-parent, his or her biological offspring, or both. To be noted is that an abundance of evidence does draw attention to an association between step-families and maltreatment (Daly & Wilson, 1980; Browne & Herbert, 1997).

The correspondence between sociobiological analyses of when abuse might be in a parent's reproductive interest, and the conditions that have been found to make abuse more likely, have been reviewed in detail by Belsky (1993). The closeness of this correspondence should not mislead us into thinking that child abuse and neglect are a biological inevitability. First, the argument must be treated with caution because the theorists who speculate about our earlier evolutionary situation already know the circumstances in which abuse is most likely to occur. We should also consider the route by which selection pressure during the development of our species connects to parental behaviour in 2002.

The existence of a selection pressure, for example to give most resources to the offspring who are most likely to survive, will not in itself create a direct motivation. It will have built into the species those tendencies that will most easily achieve the (evolutionarily) desired result. The argument that we should look for mechanisms that will achieved the needed behaviour with the minimum of genetic specification has been developed, in relation to attachment formation, by Stratton (1983). This approach might lead us, for example, to a simple tendency to reject children who are perceived as unattractive, combined with an existing tendency to judge people similar to oneself, and maybe one's partner, as attractive. Another tendency could be to react negatively to people, including one's own children, who appear weak or defective. Such tendencies (and note that we are speaking throughout of "tendencies" not compulsions) could be a cost-effective route to achieving a significant biological objective with the minimum of genetic specification. The usefulness of evolutionary explanations thus comes when they alert us to look for the human tendencies that connect selection pressures to current parental behaviours. These tendencies are more likely to be the direct causes rather than correlates of abuse that are merely a function of specific aspects of current society. So, for example, we are directed to tackling feelings of parents that the child is seriously threatening their own resources, rather than attempting to prevent abuse and neglect by eliminating unemployment. More broadly, the sociobiological perspective claims that if we can specify the conditions that amplify conflicts of (biological) interest between parent and child then we will understand better the conditions that foster child maltreatment. Derivatively, then, conditions that reduce such conflict should prevent maltreatment.

So evolutionary theory complements sociological and psychological theorising, as well as humanistic concern, in drawing attention to risks associated with rearing children under conditions of limited social and economic resources and to issues of fertility. When resources are limited and are insufficient—or perceived to be—to meet the basic needs of parents and children, parents may "choose" to overlook some needs of their offspring and/or to discriminate between them. That they do this is not because they are mean, nasty or morally flawed, or only because they are sociologically stressed and psychologically depleted. It may also be because an ancient evolutionary heritage has provided them with the faculties to monitor these features of themselves and their environment, calculate (unconsciously) what is in their own, personal, reproductive best interests—or once would have been—and behave accordingly (cf. Burgess & Draper, 1989).

CONCLUSION AND FUTURE DIRECTIONS

Our main conclusion from the preceding developmental-contextual analysis of the ecology of child maltreatment is that physical child abuse and neglect are multiply determined by factors operating at multiple levels of analysis (developmental, immediate situational, demographic, cultural-historical, evolutionary). None of the factors are without effect but none is an inevitable cause of abuse. Each is a contributor to the transactional process by which individuals come to their particular adaptations and we have seen that certain constellations carry greater risks of abuse or neglect.

Fortunately, because of the "discovery" that child maltreatment is multiply determined, no "magic bullet" needs to be identified and targeted before intervention efforts can be initiated. This same central fact about maltreatment, however, poses many challenges. Although the multi-determined nature of child maltreatment suggests that there are many targets to focus prevention and remediation efforts upon, it simultaneously alerts us to the fact that directing efforts at any single target is not likely to be particularly successful. Randall and Henggeller (1999) in the broader context of child and family treatment reached a similar conclusion with their formulation of "multisystemic therapy" which, like this chapter, took its inspiration from Bronfenbrenner's theory of social ecology.

We would predict that providing parent training, for example, without regard for the dire economic circumstances of a family, is unlikely to prevent maltreatment over the long term. Analogously, deferring early parenthood will probably not prove entirely successful if issues of emotional deprivation in a parent's childhood and social isolation in the parent's current living situation are not addressed. Nevertheless, because the demographic data clearly indicate that poverty and early and extensive childbearing provide fertile soil in which child maltreatment can grow, it is difficult to imagine that major strides can be made in the battle to prevent, much less remediate, child maltreatment so long as impoverished young women are rearing multiple and closely-spaced offspring on their own and/or without sufficient social supports. This observation suggests that fertility planning, education, employment and economic assistance will be required if serious progress is to be made in the battle to prevent child maltreatment.

The fact that not every young, poor or single parent, or even young and poor and single parent, mistreats their child clearly suggests that more may be required than interventions that reduce impoverishment and fertility. Because of developmental histories which, on the one hand, may predispose parents to high levels of negative emotionality and reactivity and, on the other, provide them with insecure expectations about the world while simultaneously failing to provide them with skills to be sensitive caregivers or functional neighbours, efforts which target these derivatives of troubled childhoods should also prove helpful in reducing the risk of maltreatment. The extent to which such interventions foster supportive social and emotional bonds between at-risk parents and others are likely to increase the long-term effectiveness of any such efforts to promote more nurturant parenting.

Although it is rather easy to make such broad, sweeping assertions about the implications of research on the etiology of child maltreatment for intervention efforts, it is something else entirely to actually identify tactics and strategies that might work. The implication of this analysis of etiology is that whatever programmes or efforts are tried, they must aim at multiple targets at different systemic levels simultaneously before we can expect success.

REFERENCES

Ammerman, R. T., & Patz, R. J. (1996). Determinants of child abuse potential: Contribution of parent and child factors. *Journal of Clinical Child Psychology*. **25**, 300–307.

Azar, S. T., Poilaitis, T., Lauretti, A., & Pouquette, C. (1998). The current status of etiological theories in intrafamilial child maltreatment. In J. R. Lutzker (Ed.) *Handbook of Child Abuse Research and Treatment*. New York: Plenum.

Baumrind, D. (1995). Psychological characteristics of abusive parents. In *Child Maltreatment and Optimal Caregiving in Social Contexts* (pp. 75–81). New York: Garland Publishing.

Belsky, J. (1980). Child maltreatment: An ecological integration. *American Psychologist*, **35**, 320–335.

Belsky, J. (1988). Child maltreatment and the emergent family system. In K. Browne, C. Davies & P. Stratton (Eds.) *Early Prediction and Prevention of Child Abuse and Neglect*. Chichester: Wiley.

Belsky, J. (1993). The etiology of child maltreatment: a developmental-ecological analysis. *Psychological Bulletin*, **114**, 413–434.

Belsky, J., & Barends, N. (2002). Personality and Parenting. In M. Bornstein, *Handbook of Parenting*, 2nd Ed. (pp. 415–438). Mahwah, NJ: Erlbaum.

Belsky, J., & Pensky, E. (1988). Developmental history, personality and family relationships: Toward an emergent family system. In R. Hinde & J. Stevenson-Hinde (Eds.), *Relationships within families* (pp. 193–217). Oxford: Clarendon Press.

Belsky, J., & Vondra, J. (1989). Lessons from child abuse: The determinants of parenting. In D. Cicchetti & V. Carlson (Eds.), *Current research and theoretical advances in child maltreatment* (pp. 153–202). Cambridge: Cambridge University Press.

Bousha, D., & Twentyman, C. (1984). Mother–child interactional style in abuse, neglect, and control groups. *Journal of Abnormal Psychology*, **93**, 106–114.

Bowlby, J. (1980). *Attachment and loss: Vol. 3. Loss, sadness and depression.* New York: Basic.

Bronfenbrenner, U. (1979). *The ecology of human development.* Cambridge, MA: Harvard University Press.

Brown, J., Cohen, P., Johnson, J. G., & Salzinger, S. (1998). A longitudinal analysis of risk factors for child maltreatment. *Child Abuse and Neglect*, **22**, 1065–1078.

Browne, K. D. & Herbert, M. (1997). *Prevention of Family Violence.* Chichester: Wiley.

Burgess, R. L., & Conger, R. D. (1978). Family interaction in abusive, neglectful, and normal families. *Child Development*, **49**, 1163–1173.

Burgess, R. L., & Draper, P. (1989). The explanation of family violence: The role of biological, behavioral, and cultural selection. In L. Ohlin & M. Tonry (Eds.), *Family violence* (pp. 59–116). Chicago: University of Chicago Press.

Coohey, C., & Braun, N. (1997). Toward an integrated framework for understanding child physical abuse. *Child Abuse and Neglect*, **21**, 1081–1094.

Corse, S., Schmid, K., & Trickett, P. (1990). Social network characteristics of mothers in abusing and nonabusing families and their relationships to parenting beliefs. *Journal of Community Psychology*, **18**, 44–59.

Crittenden, P. M. (1981). Abusing, neglecting, problematic, and adequate dyads: Differentiating by patterns of interaction. *Merrill-Palmer Quarterly*, **27**, 1–18.

Crouch, J. L., Milner, J. S., & Thomsen, C. (2001). Childhood physical abuse, early social support, and risk for maltreatment: Current social support as a mediator of risk for child physical abuse. *Child Abuse and Neglect*, **25**, 93–107.

Daly, M., & Wilson, M. (1980). Discriminative parental solicitude: A biological perspective. *Journal of Marriage and the Family*, **42**, 277–288.

Daly, M., & Wilson, M. (1981). Child maltreatment from a sociobiological perspective. *New Directions in Child Development: Developmental perspectives on child maltreatment*, **11**, 93–112.

Egeland, B., & Jacobvitz, D. (1984). *Intergenerational continuity in parental abuse: Causes and consequences.* Paper presented at the Conference on Biosocial Perspectives in Abuse and Neglect, York, Maine.

Egeland, B., Jacobvitz, D., & Papatola, K. (1987). Intergenerational continuity of abuse. In R. Gelles & J. Lancaster (Eds.), *Child abuse and neglect: Biosocial dimensions* (pp. 255–276). New York: Aldine.

Eth, S. (1996). A developmental-interactional model of child abuse. In C. R. Pfeffer (Ed.), *Severe stress and mental disturbance in children* (pp. 475–495). Washington, DC: American Psychiatric Press.

Fontana, V. (1973). The diagnosis of the maltreatment syndrome in children. *Pediatrics*, **51**, 780–782.

Frodi, A. M. (1981). Contribution of infant characteristics to child abuse. *American Journal of Mental Deficiency*, **85**, 341–349.

Garbarino, J. (1977). The price of privacy: An analysis of the social dynamics of child abuse. *Child Welfare*, **56**, 565–575.

Garbarino, J., & Kostelny, K. (1992). Child maltreatment as a community problem. *Child Abuse and Neglect*, **16**, 455–464.

Garbarino, J., & Sherman, D. (1980). High-risk neighborhoods and high-risk families: The human ecology of child maltreatment. *Child Development*, **51**, 188–198.

Gelfand, D., & Teti, D. (1990). The effects of maternal depression on children. *Clinical Psychology Review*, **10**, 329–353.

Gelles, R. (1973). Child abuse as psychopathology: A sociological critique and reformulation. *American Journal of Orthopsychiatry*, **43**, 611–621.

Gelles, R. J., & Cornell, C. P. (1997). *Intimate Violence in Families*, 3rd. Edn. Beverly Hills, California: Sage.

Gelles, R. J., & Harrop, J. W. (1991). The risk of abusive violence among children with non-genetic caretakers. *Family Relations*, **40**, 78–83.

Gil, D. (1973). *Violence against children.* Cambridge, MA: Harvard University Press.

Hanks, H & Stratton, P. (2002). Consequences and indicators of child abuse. In K. Wilson & A. James (Eds.), *The Child Protection Handbook.* Edinburgh: Ballière Tindall.

Hunter, R., & Kilstrom, N. (1979). Breaking the cycle in abusive families. *American Journal of Psychiatry*, **136**, 1320–1322.

Hunter, R. S., Kilstrom, N., Kraybill, E. N., & Loda, F. (1978). Antecedents of child abuse and neglect in premature infants: A prospective study in a newborn intensive care unit. *Pediatrics*, **61**, 629–635.

Kaufman, J., & Zigler, E. (1987). Do abused children become abusive parents? *American Journal of Orthopsychiatry*, **57**, 186–192.

Kaufman, J., & Zigler, E. (1989). The intergenerational transmission of child abuse. In D. Cicchetti & V. Carlson (Eds.), *Child maltreatment: Theory and research on the causes and consequences of child abuse and neglect* (pp. 129–150). New York: Cambridge University Press.

Kavanagh, K., Youngblade, L., Reid, J., & Fagot, B. (1988). Interactions between children and abusive versus control parents. *Journal of Clinical Child Psychology*, **17**, 137–142.

Klein, M., & Stern, L. (1971). Low birth weight and the battered child syndrome. *American Journal of Diseases of Childhood*, **122**, 15.

Korbin, J. E. (1991). Cross-cultural perspectives and research directions for the 21st century. *Child Abuse and Neglect*, **15**, 67–77.

Lawson, K. A., & Hays, J. R. (1989). Self-esteem and stress as factors in abuse of children. *Psychological Reports*, **65**, 1259–1265.

Melnick, B., & Hurley, J. (1969). Distinctive personality attributes of child abusing mothers. *Journal of Consulting and Clinical Psychology*, **33**, 746–749.

Polansky, N. A., Chalmers, M. A., Buttenwieser, E., & Williams, D. P. (1981). *Damaged parents*. Chicago: University of Chicago Press.

Polansky, N. A., Gaudin, J. M., Ammons, P. W., & Davis, K. B. (1985). The psychological ecology of the neglectful mother. *Child Abuse and Neglect*, **9**, 265–275.

Putallaz, M., Costanzo, P. R., Grimes, C. L., & Sherman, D. M. (1998). Intergenerational continuities and their influences on children's social development. *Social Development*, **7**, 389–427.

Raine, A., Brennan, P., & Mednick, S. A., (1994). Birth complications combined with early maternal rejection at age 1 predispose to violent crime at age 18 years. *Archives of General Psychiatry*, **51**, 984–988.

Randall, J. & Henggeller, S. W. (1999). Multisystemic therapy. In S. W. Russ & T. H. Ollendick (Eds.). *Handbook of Psychotherapies with Children and Families*. New York: Kluwer/Plenum.

Steele, B. (1976). Violence within the family. In C. H. Kempe & A. E. Helfer (Eds.), *Child abuse and neglect: The family and the community* (pp. 3–24). Cambridge, MA: Ballinger.

Steele, B. F., & Pollack, C. B. (1968). A psychiatric study of parents who abuse infants and small children. In R. E. Helfer & C. H. Kempe (Eds.), *The battered child* (pp. 89–133). Chicago: University of Chicago Press.

Stratton, P. M., (1977). Criteria for assessing the influence of obstetric circumstances on later development. In T. Chard & M. Richards (Eds.), *Benefits and Hazards of the New Obstetrics*. 139–156, London: SIMP.

Stratton, P. M., (1983). Biological pre-programming of infant behaviour. *Journal of Child Psychology and Psychiatry*, **24**, 301–309.

Stratton, P., & Hanks, H. (1991). Incorporating circularity in defining and classifying child maltreatment. *Human Systems*, **2**. 181–200.

Stratton, P. (2002). Contemporary families as contexts for development: contributions from systemic family therapy. In J. Valsiner, & K. Connolly (Eds.), *Handbook of Developmental Psychology*. New York: Sage (in press).

Straus, M. A., & Stewart, J. H. (1999). Corporal punishment by American parents: National data on prevalence, chronicity, severity, and duration, in relation to child and family characteristics. *Clinical Child and Family Psychology Review*, **2**, 55–70.

Trickett, P. K., & Kuczynski, L. (1986). Children's misbehaviors and parental discipline strategies in abusive and nonabusive families. *Developmental Psychology*, **22**, 115–123.

Vasta, R. (1982). Physical child abuse: A dual-component analysis. *Developmental Review*, **2**, 125–149.

Whipple, E. E., & Webster-Stratton, C. (1991). The role of parental stress in physically abusive families. *Child Abuse and Neglect,* **15,** 279–291.

Widom, C. S. (1989). Does violence beget violence? A critical examination of the literature. *Psychological Bulletin,* **106,** 3–28.

Ziegert, K. A. (1983). The Swedish prohibition of corporal punishment: A preliminary report. *Journal of Marriage and the Family,* **45,** 917–926.

Zigler, E., & Hall, N. (1989). Physical child abuse in America. In D. Cicchetti & V. Carlson (Eds.), *Child maltreatment* (pp. 38–75). New York: Cambridge University Press.

Zuravin, S. J. (1988). Child maltreatment and teenage first births: A relationship mediated by chronic sociodemographic stress? *American Journal of Orthopsychiatry,* **58,** 91–103.

Zuravin, S. J. (1991). Unplanned childbearing and family size: Their relationship to child neglect and abuse. *Family Planning Perspectives,* **23,** 155–161.

Zuravin, S. J., & Greif, G. L. (1989). Normative and child-maltreating AFDC mothers. *Social Casework: The Journal of Contemporary Social Work,* 76–84.

7

IF I KNEW THEN WHAT I KNOW NOW: INTEGRITY AND FRAGMENTATION IN THE TREATMENT OF CHILD ABUSE AND NEGLECT

Patricia Crittenden

Family Relations Institute, Miami, USA

Thirty years ago, in June, my husband and I kissed our two foster daughters good-bye and watched them go out of the door, out of our lives. It was the painful conclusion to a failed process of treatment. After numerous types of treatment, our life with the elder of our foster children had continued its downward spiral. Then, as their stay with us was drawing to a close, I found that I had unexpected sympathy with their mother. A few months later, I went back to work as a teacher of young handicapped children. But a transition had begun, one that would change my career, causing me to spend the next 30 years trying to answer for myself, for other biological, foster and adoptive parents, for maltreated children, and for professionals, the questions raised by our failure and the failure of the service system to ameliorate the interpersonal problems associated with child abuse and neglect.

But the story didn't end there. Twenty-five years later, I received a call from a young woman who spoke hesitantly and with a child's voice. She was searching for her mother because her three-year-old daughter was in psychological treatment and she wondered if the problem was genetic. In talking with her, I discovered that her husband abused her, that she and her younger sister had been abandoned by their third set of adoptive parents when she was only 16, that her sister now lived on the streets with her newborn infant, having had two previous children removed, with each child having a different father. After 28 years in the treatment system, the elder of my foster children was looking for an explanation for the next generation of problems.

Early Prediction and Prevention of Child Abuse: A Handbook.
Edited by Kevin Browne, Helga Hanks, Peter Stratton and Catherine Hamilton. © 2002 John Wiley & Sons, Ltd.

What had happened? Why hadn't I been able find a way to heal these two little girls with love—or treatment? Why had their mother abused and abandoned them? Why did several foster and adoptive homes abandon them? What went wrong? Why couldn't any of the army of social workers, psychologists, and psychiatrists who had seen them over 25 years help? What did professionals need to know that we didn't know then?

These questions have led me to answers that now color the way I see human suffering and human adaptation. In this chapter, I discuss what I think is critical to stopping the pain. I am not going to review the literature or articulate theory. I have done that many times before (cf. Crittenden, 1998; 2000) as have my colleagues. Instead, I will try to integrate what I know personally with what I have learned from working with maltreating parents, reading my colleagues' work, and carrying out my own research. I will try to condense what I know into a few guidelines for working with maltreating parents and their children. The litmus test is the private one that remains in the back of my mind: Would knowing this have made a difference to me or to any of the families with whom I have worked?

WHAT IS THE PROBLEM?

Who are maltreating parents?   Forty years of research on child abuse and neglect have made a few things clear. Most maltreating parents want for their children what the rest of us want for ours: safety and comfort. Most of us have, at least occasionally, done to our children what maltreating parents do to theirs: struck them, not responded when a response was needed, responded inappropriately. Most maltreating parents are not mentally ill and most of us are not entirely free of distortion. Finally, maltreating parents generally know as much about children's behavior and parenting techniques as do other parents of their socioeconomic status. Maltreating parents aren't uncaring, bizarre, mentally ill, or uninformed. When you get to know them, they turn out to be quite human, quite deserving of our sympathy. The distinctions between us and them, that seemed so clear 40 years ago, have become increasingly murky. Nevertheless, it seems to me that maltreating parents differ from other parents in two important ways. First, they were exposed to more danger as children and, in adulthood, they live in more dangerous circumstances and are more anxious about the threat of danger. Second, throughout their lives, they have experienced little comfort. Danger and lack of comfort have come to stand out for me as central to understanding child abuse and neglect and to treating the suffering caused by it.

What are we treating when we treat maltreating parents or their children?   There is a litany of diagnostic terms applied to maltreated children: anxious, depressed, traumatized, ADHD, PTSD, etc. In the end, these diagnoses rarely enable parents to live comfortably with their children's behavior. At best, they reduce parental feelings of guilt without solving the problems of daily interaction. Further, in spite of an impressive array of treatments, it is still rare to be able to completely eradicate symptomatic behavior. This is in spite of several decades of trying treatments ranging from community to family to individual levels and from numerous theoretical perspectives. Most treatments work for some people and most demonstration projects show positive effects, but a true solution has not been found.

Over the last three decades, I've come to think differently about diagnosis. Instead of wanting to know what a parent or child fails to do properly or what is abnormal about them, I want to know what they are doing and why they are doing it. I want to understand how their behavior functions in the light of their problems. This sort of reasoning has enabled me to view behavior strategically, to see clusters of behavioral functions that are implemented in predictable ways. It has led me to think a great deal about interpersonal strategies for reducing danger and achieving comfort.

HOW DO MALTREATING PARENTS AND CHILDREN TRY TO SOLVE THE PROBLEMS OF DANGER AND LACK OF COMFORT?

Strategic behavior in maltreating families   The central thrust of my work has been to develop a Dynamic-Maturational model of the strategies that individuals use to organize self-protective and reproductive behavior (Crittenden, 1997). This model is developmental and begins with very simple strategies that, over time, are elaborated by the inclusion of distorting twists and substitutions in information and behavior. These reflect the distortions and deceptions, around danger and achieving comfort, that individuals have experienced in their own lives. By early adulthood, a wide array of strategies can be implemented. Three groups of strategies, labeled A, B, and C, have been identified (Ainsworth et al., 1978.)

The Type A strategies use true or distorted temporal predictions, i.e., true or distorted cognition, and sometimes false positive affect, but consistently omit negative affect from mental processing and behavior. Type A people seem inhibited emotionally and quite predictable. Their basic self-protective strategy is to "Do the right thing from the perspective of other people and without regard to one's own feelings or desires." There are many forms of the Type A pattern.

Some are just cool and businesslike (A1-2, Figure 7.1), whereas others are compulsive caregivers who rescue or care for others, especially those who appear weak and needy (A3). Some are compulsively compliant or obedient, especially toward angry and threatening people (A4). Others become compulsively self-reliant (A6). Usually this develops in adolescence after the individual has discovered that they cannot regulate the behavior of important, but dangerous or non-protective, caregivers. They withdraw from close relationships as soon as they are old enough to care for themselves. Among these, a few will become compulsively promiscuous (A5). Again this develops in adolescence when intimate relationships have been treacherous and strangers appear to offer the only hope of closeness and sexual satisfaction. The two most distorted subpatterns (that develop only in early adulthood) are delusional idealization of imaginary protective figures (A7) and an externally assembled self (A8). Both are associated with pervasive and sadistic early abuse and neglect.

The Type C strategies are used when individuals do not know what the right thing to do is—usually because outcomes are inconsistent and unpredictable. Not knowing what to do when one feels threatened elicits anxiety. The Type C pattern

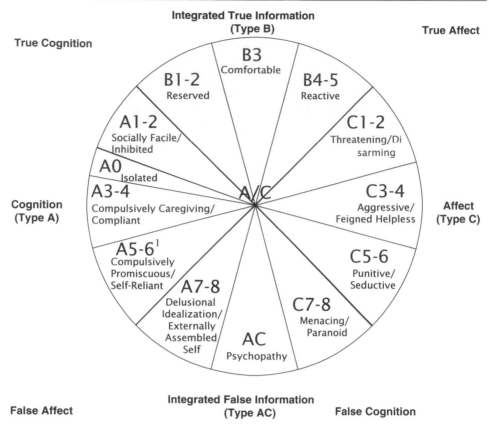

FIGURE 7.1 A Dynamic-Maturational model of patterns of attachment in adulthood
Note the reversal of A5-6 compared to previous versions of this model
Copyright: Patricia M. Crittenden, 2001. Reprinted with permission.

uses negative affect as the primary source of information and omits cognition, because outcomes have proved unpredictable. The basic form of the strategy is: "Act in accordance with your feelings and resist the attempts of others to induce you to act otherwise."

Feelings, however, are not direct and clear guides to behavior. Anxiety elicits arousal, hypervigilance, and readiness to respond, but does not suggest a response. Indeed, anxiety can be thought of as a mixture of three feelings that elicit incompatible responses. Anger motivates aggressive approach; fear motivates flight; and desire for comfort motivates approach with affection. Any one of these might solve the problem, but enacted together, behavior will almost certainly be incoherent and ineffective. Most anxious people resolve this conflict by distorting the display of feelings to create a coercive strategy. The strategy consists of splitting, exaggerating, and alternating the display of mixed negative feelings to attract attention and then manipulate the feelings and responses of others. The alternation is between presentation of a strong, angry invulnerable self who blames others for the problem (C1,3,5, Figure 7.1) with the appearance of a fearful, weak, and vulnerable self who entices others to give succorance (C2,4,6). The angry presentation elicits compliance and guilt in others, whereas vulnerability elicits rescue. This alternating pattern is often seen in bully–victim pairs, within gangs, and in violent couples where the hidden half of the pattern is usually forgotten or forgiven—until the presentation reverses. At the extreme, this pattern, too, becomes delusional with delusions of infinite revenge over ubiquitous enemies (a menacing strategy, C7) or the reverse, paranoia regarding the enemies (C8). These last two do not become organized before early adulthood.

The Type B strategy involves a balanced integration of temporal prediction with affect. In childhood, the information used is true, but, as children are exposed to the range of strategies used by others outside the family, Type B children have the opportunity to observe a wide range of distorted strategies. By adulthood, two sorts of Type B strategies can be differentiated. Naive B's simply had the good fortune to grow up in safety and comfort. Mature B's, on the other hand, (1) have reached neurological maturity (in the mid- to late 20's), (2) function in life's major roles, i.e., child, spouse, parent, and (3) carry out an on-going process of psychological integration across relationships, roles, and contexts (including those not experienced directly). Where naive B's tend to be simplistic, mature B's grapple with life's complexities.

A central notion underlying the Dynamic-Maturational model is that exposure to danger, particularly inescapable and unpredictable danger, and deception regarding comfort lead to the development of the most distorted and complex strategies (Crittenden, 1999). After puberty, achievement of sexual satisfaction and reproductive success become integrated with the protective function of attachment. This means that the highly distorted strategies, those associated with prior endangerment, will usually include some form of sexual dysfunction.

Are these strategies actually used by maltreating parents and children?   A number of studies have applied these ideas to maltreating families and, although the data are incomplete, the studies indicate that these strategies fit behavior and relationships of both normative and maltreating families at many ages (Black et al., 2000; Carlson et al., 1989; Ciotti et al., 1998; Crittenden, 1985; Crittenden & Bonvillian, 1984; Crittenden & DiLalla, 1988; Egeland & Sroufe, 1981; Jacobsen & Miller, in press; Leadbeater et al., 1996; Seefeldt, 1997; Vondra et al., in press; Ward et al., 1993). These studies also indicate how few maltreating parents or children use strategies in the upper and lower quadrants of the model and, conversely, how many use the A3-6 and C3-6 patterns, or combinations of these. That is, maltreating parents and children are rarely in the "normal" or desirable range, but neither are they usually in the psychopathological range. They display distortion in the mental processes, but are not crazy or delusional.

WHAT DIFFERENCE DOES IT MAKE TO RECOGNIZE AND UNDERSTAND THESE STRATEGIES?

Assuming that these strategies describe the behavior of individuals in maltreating families reasonably well, what is gained from knowing this?

Attribution of meaning   First, behavior becomes meaningful. Troublesome behavior can be understood as an attempt to solve a problem and to communicate meaningfully with others about the problem. When the function and organization of symptomatic behavior are understood, others become able to think productively about alternative responses to the behavior, responses directed toward its function.

A compassionate approach   Second, even a superficial knowledge of maltreating parents' history, the effects of past exposure to danger on mental functioning, and the immediate conditions surrounding maltreatment makes it clear that blame is misplaced when assigned only to the parents. From a practical perspective, guilt, when applied or accepted, interferes with the resolution of problems. Unfortunately, the treatment system too often is accessed through an accusatory process and sometimes confession and admission of guilt are required before treatment is offered. This looks uncomfortably similar to the bullying C3/5 strategy. A descriptive approach that seeks to understand parents' and children's intentions and to change conditions in ways that yield greater safety and comfort might be more productive.

In my work with maltreating mothers, I became convinced that, in spite of their appearance of not caring or their aggressive assertion of righteous innocence, most felt rejected by their children and guilty of behaving in ways that caused rejection. Most were confused about how this had happened. Having been rejected and hurt as children, they had imagined that, as parents, they would correct what their parents did wrong. Instead, they found their expectations destroyed by ugly outcomes that they could not explain. Much of my ability to win their trust and enable them to try new approaches came from my unspoken knowledge of their suffering and my appreciation of their intentions and strengths. Awareness of their perspective is a crucial base upon which to build a bridge from where they are to where they'd like to be. Compassion from others when you have reached a very low point in your life may be crucial to being able to accept help.

Focus on relationships—both current and past   Third, all the Dynamic-Maturational strategies are interpersonal. Child abuse and neglect is itself an interpersonal occurrence. This highlights the importance of relationships with other people, especially parents, for being safe and feeling secure. This is true for biological, foster, or adoptive parents. It is also true for therapists who function as temporary and surrogate attachment figures. The point is that to resolve a child's distorted interpersonal strategy, the strategies of their attachment figures must also be addressed. Knowing what parents perceive as dangerous and how they respond strategically to threat, including how they seek comfort and when they give comfort, is crucial to changing their relationship with the child and the child's strategy. I find it disturbing that, although we now know a great deal about maltreated children and their parents, we lack comparable information about foster and adoptive parents and about professionals. Knowing the interpersonal strategies of the specific individuals who work with specific maltreating families may be critical to the effectiveness of their intervention.

Intervention around danger and comfort   Fourth, the Dynamic-Maturational model suggests directions for intervention. Specifically, if there is danger, it must be lessened before change in behavior can be expected. Although this seems obvious, reducing one danger sometimes creates another. For example, the threat of parental violence may be reduced by foster care, but this creates the danger of loss of attachment figures. The child may organize a new and equally distorted strategy to deal with this threat. In other cases, danger is effectively ended, but the former strategy is maintained. This often occurs when danger was unpredictable and comfort deceptive. A means for the individual to control the danger and identify genuine comfort is needed; in its absence, anxiety and the strategies for reducing anxiety will remain. It strikes me as sadly paradoxical that some of the interventions for the most seriously harmed children would be perceived by them as increasing the danger and offering a false promise of comfort through superficial relationships. Increasing children's anxiety and presuming that case workers can provide comfort and continuity is probably counter-productive.

Opposite strategies may call for opposite treatments Finally, if the Dynamic-Maturational model of Type A versus Type C strategies (and the underlying theory of information processing, see Crittenden, 1997; 2000) is reasonably accurate, then the A and C strategies are psychological opposites. A central implication of this is that a treatment approach that reduced the Type A distortion might increase the Type C distortion and vice versa. There are no data yet that test this proposition, but it is a crucial proposition because it suggests that applying a specific technique to a group of children or parents that was mixed with regard to Type A and Type C organizations could be beneficial to some individuals and detrimental to others. Elsewhere my colleagues and I have outlined this perspective more fully with regard to maltreated children and their parents (Crittenden et al., 2001).

WHAT MOTIVATES PARENTS TO ACT THE WAY THEY DO?

At the height of behaviorism, that question would have been answered with the word "consequences." Surely that is a primary motivation and in the Dynamic-Maturational model, I have labeled it "cognitive" information about the temporal order of events. It is the basis for the behavior of individuals using the Type A strategies. More recently, affect has been recognized as an equally important motivation. This motivation is, I think, much less well understood. Here I discuss confusion among affective states, leading to inappropriate behavior and unclear communication to others about one's internal state and intentions. I address three confusions: confusion of positive and negative affect, confusion among negative affects, and confusion of sexual desire and satisfaction with other affects. Because they are the least understood and most disturbing, I treat confusions regarding sexuality in detail.

Confusion of false positive affect and true negative affect When children discover that expression of negative affect leads to abandonment or aggression, they learn to inhibit the display of true negative feelings. This can occur as early as the first days of life. By about 18–24 months of age, toddlers are capable of displaying positive affect that they do not feel if the consequence is parental attention and approval.

Such children, using a Type A strategy, display false positive affect because it makes them safer and more comfortable. Under these conditions, both adults and children can become confused about the child's actual feelings.

Mixed negative feelings Feelings motivate us strongly, but their message is often unclear. When one is highly anxious, one seeks to lower arousal. The focus, in other words, is on changing feeling states when, in fact, a change in safety is needed. This confusion of the affective signal of safety with safety itself can lead to misdirected behavior. The difficulty is exacerbated by lack of clarity among feelings states, particularly anger, fear, and desire for comfort. Moreover, when past comfort seeking has provoked danger, anger and fear may dominate motivation. It is not uncommon that one feeling and its non-verbal expression is exaggerated while the opposite signal is inhibited. This clarifies the disposition to act, but obscures motivation. Professionals need to know that angry people are usually frightened, frightened people are often angry, and both need comfort.

Anxious arousal and sexual arousal Sexual arousal creates another source of confusion. Sexual arousal shares with anxiety the state of aroused anticipation and heightened attention. It shares with anger and desire for comfort the search for a person on whom or with whom to act. Moreover, just as aggression, flight, and soothing change a person's anxious state, sexual activity transforms sexual arousal into sexual satisfaction and lowered arousal. The parallels between anxious and sexual arousal and between comfort and sexual satisfaction create the potential for psychological and behavioral confusion. When is the source of arousal sexual and when not? Can anxious arousal be soothed by sexual activity? Comforting behavior is startlingly similar to sexual behavior. Close bodily contact, gentle, soothing touch, soft voices, and private, safe places are associated with comfort. Another person who feels similarly to you and whose rhythmic, rocking movements are in synchrony with your own yields comfort. The details of this list are important because these activities draw us into intimate relationships. Children need to be comforted and comfortable. So do adults. Being close to another person, especially someone wiser, stronger, and committed to our welfare, not only makes us comfortable, it also protects us from danger. Isolation from protective and comforting people is both itself dangerous and also a signal of danger that elicits feelings of anxiety. In homes where anxiety is constant and danger threatens often, comfort is needed desperately and comforting people are rarely available. When protection fails to draw people together in comforting relationships, sex can sometimes accomplish the goal.

Not only are anxious arousal and sexual arousal difficult to differentiate as internal states and enacted behavior, the non-verbal signals that communicate desire for comfort and desire for sexual contact are overlapping and ambiguous. Because the mouth and genitalia are highly enervated, touching them elicits responses more consistently and intensively than touching other parts of the body. For example, gentle stroking of genitals calms distressed infants. This is a commonly used, but rarely discussed, tactic employed by some mothers and newborn nursery nurses. By about eight months of age, infants become able to do this for themselves. For the remainder of the life-span, masturbation is a frequently used means of reducing excessive arousal and achieving self-comfort.

Sexualized behavior can also be used to achieve the opposite goal, that of increased arousal and attention. Use of the CARE-Index videotape procedure with many hundreds of normative, maltreating, and disturbed mothers indicates a consistent pattern in mothers' use of kissing and sexualized touching. When mothers have made numerous bids for their infants' attention and yet the infants remain inattentive or actively avoidant, mothers quite universally dart in with a kiss. Distal kisses on the cheek are used initially, but, if the infant remains distant, kisses to the infant's mouth often follow. If this fails, the mother may use her tongue to stroke the inside of the infant's lips or mouth. This appears sexual, but the functional sequence is one of seeking attention when the mother feels rejected. It should be noted that this technique almost always elicits infant attention, albeit sometimes negative attention.

By the second year of life, toddlers begin to behave in ways that can be confused with sexual invitation. Toddlers use coy behavior to elicit attention and caregiving from protective adults. Coy behavior, however, is also used after puberty to flirt sexually. This can lead to confused communications, particularly with adults who fragment their functioning by responding too readily to signals tied to sexuality. By failing to take the child's perspective, such adults could perceive that they were being invited into a sexual relationship with a precocious child, when in actuality, they were being invited into a protective relationship with an anxious child. Children too can become confused. They want attention and enjoy being touched and stroked. But they want to be calmed, not aroused, and they have no particular desire for genital contact. Many will have mixed feelings. This confusion is worrisome when carried into adulthood.

Puberty and the onset of sexual desire create new ways to achieve comfort. Sexual closeness shares many features with comfort, such that the description above of comforting behavior can fit either the image of a mother comforting her fretful infant or of lovers beginning the progression to sexual intercourse. The processes are not identical, particularly because one leads to lowered arousal and the other to increased arousal. But they are very similar behaviorally and, emotionally, sexual satisfaction feels very much like comfort. Moreover, in both cases, relationships are strengthened by intimate activity. Sexuality, in other words, opens the door both to sexual desire and behavior (that serve the function of reproduction) and also to new ways of achieving closeness and comfort in relationships where there is little safety and less comfort.

WHAT DIFFERENCE DOES IT MAKE TO RECOGNIZE THE CONFUSION OF MOTIVATION THAT ACCOMPANIES CONFUSED FEELINGS?

Appearance versus reality   Not everything is as it appears to be. Everyone knows this. The details of identifying the inaccurate appearance, however, are not easily mastered. Many abused and neglected children appear happy and agreeable in just those moments when we would expect them to be distressed or resistant. Is their positive affect a reflection of their real feelings or is it a false presentation that hides true negative feelings? Knowing that the appearance could be false would help other people to respond to the child more appropriately. Failure to recognize this false resilience caused me to misjudge how one of my foster children truly felt and, for her first year with us, prevented our seeking help for her. Instead, we accepted the desired appearance that she was happy and contented. I wish I had known then—or been told—what I know now about the compulsive Type A strategies. Their use by my foster daughter made me feel good (and that is their function) and I asked no further questions. Negative affect is appropriate in some circumstances and its absence should alert us to the possibility of problems.

For other children, the confusion will be between anger and fear. If the Dynamic-Maturational model is accurate, aggressive children are very often fearful and desirous of comfort. Being misled by appearances, we treat aggression and anger as if they were the problem. Timid children rarely look angry; all too often we overlook such children, never suspecting the rage that lies under the surface. The cost of this error of interpretation may be drug abuse, depression, suicide, even homicide. Sexually abused, precocious, and promiscuous children and adolescents are all likely to experience anxiety and desire for comfort and protection; it seems important that we consider this interpretation of their behavior.

Maltreating parents show similar distortions of appearance. Rigidly punitive parents may act aggressively because of their fear of harm to their disobedient, rowdy, or risk-taking children. Having been severely punished themselves in childhood, disobedience becomes a signal of danger. When their children disobey, their minds are propelled into action by fear at the violated rule. The remembered fear and the present fear become one; the punishment they received and that which they deliver become one. Later, they will only be able to say that the child misbehaved and must learn to obey. We perceive rigidity of rules in an angry, aggressive person. We may be unaware that fear and memories of being the victim were in the abuser's mind at the critical moment when thought stopped and action started.

When sexual abuse is intrafamilial, sexual contact becomes a part of the relationship between adult and child. In the future, however, the victims are likely to attract other abusers. The distorted processes of interpersonal communication and maintenance of relationship appear to ripple through other relationships. Confused feelings cause slippage of behavior across motivational systems until it becomes difficult to understand what was actually wanted or achieved. For both child victims and adult perpetrators, desire for comfort is likely to underlie at least some sexually distorted behavior such that comfort seeking becomes implicitly tied to sexual desire and activity. If treatment fails to address children's confusing behavior and adults' confusion of anxiety and sexual desire, it may fail to address crucial realities that motivate sexual abuse of children and that contribute to its effects on their later development.

Aborted information processing and danger   All of the confusions described above can be resolved by exploring past and present experience through a process of mental integration and by learning new interpersonal skills that will change how relationships are experienced. So simple! So very difficult to actually achieve. The conditions that halt mental processing most quickly are perception of danger and sexual opportunity. This is universal, but very informative regarding maltreating parents and maltreated children. Their lives have been lived with and near danger, from their neighborhoods to their bedrooms. The more individuals are in danger (or think they are), the more they must act quickly and in the safest way possible. Taking time to reflect can take time away from self-protection. Under conditions of danger, there is a strong advantage to acting prior to thinking.

It has become clear to me that most abuse involves perception of danger, most neglect of believing oneself to be helplessly unprotected, and most familial sexual abuse a misguided attempt to feel comfortable and close to others. In the face of danger, humans feel anger, fear, and desire for comfort. Comfort, on the other hand, is the emotional signal that there is no danger; in comfort and safety, we can afford the luxury of integrative reflection. There is very little comfort in the homes and lives of maltreated children and their parents.

WHY DO PROFESSIONALS DO WHAT THEY DO?

Mental health professionals   Given all that we know about maltreating parents, maltreated children, and the importance of relationships to both dysfunction and healing, it is concerning that we have not examined closely the psychological functioning of the professionals who work with maltreating families. What we do know suggests limitations to our ability to resolve the problems in these families.

Child protection workers tend to be young, are often unmarried and without children, lack appropriate professional training, and stay in their jobs only a few years. Much less is known about their psychological functioning. Although they could use naive Type B strategies, it is unlikely that they have had the opportunity to develop a maturely balanced strategy. Consequently, most are dependant upon on-the-job training for guidance in dealing with maltreating families. Instructional guidelines and procedural manuals line their desks, but cannot substitute for the inner judgment they have not had time to develop.

More is known about psychologists and psychiatrists. Compared to the normative population, they have experienced more trauma and loss, have more depression and anxiety, and more often attempt and commit suicide. A significant proportion suffer from diagnosable forms of psychological disturbance. Others are certainly mature and wise guides to managing life's complexities. But we do not systematically identify these individuals and there is no reason to believe that they predominate among those who treat cases of child abuse and neglect. Compounding this problem is the fact that most therapists are middle class and most maltreating families are not. As any child protection worker knows, life in these families and in their neighborhoods is nothing like life in the middle class. When therapists offer treatment only in their offices and predominantly to individuals, they are vulnerable to simplifying the problem of maltreatment in ways that reduce their potential to be helpful.

Foster parents   It is startling how little is known about foster parents. Some demographic information is available (they are generally low income, have limited education, etc.). A bit is known about their motivations. It is often stated that particular foster parents are in it for the money; there are better low paying jobs than fostering troubled children. For others, the reasons given are altruistic. Again, there are other ways to benefit society. Why was fostering selected?

The psychological functioning of foster parents is unknown. It matters because their role with maltreated children is intensely personal and psychologically powerful. They have psychological effects upon the children whom they raise—and we know almost nothing about what those effects might be. Nevertheless, statistically, they are an atypical population, i.e., very few parents offer to foster other parents' children. Preliminary data in a small doctoral dissertation suggest that many have unresolved losses from their own childhoods. Others first begin to foster as their own children are leaving home as young adults. This is a natural time of increased availability, but does it sometimes reflect a need to replace something that is being lost? Given that all foster children suffer from loss and that foster parents must be prepared to lose their foster children, lack of resolution of loss may be very relevant to the care foster parents offer. We know next to nothing about this.

Redefining the problem   Aside from biological parents, foster parents are the most powerful treatment system at our disposal. Generally, however, we consider them more like refrigerators, simply keeping children safe until permanent decisions can be made. In reality, foster parents become attachment figures simply because they are with children every day and every night, especially when children are tired, hurt, or frightened. Foster parents have a special opportunity to help troubled children.

Foster care is also the most dangerous treatment strategy. Simply placing children away from their parents constitutes a major threat from the perspective of children. If perception of danger elicits self-protective behavior, placement in foster care should do so in the extreme. In addition, placement disrupts children's already anxious relationship with their biological parents, making it more difficult to heal in the future. Concurrently, the biological parents' bond is disrupted; they become worried about losing their children forever and this elicits self-protective behavior on their part. Finally, the risk of abuse or neglect in foster care is higher than in the population at large, as is the risk of abandonment in the form of multiple placements.

Because these risks are well known, foster care is the intervention of last resort. Can we reduce the risk? Informing foster parents of the strategic patterning of children's behavior might help them to tolerate and reduce this atypical behavior. It might also help them to organize their homes in ways that would provide children with the safety and comfort that they seek.

The issue may be one of integrity. Conflicting interests and needs define the situation of foster parents. How do foster parents, who may have unresolved losses, maintain psychological integrity in the context of volunteering to surrender family integrity? What strategy can best enable them to form the essential bonds of attachment with children and, at the same time, relinquish the children willingly when they return to their biological parents or other permanent home? How do foster parents protect themselves from repeated losses and still accept and care for additional children? There is a gradient of success in fostering with some couples managing very well and others having either trouble with the children or trouble with their departure. How do the best foster parents maintain their own psychological integrity and promote such integrity in their foster children?

How best can we select, support, and use foster parents?   Knowing more about foster parents and fostering could be very helpful in matching children to foster parents and in supporting placements. The issue could be framed in terms of the strategies described in the Dynamic-Maturational model. Some pairs of strategies match easily whereas others clash. Knowing both children's and foster parents' strategies could provide one basis for selecting a specific placement in preference to another. After placements have been made, knowing the adults' and children's preferred strategies might enable professionals to fine-tune their guidance to fit each particular dyad and family context. It is not a matter of weeding out "bad" foster and adoptive parents; it is a matter of matching them psychologically to those specific children who can trust and learn from them and assisting them to apply their strategies in uniquely helpful ways to each child.

Another approach, one that is often used with young adolescent mothers, is to have foster parents foster the entire maltreating family. There could be several advantages to selecting foster parents who can conceptualize their role as protecting families, as opposed to protecting children from their families. First, a source of conflicting interests would be reduced. Second, foster children might feel less stressed around visitation. Third, an ameliorative relationship between the families could help the maltreating family, not only during the placement, but potentially into the future as well. Studies of the effects of paraprofessionals' committed involvement with specific maltreating families suggest the healing power of a caring adult for both maltreating parents and their children. An advantage is that paraprofessionals tend to deal more directly and fully with families than do professionals who respect client–professional boundaries and boundaries between professional disciplines. The issue is integrity again. Paraprofessionals who are trained and supervised adequately are more likely to respond to the whole family than professionals whose scope is more narrowly defined.

Having had foster children and worked with maltreating mothers and families, I now wish that my husband and I had been encouraged to get to know our foster daughters' mother and father. The dismay that I feel now over the events of the last 30 years might have been satisfaction at having assisted a young couple to keep, raise, and love their children. It seems to me now that it would have been worth a try. After all who, more than the foster parents, could know and empathize with the unique challenges presented by maltreated children?

WHAT HAVE WE LEARNED? WHAT DO WE STILL NEED TO KNOW AND DO?

I began by asking what we needed to know about abuse and neglect that we did not know 30 years ago. In that time, we have learned a tremendous amount. My own work has taught me about the strategies that endangered children and their parents organize to protect themselves and feel more comfortable. Knowing about these when we had foster children would have helped me to understand and modify the behavior that created so many problems. Indeed, the entire approach of seeing atypical interpersonal functioning as a strategic route to achieving self-protection and comfort would enable those who provide treatment to be more helpful to both children and their parents. Knowing that endangered children and adults often disguise their true feelings by distortion, inhibition, and falsification would have enabled me to interpret my foster children's behavior more accurately and, thus, respond more helpfully. Knowing why endangered people represent their experience as they do could enable professionals to work from that representation toward more accurate representation, as opposed to confronting parents' representations as inaccurate. Knowing that early endangerment and lack of comfort affect parents' strategies for protecting their children would generate more compassion for maltreating parents. This, in turn, could enable professionals to form more supportive relationships with the parents to assist them to realize their dreams for their children. More than before, we now understand that relationships are critical to human well-being and to the process of achieving well-being. Finally, we know how dangerous it can be, in terms of further maltreatment and emotional functioning, to remove children from their families. Even when it is necessary, it comes at a cost to the children. Knowing better how to support maltreating parents could enable us to place fewer children in foster care.

Nevertheless, there are still important gaps in our knowledge. We know far too little about the interpersonal strategies and goals of those who offer treatment (including foster parents) and how these strategies affect therapeutic and fostering relationships. Having this information could be critical to matching personnel to parents and children, to constructing individualized treatment plans, and to offering personalized supervision. Similarly, we understand too little about how we might foster entire families, thus, avoiding removal of some children. We also know too little about the specific effects of our treatment techniques, including whether they function similarly for all people. If my hypothesis of opposite effects of some techniques on individuals who use Type A or Type C strategies is accurate, we could prevent iatrogenic harm by applying techniques differentially. Finally, we need to know the limits of our current ability to help. Some cases are beyond the means currently at our disposal for changing behavior. In most cases, the parents will be those who themselves were the most endangered, the most deceptively, for the longest periods of time from the earliest years of life. Our compassion for them and awareness that they too are victims and are deserving of our help should not blind us to our current inability to help them or to protect their children. We should act quickly to place their children in permanent homes in which they can grow up in safety and comfort.

If I try to summarize what I think I have learned, it might be that danger and lack of comfort often lead to fragmentation of mental functioning and of relationships. Treatment should be focused on integration—of information, of psychological functions, and of families and their relationships. Without such integration, integrity is impossible. For professionals, forgetting the humanity of maltreating parents fragments our mental functioning and their families. Nevertheless, maintaining integrity for ourselves by recognizing complexity and suffering in their lives is very difficult. This leads me to conclude that there is an inherent incompatibility between the legal and moral responses to child maltreatment and a mental health response. The legal system focuses on guilt, prohibition, and punishment, but cannot teach people what to do or make them feel safe and comfortable. The treatment system can be a non-judgmental means to offer parents and children new strategies that promote safety and comfort. Because these approaches are in conflict, the systems should be accessed separately. In most cases, however, the child potection system provides entry to both. This creates problems. Perhaps judgment and punishment should be reserved not for the guilty, but for those relentlessly dangerous individuals whom we do not yet know how to help and from whom we must protect children.

Fragmentation of the problem and of our solutions cannot solve, and often exacerbates, the problem of child maltreatment. The familiar dichotomies of perpetrator/victim, right/wrong, parent/professional, and adult/child distort the truth. If I have learned anything in these 30 years, it is that it is easy to blame, but impossible to be fair or to promote children's well-being when doing so. It is easy to punish, but hard to heal. Reductionist dichotomies fragment the mind, fragment the complexity of reality, and fragment our families. Possibly justice is a continual process of using the best that we have to generate better in a world that has unavoidable danger, but whose comfort depends only upon our wisdom and compassion.

REFERENCES

Ainsworth, M. D. S., Blehar, M., Waters, E., & Wall, S. (1978). *Patterns of attachment: A psychological study of the Strange Situation*. Hillsdale, NJ: Erlbaum Assoc.

Black, K. A., Jaeger, E., McCartney, K., & Crittenden, P. M. (2000). Attachment models, peer interaction behavior, and feelings about the self: Indications of maladjustment in dismissing/preoccupied (Ds/E) adolescents. In P. M. Crittenden and A. H. Claussen (Eds). *The organization of attachment relationships: Maturation, culture, and context* (pp. 300–324). New York: Cambridge University Press.

Carlson, V., Cicchetti, D., Barnett, D., & Braunwald, K. (1989). Disorganized/disoriented attachment relationships in maltreated infants. *Developmental Psychology*, **25**, 525–531.

Ciotti, F., Lambruschi, F., Pittino, B., & Crittenden, P. (1998). La valutazione della relazione precoce madre–bambino in una popolazione di madri con una storia di tossicodipendenza attraverso l'uso del CARE-Index. *Psicoterapia Cognitiva e Comportamentale*, **4**, 53–59.

Crittenden, P. M. (2000). A dynamic-maturational exploration of the meaning of security and adaptation: Empirical, cultural, and theoretical considerations. In P. M. Crittenden and A. H. Claussen (Eds). *The organization of attachment relationships: Maturation, culture, and context* (pp. 358–384). New York: Cambridge University Press.

Crittenden, P. M. (1998). Dangerous behavior and dangerous contexts: A thirty-five year perspective on research on the developmental effects of child physical abuse. In P. Trickett (Ed.) *Violence to children* (pp. 11–38). Washington, DC: American Psychological Association.

Crittenden, P. M. (1997). Toward an integrative theory of trauma: A dynamic-maturational approach. In D. Cicchetti and S. Toth (Eds). *The Rochester Symposium on Developmental Psychopathology, Vol. 10. Risk, Trauma, and Mental Processes* (pp. 34–84). Rochester, NY: University of Rochester Press.

Crittenden, P. M. (1999). Danger and development: The organization of self-protective strategies. In J. I. Vondra and D. Barnett, (Eds). A typical attachment in infancy and early childhood among children at developmental risk. *Monographs of the Society for Research on Child Development* (pp. 145–171).

Crittenden, P. M. (1985). Social networks, quality of child-rearing, and child development. *Child Development*, **56**, 1299–1313.

Crittenden, P. M. & Bonvillian, J. D. (1984). The effect of maternal risk status on maternal sensitivity to infant cues. *American Journal of Orthopsychiatry*, **54**, 250–262.

Crittenden, P. M. & DiLalla, D. L. (1988). Compulsive compliance: The development of an inhibitory coping strategy in infancy. *Journal of Abnormal Child Psychology*, **16**, 585–599.

Crittenden, P. M., Landini, A., & Claussen. A. H. (2001). A dynamic-maturational approach to treatment of maltreated children. In J. Hughes, J. C. Conley, and A. La Greca (Eds.), *Handbook of Psychological Services for Children and Adolescents* (pp. 373–398), New York: Oxford University Press.

Egeland, B., & Sroufe, L. A. (1981). Attachment and early maltreatment. *Child Development,* **52,** 44–52.

Jacobsen, T., & Miller, L. J. (in press). Compulsive compliance in a young maltreated child. *Journal of the American Academy of Child and Adolescent Psychiatry.*

Leadbeater, B. J., Bishop, S. J., & Raver, C. C. (1996). Quality of mother–toddler interaction, maternal depressive symptoms, and behavior problems of adolescent mothers. *Developmental Psychology,* **32,** 280–288.

Seefeldt, L. (1997). Models of parenting in maltreating and non-maltreating mothers. Dissertation presented to the Faculty of the School of Nursing, University of Wisconsin-Milwaukee. Milwaukee, USA.

Vondra, J. I., Shaw, D. S., Swearingen, L., Cohen, M., & Owens, E. B. (in press). Attachment stability and emotional and behavioral regulation from infancy to preschool age. *Development and Psychopathology.*

Ward, M. J., Kessler, D. B., & Altman, S. C. (1993). Infant–mother attachment in children with failure to thrive. *Infant Mental Health Journal,* **14,** 208–220.

8

EDUCATING AND CHANGING PARENTS: STRENGTHENING THE PRIMARY SAFETY NET FOR CHILDREN

Deborah Daro
University of Chicago, USA

INTRODUCTION

Given the primacy of parental responsibility for both nurturing and protecting children, it is not surprising to find parent education and support programs at the heart of child abuse prevention efforts (Gray & DiLeonardi, 1982; Helfer, 1982; Daro, 1988). A plethora of home-based and classroom educational programs, community-based parent support groups and advocacy efforts designed to strengthen the political voice of parents have long been part of comprehensive child abuse prevention policies (Cohn, 1983). While such efforts have successfully strengthened parental capacity and reduced propensity toward abuse, programs often underestimate the need for alternative service delivery strategies due to a parent's different levels of need and receptivity to various educational messages. Parents come from all socio-economic groups and an increasingly wide range of ages, educational sophistication, family structures and work arrangements. Some parents have many hours with their children; some have precious few. Some are surrounded by supportive family members and friends; some rear their children in lonely isolation. Some enjoy excellent community-based social, educational and recreational services; others have playgrounds filled with broken glass and streets lined with boarded up buildings.

Educating this diverse group of parents so as to reduce their risk for abusive or neglectful behaviors requires a multifaceted approach, one that seeks change at

Early Prediction and Prevention of Child Abuse: A Handbook.
Edited by Kevin Browne, Helga Hanks, Peter Stratton and Catherine Hamilton. © 2002 John Wiley & Sons, Ltd.

both the individual and community levels (Daro, 2000). The purpose of this chapter is to offer a framework for defining and implementing a range of parent education strategies such that all parents have access to essential information and support. After a brief overview of the factors influencing parental capacity, the chapter reviews the relative strengths and limitations of parent education strategies that employ different service delivery systems and target different parent populations. Shifting to issues of community capacity building, the chapter then outlines the role community norms and values can play in creating a richer parent learning environment, one that encourages shared responsibility for child well being and parent support. The chapter concludes with the challenges this dual framework suggests for expanding and improving child abuse prevention systems.

UNDERSTANDING PARENTAL CAPACITY

A number of factors go into determining an individual's parenting style. As outlined by Belsky and Vondra (1989), theories of parental practice have evolved from a reliance on "linear or main effect" frameworks into models which recognize the interdependence or interaction of multiple causal agents. Efforts to model this process generally include some combination of developmental history, personality factors, social interactions or social networks, familial relationships and child characteristics (Belsky and Stratton, Chapter 6).

Figure A offers one approach for understanding the constellation of factors that directly and indirectly influence parental behavior. As illustrated in this model, parental abilities and actions stem from a number of factors, each of which influences and is influenced by the others. At the most basic level, a parent needs to have the capacity to love or empathize with a child in order to establish any relationship (Olden, 1953; 1958). Often adults who were abused as children, who were raised without the nurturance or support of an identified primary caretaker or whose initial observations of adult interactions were scenes of extreme violence, lack this basic capacity (Steele, 1997). While parents who exhibit a lack of emotional attachment to their children are generally viewed as poor candidates for prevention services, instructional programs can provide high risk parents with a general framework for assessing their child's minimal needs, providing these efforts are augmented by substantial therapeutic intervention and continuous support (Jones, 1997).

While psychological well being is one component of parental capacity, equally important is the knowledge and skills individuals have regarding basic child development, child management and problem solving. It is important for parents to know, in at least general terms, the differing cognitive and physical abilities and needs of children at different stages of development. If knowledge is the only barrier between good intentions and positive parenting, simple, educational programs are well suited to filling this gap. Indeed, conveying this type of basic knowledge to parents through written material or group presentations may be one of the easiest ways to improve parenting potential (Dunst, 1995; Weiss & Jacobs, 1988, Sanders & Cann Chapter 9).

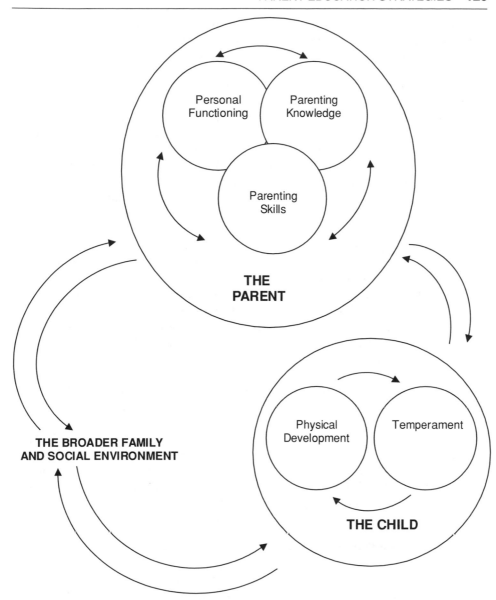

FIGURE 8.1   A conceptual model of parenting

However, for many parents the inability to care for their children is not simply a matter of insufficient knowledge. Parents who lacked the benefits of positive adult relationships in their own childhood, for example, often require extensive assistance in mastering basic child care techniques and in providing consistent emotional support to their children (Polansky, 1981; Rutter, 1989). In these cases, identifying and addressing the barriers parents face in meeting their child's needs can be a complex and time consuming task for practitioners. As discussed below, modeling the implementation of basic parenting information is one of the most effective ways to assist parents in integrating their newly acquired knowledge into consistent behavioral change (Bandura, 1986; Wolfe, 1994).

In every parent–child relationship, this constellation of adult characteristics interacts with each child's unique personality and temperament. In some cases, this interaction is positive and self-satisfying. In other cases, this interaction enhances the likelihood for maltreatment. Some babies are more difficult and temperamental than others. Low birth weight babies, premature infants or developmentally delayed children can be challenging for all parents but particularly so for those parents with limited personal capabilities (Kolko, 1996). Further, as with all relationships, some mothers and babies are simply more compatible and better suited to each other (Webster-Stratton, 1990). As children mature, they often make choices or seek a level of independence at odds with their parents' wishes or expectations, leading to elevated levels of conflict (Garbarino, 1989). Effectively educating parents, therefore, requires that attention be paid to the manner in which the child and parent temperaments complement or disrupt the parenting process and how this interaction changes over time.

Beyond the complex but very narrow dyad of parent and child lies a host of environmental factors that contribute to an individual's perception of what constitutes adequate parenting and, more importantly, his or her ability to realize these standards of care. Family and friendship networks can provide a rich reservoir of supports for a new parent or present formidable barriers to adopting new methods of care or discipline (Thompson, 1995). In addition, the total pool of community resources available to parents expands or limits their ability to address their children's evolving educational and health care needs. Communities with a large number of quality day care facilities, schools, health care centers, housing and employment opportunities offer families greater resources to care for their children than do communities lacking these characteristics (Melton & Berry, 1994). Even the most knowledgeable and skillful parents will have problems ensuring the health and well being of their children if they are unable to find employment or if their housing complex or community is riddled with crime.

Implications for Program Planning

For purposes of planning interventions and understanding their potential impacts, it is useful to categorize parents into three groups. This typology, which is more fully discussed elsewhere (Daro, 1993), divides families in the following manner:

- Consumer families are those parents who recognize their limitations with respect to child development knowledge, parenting skills and the use of formal and informal supports. While they may not always articulate their specific shortcomings, they are able to secure, often on their own, the help they need to compensate for deficits in their parental capacity.
- Dependent families may not know they need assistance or, if they do know that they need additional help, may not know where to find help or how to effectively access the help they can locate. They are generally not good at readily applying

a theoretical concept to their own child's behavior or adjusting a technique to suit their child's developmental progress. These families need more directed assistance in assessing their needs and in locating and accessing educational and supportive services.

- Broken families are those families whose members have failed to integrate the social, emotional and cognitive competencies needed for healthy development. These parents often exhibit serious functional problems such as extreme disorganization, substance abuse and violent behavior. As a result, their children may be taken into temporary custody by government agencies or they will be forced to relinquish all their parental rights. For those children remaining in these families, however, their safety often hinges on the ability of supportive and therapeutic services to engage and retain their parents over an extended time period.

This typology suggests that, to be effective, parenting education programs need to encompass a variety of strategies. For some parents, simply making them aware of new information or service options may be sufficient to ensure adequate support. For other parents, assistance will need to be targeted, well focused and repeatedly offered. While it appears prudent to begin parent education efforts at the time a child is born or a mother is pregnant, each developmental stage (e.g., toddlers, latency age, school age and adolescence) presents unique challenges and informational needs. Similarly, parents experiencing divorce, domestic violence and other disruptions in their lives may find themselves in need of specific guidance and skills as to how to navigate these changes without placing their child at further risk (Baumrind, 1991; Cowan & Cowan, 1992; Kagan, 1998; Wilson, 1999).

In addition to these developmental and personal capacity dimensions, parenting education efforts also must recognize the powerful role cultural traditions and community norms play in what parents view as abusive behavior and on the acceptance of alternative behaviors (Guterman, 2001; Specht & Courtney, 1994; Wasik & Bryant, 2001). It is often unclear how a given family, culture or community will respond to different interpersonal and environmental risk factors. While some of these factors have universal effects, most influence parenting patterns and parent–child relationships in diverse ways. Because many parent education efforts occur in the absence of any observable parental failure or acts of maltreatment, these programs also must be non-judgmental, offering assistance rather than reform or "cure". Achieving this type of supportive character is facilitated when a program reflects community norms and values with respect to both the help seeking and help giving processes (Slaughter-Defoe, 1993).

The prevention field is replete with examples of parenting education efforts that have effectively adjusted their content and service delivery style to reflect these vast differences in parental expectations, capacity and needs. In investigating the features of successful programs, many have written about the need for programs to establish clear, coherent linkages among participant needs, program goals, program structure and staff skills (Berlin et al., 1998; Fulbright-Anderson et al., 1998; Olds, et al., 1999; Weiss, 1995). Others have emphasized the need for greater attention to the role community values and resources play in a child's development

(Earls, 1998; Melton & Berry, 1994; Schorr, 1997) and the importance of continuous adherence to quality standards in both structuring programs and hiring and supervising staff (Dunst, 1995; Schorr, 1997; Wasik & Bryant, 2001). Within these parameters, child abuse prevention advocates have designed and implemented a number of diverse and effective prevention efforts that target both the behaviors of individual parents as well as the contexts in which they live. The balance of this chapter briefly summarizes the empirical evidence for these diverse strategies and discusses the implication of this body of research on program and policy planning.

EDUCATING PARENTS DIRECTLY

Volumes have been written about the efficacy of individual prevention strategies and broad prevention systems, as reflected in other chapters within this volume. The emphasis in this chapter is on examining the relative merits of these diverse strategies in light of the family typology outlined above. For purpose of framing this discussion, Table 8.1 briefly outlines the underlying logic, evidence of possible impacts and limitations of four commonly discussed strategies for delivering parenting information and enhancing parental capacity. As outlined in this table, efforts to build upon existing institutional contacts with families and group-based interventions offer the least intrusive methods to educate parents. For those parents who can avail themselves of these opportunities, the strategies offer a non-stigmatizing, strength-based method to secure information and support. For families without this personal capacity, home visitation services and models that combine therapeutic and educational strategies offer an opportunity to package parenting information in a way more consistent with what a family may need. The individualized nature of these services and their level of intensity offer a greater likelihood for success with those families that share many of the demographic and situational factors that place them at high risk for abusive or neglectful behaviors.

While each model has produced some changes in targeted outcome areas with selected populations, strong empirical support for any of these strategies is either very limited or non-existent. In some cases, the absence of outcomes reflects measurement difficulties (e.g., the absence of solid baseline data, the lack of standardized assessment measures in certain domains, incomplete or inaccurate administrative data systems, etc.). In other cases, the evaluations of these strategies have not incorporated rigorous designs (e.g., controlled randomized trials or quasi-experimental designs) or identified samples large enough to detect more subtle changes in attitudes or behaviors. In other cases, implementation difficulties such as high staff turnover rates, poor participant identification procedures, or dramatic changes in community context have limited a strategy's potential. Despite their individual limitations, diverse parent education efforts delivered with quality can complement each other such that the majority of parents can be provided a consistent and reliable resource for understanding and responding to their child's physical, social and emotional needs.

TABLE 8.1 Relative merits of alternative parenting education models

Strategy	Underlying logic	Strengths or Promise	Limitations
Building on Existing Institutional Supports for *All* Parents	Major institutions provide an infrastructure prevention advocates can use to deliver universal services. Because many families with risk markers already have contact with these institutions, embedding prevention within the systems allows for more targeted support without stigmatizing families.	Some evidence exists that pediatric care centers and prenatal clinics offer effective vehicles for insuring that high risk families receive more consistent heath care. Public education settings can be used to improve parenting knowledge and create more positive and effective parental responses to high risk behavior by teens.	Most institutions continue to focus on the most at-risk families or those who have already demonstrated abusive behavior. Sustaining the ability to deliver individualized services in a high quality manner is difficult within a highly structured, bureaucratic context
Group-Based Services	Reduces family isolation and promotes informal supports. Allows parents to "learn from each other" and creates a new cultural context for enhanced parenting.	Evidence of improved social integration, parenting knowledge and life skills, particularly for teens. Strong universal appeal in that most parents seek approval of their parenting from peers.	Difficult for high-risk families to sustain involvement due to logistical barriers (e.g. transportation, adapting to a fixed schedule, etc.). Services difficult to tailor to each individual parent.
Home Visitation	Focuses in enhancing parent–child interaction and building solid attachment. Allows provider to observe mother–child in "natural" environment and to tailor services to family's needs. Overcomes "system" barriers to service access	Brain research underscores importance of 0–3 period. Reasonable empirical evidence of efficacy for new parents in terms of parent–child interactions, maternal behavior and child development. May engage higher risk population.	Outcomes are not consistently achieved within or across models. Poor engagement rates. Labor intensive, high-cost service relative to other strategies. Method can be isolating for worker
Parent Education and Therapeutic Strategies	Parents whose psychological and social skills are limited or who are engaged in high-risk behaviors need to overcome these obstacles before assuming parental responsibilities. While some percentage of these families may not respond to any form of intervention, many families can be assisted if services are sufficiently intensive.	In highly specified settings, these interventions have produced significant gains in parental capacity and reduced incidence of child maltreatment. While not always statistically significant, intensive therapeutic and educational services with high-risk families have reduced the time a child spends in foster care.	Despite thoughtful and intensive intervention, many families with an extended history of abusive behaviors eventually lose their children to state systems of care. The high cost of these interventions are difficult to justify given the absence of solid empirical evidence of success.

Using Existing Institutions to House Parent Education Efforts

Normalizing the help seeking process for parents requires, in part, that such efforts build upon those institutional supports with which parents already have contact (Kagan, 1996). Two such systems include local primary and secondary schools and pediatric health services. With respect to the educational system, primary prevention strategies targeting all parents with school-aged children offer the advantage of providing a more universal level of support without the stigma commonly associated with secondary prevention efforts. For example, the Preparing for the Drug Free Years (PDFY) is a universal, family-focused preventive intervention that is designed to enhance parent and adolescent competencies and to reduce adolescent problem behavior. Repeated randomized trials of this program found it produced significant change in the parent's application of substance-related rules and consequences; positive involvement with their child; and anger or conflict management (Spoth et al., 1998).

With respect to pediatric practice, a number of privately funded experiments have been developed to test the feasibility of placing parent educators and child development specialists within medical clinics and practitioner offices. While evaluative data on most of these efforts is limited to process and implementation studies as oppose to participant impacts, early findings suggest promise. The Detroit Family Project, for example, utilizes a system of parent facilitators who rotate among waiting rooms at the city's health clinics where young families gather (e.g., obstetrics/gynecology and pediatrics) as well as WIC (Woman, Infant and Children) food coupon distribution centers. Each facilitator has a small cart containing snacks, handouts and brochures, books and toys for children and a small flipchart. Once in a waiting room, the parent facilitator will offer snacks and initiate an informal discussion among small groups of parents. These discussions will respond to a need raised by one of the participants or center on a simple, predetermined parenting or child development message. In either case, the parent facilitator will leave parents with written material on a topic and suggestions as to where he or she may obtain additional information. Many of those offered this service have indicated that they had not received any information on parenting or child development prior to meeting the parent facilitator (Whitelaw Downs & Walker, 1996).

Another effort to influence pediatric practice is Healthy Steps for Young Children, a multi-site program supported by a large U.S. philanthropic organization (the Commonwealth Fund) and the American Academy of Pediatrics. Developed at Boston University's School of Medicine, the program adds a Healthy Steps Specialist to the traditional pediatric practice team offering parents such additional assistance as enhanced strategies in well-child care, home visiting, new written materials, a telephone information line, parent groups and linkages to community resources (Zuckerman et al., 1997). In addition to providing parents with an opportunity to discuss their concerns directly and to receive specific service referrals, the program provides parents with tools to monitor their child's growth and development including: semi-annual child development assessments; various informational handouts; and a detailed child health and development record.

These procedures, integrated into standard pediatric practice, encourage parents to seek out assistance and use medical and social service personnel as resources in improving their parental capacity. While some percentage of families will need additional assistance in effectively utilizing the resources being suggested, the method underscores a universal need parents have for more current and consistent information regarding their child's development and how best to respond to these evolving needs. A comprehensive, 15-site evaluation of the initiative is under way, with results available in late 2002.

Group-Based Interventions

It has been estimated that more than 100 000 groups of parents voluntarily meet every year in the United States in an attempt to learn more about how to better care for their children (Carter, 1995). In addition to its educational function, this service delivery strategy provides parents the opportunity to share experiences, concerns and solutions. "The universal parental search for normalcy and support—something most readily available from other parents—can often find its fullest expression through this process." (Carter & Harvey, 1996:3). Parents remain committed and engaged in this intervention because they have now formed a connection or friendship to a specific group of parents not simply a sense of loyalty to an individual provider. When these connections are established, parent groups begin building the type of reciprocity and mutual support viewed by many as essential to achieving a higher standard of care for children (Melton & Berry, 1994).

While solid empirical evidence supporting the method's efficacy with families facing significant difficulties is limited (Chalk & King, 1998), the strategy has effectively enhanced parental capacity among those able to seek out and sustain engagement in these efforts (Baker et al., 1999; Daro, 1988; 1993; Carter & Harvey, 1996; Wolfe, 1994). These gains include more appropriate expectations for their children; increased awareness of their child's needs; and reduced support for corporal punishment. In addition, the vast majority of young mothers enrolled in these programs complete or continue their education, seek and remain in full-time employment, and delay subsequent pregnancies (Treichel, 1996).

Repeated process and outcome evaluations of these strategies have suggested some aspects of program delivery appear more related to program outcomes. For example, an assessment of MELD (formerly the Minnesota Early Learning Design) found the following service features central to achieving positive outcomes: group facilitation by parents who have experienced life situations similar to those of group members; long-term service availability (e.g., two or more years); persistent focus on parent strengths; emphasis on solid decision-making rather than quick fixes; and a commitment to ongoing staff training and supervision (Ellwood, 1988; Hoelting et al., 1996).

Home Visitation Programs

The delivery of health and social services through home-based interventions has a long and rich history in many countries and contexts (Guterman, 2001; Kamerman & Kahn, 1993; Wasik & Bryant, 2001). Offering services in a parent's home has a number of distinct advantages, particularly for those families unable to effectively seek out services on their own or who are reluctant to engage in group-based interventions. Home visits offer the provider an excellent opportunity to assess the safety of the child's living environment and to work with the mother in a very concrete way to improve parent–child interactions. The method also affords the participant a degree of privacy and the practitioner an increased flexibility.

Over the past decade, this intervention strategy has become the focal point of child abuse prevention efforts. Encouraged by a growing body of theoretical and clinical evidence underscoring the importance of a child's first few years of life, dozens of national models and scores of state sponsored initiatives have blossomed across the United States. Considering only the six most common of these models, it is estimated that as many as 550 000 children are reached annually by home visitation programs for pregnant women and families with young children (Gomby et al., 1999).

Unlike other parent education efforts, this strategy has produced significant and substantial improvements among parents that have many of the demographic and environmental markers that place them at high risk for abuse (Daro, 1993; Gutterman, 1997; Infant Health and Development Program, 1990; Karoly et al.,1998; Ramey & Ramey, 1998; Seitz et al., 1985). Indeed, home visitation has been cited by several policy analysts and advocates as offering a particularly promising service delivery approach for educating parents and reducing abuse potential (GAO, 1990; U.S. Advisory Board, 1990; 1991; 1995; Zero to Three, 1999).

David Olds, Harriet Kitzman and their colleagues have documented the strongest empirical evidence for this method. Repeated evaluations of their model find that intensive nurse home visits initiated during pregnancy and continuing for two years reduces abuse potential, improves maternal health behavior and enhances child development (Kitzman et al., 1997; Olds et al., 1986; Olds, et al., 1997; Olds et al. Chapter 10). Other home visitation research with new parents also has found that this strategy when delivered in an intensive manner with an attention to quality can produce positive outcomes for at least a subgroup of program participants (Daro & Harding, 1999; Gray et al., 1979; Heinicke et al., 1998; Lutzker & Rice, 1987; Larson 1980; and Larner 1992). In contrast, more recent reviews of this evidence and additional evaluative work on home visitation models suggest a more mixed performance picture (Gomby et al., 1999; Guterman 2001; Leventhal, 2001). Despite these concerns, sustained and intensive home visitation services remain the most important and promising vehicle for altering parental capacity among parents facing the greatest difficulties.

Combining Education and Therapy

As discussed above, parents who have a number of psychosocial problems and an established history of abusive and neglectful behavior may well require a level of service intensity far beyond what is commonly found within the context of largely voluntary parent education and support services. While families can be court ordered into these "voluntary" programs, there is little evidence that such action produces meaningful change in parental attitudes or behaviors. In addition, the inclusion of mandatory families in these programs may alter the service delivery dynamics and make it difficult to sustain a prevention program's "strength-based" philosophy.

In working with the most dysfunctional families, one successful approach has been to combine parenting instruction with a therapeutic approach (Gambrill, 1983). These types of group-based programs have proven a useful addition to more individualized interventions generally offered families being served through the mental health and child protective service systems (Hogue & Liddle, 1999). In these cases, an individual provider or therapist may attend group meetings with the parent, accompany the parent on service referrals and serve as an interpreter of the information the parent receives in the group-based program. This dual strategy allows these parents to benefit from the mutual support inherent in a group setting while still retaining access to more individualized methods focusing on the parent's complex psychosocial and emotional needs.

Testing this notion, Wolfe et al. (1988) achieved notable success by combining group-based family support services with individual training in child management for families referred by local child protective service agencies. Three months following the intervention, mothers who received individual parent training in addition to group services for an average of 20 weeks reported fewer and less intense child behavior problems and indicated fewer adjustment problems associated with the risk of maltreatment than did the controls who attended only the group services for an average of 18 weeks. This pattern was supported by caseworker ratings at one-year follow-up, which showed greater improvement and a lowered risk of maltreatment among clients who received both interventions.

EDUCATING PARENTS THROUGH COMMUNITY CHANGE

The varied success of parent education efforts with all populations has led many to broaden their service focus to include the communities in which parents live. Commenting on the positive results from targeted early intervention programs noted by Olds and his colleagues, Felton Earls emphasized this point by speculating on "how much stronger the effects of this early intervention would have been if the program had continued beyond the child's second year of life or if efforts had been made to engage the wider social settings in which the families lived." (Earls, 1998, p. 1272).

Over the past ten years, a growing body of work has developed which attempts to measure and better articulate the mechanisms by which neighborhoods influence child development and support parents. In summarizing this work, the Working Group on Communities, Neighborhoods, Family Process and Individual Development (Brooks-Gunn et al., 1997) concluded that neighborhood mattered both directly (e.g., schools, parks, other primary supports) and indirectly in shaping parental attitudes and behaviors and in affecting a parent's self-esteem and motivational processes.

Neighborhood context also has long been viewed as an important mediating variable in explaining differential levels of maltreatment among neighborhoods that share a common socioeconomic profile. A study of contrasting neighborhoods in Omaha, Nebraska by Garbarino & Sherman (1980) found that the communities with the same predicted but different observed rate of child maltreatment reports differed dramatically in terms of its human ecology. Specifically, the community with a higher rate of reported maltreatment was less socially integrated, had less positive neighboring, and represented more stressful day-to-day interactions. More recently, researchers have begun examining the mechanisms through which neighborhoods might explicitly support parents and children. One particularly promising research strategy has been the concept of social capital (Coleman, 1988). Coulton et al. (1995) have implemented a series of studies examining the role of neighborhood in shaping parental practices and influencing child outcomes. Using census and administrative agency data for 177 urban census tracts in Cleveland, variation in rates of officially reported child maltreatment was found to be related to structural determinants of community social organization: economic and family resources; residential instability; household and age structure; and geographic proximity of neighborhoods to concentrated poverty. Children who live in neighborhoods that are characterized by poverty, excessive number of children per adult resident, population turnover and the concentration of female-headed families are at highest risk of maltreatment.

As might be expected, residents of neighborhoods with high rates of child maltreatment reports and other adverse outcomes perceived their neighborhoods as settings in which they and their neighbors were the least able to intervene in or control the behavior of neighborhood children. In justifying their lack of action, residents in the high maltreatment communities were more likely to express concerns that the child or adolescent being corrected would verbally or physically retaliate. In contrast, residents in low maltreatment communities were more likely to monitor the behavior of local children because they saw such action as part of their responsibility to "protect" children from violent or dangerous neighborhood conditions (traffic, broken glass, etc.) (Korbin & Coulton, 1997).

In examining the impacts of neighborhood on levels of violence, Sampson et al. (1997) found lower crime rates in those neighborhoods in which residents were able to achieve a level of shared values and demonstrate a willingness to intervene on behalf of the collective good. Using the term "social cohesion", the authors hypothesized that social and organizational characteristics of neighborhoods explained variations in crime rates that were not solely attributable to the aggregated demographic characteristics of individuals. The sample included personal interviews with some 8782 Chicago residents living in one of 343 distinct "neighborhood clusters" which differed in terms of race and socio-economic status. Interviews were used to construct a measure of "informal social control" (i.e., the degree to which residents expressed a likelihood that their neighbors could be counted upon to help in various ways such as correcting adolescent behavior, advocating for necessary services or intervening in fights) and "social cohesion" (i.e., neighbors could be counted upon to help each other or could be trusted). Together, three dimensions of neighborhood stratification—concentrated disadvantage, immigration concentration and residential stability—explained 70% of the neighborhood variation in collective efficacy. Collective efficacy in turn mediates a substantial portion of the association of residential stability and disadvantage with multiple measures of violence. In other words, while large structural issues play a critical role in establishing the social milieu in neighborhoods, neighborhoods that are able to establish a sense of community and mutual reciprocity develop a unique and potentially powerful tool to reduce violence and support parents.

MOVING FORWARD: NEW FRAMEWORK, MAJOR CHALLENGES

Caring for one's child is a deeply personal experience. How individuals rear their children is a function of how they were raised as a child, their knowledge of child development, and their capacity to put the needs of another above their own needs. It is a process shaped by the attitudes and support within a parent's family, culture and community. If parent education and support programs hope to influence these mechanisms, they must utilize multiple strategies and be implemented with a keen attention to quality. They also must reflect a common sense of purpose and shared commitment to providing opportunities for all parents at a level of service intensity and style commensurate with their contextual, knowledge and skill building needs.

Limitations in the existing efforts to educate and support parents call for new thinking in how such efforts are crafted and presented to potential participants. Three key principles are important. First, such efforts need to offer community planners flexible, empirically based criteria for "building" their own prevention programs. Simply adopting predetermined, monolithic intervention strategies has not produced a steady expansion of high quality, effective interventions (Brookings Institute, 1998; Schorr, 1997). Replication efforts need to include a specific planning phase in which local stakeholders (e.g., potential participants, local service providers, funders, the general public, etc.) assess the scope of maltreatment in their community, identify local human and social service resources, and craft a service delivery system in keeping with local realities.

Second, intensive efforts for those families facing the greatest challenges need to be nested within a more broadly defined network of support services. Successfully engaging and retaining those parents facing the greatest challenges will not result from more stringent efforts to identify and serve only these parents. Until systems are established which normalize the parent support process by assessing and meeting the needs of all new parents, prevention efforts will continue to struggle with issues of stigmatization and deficit-directed imagery.

Finally, prevention programs need to focus not merely on changing individual behaviors but also on using these services as a springboard for systemic reforms in health and social service institutions. Establishing a series of solid, well-implemented direct service programs is one level of change. Integrating these efforts into a coherent system of support that can be used to leverage broader, institutional change is a more challenging and less obvious process. While many private and public agencies have engaged in efforts to alter the way major institutions interface with families, few consistent success stories exist (Kagan, 1996; Schorr, 1997; St. Pierre et al., 1997). Developing and sustaining such systemic success stories is essential. At present, the vast majority of public and social investment in addressing the problem of child abuse is focused on tertiary care. In the absence of any dramatic shift in mission, agency directors and line staff have no incentive to retool their operations or to alter their funding streams to accommodate the alternative service delivery methods and values represented by prevention advocates. Prevention efforts will remain marginalized and, ultimately, ineffective until this imbalance is corrected.

REFERENCES

Baker, A., Piotrkowski, C. & Brooks-Gunn, J. (1999). "The Home Instruction Program for Preschool Youngsters (HIPPY)." *The Future of Children.* **9**:1 (Spring/Summer), pp. 116–133.

Bandura, A. (1986). *Social Foundations of Thought and Action: A Social Cognitive Theory.* Englewood Cliffs, NJ: Prentice-Hall.

Baumrind, D. (1991). "Effective parenting during the early adolescent transition." In Cowan, P.A. & Heatherington, E.M. (Eds.). *Family Transitions.* Hillsdale, NJ: Erlbaum, pp. 111–164.

Belsky, J. & Vondra, J. (1989). "Lessons for child abuse: The determinants of parenting." In Cicchetti, D. and Carlson, V. (Eds.). *Child Maltreatment: Theory and Research on the Causes and Consequences of Child Abuse and Neglect.* Cambridge: Cambridge University Press, pp. 153–202.

Berlin, L., O'Neal, C. & Brooks-Gunn, J. (1998). "What makes early intervention programs work? The program, its participants and their interaction." *Zero to Three.* **18**:4 (February/March), pp. 4–15.

Brookings Institute. (1998). *Learning What Works: Evaluating Complex Social Interventions. Report on the Symposium held October 22, 1997.* Prepared by the Brookings Institute and Harvard University, Project on Effective Interventions. Washington DC: The Brookings Institute.

Brooks-Gunn, J., Ducan, G. & Aber, J.L. (1997). *Neighborhood Poverty. Volume II: Policy Implications in Studying Neighborhoods.* New York: Russell Sage Foundation.

Carter, N. (1995). *Parenting Education in the United States: An Investigative Report.* Philadelphia: Lew Charitable Trusts.

Carter, N. & Harvey, C. (1996). "Gaining perspective on parenting groups." *Zero To Three.* **16**:6 (June-July), pp.1, 3–8.

Chalk, R. & King, P. (Eds.). (1998). *Violence in Families: Assessing Prevention and Treatment Programs.* Washington, DC: National Academy Press.

Cohn, A. (1983). *An Approach to Preventing Child Abuse: Second Edition.* Chicago, IL: National Committee to Prevent Child Abuse.

Coleman, J. (1988). "Social capital in the creation of human capital." *American Journal of Sociology.* **94**(Supplement), pp. S95–S120.

Coulton, C., Korbin, J., Su, M. & Chow, J. (1995). "Community level factors and child maltreatment rates." *Child Development,* **66**, pp. 1262–1276.

Cowan, C. & Cowan, P. (1992). *When Partners Become Parents: The Big Life Change for Couples.* New York: Basic Books.

Daro, D. (1988). *Confronting Child Abuse.* New York: The Free Press.

Daro, D. (1993). "Child maltreatment research: Implications for program design." In Cicchetti, D. and Toth, S. (Eds.). *Child Abuse, Child Development, and Social Policy.* Norwood, NJ: Ablex Publishing Corporation, pp. 331–367.

Daro, D. (2000). "Child abuse prevention: New directions and challenges." In Hansen, D. (Ed.). *Motivation and Child Maltreatment Vol. 46 of the Nebraska Symposium on Motivation.* Lincoln, NB: University of Nebraska, pp. 161–220.

Daro, D. & Harding, K. (1999). "Healthy Families America: Using research in going to scale." *The Future of Children.* **9**:1 (Spring/Summer), pp. 152–176.

Dunst, C. (1995). *Key Characteristics and Features of Community-Based Family Support Program.* Chicago, IL: The Family Resource Coalition.

Earls, F. (1998). "Positive effects of prenatal and early childhood interventions." *Journal of the American Medical Association.* **280**:14 (October 14), pp. 1271–1273.

Ellwood, A. (1988). "Prove to me that MELD makes a difference." In Weiss, H. & Jacobs, F. (Eds.). *Evaluating Family Programs*. New York: Aldine, pp. 303–314.

Fulbright-Anderson, K., Kubisch, A. & Connell, J. (Eds.). (1998). *New Approaches to Evaluating Community Initiatives: Volume 2, Theory, Measurement and Analysis*. Queenstown, MD: The Aspen Insitute.

Gambrill, E. (1983). "Behavioral interventions with child abuse and neglect." *Progress in Behavior Modification*. **15**, pp. 1–56.

Garbarino, J. (1989). "Troubled youth, troubled families: The dynamics of adolescent maltreatment." In Cicchetti, D. & Carlson, V. (Eds.). *Child Maltreatment: Theory and Research on the Causes and Consequences of Child Abuse and Neglect*. New York: Cambridge University Press, pp. 685–706.

Garbarino, J. & Sherman, D. (1980). High-risk neighborhoods and high-risk families: The human ecology of child maltreatment. *Child Development*, **51**, pp. 188–198.

Gomby, D., Culross, P. & Behrman, R. (1999). "Home visiting: Recent program evaluations— analysis and recommendations." *The Future of Children*. **9**:1 (Spring/Summer), pp. 4–26.

Government Accounting Office (GAO). (1990). *Home Visiting: A Promising Early Intervention Strategy for At-Risk Families*. GAO/HRD-90–83. Washington, DC: Author.

Gray, E. & DiLeonardi, J. (1982). *Evaluating Child Abuse Prevention Programs*. Chicago, IL: National Committee to Prevent Child Abuse.

Gray, J.D., Cutler, C.A., Dean, J.G. & Kempe, C.H. (1979). Prediction and prevention of child abuse and neglect. *Journal of Social Issues*, **35**(2), pp. 127–139.

Guterman, N. (2001). *Stopping Child Maltreatment Before It Starts: Emerging Horizons in Early Home Visitation Services*. Thousand Oaks, CA: Sage.

Guterman, N. (1997). "Early prevention of physical abuse and neglect: Existing evidence and future directions." *Child Maltreatment*. **2**(1), pp. 12–34.

Heinicke, C., Goorsky, M., Moscov, M., Dudley, K., Gordon, J. & Gurthrie, D. (1998). "Partner support as a mediator of intervention outcome." *American Journal of Orthopsychiatry*. **68**:4 (October), pp. 534–541.

Helfer, R. (1982). "A review of the literature on preventing child abuse and neglect." *Child Abuse and Neglect*. **6**, pp. 251–261.

Hoelting, J., Sandell, E., Letourneau, S., Smerlinder, J. & Stranik, M. (1996). "The MELD experience with parent groups." *Zero To Three*. **16**:6 (June-July), pp. 9–18.

Hogue, A. & Liddle, H. (1999). "Family-based preventive intervention: An approach to preventing substance use and antisocial behavior." *American Journal of Orthopsychiatry*. **69**:3 (July), pp. 278–293.

Infant Health and Development Program. (1990). Enhancing outcomes of low-birth weight preterm infants. *Journal of the American Medical Association*. **263** (22), pp. 3035–3042.

Jones, D. (1997). "Treatment of the child and the family where child abuse or neglect has occurred." In Helfer, M.E., Kempe, R. & Krugman, R. (Eds.). *The Battered Child: Fifth Edition*. Chicago, IL: University of Chicago Press, pp. 521–542.

Kagan, J. (1998). *Three Seductive Ideas*. Cambridge, MA.: Harvard University Press.

Kagan, S.L. (1996). "America's family support movement: A moment of change." In Zigler, E., Kagan, S. and Hall, N. (Eds.). *Children, Families & Government: Preparing for Twenty-first Century*. Cambridge: Cambridge University Press, pp. 156–170.

Kamerman, S. & Kahn, A. (1993). "Home health visiting in Europe." *The Future of Children*. **3**:3 (Winter), pp. 39–52.

Karoly, L.A., Greenwood, P.W., Everingham, S.S., Hoube, J., Kilburn, M.R., Rydell, C.P., Sanders, M. & Cheisa, J., (1998). *Investing in Our Children: What we Know and Don't Know About the Costs and Benefits of Early Childhood Interventions*. Santa Monica, CA: Rand.

Kitzman, H., Olds, D., Henderson, C., Hanks, C., Cole, R., Tatelbaum, R., McConnochie, K., Sidora, K., Luckey, D., Shaver, D., Engelhart, K., James, L. & Barnard, K. (1997). "Effects of prenatal and infancy home visitations by nurses on pregnancy outcomes, childhood injuries and repeated childbearing." *Journal of the American Medical Association*, **278** (22), pp. 644–652.

Kolko, D. (1996). "Child physical abuse." In Briere, J., Berliner, L., Bulkley, J., Jenny, C. & Reid, T. (Eds.). *The APSAC Handbook on Child Maltreatment*. Thousand Oaks, CA: Sage Publications, pp. 21–50.

Korbin, J. & Coulton, C. (1997). "Understanding the neighborhood context for children and families: Combining epidemiological and ethnographic approaches." In Brooks-Gunn, J., Ducan, G. & Aber, J.L. (Eds.). *Neighborhood Poverty. Volume II: Policy Implications in Studying Neighborhoods*. New York: Russell Sage Foundation, pp. 65–79.

Larner, M. (1992). "Realistic expectations: Review of evaluation findings." In Larner, M., Halpern, R. & Harkavy, O. (Eds.). *Fair Start for Children: Lessons Learned from Seven Demonstration Projects*. New Haven: Yale University Press, pp. 218–245.

Larson, C. (1980). "Efficacy of prenatal and postpartum home visits on child health and development". *Pediatrics*. **66** (2), pp. 191–197.

Leventhal, J. (2001). "The prevention of child abuse and neglect: Successfully out of the blocks". *Child Abuse and Neglect*. **25**, pp. 431–440.

Lutzker, J. & Rice, J. (1987). "Using recidivism data to evaluate Project 12-ways: An ecobehavioral approach to the treatment and prevention of child abuse and neglect." *Journal of Family Violence*. **2** (4), pp. 283–290.

Melton, G. & Berry, F. (1994). *Protecting Children From Abuse and Neglect: Foundations for a New National Strategy*. New York: Guilford Press.

Olden, C. (1953). "On adults' empathy with children." *Psychoanalytic Study of the Child*. **8**, pp. 111–126.

Olden, C. (1958). "Notes on the development of empathy." *Psychoanalytic Study of the Child*. **13**, pp. 505–518.

Olds, D., Eckenrode, J., Henderson, C.R. Jr. et al. (1997). "Long-term effects of home visitation on maternal life course, child abuse and neglect and children's arrests: Fifteen-year follow-up of a randomized trial." *Journal of the American Medical Association*. **278**:8, pp. 637–643.

Olds, D., Henderson, C., Chamberlin, R. & Tatelbaum, R. (1986). "Preventing child abuse and neglect: A randomized trial of nurse home visitation." *Pediatrics*. **78**:1, pp. 65–78.

Olds, D., Henderson, C., Kitzman, H., Eckenrode, J., Cole, R. & Tatelbaum, R. (1999). "Prenatal and infancy home visitation by nurses: Recent findings." *The Future of Children*. **9**:1 (Spring/Summer), pp. 44–65.

Polansky, N. (1981). *Damaged Parents*. Chicago: University of Chicago Press.

Ramey, C. & Ramey, S. (1998). "Early intervention and early experience." *American Psychologist* **53**(2), pp. 109–120.

Rutter, M. (1989). "Intergenerational continuities and discontinuities in serious parental difficulties." In Cicchetti, D. & Carlson, V. (Eds.). *Child Maltreatment: Theory and Research on the Causes and Consequences of Child Abuse and Neglect*. Cambridge: Cambridge University Press, pp. 317–348.

St. Pierre, R., Layzer, J., Goodson, B. & Bernstein, L. (1997). *National Impact Evaluation of the Comprehensive Child Development Program: Final Report*. Cambridge, MA: Abt Associates Inc.

Sampson, R., Raudenbush, S. & Earls, F. (1997). "Neighborhoods and violent crime: A multilevel study of collective efficacy." *Science*. **277** (August 15), pp. 918–924.

Schorr, L. (1997). *Common Purpose: Strengthening Families and Neighborhoods to Rebuild America*. New York: Anchor Books.

Seitz, V., Rosenbaum, L.K. & Apfel, N.H. (1985). "Effects of family support intervention: A ten-year follow-up." *Child Development*. **56**, pp. 376–391.

Slaughter-DeFoe, D. (1993). "Home visiting with families in poverty: Introducing the concept of culture." *The Future of Children*. **3** (3), pp. 172–183.

Specht, H. & Courtney, M. (1994). *Unfaithful Angels: New Social Work Has Abandoned Its Mission*. New York, NY: The Free Press.

Spoth, R., Redmond, C., Shin, C., Lepper, H., Haggerty, K. & Wall, M. (1998). "Risk moderation of parent and child outcomes in a preventive intervention: A test and replication." *American Journal of Orthopsychiatry*. **68**:4 (October), pp. 565–579.

Steele, B. (1997). "Psychodynamic and biological factors in child maltreatment". In Helfer, M.E., Kempe, R. & Krugman, R. (Eds.). *The Battered Child: Fifth Edition*. Chicago, IL: University of Chicago Press, pp. 73–103.

Thompson, R. (1995). *Preventing Child Maltreatment through Social Support: A Critical Analysis*. Thousand Oaks, CA: Sage.

Treichel, D. (1996). *A National Study of Demographics and Program Outcomes: The MELD for Young Moms Program*. Minneapolis, MN: MELD.

US Department of Health and Human Services, US Advisory Board on Child Abuse and Neglect. (1990). *Child Abuse and Neglect: Critical First Steps in Response to a National Emergency*. Washington, DC: US Government Printing Office, August.

US Department of Health and Human Services, US Advisory Board on Child Abuse and Neglect. (1991). *Creating Caring Communities: Blueprint For An Effective Federal Policy for Child Abuse and Neglect*. Washington, DC: US Government Printing Office.

US Department of Health and Human Services, US Advisory Board on Child Abuse and Neglect. (1995). *The Continuing Child Protection Emergency: A Challenge to the Nation*. Washington, DC: US Government Printing Office.

Wasik, B. & Bryant, D. (2001). *Home Visiting: Second Edition*. Thousand Oaks, CA: Sage Publications.

Webster-Stratton, C. (1990). "Stress: A potential disrupter of parent perceptions and family interactions." *Journal of Clinical Child Psychology*. **19**, pp. 302–312.

Weiss, C. (1995). "Nothing as practical as good theory: Exploring theory-based evaluation for comprehensive community initiatives for children and families." In Connell, J., Kubisch, A., Schorr, L. & Weiss, C. (Eds.). *New Approaches to Evaluating Community Initiatives: Concepts, Methods and Contexts*. Washington DC: The Aspen Institute, pp. 65–92.

Weiss, H. & Jacobs, F. (Eds.). (1988). *Evaluating Family Programs*. New York: Aldine.

Whitelaw Downs, S. & Walker, D. (1996). "Family support while you wait: Lessons from the Detroit Family Project." *Zero to Three*. **16**:6 (June/July), pp. 25–32.

Wilson, J. (1999). "Thinking about parent and child." *The Public Interest*. **135** (Spring), pp. 18–29.

Wolfe, D. (1991). Preventing Physical and Emotional Abuse of Children. New York: Guilford Press.

Wolfe, D. (1994). "The role of intervention and treatment services in the prevention of child abuse and neglect." In Melton, G. & Berry, F. (Eds.). *Protecting Children from Abuse and Neglect: Foundations for a New National Strategy*. New York: Guilford Press, pp. 224–303.

Wolfe, D., Edwards, B., Manion,I. & Koverola, C. (1988). "Early intervention for parents at risk of child abuse and neglect: A preliminary investigation". *Journal of Consulting and Clinical Psychology*. **56**:1, pp. 40–47.

Zero to Three (1999). *Home Visiting: Reaching Babies and Families Where They Live*. Washington D.C.: Zero to three.

Zuckerman, B., Kaplan-Sanoff, M., Parker, S. & Taaffe Young, K. (1997). "The Healthy Steps for Young Children program." *Zero to Three*. **17**:6 (June-July), pp. 20–25.

9

PROMOTING POSITIVE PARENTING AS AN ABUSE PREVENTION STRATEGY

Matthew Sanders
University of Queensland, Australia
Warren Cann
Victorian Parenting Centre, Australia

The development of interventions that promote positive, caring, and consistent parenting practices has been repeatedly highlighted as central to any serious attempt to reduce the incidence of child maltreatment in the community (Azar, 1997). Traditionally, maltreating parents have not participated in parenting programs available in the community and of those parents who do it is an unfortunate reality that many of these parents are resistant and are at greater risk of dropping out of parenting interventions. The lack of success of traditional parent training programs in engaging parents who are at risk of maltreating their children or families who have been notified to protective services for child maltreatment suggests that special efforts need to be made to engage families who might benefit from such interventions. This chapter argues that the reduction of abuse potential of parents must be tackled within an ecological framework within which a comprehensive multi-level model of parenting and family support is available at a population level. One such model is the Triple P-Positive Parenting Program. The applicability of this model to a child abuse prevention agenda is discussed.

ORIGINS OF DYSFUNCTIONAL PARENTING PRACTICES

Physical maltreatment of children was once conceptualized almost exclusively in terms of parental psychopathology (Wolfe, 1994). More recent theories of abuse

Early Prediction and Prevention of Child Abuse: A Handbook.
Edited by Kevin Browne, Helga Hanks, Peter Stratton and Catherine Hamilton. © 2002 John Wiley & Sons, Ltd.

now recognize the complex interaction of cultural, community, family, parent and child factors in the etiology of child abuse. Community surveys still reliably find that the majority of parents believe in and use physical discipline (Straus & Stewart, 1999). A recent randomized telephone survey of a representative sample of 1218 Australian parents found that 70% of parents had used smacking at least once and 15% had implemented physical punishment with an implement other than their hand (Sanders et al., 1999). Straus and Stewart (1999) reported data on a nationally representative sample of US parents showing a high overall prevalence rate of corporal punishment, with a peak prevalence for parents of three- and four-year old children (94%).

In addition to personal adjustment difficulties, parents who are abusive exhibit deficits in parenting responsiveness, knowledge and skills. They are less empathetic toward their children (Miller & Eisenberg, 1988) and less sympathetic to infant crying (Frodi & Lamb, 1980). Compared to non-abusive controls, abusive parents spend less time interacting and exhibit lower rates of positive behavior toward their children (Moltershom et al., 1992). Lacking a flexible range of effective responses to children's misbehavior, abusive parents make less use of explaining and reasoning (Chilamkurti & Milner, 1993) and are more likely to use harsh, punitive and inconsistent discipline practices (Trickett & Kucznski, 1986).

Distorted cognitive processes that result in negative interpretations of children's behavior also appear to play a direct role in the origin and maintenance of abusive responses to children's behavior. Abusive parents appear to exaggerate the rate of problem behavior in their children (Mash et al., 1983) and judge transgressions more harshly than normal controls (Chilamkurti & Milner, 1993). The causal attributions abusive parents make about their children's behavior are more likely to be negative. High levels of anger and harsh discipline can occur in situations in which children fail to live up to initially unrealistic expectations of maturity and self-regulation (Hawkins & Duncan, 1985). Children's misbehavior is more likely to be seen as deliberate and intended to harm the parent (Azar, 1986) and as a consequence of a stable internal characteristic of the child (Larrance & Twentyman, 1983).

Cognitive factors have also been identified as being associated with non-responsiveness to treatment. Limited parenting skills and harsh discipline practices associated with parental depression, low self esteem, unrealistic expectations of children and blaming the child for the problem behavior have been found to be associated with poor response to treatment of high risk families (Ayoub et al., 1992).

Interactional models of the aetiology of abuse have emphasised the bidirectional nature of social, parental and child factors (e.g., Belsky & Stratton, Chapter 6; Sameroff & Chandler, 1975). In addition to the parenting variables described above, various child related factors appear to contribute directly to the risk of abuse and neglect. Prematurity (Browne & Saqi, 1988) and behavioral difficulties (Trickett & Kuczynski, 1986) appear to increase the risk of abuse. Physical abuse has been found to be associated with crying and toileting difficulties (Schmitt, 1997), sleeping and eating difficulties (Herrenkohl & Herrenkohl, 1979), distractibility (Wolfe, 1988), impulsivity (Daro, 1988), non-compliance (Herrenkohl et al., 1983) and aggression (Kudushin & Martin, 1981). Early adversity or difficult to manage childhood behavior may impair attachment and challenge the coping skills of parents who have limited social and personal resources (Ammerman & Patz, 1996).

THE IMPORTANCE OF A PREVENTION APPROACH
TO CHILD MALTREATMENT

Effective interventions are needed to prevent the short- and long-term consequences of abuse for children, their families and the broader community. The need
for effective prevention is further highlighted by limitations to known treatment
approaches and the difficulties associated with treating the sequelae of abuse in
children. Concerns have been expressed about the long-term effectiveness of treatment programs. Re-abuse rates following treatment ranging from 18.5% to 66%
have been reported in the literature (Ayoub et al., 1992). The difficulties of engaging and maintaining abusive families in treatment have been well documented and
up to one third will maltreat their children whilst undergoing treatment (Cohn &
Daro, 1987). The most seriously at risk parents, those who persistently deny the
problem, refuse help, have severe personality or psychiatric disorders, and have
been involved in severe abuse may in fact be impossible to treat (Jones, 1987 cited
in Oates & Bross, 1995). Disappointed by the outcomes of remedial and treatment
approaches, some authors have concluded that treatment may indeed be too late
(e.g., Cohn & Daro, 1987). Whilst well established negative parent–child interaction
patterns are difficult to change, promoting positive parent–child relationships is a
viable and valid abuse prevention strategy (Wolfe, 1994).

THE ROLE OF PARENTING INTERVENTIONS IN THE
PREVENTION AND TREATMENT OF CHILD MALTREATMENT

Ecological models suggest that effective prevention of child abuse will require a
multi-faceted approach that involves intervention at the community, family, parent and individual child level. Societal interventions are required to reduce family
adversity factors such as poverty, substance abuse and alienation. Parenting interventions are required to reduce the incidence of abuse by promoting positive
parent–child relationships, increasing the confidence and competence of parents
and modifying patterns of behaviour that may be precursors to abuse. It is now
widely recognized that intensive, flexible and multi-component parenting intervention programs are required for the most dysfunctional families in the community
(Ayoub et al., 1992).

Essential Characteristics of Effective Parenting Interventions
for the Prevention of Child Abuse

On the basis of research into risk and protective factors parenting initiatives are
more likely to be successful with maltreating parents when the following principles
are adhered to:

1. Parenting interventions should empower parents. Effective parenting interventions should enhance the competence and confidence of parents, promote self-
   sufficiency and reduce dependency on external sources of support.

2. Parenting interventions should build on existing strengths. Successful interventions recognize and build on existing competencies, and assume that all parents have the potential to be independent problem-solvers.

3. Parenting interventions should address known risk variables for coercive parenting. Parenting interventions must increase the quantity and quality of parent–child interactions and provide effective discipline strategies as an alternative to cycles of escalating coercive behavior. At-risk families may also require education in child development, interventions at the cognitive level to modify negative expectancies and causal attributions, and assistance in managing stress and anger control techniques. Negative lifestyle influences and habits relating to substance abuse, marital discord and a history of relationship violence between parents may need specific attention.

4. Parenting interventions must be accessible. A multi-level system of intervention is required to ensure a flexible range of short- and long-term responses based on the level of family functioning. A public health perspective should be adopted to ensure that all families have access to parenting information and support from the services they use on a regular basis.

5. Parenting interventions should be timed developmentally to optimize impact. Interventions timed prior to interactional patterns becoming ingrained and more difficult to modify are preferred. Parenting interventions can also be timed to coincide with developmental stages in children known to be associated with increased risk. Interventions which target the prenatal period and subsequently provide parenting support through important early developmental stages, such as infancy and toddlerhood, are likely to have the greatest impact (Olds et al., 1997).

6. Parenting interventions should be culturally appropriate. Effective parenting interventions must have the capacity to be sensitive to the cultural background of families. Beliefs about the legitimacy of corporal punishment are stronger is some minority groups (e.g., Straus & Stewart, 1999).

Triple P Positive Parenting Program: A Multi-Level Child Abuse Prevention Strategy?

The Triple P-Positive Parenting Program is a multi-level, preventively oriented parenting and family support strategy developed by the first author and colleagues at The University of Queensland in Brisbane, Australia. The program aims to prevent severe behavioral, emotional and developmental problems in children by enhancing the knowledge, skills and confidence of parents. It incorporates five levels of intervention on a tiered continuum of increasing strength (see Table 9.1) for parents of preadolescent children from birth to age 12:

- Level 1   a universal parent information strategy, provides all interested parents with access to useful information about parenting through a coordinated media and promotional campaign. This level of intervention aims to increase community awareness of parenting resources and receptivity of parents to participating in programs.

- Level 2   a brief, one-to two-session primary health care intervention providing early anticipatory developmental guidance to parents of children with mild behavioral difficulties.
- Level 3   a four-session intervention, targets children with mild to moderate behavioral difficulties and includes active skills training for parents.
- Level 4   an intensive eight- to ten-session individual or group parent training program for children with more severe behavioral difficulties.
- Level 5   an enhanced behavioral family intervention program for families where parenting difficulties are complicated by other sources of family distress (e.g., marital conflict, parental depression or high levels of stress).

The rationale for this tiered multi-level strategy is that there are differing levels of dysfunction and behavioral disturbance in children, and parents have differing needs and desires regarding the type, intensity and mode of assistance they may require. The multi-level strategy is designed to maximize efficiency, contain costs, avoid waste and over-servicing and to ensure the program has wide reach in the community. Also the multi-disciplinary nature of the program involves the better utilization of the existing professional workforce in the task of promoting competent parenting.

The program targets five different developmental periods from infancy to adolescence. Within each developmental period the reach of the intervention can vary from being very broad (targeting an entire population) or quite narrow (targeting only high-risk children). This flexibility enables practitioners to determine the scope of the intervention given their own service priorities and funding (see Figure 9.1).

THEORETICAL BASIS OF TRIPLE P

Triple P is a form of behavioral family intervention based on social learning principles (e.g., Patterson, 1982). This approach to the treatment and prevention of childhood disorders has the strongest empirical support of any intervention with children, particularly those with conduct problems (see Sanders, 1996; Taylor & Biglan, 1998). Triple P aims to enhance family protective factors and to reduce risk factors associated with severe behavioral and emotional problems in preadolescent children. Specifically the program aims to: (1) enhance the knowledge, skills, confidence, self sufficiency and resourcefulness of parents; (2) promote nurturing, safe, engaging, non-violent and low-conflict environments for children; (3) promote children's social, emotional, language, intellectual and behavioral competencies through positive parenting practices.

The program content draws on:

1. social learning models of parent–child interaction that highlight the reciprocal and bidirectional nature of parent–child interactions (e.g., Patterson, 1982).
2. research in child and family behavior therapy and applied behavior analysis which has developed many useful behavior change strategies, particularly research which focuses on rearranging antecedents of problem behavior through designing more positive engaging environments for children (Risley et al., 1976; Sanders, 1996).

TABLE 9.1 The Triple P model of parenting and family support

Level of Intervention	Target Population	Intervention Methods	Program Materials	Possible Target Behaviours
Universal Triple P	All parents interested in information about promoting their child's development.	Anticipatory well child care involving the provision of brief information on how to solve developmental and minor behaviour problems. May involve self-directed resources, brief consultation, group presentations and mass media strategies.	*Positive Parenting* booklet *Positive Parenting* tip sheet series *Families* video series *Every Parent Triple P Program Guide*	Common everyday behaviour difficulties
Selective Triple P	Parents with a specific concern about their child's behaviour or development.	Provision of specific advice for a discrete child problem behaviour. May be self-directed or involve telephone or face-to-face clinician contact or group sessions.	Level 1 materials *Primary Care Triple P Practitioner's Manual* Developmental wall chart	Bedtime routine difficulties Temper tantrums Meal time behaviour problems Toilet training
Primary Care Triple P	Parents with specific concerns about their child's behaviour or development that require active skills training.	Brief therapy program (1 to 4 clinic sessions) combining advice, rehearsal and self-evaluation to teach parents to manage a discrete child problem behaviour.	Consultation flip chart Level 1 and 2 materials	As for Level 2 Persistent eating problems Pain management

Standard Triple P	Parents of children with more severe behaviour problems. Parents wanting intensive training in positive parenting skills.	Intensive program focussing on parent–child interaction and the application of parenting skills to a broad range of target behaviours. Includes generalisation enhancement strategies. May be self-directed or involve telephone or face-to-face clinician contact or group sessions.	Level 1 to 3 materials *Every Parent's Self-Help Workbook* *Standard Triple P Practitioner's Manual and Every Parent's Family Workbook* *Group Triple P Facilitator's Manual and Every Parent's Group Workbook*	General behaviour management concerns Aggressive behaviour Oppositional Defiant Disorder Conduct Disorder Learning difficulties
Enhanced Triple P	Parents of children with concurrent child behaviour problems and family dysfunction	Intensive program with modules including home visits to enhance parenting skills, mood management strategies and stress coping skills, and partner support skills.	Levels 1 to 4 materials *Enhanced Triple P Practitioner's Manual and Every Parent's Supplementary Workbook*	Persistent conduct problems Concurrent child behaviour problems and parent problems (such as relationship conflict, depression). Child maltreatment

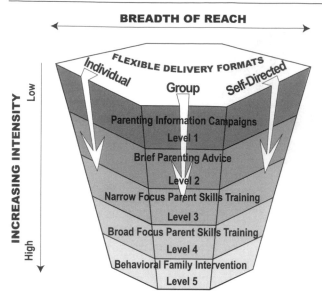

FIGURE 9.1   The Triple P Model of Graded Reach and Intensity of Parenting and Family Support Services

3. developmental research on parenting in everyday contexts. The program targets children's competencies in naturally occurring everyday contexts, drawing heavily on work which traces the origins of social and intellectual competence to early parent–child relationships (e.g., Hart & Risley, 1995).
4. social information processing models which highlight the important role of parental cognitions such as attributions, expectancies and beliefs as factors which contribute to parental self-efficacy, decision making and behavioral intentions (e.g., Bandura, 1995).
5. research from the field of developmental psychopathology which has identified specific risk and protective factors which are linked to adverse developmental outcomes in children (e.g., Hart & Risley, 1995).
6. a public health perspective to family intervention which involves the explicit recognition of the role of the broader ecological context for human development (e.g., Biglan, 1995; Mrazek & Haggerty, 1994). As pointed out by Biglan (1995) the reduction of antisocial behavior in children requires the community context for parenting to change.

TOWARDS A MODEL OF PARENTAL COMPETENCE

The educative approach to promoting parental competence in Triple P views the development of a parent's capacity for self-regulation as a central skill. This involves teaching parents skills that enable them to become independent problem solvers. Karoly (1993) defined self-regulation as follows: "Self-regulation refers to those processes, internal and or transactional, that enable an individual to guide his/her goal directed activities over time and across changing circumstances (contexts). Regulation implies modulation of thought, affect, behavior, and attention via deliberate or automated use of specific mechanisms and supportive metaskills. The processes of self-regulation are initiated when routinized activity is impeded or when goal directedness is otherwise made salient (e.g., The appearance of a challenge, the failure of habitual patterns; etc) . . . " (p. 25). This definition emphasizes that self-regulatory processes are embedded in a social context that not only provides opportunities and limitations for individual self-directedness, but implies a dynamic reciprocal interchange between the internal and external determinants of human motivation. From a therapeutic perspective self-regulation is a process whereby individuals are taught skills to modify their own behavior.

This self-regulatory framework is operationalized to include:

1. Self-sufficiency: Parents need to become independent problem-solvers so they trust their own judgment and become less reliant on others in carrying out basic parenting responsibilities.
2. Parental self-efficacy: This refers to a parent's belief that they can overcome or solve a parenting or child management problem.
3. Self-management: The tools or skills that parents use to become more self-sufficient include self-monitoring, self-determination of performance goals and standards, self-evaluation against some performance criterion and self-selection of change strategies (see Sanders & Dadds, 1993).
4. Personal agency: Here the parent increasingly attributes changes or improvements in their situation to their own or their child's efforts rather than to chance, age, maturational factors or other uncontrollable events (e.g., spouses' bad parenting or genes).

Encouraging parents to become self-sufficient means that parents become more connected to social support networks (partners, extended family, friends, child care supports) and the broader ecological context within which a family lives. It is hypothesized that the more self-sufficient parents become the more likely they are to seek appropriate support when they need it, to advocate for children, become involved in their child's schooling and to protect children from harm (e.g., by managing conflict with partners, and creating a secure, low conflict environment).

PRINCIPLES OF POSITIVE PARENTING

Five core positive parenting principles form the basis of the program. These principles address specific risk and protective factors known to predict positive developmental and mental health outcomes in children. These core principles translate into a range of specific parenting skills, which are outlined in Table 9.2.

Ensuring a safe and engaging environment   Children of all ages need a safe, supervised and protective environment that provides opportunities for them to explore, experiment and play. Triple P draws on the work of Risley and his colleagues who have articulated how the design of living environments can promote engagement and skill development of dependent persons from infancy to the elderly (Risley et al., 1976).

TABLE 9.2 Core parenting skills

Observation skills	Parent–child relationship enhancement skills	Encouraging desirable behaviour	Teaching new skills and behaviours	Managing misbehaviour	Preventing problems in high risk situations	Self-regulation skills	Mood management and coping skills	Partner support and communication skills
Monitoring children's behaviour Monitoring own behaviour	Spending quality time Talking with children Showing affection	Giving descriptive praise Giving non-verbal attention Providing engaging activities	Setting developmentally appropriate goals Setting a good example Using incidental teaching Using Ask, Say, Do Using behaviour charts	Establishing ground rules Using directed discussion Using planned ignoring Giving clear, calm instructions Using logical consequences Using quiet time Using time-out	Planning and advanced preparation Discussing ground rules for specific situations Selecting engaging activities Providing incentives Providing consequences Holding follow up discussions	Setting practice tasks Self-evaluation of strengths and weaknesses Setting personal goals for change	Catching unhelpful thoughts Relaxation and stress management Developing personal coping statements Challenging unhelpful thoughts Developing coping plans for high risk situations	Improving personal communication habits Giving and receiving constructive feedback Having casual conversations Supporting each other when problem behaviour occurs Problem solving Improving relationship happiness

Creating a positive learning environment This involves educating parents in their role as their child's first teacher. The program specifically targets how parents can respond positively and constructively to child-initiated interactions (e.g., requests for help, information, advice, attention) through incidental teaching to assist children learn to solve problems for themselves.

Using assertive discipline Behavior change procedures and specific child management strategies that are alternatives to coercive and ineffective discipline practices (such as shouting, threatening or using physical punishment) are taught to parents. Parents learn to use these skills both in the home and community settings to promote the generalization of parenting skills to diverse parenting situations (see Sanders & Dadds, 1993 for more detail).

Having realistic expectations This involves exploring with parents their expectations, assumptions and beliefs about the causes of children's behavior and choosing goals that are developmentally appropriate for the child and realistic for the parent.

Taking care of oneself as a parent Parenting is affected by a range of factors that impact on a parent's self esteem and sense of well-being. Triple P encourages parents to view parenting as part of a larger context of personal self-care, resourcefulness and well-being. Parents develop specific coping strategies for managing difficult emotions including depression, anger, anxiety and high levels of parenting stress at high-risk times for stress.

DISTINGUISHING FEATURES OF TRIPLE P

There are several other distinctive features of Triple P as a family intervention.

Principle of program sufficiency This concept refers to the notion that parents differ in the strength of intervention they may require to enable them to independently manage a problem. Triple P aims to provide the minimally sufficient level of support parents require, as indicated in Table 9.1.

Flexible tailoring to identified risk and protective factors The program enables parents to receive parenting support in the most cost-effective way possible. Within this context a number of different programs of varying intensity have been developed (see Table 9.1).

Varied delivery modalities Figure 9.1 shows that levels of Triple P interventions can be delivered in a variety of formats, including individual face to face, group, telephone assisted or self-directed programs or a combination. This flexibility enables parents to participate in ways that suit their individual circumstances and allows participation from families in rural and remote areas who typically have less access to professional services.

Wide potential reach Triple P is designed to be implemented as an entire integrated system at a population level. However, the multi-level nature of the program enables various combinations of the intervention levels and modalities within levels to be used flexibly as either universal, indicated or selective prevention strategies depending on local priorities, staffing and budget constraints.

A multi-disciplinary approach   Many different professional groups provide counsel and advice to parents. Discouraging rigid professional boundaries, Triple P was developed as a professional resource that can be used by a range of helping professionals including community nurses, family doctors, paediatricians, teachers, social workers, psychologists, psychiatrists and police officers.

DIFFERENT LEVELS OF INTERVENTION

LEVEL 1: universal Triple P (media and promotional strategy)

A universal prevention strategy targets an entire population (national, local community, neighbourhood or school) with a program aimed at preventing inadequate or dysfunctional parenting (Mrazek & Haggerty, 1994). Evidence from the public health field shows that media strategies can be effective in increasing community awareness of health issues and has been instrumental in modifying potentially harmful behavior such as cigarette smoking, lack of exercise and poor diet (Biglan, 1995).

Universal Triple P aims to use health promotion and social marketing strategies to: (1) promote the use of positive parenting practices in the community; (2) increase the receptivity of parents towards participating in the program; (3) increase favourable community attitudes towards the program and parenting in general; (4) destigmatize and normalize the process of seeking help for children with behavior problems; (5) increase the visibility and reach of the program; and (6) counter alarmist, sensationalized or parent blaming messages in the media.

To illustrate such an approach, a media campaign on parenting based around a television series ("Families") which was shown on a commercial television network in New Zealand is discussed below. The centrepiece of this media campaign was 13, 30-minute episodes of an infotainment style television series, "Families". This program was shown at prime time (7.30 pm) on a Wednesday evening on the TV 3 commercial television network in October-December, 1995.

The series used an entertaining format to provide practical information and advice to parents on how to tackle a wide variety of common behavioral and developmental problems in children (e.g., sleep problems, tantrums, whining, aggression) and other parenting issues. A five- to seven-minute Triple P segment each week enabled parents to complete a 13-session Triple P program in their own home through the medium of television. A cross-promotional strategy using radio and the print media was also used to prompt parents to watch the show and inform them of how to contact a Triple P infoline for more information about parenting. "Families" fact sheets which were specifically designed parenting tipsheets were also available through writing to a Triple P Centre or calling a Triple P information line, or through a retail chain.

This level of intervention may be particularly useful for parents who have sufficient personal resources (motivation, literacy skills, commitment, time and support) to implement suggested strategies with no additional support other than a parenting tipsheet on the topic. However, a media strategy is unlikely to be effective on its own if the parent has a child with a severe behavioral disorder or where the parent is depressed, maritally distressed or suffering from major psychopathology.

LEVEL 2: selective Triple P

Selective prevention programs refer to strategies that target specific subgroups of the general population that are believed to be at greater risk than others for developing a problem. Level 2 is a selective intervention delivered through primary care services, which are well positioned to provide brief preventively oriented parenting programs without there being the stigma often attached to seeking specialist mental health services. Parents see primary care practitioners as credible sources of information about children, with family doctors being the most likely professional to be consulted (Sanders et al., 1999).

As with all levels of Triple P, a series of parenting tipsheets are used to provide basic information to parents on the prevention and management of common problems in children of all ages. Four videotape programs complement the tipsheets for use in brief primary care consultations. All materials are written in plain English, and checked to ensure the material is understandable at a grade 6 reading level, is gender sensitive, and avoids technical language and colloquial expressions, which might constitute barriers for parents from non-English speaking backgrounds. Information is provided within a brief consultation format (up to 30-minutes), which clarifies the presenting problem, explains the materials and tailors them to the family's needs. Families are invited to return for further help if they have any difficulties.

This level of intervention is designed for the management of discrete child problem behaviors that are not complicated by other major behavior management difficulties or family dysfunction. With Level 2 interventions, the emphasis is on the management of specific child behavior rather than developing a broad range of child management skills. Key indicators for a Level 2 intervention include: (1) The parent is seeking information, hence the motivational context is good; (2) The problem behavior is relatively discrete; (3) The problem behavior is of mild to moderate severity: (4) The problem behavior has a recent onset; (5) The parents and/or child are not suffering from major psychopathology; (6) The family situation is reasonably stable; and (7) The family has successfully completed other levels of intervention and is returned for a booster session.

LEVEL 3: primary care Triple P

This is another selective more intensive prevention strategy targeting parents who have mild and relatively discrete concerns about their child's behavior or development (e.g., toilet training, tantrums, sleep disturbance). Level 3 is a four-session, 20-minute information based strategy that incorporates active skills training and the selective use of parenting tipsheets covering common developmental and behavioral problems of preadolescent children. It also builds in generalization enhancement strategies for teaching parents how to apply knowledge and skills gained to non-targeted behaviors and other siblings (see Table 9.1).

As in Level 2, this level of intervention is appropriate for the management of discrete child problem behaviors that are not complicated by other major behavior management difficulties or family dysfunction. The key difference is that provision of advice and information alone is supported by active skills training for those parents who require it to implement the recommended parenting strategies. Children would not generally meet full diagnostic criteria for a clinical disorder such as oppositional defiant disorder (ODD), conduct disorder or attention deficit hyperactivity disorder (ADHD), but there may be significant subclinical levels of problem behavior.

LEVEL 4: standard Triple P/group Triple P/telephone assisted and self-directed Triple P (intensive parenting skills training)

This indicated preventive intervention targets high-risk individuals who are identified as having detectable problems, but who do not yet meet diagnostic criteria for a behavioral disorder. It should be noted that this level of intervention can target individual children at risk or an entire population to identify individual children at risk. As in Level 3, this level of intervention combines the provision of information with active skills training and support. However, it teaches parents to apply parenting skills to a broad range of target behaviors in both home and community settings with the target child and siblings. There are several different delivery formats available at this level of intervention, as seen in Table 9.1.

Standard Triple P

This 10-session program incorporates sessions on causes of children's behavior problems, strategies for encouraging children's development and strategies for managing misbehavior. Active skills training methods include modeling, rehearsal, feedback and homework tasks. Segments from *Every Parent's Survival Guide* [video] may be used to demonstrate positive parenting skills. Home visits or clinic observation sessions are conducted in which parent's self-select goals to practise, are observed interacting with their child and implementing parenting skills, and subsequently receive feedback from the practitioner.

Group Triple P

Group Triple P is an eight-session program, ideally conducted in groups of 10–12 parents. It employs an active skills training process to help parents acquire new knowledge and skills. The program consists of four two-hour group sessions, which provide opportunities for parents to learn through observation, discussion, practice and feedback. As with Standard Triple P, segments from *Every Parent's Survival Guide* [video] are used to demonstrate positive parenting skills. These skills are then practised in small groups and parents receive constructive feedback about their use of skills in an emotionally supportive context. Following the group sessions, four 15- to 30-minute follow-up telephone sessions provide additional support to parents as they put into practice what they have learned in the group sessions.

Self-directed Triple P

In this self-directed delivery mode, detailed information is provided in a parenting workbook, *Every Parent's Self-Help Workbook* which outlines a 10-week self-help program for parents. Each weekly session contains a series of set readings and suggested homework tasks for parents to complete. This format was originally designed as an information only control group for clinical trials. However, positive reports from families have shown this program to be a powerful intervention in its own right (Markie-Dadds & Sanders, in preparation).

Some parents require and seek more support in managing their children than simply having access to information. Hence, the self-help program may be augmented by weekly 15- to 30-minute telephone consultations. This consultation model aims to provide brief, minimal support to parents as a means of keeping them focused and motivated while they work through the program and assists in tailoring the program to the specific needs of the family. Rather than introducing new strategies, these consultations direct parents to those sections of the written materials, which may be appropriate to their current situation.

Level 4 intervention is indicated if the child has multiple behavior problems in a variety of settings and there are clear deficits in parenting skills (see Table 9.1). If the parent wishes to have individual assistance and can commit to attending a 10-session program the standard Triple P program is appropriate. Group Triple P is appropriate as a universal (available to all parents) or selective (available to targeted groups of parents) prevention parenting support strategy; however, it is particularly useful as an early intervention strategy for parents of children with current behavior problems. Self-Directed Triple P is ideal for families where access to clinical services is poor (e.g., families in rural or remote areas). It is most likely to be successful with families who are motivated to work through the program on their own and where literacy or language difficulties are not present. Possible obstacles to consider include major family adversity and the presence of psychopathology in the parent/s or child. In these cases, a Level 4 intervention may be begun, with careful monitoring of the family's progress. A Level 5 intervention may be required following Level 4, and in some cases Level 5 components may be introduced concurrently.

LEVEL 5: enhanced Triple P (family intervention)

This indicated level of intervention is for families with additional risk factors that have not changed as a result of participation in a lower level of intervention. It extends the focus of intervention to include marital communication, mood management and stress coping skills for parents. Usually at this level of intervention children have quite severe behavior problems that are also complicated by additional family adversity factors.

Following participation in a Level 4 program, families requesting or deemed to be in need of further assistance are invited to participate in this individually tailored program. Three enhanced individual therapy modules may be offered to families individually or in combination: Home Visits, Coping Skills and Partner Support. Within each additional module, the components to be covered with each family are determined on the basis of clinical judgement and needs identified by the family (i.e., certain exercises may be omitted if parents have demonstrated competency in the target area).

At the time of writing several additional Level 5 modules are being developed and trialed. These include specific modules for changing dysfunctional attributions, improving home safety, modifying disturbances in attachment relationships, and strategies to reduce the burden of care of parents of children with disabilities. When complete, these additional modules will comprise a comprehensive range of additional resources for practitioners to allow tailoring to the specific risk factors that require additional intervention.

This level of Triple P is designed as an indicated prevention strategy (see Table 9.1). It is designed for families who are experiencing ongoing child behavior difficulties after completing Level 4 Triple P, or who may have additional family adversity factors such as parental adjustment difficulties and partner support difficulties that do not resolve during Level 4 interventions.

The model of parenting interventions outlined as a Level 5 intervention has recently been extended and modified for use with parents with anger control problems and parents who have been notified to child protection agencies for child maltreatment. This program includes a parenting program, partner support training and coping skills training. In addition, specific modules target parents' cognitive distortions, particularly their attributional biases, and provide anger management training to address hostility directed towards the child. At time of writing this program is being evaluated within a randomized controlled trial, using multiple methods of assessment and informants including direct observational measures of parent–child interaction, and parent report measures.

EVALUATION

The evaluation of Triple P needs to be viewed in the broader context of research into the effects of behavioral family intervention (BFI) and the parenting literature focusing on abusive parents. There have been several recent comprehensive reviews that have documented the efficacy of BFI as an approach to helping children and their families (Sanders, 1996; Taylor & Biglan, 1998). This literature will not be revisited here in detail. There is clear evidence that BFI can benefit children with disruptive behavior problems, particularly children with ODD and their parents (Forehand & Long, 1988). The empirical basis of BFI is strengthened by evidence that the approach can be successfully applied to many other clinical problems and disorders including ADHD, persistent feeding difficulties, pain syndromes, anxiety disorders, autism and developmental disabilities, achievement problems and habit disorders, as well as everyday problems of normal children (see Sanders, 1996; 1999; Taylor & Biglan, 1998 for reviews of this literature). Treatment outcome studies often report large effect sizes (Serketich & Dumas, 1996), with good maintenance of treatment gains (Forehand & Long, 1988). Treatment effects have been shown to generalize to school settings (McNeil et al., 1991) and to various community settings (Sanders & Glynn, 1981). Parents participating in these programs are generally satisfied consumers (Webster-Stratton, 1989).

A recent review of the outcome data concerning the efficacy and effectiveness of Triple P as a multi-level intervention appears in Sanders (1999). Relatively few studies have examined the applicability of the model of parent training to an abusive parenting population. However, several studies have used Planned Activities Training (PAT), a pivotal intervention used in the Triple P model of parent training with abusive parents. These studies have shown promising intervention effects within primarily single case design methodologies (see Lutzker et al., 1998 for a review).

CONCLUSION

The reduction of coercive and harmful parenting practices is an important social issue. To ensure that preventively oriented parenting programs reach families at risk of abusing their children is likely to require special efforts to be made to recruit and engage parents early in a child's development. To achieve this outcome we believe that a tiered multi-level approach that has wide reach in the community is necessary and has the best chance of engaging parents in a destigmatized normative context before serious problems arise. Continuing community tolerance for corporal punishment and coercive methods of managing children's behavior (Straus & Stewart, 1999) needs to be addressed at a population level through the active promotion of positive alternatives for disciplining children.

REFERENCES

Ammerman, R. T., & Patz, R. J. (1996). Determinants of child abuse potential: Contribution of parent and child factors. *Journal of Clinical Child Psychology*, **25**, 300–307.

Ayoub, C. C., Willett, J. B., & Robinson, D. S. (1992). Families at risk of child maltreatment: Entry level characteristics and growth in family functioning during treatment. *Child Abuse and Neglect*, **16**, 495–511.

Azar, S. T. (1986). A framework for understanding child maltreatment: An integration of cognitive behavioral and developmental perspectives. *Canadian Journal of Behavioral Science*, **18**, 340–355.

Azar, S. T. (1997). A cognitive behavioural approach to understanding and treating parents who physically abuse their children. In D. A. Wolfe., R. J. McMahon., & R. DeV. Peters. (Eds). *Child Abuse: New Directions in prevention and treatment across the lifespan*. Thousand Oaks, CA: Sage.

Bandura, A. (1995). *Self-efficacy in changing societies*. New York: Cambridge University Press.

Biglan, A. (1995). Translating what we know about the context of antisocial behaviour into a lower prevalence of such behaviour. *Journal of Applied Behavior Analysis*, **28**, 479–492.

Browne, K., & Saqi, S. (1988). Approaches to screening child abuse and neglect. In K. Browne, C. Davies, and P. Stratton, (Eds), *Early prediction and prevention of child abuse*. Chichester: John Wiley.

Chilamkurti, C., & Milner, J. S. (1993). Perceptions and evaluations of child transgressions and disciplinary techniques in high and low risk mothers and their children. *Child Development*, **64**, 1801–1814.

Cohn, A. H., & Daro, D. (1987). Is treatment too late: What ten years of evaluative research tells us. *Child Abuse and Neglect*, **11**, 433–442.

Daro, D. (1988). *Confronting child abuse: Research for effective program design*. New York: Free Press.

Forehand, R. L., & Long, N. (1988). Outpatient treatment of the acting out child: Procedures, long term follow-up data, and clinical problems. *Advances in Behavior Research and Therapy,* **10**, 129–177.

Frodi, A. M., & Lamb, M. E. (1980). Child abuser's responses to infant smiles and cries. *Child Development,* **51**, 238–241.

Hart, B., & Risley, T. R. (1995). *Meaningful differences in the everyday experience of young American children.* Baltimore: Paul H. Brookes.

Hawkins, W. E., & Duncan, D. F. (1985). Perpetuators and family characteristics related to child abuse and neglect: comparison of substantiated and unsubstantiated reports. *Psychological Reports,* **56**, 407–410.

Herrenkohl, E., & Herrenkohl, R. C. (1979). A comparison of abused children and their non-abused siblings. *Journal of the American Academy of Child Psychology,* **18**, 260–269.

Herrenkohl, R. C., Herrenkohl, E. C., & Egolf, B. P. (1983). Circumstances surrounding the occurrence of child maltreatment. *Journal of Consulting and Clinical Psychology,* **51**, 424–431.

Kadushin, A., & Martin, J. (1981). *Child abuse: An interactional event.* New York: Columbia University.

Karoly, P. (1993). Mechanisms of self-regulation: A systems view. *Annual Review of Psychology,* **44**, 23–52.

Larrance, D. T., & Twentyman, C. T. (1983). Maternal attributions and child abuse. *Journal of Abnormal Psychology,* **92**, 449–457.

Lutzker, J. R., Huynen, K. B., & Bigelow, K. M. (1998). Parent Training. In V. B. Van Hasselt & M. Hersen, (Eds), *Handbook of psychological treatment protocols for children and adolescents. The LEA series in personality and clinical psychology.* (pp. 467–500). Mahwah, NJ: Lawrence Erlbaum.

Markie-Dadds, C., & Sanders, M. R. (2001). Self-directed Triple P (Positive Parenting Program) for mothers with children at-risk of developing conduct problems. Submitted to *Child and Family Behaviour Therapy.*

Mash, E. J., Johnston, C., & Kovitz, K. (1983). A comparison of the mother–child interactions of physically abused and non-abused children during play and task situations. *Journal of Clinical Child Psychology,* **12**, 337–346.

McNeil, C. B., Eyberg, S., Eisenstadt, T. H., Newcomb, K., & Funderbunk, T. (1991). Parent child interaction therapy with behaviour problem children: Generalisation of treatment effects to the school setting. *Journal of Clinical Child Psychology,* **20**, 140–151.

Miller, P. A., & Eisenberg, N. (1988). The relation of empathy to aggressive and externalizing/anti-social behaviour. *Psychological Bulletin,* **103**, 324–344.

Moltershom, W. W., Patchner, M. A., & Milner, J. S. (1992). Family functioning and child abuse potential. *Journal of Consulting and Clinical Psychology,* **48**, 445–454.

Mrazek, P., & Haggerty, R. J. (1994). *Reducing the risks for mental disorders.* Washington: National Academy Press.

Oates, R. K., & Bross, D. C. (1995). What have we learned about treating child physical abuse? A literature review of the last decade. *Child Abuse and Neglect,* **19**, 463–473.

Olds, D. L., Eckenrode, J., Henderson, C. R., Kitzman, H., Powers, J., Cole, R., Sidora, K., Morris, P., Pettitt, P., & Luckey, D. (1997). Long-term effects of home visitation on maternal life course and child abuse and neglect. *Journal of American Medical Association,* **27**, 637–643.

Patterson, G. R. (1982). *Coersive family process.* Eugene, OR: Castalia.

Risley, T. R., Clark, H. B., & Cataldo, M. R. (1976). Behavioral technology for the normal middle class family. In E. J. Mash, L. A. Hamerlynck, & L. C. Handy. (Eds), *Behavior Modification and Families* (pp. 34–60). New York: Brunner/Mazel.

Sameroff, A., & Chandler, M. (1975). Reproductive risk and the continuum of caretaking causality. In F. Horowitz (Ed.), *Review of child development research. (Vol. 4).* Chicago: University of Chicago.

Sanders, M. R. (1996). New direction in behavioral family intervention with children. In T. H. Ollendick & R. J. Prinz (Eds), *Advances in clinical child psychology, Vol. 18,* (pp. 283–330). New York: Plenum.

Sanders, M. R. (1999). The Triple P-Positive Parenting Program: Towards an empirically validated multilevel parenting and family support strategy for the prevention of behavior and emotional problems in children. *Clinical Child and Family Psychology Review*, 2, 71–90.

Sanders, M. R., & Dadds, M. R. (1993). *Behavioral family intervention*. Boston: Allyn & Bacon.

Sanders, M. R., & Glynn, E. L. (1981). Training parents in behavioural self-management: An analysis of generalization and maintenance effects. *Journal of Applied Behavior Analysis*, 14, 223–237.

Sanders, M. R., Tully, L. A., Baade, P. D., Lynch, M. E., Heywood, A. H., Pollard, G. E., & Youlden, D. R. (1999). A survey of parenting practices in Queensland: Implications for mental health promotion. *Health Promotion Journal*, 9, 105–114.

Schmitt, B. D. (1997). Seven deadly sins of childhood: advising parents about difficult developmental phases. *Child Abuse and Neglect*, 11, 421–432.

Serketich, W. J., & Dumas, J. E. (1996). The effectiveness of behavioral parent training to modify antisocial behaviour in children: A meta-analysis. *Behavior Therapy*, 27, 171–186.

Straus, M. A., & Stewart, J. H. (1999). Corporal punishment by American parents: National data on prevalence, chronicity, severity, and duration, in relation to child and family characteristics. *Clinical Child and Family Psychology Review*, 2, 55–70.

Taylor, T. K., & Biglan, A. (1998). Behavioural family interventions for improving child-rearing: A review of the literature for clinicians and policy makers. *Clinical Child and Family Psychology*, 1, 41–60.

Trickett, P. K., & Kuczymski, L. (1986). Children's misbehaviour and parental discipline strategies in abusive and non-abusive families. *Developmental Psychology*, 22, 115–123.

Webster-Stratton, C. (1989). Systematic comparison of consumer satisfaction of three cost effective parent training programs for conduct problem children. *Behavior Therapy*, 20, 103–115.

Wolfe, D. A., (1988). Child abuse and neglect. In E. J. Mash & L. G. Terdal, (Eds). *Behavioral assessment of childhood disorders*. New York: Guilford.

Wolfe, D. A. (1994). The role of intervention and treatment services in the prevention and treatment of child abuse and neglect. In G. B. Melton and F. D. Barry, (Eds). *Protecting children from abuse and neglect*. New York: Guilford.

10

PREVENTING CHILD ABUSE AND NEGLECT WITH PRENATAL AND INFANCY HOME VISITING BY NURSES

David Olds
University of Colorado, USA

Charles Henderson
Cornell University, USA

John Eckenrode
Cornell University, USA

INTRODUCTION

Annually, about 1 million children, or 15 of every 1000 children, are maltreated in the USA (Sedlak & Broadhurst, 1996). Low-income children are particularly vulnerable, as poverty has been linked with increased parental stress and negative parenting behavior (McLoyd, 1990). Home visiting, as a means of delivering services to families with young children has, in recent years, been identified as the most promising method of preventing child maltreatment (US Advisory Board on Child Abuse and Neglect, 1990). Recent reviews of home visiting programs indicate, however, that they are not uniformly effective in improving parent and child functioning (Gomby et al., 1999).

A program of prenatal and infancy home visiting by nurses, nevertheless, has produced consistent evidence that it reduces child abuse and neglect and injuries to children in two randomized controlled trials over the past 24 years (Olds et al., 1986b; Olds et al., 1997; Kitzman et al., 1997). While the program seeks to prevent

Early Prediction and Prevention of Child Abuse: A Handbook.
Edited by Kevin Browne, Helga Hanks, Peter Stratton and Catherine Hamilton. © 2002 John Wiley & Sons, Ltd.

more than child abuse and neglect, much of the attention given this program has resulted from the evidence that it has prevented child maltreatment.

We think it is a mistake, however, to label this service as a child abuse prevention program. One of the reasons that families are willing to participate in this program is that it is presented as a broad-based program of support to parents in which the nurses are able to help women with their concerns about pregnancy, labor, delivery, and the health and care of their newborns. If the program were presented to parents as a child abuse and neglect prevention strategy, many parents would refuse participation because they would identify themselves as potential abusers. Given the intense interest in the prevention of child abuse and neglect, we offer here evidence supporting the effectiveness of this program in reducing child maltreatment, with the caveat that an exclusive identification of this program in this way ultimately will damage its potential to reach those families who need it the most.

Results of a randomized trial conducted in Elmira, New York, in the 1970's and 80's indicated that the program, now known as the Nurse Family Partnership, had the potential to reduce a variety of adverse outcomes for low-income women, their children and families (Olds et al., Chamberlin, 1986a; Olds et al., 1986b; Olds et al., 1988b). In spite of these promising findings in a variety of maternal and child health domains, we were reluctant to offer the Nurse Family Partnership for public investment until three fundamental questions were addressed: First, would the early beneficial effects of the Elmira program endure after the program ended? Second, were the positive findings from the Elmira program generalizable to minorities living in a major urban area? And third, could we develop the program training and protocols and help new communities develop the program well enough to reproduce reliably the essential elements of the program tested in the randomized trials?

This chapter summarizes findings from our program of research that bear upon the prevention of child abuse and neglect and addresses the three questions specified above. We first begin with an outline of the epidemiological and theoretical foundations of the program and its content and methods.

A RESEARCH-BASED AND THEORY-DRIVEN MODEL

The program tested in the two randomized trials described below has been firmly grounded in epidemiology and theories of child development and behavioral change (Olds et al., 1998a).

Research-Based

Research has guided decisions about the families to be served and the content of the program. Each of the studies has examined program impact with women who have had no previous live births, and each has focused recruitment on women who were low income, unmarried, and adolescents. Women with these characteristics were recruited because the problems the program was designed to address (e.g., poor birth outcomes, child abuse and neglect, and diminished economic

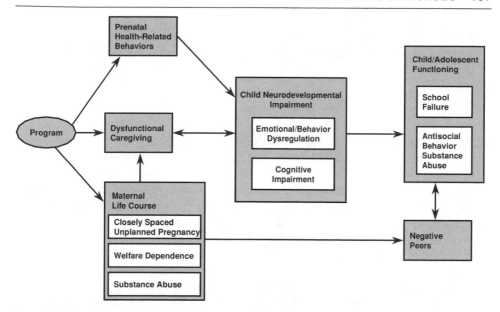

FIGURE 10.1   Conceptual model of program influences on maternal and child health and development

self-sufficiency of parents) are concentrated in those populations (Elster & McAnarney, 1980; Overpeck et al., 1998; Furstenberg et al., 1987). Moreover, we focused on women who had no previous live births because such women were thought to be more receptive to home-visitation services concerning pregnancy and child rearing than were women who had already given birth. In addition, as parents learned parenting and other skills through the program, they would be better able to care for subsequent children, and the program might have an even greater positive effect. Finally, if the program helped parents plan subsequent births, then it would be easier for parents to finish their educations and find work because of fewer problems with child care (Furstenberg et al., 1987), and the children would benefit from more focused parental nurture and guidance (Tygart, 1991).

The content of the program is also research-based. The program seeks to modify those risk factors that are associated with the negative outcomes the program seeks to address: poor birth outcomes, child abuse and neglect, welfare dependence, and poor maternal life course. Figure 10.1 summarizes how these influences are thought to reinforce one another over time.

MODIFIABLE RISKS FOR POOR BIRTH OUTCOMES (LOW BIRTHWEIGHT, PRETERM DELIVERY, AND FETAL IMPAIRMENT)

Prenatal exposure to tobacco, alcohol, and illegal drugs are established risks for poor fetal growth (Kramer, 1987) and, to a lesser extent, preterm birth (Kramer, 1987) and neurodevelopmental impairment (such as attention-deficit disorder, or poor cognitive and language development) (Olds, 1997; Streissguth et al., 1994;

Olds et al., 1994a; Olds et al., 1994b; Milberger et al., 1996; Wakschlag et al., 1997). The nurses therefore sought to reduce mothers' use of these substances, to increase women's use of the primary care system to obtain prompt and reliable treatment of emerging obstetrical conditions, and to reduce stressful family conditions that may interfere with family functioning and that may adversely affect the child's developing nervous system.

MODIFIABLE RISKS FOR CHILD ABUSE AND NEGLECT AND INJURIES TO CHILDREN

Mothers' psychological immaturity and mental health problems can reduce their ability to care for their infants (Newberger & White, 1990). Parents who grew up in households with punitive, rejecting, abusive, or neglectful caregiving are considered at heightened risk (Rutter, 1989; Egeland et al., 1988). In addition, unemployment (Gil, 1970), poor housing and household conditions (Gil, 1970), marital discord (Gil, 1970), and isolation from supportive family members and friends (Garbarino, 1981) are all associated with higher rates of abuse and neglect, perhaps because they create stressful conditions in the household that interfere with parents' ability to care for their children (Bakan, 1971). The program guidelines therefore contain specific strategies to reduce these risks.

MODIFIABLE RISKS FOR WELFARE DEPENDENCE AND COMPROMISED MATERNAL LIFE-COURSE DEVELOPMENT

One of the major risks for compromised maternal educational achievement and workforce participation is rapid, successive pregnancies, particularly among unmarried women (Furstenberg et al., 1987). Such pregnancies often occur when women have limited visions for their futures in the areas of education and work (Musick, 1993), as well as a limited belief in their control over their life circumstances and over their contraceptive practices in particular (Levinson, 1986). The nurses therefore help women envision a future consistent with women's own values and aspirations; they help women evaluate different contraceptive methods, child care options, and career choices; and they help women develop concrete plans for achieving their goals.

MODIFIABLE RISKS FOR EARLY-ONSET ANTISOCIAL BEHAVIOR

Many of the factors listed above are risk factors for early-onset antisocial behavior (Olds et al., 1998b), a type of disruptive behavior that frequently characterizes children who grow up to become violent adolescents and, sometimes, chronic offenders (Moffitt, 1993a; Raine et al., 1994). Children who develop early-onset disorder, for example, are more likely to have subtle neurodevelopmental deficits (sometimes due to poor prenatal health) (Olds, 1997; Streissguth et al., 1994; Milberger et al., 1996; Wakschlag et al., 1997) combined with abusive and rejecting care early in life (Moffitt, 1993; Raine et al., 1994). They are more likely to come from large families, with closely-spaced children (Tygart, 1991) where parents themselves are involved in substance abuse and criminal behavior (Moffitt, 1993a).

Theory-Driven

The program is grounded in theories of human ecology (Bronfenbrenner, 1979), self-efficacy, (Bandura, 1977), and human attachment (Bowlby, 1969). Together, these theories suggest that behavior change is a function of families' social context as well as the individual's beliefs, motivations, and emotions—a view that has implications for program design.

Human ecology theory, for example, emphasizes that children's development is influenced by how their parents care for them, and that, in turn, is influenced by characteristics of their families, social networks, neighborhoods, communities, and the interrelations among them (Bronfenbrenner, 1979). Drawing from this theory, nurses attempt to enhance the material and social environment of the family by involving other family members, including fathers, in the home visits, and by linking families with needed health and human services.

Parents help select and shape the settings in which they find themselves, however (Plomin, 1986). Self-efficacy theory provides a useful framework for understanding how women make decisions about their health-related behaviors during pregnancy, their care of their children, and their own personal development. This theory suggests that individuals choose those behaviors that they believe (1) will lead to a given outcome, and (2) they themselves can successfully carry out (Bandura, 1977). Therefore, the curriculum was designed first to help women understand what is known about the influence of particular behaviors on their own health and on the health and development of their babies. Second, the nurses help parents establish realistic goals and small achievable objectives that, once accomplished, increase parents' reservoir of successful experiences. These successes, in turn, increase women's confidence in taking on larger challenges.

Finally, the program is based on attachment theory, which posits that infants are biologically predisposed to seek proximity to specific caregivers in times of stress, illness, or fatigue in order to promote survival (Bowlby, 1969). Attachment theory also hypothesizes that children's trust in the world and their later capacity for empathy and responsiveness to their own children once they become parents is influenced by the degree to which they formed an attachment with a caring, responsive, and sensitive adult when they were growing up (Main et al., 1985). The program therefore explicitly promotes sensitive, responsive, and engaged caregiving in the early years of the child's life (Barnard, 1990; Dolezol & Butterfield, 1994). In addition, home visitors try to help mothers and other caregivers review their own childrearing histories and make decisions about how they wish to care for their children in light of the way they were cared for as children. Finally, the visitors seek to develop an empathic and trusting relationship with the mother and other family members because experience in such a relationship is expected to help women eventually trust others and to promote more sensitive, empathic care of their children.

Nurses as Home Visitors

Nurses were selected to be the home visitors because of their formal training in women's and children's health and their competence in managing the complex clinical situations often presented by at-risk families. Nurses' abilities to competently address mothers' and family members' concerns about the complications of pregnancy, labor, and delivery, and the physical health of the infant are thought to provide nurses with increased credibility and persuasive power in the eyes of family members. Moreover, through their ability to teach mothers and family members to identify emerging health problems and to use the health-care system, nurses enhance their clinical effect through the early detection and treatment of disorders.

OVERVIEW OF RESEARCH DESIGNS, METHODS, AND FINDINGS

The Elmira study was conducted in a small, semi-rural county of approximately 100 000 residents in the Appalachian region of New York State. Five hundred primarily low-income women were invited to participate and 400 enrolled, 85% of whom were either low-income, unmarried, or younger than 19 years of age at registration; none had a previous live birth. Eighty-nine percent of the sample was white (Olds et al., 1986a). The Memphis trial was designed to determine if the encouraging results of the Elmira program could be replicated when the program was conducted through an existing health department and when it served low-income African-American women, children, and their families living in a major urban area (Kitzman et al., 1997). In the Memphis trial, 98% of the women were unmarried, 85% were below the US federal poverty guidelines, and 89% were African-American.

In both studies there were no sociodemographic differences between those who enrolled and those who declined, although participation was higher among African-Americans than whites. The samples were stratified on the basis of maternal race, marital status, and geographic region of residence and then randomly assigned to nurse-visited and comparison groups. High rates of sample retention increase our confidence in the findings reported below.

We looked for consistency in program effect across different sources of data and the two trials before assigning much importance to any one finding. Findings that are corroborated by data from different sources and that apply to different populations have increased validity.

Elmira Results

DYSFUNCTIONAL CAREGIVING

Overall, nurse-visited children were seen in the emergency department 27% fewer times during the first year of life (0.74 versus 1.02 visits, $p = 0.04$), a difference that was greater for children born to poor, unmarried teens (0.95 versus 1.66 visits, $p = 0.04$). A review of the medical records revealed that these differences were

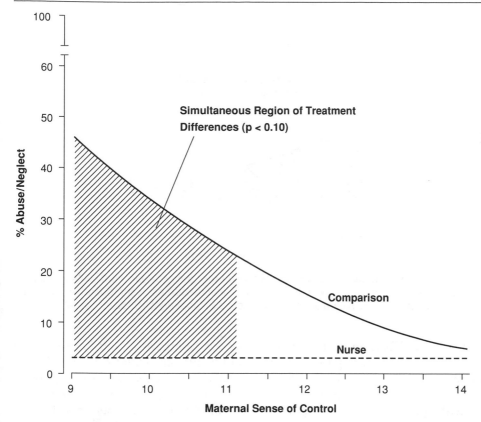

FIGURE 10.2 Concentration of program effects on child abuse and neglect in low-income, unmarried teens with little sense of mastery. Reproduced with permission from *Pediatrics*, Vol. 78, Page(s) 65–78, Figure 1, Copyright 1986.

accounted for by fewer visits for upper respiratory infections (and thus reflected more appropriate use of the emergency department). During the second year of life, nurse-visited children were seen in the emergency department 32% fewer times (0.74 versus 1.09 visits, $p = 0.01$), a difference that was explained in part by a 56% reduction in visits for injuries and ingestions (0.15 versus 0.34 visits, $p = 0.03$). Perhaps most importantly, nurse-visited children born to low-income, unmarried teens had 80% fewer verified cases of child abuse and neglect during the first two years of the child's life than did their counterparts in the control group (1 case or 4% of the nurse-visited teens, versus 8 cases or 19% of the control group, $p = 0.07$).

As can be seen in Figures 10.2 and 10.3, the effect of the program on child abuse and neglect in the first two years of life and on emergency department encounters in the second year of life was greatest among children whose mothers had little belief in their control over their lives when they first registered for the program. The numbers on the vertical axis show the rates of the outcome (child abuse or emergency visits) while the numbers on the horizontal axis display mothers' scores for their control beliefs measured at registration (Rotter, 1966), with higher scores indicating greater belief in their control over their life circumstances. The lines

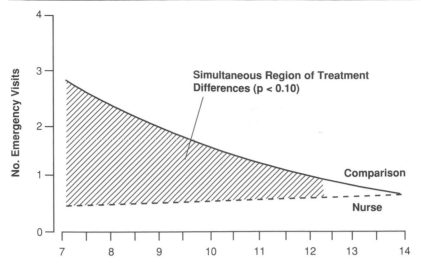

FIGURE 10.3 Concentration of program effects on emergency department visits for injuries among children born to women with few psychological resources. Reproduced with permission from *Pediatrics*, Vol. 78, Page(s) 65–78, Figure 2, Copyright 1986.

on the top and bottom of these figures marked Comparison and Nurse can be thought of as representing the mean rates of the outcome (child abuse/neglect or emergency visits) at different levels of maternal control beliefs for the Comparison and Nurse-Visited mothers respectively. The shaded regions show where we can say with specified levels of confidence ($p < 0.10$, two-tailed tests) that the two groups differed.

During the two years after the program ended, its impact on health-care encounters for injuries endured: irrespective of risk, children of nurse-visited women were less likely than their control group counterparts to receive emergency room treatment (a per-child average of 1.00 versus 1.53 visits, $p < 0.001$) and to visit a physician for injuries and ingestions (per child average of 0.34 versus 0.57 visits, $p = 0.03$) (Olds et al., 1995). The impact of the program on state-verified cases of child abuse and neglect, on the other hand, disappeared during that two-year period, probably because of an increased detection of child abuse and neglect in nurse-visited families due to the nurses' linkage of families with needed services (including child protective services) at the end of the program at the child's second birthday (Olds et al., 1995). When child abuse or neglect was identified in the first four years of the child's life, the nurse-visited cases were found to be less serious, again probably because of the early identification of less serious forms of maltreatment in nurse-visited families (Olds et al., 1995).

Results from a 15-year follow-up of the Elmira sample (Olds et al., 1997) indicate that the Group 4–comparison differences in rates of state-verified reports of child abuse and neglect grew between the children's fourth and fifteenth birthdays. Overall, during the 15-year period after delivery of their first child, in contrast to women in the comparison group, those visited by nurses during pregnancy and infancy were identified as perpetrators of child abuse and neglect in an average of 0.29 versus 0.54 verified reports per program participant ($p < 0.001$). This difference

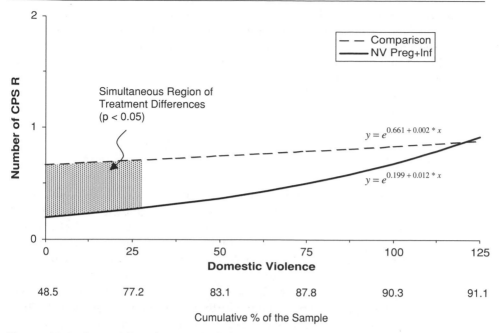

FIGURE 10.4 Attenuation of program effects on child abuse and neglect in families with moderate to high levels of domestic violence.

for the entire time period overrode the disappearance of program effects during the two-year period immediately following the end of the program. This program effect was greater for women who were poor and unmarried at registration (0.11 versus 0.53 reports per program participant, $p < 0.001$) (Olds et al., 1997).

While this reduction in child abuse and neglect was quite promising, the program did not eliminate maltreatment. We therefore turned our attention to an analysis of why the program was not successful in preventing child abuse and neglect for certain families and hypothesized that the presence of domestic violence in the home would attenuate the preventive effects of the program. This analysis showed that the program had no impact on the incidence of domestic violence, but domestic violence did moderate the impact of the program on child abuse and neglect (Figure 10.4).

As indicated in Figure 10.4, the program effect on child abuse and neglect was reduced in those households in which domestic violence was higher during the 15-year period following the birth of the first child.

There were significantly fewer cases of child maltreatment in the nurse-visited group than the comparison group among mothers who reported 28 or fewer incidents of violence over the 15-year period. Program effects were non-significant for mothers reporting more than 28 incidents of domestic violence over 15 years. It has been clear from the first publication regarding program effects on child abuse and neglect that the program did not eliminate child abuse and neglect entirely. This analysis gives us clues as to why. We see that there is something about households in which there are moderate to high levels of domestic violence that interferes with the program's prevention of child maltreatment. As a result of this analysis, we have intensified our efforts to help women cope with domestic violence and to promote effective communication between partners, including strategies to reduce the likelihood that miscommunication will escalate. It is important to note that the domestic violence did not moderate reported program effects in any other area of maternal or child functioning at the 15-year follow-up. The moderation was specific to child abuse and neglect.

MATERNAL LIFE COURSE 15 YEARS AFTER DELIVERY OF FIRST CHILD

At the 15-year follow-up, no differences were reported for the full sample on measures of maternal life course such as subsequent pregnancies or subsequent births, the number of months between first and second births, receipt of welfare, or months of employment. Poor unmarried women, however, showed a number of enduring benefits. In contrast to their counterparts in the comparison condition, those visited by nurses both during pregnancy and infancy averaged fewer subsequent pregnancies (1.5 versus 2.2, $p = 0.03$), fewer subsequent births (1.1 versus 1.6, $p = 0.02$), longer time between the birth of their first and second children (65 versus 37 months, $p = 0.001$), fewer months on welfare (60 versus 90 months, $p = 0.005$), fewer months receiving food stamps (46.7 versus 83.5, $p = 0.001$); fewer behavioral problems due to substance abuse (0.41 versus 0.73, $p = 0.03$), and fewer arrests (0.18 versus 0.58 arrests by self-report, $p < 0.001$; 0.16 versus 0.90 arrests based on New York State records, $p < 0.001$) (Olds et al., 1997).

ANTISOCIAL BEHAVIOR AMONG THE 15-YEAR-OLD ADOLESCENTS

The follow-up study also assessed children of the original participants, when the children were 15 years of age (Olds et al., 1998b). There were no differences between nurse-visited and comparison-group adolescents for the whole sample, but there were differences among the children of poor, unmarried women. In contrast to adolescents born to poor, unmarried women in the comparison group, those visited by nurses during pregnancy and infancy reported fewer instances of running away (0.24 versus 0.60, $p = 0.003$), fewer arrests (0.20 versus 0.45, $p = 0.03$), fewer convictions/violations of probation (0.09 versus 0.47, $p < 0.001$), fewer life-time sex partners (0.92 versus 2.48, $p = 0.003$), fewer cigarettes smoked per day (1.50 versus 2.50, $p = 0.10$), and fewer days having consumed alcohol in the last six months (1.09 versus 2.49, $p = 0.03$). Parents of nurse-visited children reported that their children had fewer behavioral problems related to use of drugs and alcohol (0.15 versus 0.34, $p = 0.08$) (Olds et al., 1998b).

COST ANALYSIS

The Rand Corporation has conducted an economic evaluation of the program that extrapolates the results of the 15-year follow-up study to estimate cost savings generated by the program (Karoly, 1998). While there were no net savings to government or society for serving families in which mothers were married and of higher social class, the savings to government and society for serving families in which the mother was low-income and unmarried at registration exceeded the cost of the program by a factor of four over the life of the child. The return on the investment was realized well before the child's fourth birthday, and the primary cost savings were found in reduced welfare and criminal justice expenditures and in increases in tax revenues.

Memphis Results

DYSFUNCTIONAL CAREGIVING

In the Memphis trial, the rates of state-verified cases of child abuse and neglect were too low during the first two years of the child's life for verified child abuse and neglect reports to serve as a valid outcome. We, therefore, hypothesized that we would see program effects on childhood injuries consistent with the prevention of child maltreatment and with the pattern of program effects on maltreatment and emergency department visits observed in Elmira.

During their first two years, nurse-visited children overall had fewer health-care encounters in which injuries and ingestions were detected than did children in the comparison group (0.43 versus 0.56, $p = 0.05$), an effect that was accounted for primarily by a reduction in outpatient clinic encounters. Nurse-visited children also were hospitalized for fewer days with injuries and/or ingestions than were children in the comparison group (0.04 versus 0.18, $p < 0.001$).

As can be seen in Figures 10.5 and 10.6, the effect of the program on both total health-care encounters and number of days children were hospitalized with injuries and ingestions was greater for children born to women with few psychological resources. As with Figures 10.2 and 10.3, the numbers on the vertical axis show the rates of the outcome (in this case number of health-care encounters where injuries or ingestions were detected or days hospitalized with injuries or ingestions) while the numbers on the horizontal axis display mothers' scores on the psychological-resource scale. To assist with its interpretation, the psychological resources scale has been standardized to a mean of 100 for this sample, with a standard deviation of 10. The lines on the top and bottom of these figures marked Comparison and Nurse can be thought of as the mean rates of the outcome (injury visits or days hospitalized with injuries) at different levels of maternal psychological resources for Comparison and Nurse-Visited mothers respectively. The shaped regions show where we can say with confidence ($p < 0.05$) that the two groups differed. As in the Elmira study, the impact of the program on outcomes indicative of dysfunctional caregiving was greater among women with fewer coping resources.

An examination of the children's hospital records provides insight into reasons that nurse-visited children were hospitalized for fewer days than children in the comparison group. As can be seen in Table 10.1, nurse-visited children tended to be older when hospitalized and to have less severe conditions. The three nurse-visited children who were hospitalized with injuries and ingestions were

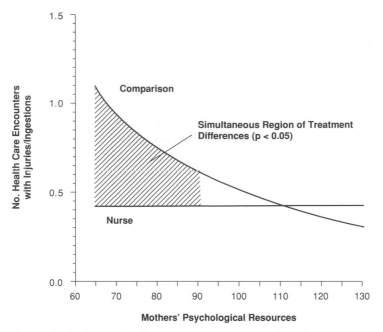

FIGURE 10.5 Intensification of program effect on health care encounters for injuries and ingestions concentrated among children born to mothers with few psychological resources *Advances in Infancy Research, Volume 12*, Carolyn Rovee-Collier, Lewis P. Lipsitt, and Harlene Hayne. Copyright 1998 by Ablex Publishing Company, 100 Prospect Street, Stamford, Connecticut 06 961-1640. Reproduced with permission of Greenwood Publishing Group, Inc., Westport, CT.

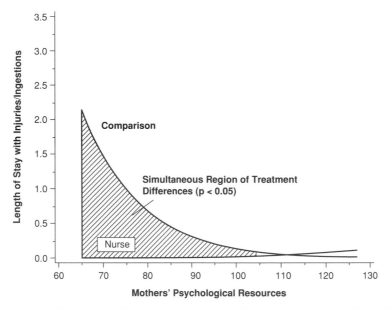

FIGURE 10.6 Intensification of program effect on days hospitalized for injuries and ingestions concentrated on children born to women with few psychological resources *Advances in Infancy Research, Volume 12*, Carolyn Rovee-Collier, Lewis P. Lipsitt, and Harlene Hayne. Copyright 1998 by Ablex Publishing Company, 100 Prospect Street, Stamford, Connecticut 06 961-1640. Reproduced with permission of Greenwood Publishing Group, Inc., Westport, CT.

TABLE 10.1   Results from the Memphis study: Diagnoses for hospitalizations in which injuries and ingestions were detected—by treatment condition. Adapted with permission from *JAMA*, August 27, 1997, 278; 644–52, Table 6, *Copyrighted 1997, American Medical Association.*

Diagnosis	Age (in months)	Sex	Length of Hospital Stay (in days)
Nurse-Visited (n = 206)			
First and second degree burns to face	12.0	M	2
Coin ingestion	12.1	M	1
Ingestion of iron medication	20.4	F	4
Comparison Group (n = 465)			
Head trauma	2.4	M	1
Fractured fibula/ congenital syphilis	2.4	M	12
Strangulated hernia with delay in seeking care/ first degree burn to lips	3.5	M	12
Bilateral subdural hematoma[a]	4.9	F	19
Fractured skull	5.2	F	5
Bilateral subdural hematoma (unresolved)/aseptic meningitis—second hospitalization[a]	5.3	F	4
Fractured skull	7.8	F	3
Coin ingestion	10.9	M	2
Child abuse/neglect suspected	14.6	M	2
Fractured tibia	14.8	M	2
Second degree burns to face/neck	15.1	M	5
Second and third degree burns to leg[b]	19.6	M	4
Gastroenteritis/head trauma	20.0	F	3
Burns—second hospitalization[b]	20.1	M	6
Finger injury/osteomyelitis	23.0	M	6

[a] One child was hospitalized twice with a single bilateral subdural hematoma
[b] One child was hospitalized twice for burns resulting from a single incident
(Reprinted with permission from Kitzman, H., Olds, D., Henderson, C.R., et al. Effect of prenatal and infancy home visitation by nurses on pregnancy outcomes, childhood injuries, and repeated childbearing. A randomized controlled trial. *The Journal of the American Medical Association*, 1997; 278(8): 644–652.)

admitted when they were 12 months of age or older, while six of the 14 comparison children were hospitalized when they were younger than six months of age. Eight of the 14 comparison-group hospitalizations involved either fractures and/or head trauma, while none of the nurse-visited hospitalizations did. In interpreting the number of hospitalizations, it is important to note that the Comparison group (n = 465) had a larger number of cases than the Nurse-Visited Group (n = 206).

These profiles suggest that many of these hospitalized comparison-group children suffered from more seriously deficient care than did children visited by nurses, a conclusion that is corroborated by differences between the nurse-visited and comparison group in maternal reports of breast-feeding and beliefs about caregiving, observations of the home environments, and the two-year-olds' behavior towards their mothers. For example, nurse-visited mothers reported that they attempted breast-feeding more frequently than did women in the comparison group

(26% versus 16%, $p = 0.006$), although there were no differences in duration of breast-feeding. By the 24th month of the child's life, in contrast to their comparison-group counterparts, nurse-visited women held fewer beliefs about child-rearing that are associated with child abuse and neglect ($p = 0.003$). Moreover, the homes of nurse-visited women were rated on the HOME scale (Olds et al., 1995; Caldwell & Bradley, 1979) as more conducive to children's development (32.3 versus 30.9 points, $p = 0.003$). There was no program effect on observed maternal teaching behavior, but children born to nurse-visited mothers with low levels of psychological resources were observed to be more communicative and responsive toward their mothers than were their comparison-group counterparts (17.9 versus 17.2, $p = 0.03$).

MATERNAL LIFE COURSE

At the 24th month of the first child's life, nurse-visited women reported fewer second pregnancies (36% versus 47%, $p = 0.006$) and fewer subsequent live births (22% versus 31%, $p = 0.01$) than did women in the comparison group. Nurse-visited women and their first-born children relied upon welfare for slightly fewer months during the second year of the child's life than did comparison-group women and their children (7.8 months versus 8.4 months, $p = 0.07$), although there were no differences during the child's first year of life. By the fifth year after delivery of their first child, in contrast to women assigned to the comparison condition, women visited by nurses had fewer subsequent pregnancies (1.15 versus 1.34, $p = 0.03$), fewer closely spaced subsequent pregnancies (0.22 versus 0.32, $p = 0.03$), longer intervals between the birth of the first and second child (30.25 versus 26.60 months, $p = 0.004$); fewer months of using Aid to Families with Dependent Children (AFDC) (32.55 versus 36.19, $p = 0.01$) and food stamps (41.57 versus 45.04, $p = 0.005$); higher rates of living with a partner (43% versus 32%, $p = 0.006$) and living with the father of the child (19% versus 12%, $p = 0.03$); and partners who had been employed for longer durations (35.15 versus 26.45 months, $p = 0.045$). There were trends for nurse-visited women to have had fewer therapeutic abortions (0.05 versus 0.10, $p = 0.07$), fewer NICU or special-care nursery admissions for subsequent births (0.14 versus 0.20, $p = 0.09$), and to be married more frequently at the 54-month interview (0.15 versus 0.10, $p = 0.09$) (Kitzman et al., 2000).

SUMMARY OF RESULTS, POLICY IMPLICATIONS, AND PROGRAM REPLICATION

Many of the beneficial effects of the program found in the Elmira trial that were concentrated in higher risk groups were reproduced in the Memphis replication. Overall, the Elmira and Memphis trials demonstrate that the nurse home visitation program achieved two of its most important goals—the reduction in dysfunctional care of children and the improvement of maternal life course.

The impact of the program on the rates of dysfunctional caregiving among higher risk families found in Elmira was substantially replicated in Memphis where the population served was at much higher risk overall. Recall that the beneficial effects of the program in Elmira on dysfunctional care during the child's first two years of life (reflected in rates of state-verified cases of child abuse and neglect and on emergency department encounters) were concentrated on women who were unmarried and from poor households and were further concentrated among those who, at registration, had little belief in their control over their lives. In Memphis (where 98% of the sample was unmarried and all were from poor families), corresponding effects were found for health-care encounters in which injures were detected, for observations of the home environments, and for parents' reports of caregiving and childrearing beliefs. These beneficial effects in Memphis, while strong enough to emerge as program "main effects," were concentrated among women with lower levels of psychological resources at the time of registration.

The Elmira program produced important effects on a host of maternal life-course outcomes from the birth of the first child to that child's 15th birthday. Among women who were unmarried and from low socio-economic status households at registration, those who were visited by nurses during pregnancy and infancy had fewer subsequent children, fewer months on welfare, fewer behavioral impairments from use of alcohol and drugs, fewer arrests and convictions, and fewer days jailed during the 15-year period after birth of their first child. It appears that the reduced rate of subsequent pregnancy positioned these mothers to eventually find work, become economically self-sufficient, and eventually avoid substance abuse and criminal behavior (Olds, 1997). In Memphis, the program reproduced that same key maternal life-course outcome—a reduction in the rate of subsequent pregnancy—albeit at less dramatic levels (a 23% reduction in Memphis versus a 67% reduction for the same time period in Elmira).

Given the simultaneous impact of the program on the rates of child abuse and neglect and compromised maternal life-course (major risks for early-onset conduct disorder) (Moffitt et al., 1996), it is not all that surprising that the 15-year-old children born to women who were unmarried and low socio-economic status exhibited fewer arrests and convictions and lower rates of cigarette smoking, alcohol use, and promiscuous sexual activity.

Policy Implications

One of the clearest messages that has emerged from this program of research is that the functional and economic benefits of the nurse-home-visitation program are greatest for families at greater risk.

This pattern of results challenges the position that these kinds of programs ought to be made available on a universal basis. Not only is the universal approach likely to be wasteful from an economic standpoint, but it may lead to a dilution of services for those families who need them the most, because of insufficient resources to serve everyone well.

As noted above, recent reviews of the home visiting literature have led us to doubt the effectiveness of home-visitation programs that do not adhere to the elements of the model studied in these trials, including especially the hiring of nurses and the use of carefully constructed program protocols designed to promote adaptive behavior. These results should give policy-makers and practitioners pause as they consider investments in home visitation programs without careful consideration of program structure, content, and methods.

With the increased focus on brain development in the first three years of life (Families and Work Institute, 1996), there is increased pressure to fund programs at this stage in the life cycle. It would be a mistake to do so, however, without solid scientific evidence that the particular model promoted is able to achieve its intended effects.

Replication and Scale-Up of the Nurse Home Visitation Program

Given the consistently positive results from these two trials, we have begun to help new communities develop the Nurse Family Partnership outside of research contexts. The program is currently operating in 24 states and over 200 local communities. Even when communities choose to develop programs based on models with good scientific evidence, programs run the risk of being watered down as they are disseminated. Consequently, we have invested considerable effort in helping new communities develop the organizational and community capacities to conduct the program well; in providing in-depth training and on-going technical assistance to the nurses delivering the program; in monitoring the performance of the programs with a comprehensive clinical information system (CIS), and in using data from the CIS to improve the performance of the programs with continuous improvement strategies over time. In this way, we hope to prevent child abuse and neglect and other adverse maternal and child outcomes in an increasingly large number of communities in the United States.

ACKNOWLEDGMENTS

The work reported here was made possible by support from many different sources. These include the Administration for Children and Families (90PD0215/01 and 90PJ0003), Biomedical Research Support (PHS S7RR05403-25), Bureau of Community Health Services, Maternal and Child Health Research Grants Division (MCR-360403-07-0), Carnegie Corporation (B-5492), Colorado Trust (93059), Commonwealth Fund (10443), David and Lucile Packard Foundation (95-1842), Ford Foundation (840-0545, 845-0031, and 875-0559), Maternal and Child Health, Department of Health and Human Services (MCJ-363378-01-0), National Center for Nursing Research (NR01-01691-05), National Institute of Mental Health (1-K05-MH01382-01 and 1-R01-MH49381-01A1), Pew Charitable Trusts (88-0211-000), Robert Wood Johnson Foundation (179-34, 5263, 6729, and 9677), US Department of Justice (95-DD-BX-0181), and the W. T. Grant Foundation (80072380, 84072380, 86108086, and 88124688).

REFERENCES

Bakan, D. (1971). *Slaughter of the innocents: A study of the battered child phenomenon*. San Francisco, CA: Jossey-Bass.

Bandura, A. (1977). Self-efficacy: Toward a unifying theory of behavioral change. *Psychological Review*, **84**, 191–215.

Barnard, K.E. (1990). *Keys to caregiving*. Seattle, WA: University of Washington Press.

Belsky, J. (1981). Early human experience: A family perspective. *Developmental Psychology,* **17,** 3–23.

Bowlby, J. (1969). *Attachment and loss; Vol 1. Attachment.* New York: Basic Books.

Bronfenbrenner, U. (1979). *The ecology of human development: Experiments by nature and design.* Cambridge, MA: Harvard University Press.

Caldwell, B. & Bradley, R. *Home observation for measurement of the environment.* Little Rock, AK: University of Arkansas, 1979.

Dolezol, S. & Butterfield, P.M. (1994). *Partners in parenting education.* Denver, CO : How to Read Your Baby.

Egeland, B., Jacobvitz, D. & Sroufe, L.A. (1988). Breaking the cycle of abuse. *Child Development,* **59,** 1080–1088.

Elster, A. & McAnarney, E. (1980). Medical and psychosocial risks of pregnancy and childbearing during adolescence. *Pediatric Annals,* **9,** 13.

Furstenberg, F.F., Brooks-Gunn, J. & Morgan, S.P. (1987). *Adolescent mothers in later life.* Cambridge: Cambridge University Press.

Garbarino, J. (1981). An ecological perspective on child maltreatment. In L. Pelson (Ed.) *The social context of child abuse and neglect.* New York: Human Sciences Press.

Gil, D. (1970). *Violence against children: Physical child abuse in the United States.* Cambridge, MA: Harvard University Press.

Karoly, L.A., Greenwood, P.W., Everingham, S.S., Hoube, J., Kilburn, M.R., Rydell, C.P., Sanders, M. & Chiesa, J. (1998). *Investing in our Children: What We Know and Don't Know About the Costs and Benefits of Early Childhood Interventions.* Santa Monica, CA.: The RAND Corporation.

Kitzman, H., Olds, D.L., Henderson, Jr., C.R., Hanks, C., Cole, R., Tatelbaum, R., McConnochie, K.M., Sidora, K., Luckey, D.W., Shaver, D., Engelhardt, K., James, D. & Barnard, K. (1997). Effect of prenatal and infancy home visitation by nurses on pregnancy outcomes, childhood injuries, and repeated childbearing: A randomized controlled trial. *The Journal of the American Medical Association,* **278,** 644–652.

Kitzman, H., Olds, D.L., Sidora, K., Henderson, Jr., C.R., Hanks, C., Cole, R., Luckey, D.W., Bondy, J., Cole, K., & Glazner, J. (2000). Enduring effects of nurse home visitation on maternal life course. *The Journal of the American Medical Association,* **283,** 1983–1989.

Kramer, M.S. (1987). Intrauterine growth and gestational duration determinants. *Pediatrics,* **80,** 502–511.

Levinson, R.A. (1986). Contraceptive self-efficacy: A perspective on teenage girls' contraceptive behavior. *J Sex Res,* **22,** 347–369.

Main, M., Kaplan, N. & Cassidy, J. (1985). Security in infancy, childhood, and adulthood: A move to the level of representation. In I. Bretherton & E. Waters (Eds.), Growing points of attachment theory and research. *Monographs of the Society for Research in Child Development,* **50**(1–2, Serial No 209), 66–104.

Milberger, S., Biederman, J., Faraone, S., Chen, L. & Jones, J. (1996). Is maternal smoking during pregnancy a risk factor for attention deficit hyperactivity disorder in children? *American Journal of Psychiatry,* **153,** 1138–1142.

Moffitt, T.E. (1993a). Adolescence-limited and life-course-persistent antisocial behavior: A developmental taxonomy. *Psychological Review,* **100,** 674–701.

Moffitt, T.E., Caspi, A., Dickson, N., Silva, P. & Stanton, W. (1996). Childhood – onset versus adolescent – onset antisocial conduct problems in males: National history from ages 3 to 18 years. *Development and Psychopathology,* **8,** 399–424.

Musick, J.S. (1993). *Young, poor and pregnant.* New Haven, CT: Yale University Press.

Newberger, C.M. & White, K.M. (1990). Cognitive foundations for parental care. In D, Cicchetti & V. Carlson (Eds.). *Child Maltreatment: Theory and research on the causes and consequences of child abuse and neglect* (pp. 302–316). Cambridge, England: Cambridge University Press.

Olds, D., Henderson, C.R. Jr., Cole, R., Eckenrode, J., Kitzman, H., Luckey, D., Pettitt, L., Sidora, K., Morris, P. & Powers, J. (1998a). Long-term effects of nurse home visitation on children's criminal and antisocial behavior: 15-year follow-up of a randomized trial. *The Journal of the American Medical Association,* **280,** 1238–1244.

Olds, D.L. (1997). Tobacco exposure and impaired development: A review of the evidence. *Mental Retardation and Developmental Disabilities Research Reviews, 3*, 1–13.

Olds, D.L., Eckenrode, J., Henderson, Jr., C.R., Kitzman, H., Powers, J., Cole, R., Sidora, K., Morris, P., Pettitt, L.M. & Luckey, D. (1997). Long-term effects of home visitation on maternal life course and child abuse and neglect: 15-year follow-up of a randomized trial. *The Journal of the American Medical Association, 278*, 637–643.

Olds, D.L., Henderson, C.R, Jr., Kitzman, H., Eckenrode, J., Cole, R., Tatelbaum, R., Robinson, J., Pettit, L.M., O'Brien, R. & Hill, P. (1998b). Prenatal and infancy home visitation by nurses: A program of research. In C. Rovee-Collier, L.P. Lipsitt & H. Hayne (Eds.), *Advances in Infancy Research, Volume 12* (pp 79–130). Stamford: Ablex Publishing Corp.

Olds, D.L., Henderson, C.R. & Tatelbaum, R. (1994a). Intellectual impairment in children of women who smoke cigarettes during pregnancy. *Pediatrics, 93*, 221–227.

Olds, D.L., Henderson, C.R. & Tatelbaum, R. (1994b). Prevention of intellectual impairment in children of women who smoke cigarettes during pregnancy. *Pediatrics, 93*, 228–233.

Olds, D.L., Henderson, C.R., Chamberlin, R. & Tatelbaum, R. (1986b). Preventing child abuse and neglect: A randomized trial of nurse home visitation. *Pediatrics, 78*, 65–78.

Olds, D.L., Henderson, C.R., Kitzman, H. & Cole, R. (1995). Effects of prenatal and infancy nurse home visitation on surveillance of child maltreatment. *Pediatrics, 95*, 365–372.

Olds, D.L., Henderson, C.R., Tatelbaum, R. & Chamberlin, R. (1986a). Improving the delivery of prenatal care and outcomes of pregnancy: A randomized trial of nurse home visitation. *Pediatrics, 77*, 16–28.

Olds, D.L., Henderson, C.R., Tatelbaum, R. & Chamberlin, R. (1988a). Improving the life-course development of socially disadvantaged mothers: A randomized trial of nurse home visitation. *American Journal of Public Health, 78*, 1436–1435.

Olds, D.L., Pettitt, L.M., Robinson, J., Henderson, C. Jr., Eckenrode, J., Kitzman, H., Cole, B. & Powers. J. (1998b). Reducing risks for antisocial behavior with a program of prenatal and early childhood home visitation. *Journal of Community Psychology, 26*, 65–83.

Overpeck, M.D., Brenner, M.D., Trumble, A.C., Trifiletti, L.B. & Berendes, H.W. (1998). Risk factors for infant homicide in the United States. *New England Journal of Medicine, 339*, 17:1121–1216.

Plomin, R. (1986). *Development, genetics, and psychology.* Hillsdale, NJ: Lawrence Erlbaum Associates.

Raine, A., Brennan, P., & Mednick, S.A. (1994). Birth complications combined with early maternal rejection at age 1 year predispose to violent crime at age 18 years. *Archives of General Psychiatry, 51*, 984–988.

Rethinking the Brain-New Insights into Early Development, Executive summary, Families and Work Institute, The University of Chicago, June 1996.

Rotter, J.B. (1966). Generalized expectancies for internal versus external control of reinforcements. *Psychological Monographs: General and Applied, 80*, 1.

Rutter, M. (1989). Intergenerational continuities and discontinuities in serious parenting difficulties. In. D. Cicchetti & V. Carlson (Eds.), *Child maltreatment - Theory and research on the causes and consequences of child abuse and neglect* (pp. 315–348). Cambridge, MA: Cambridge University Press.

Streissguth, A.P., Sampson, P.D., Barr, H.M., Bookstein, F.L. & Olson, H.C. (1994). The effects of prenatal exposure to alcohol and tobacco: Contributions from the Seattle longitudinal prospective study and implications for public policy. In H.L. Needleman & D. Bellinger (Eds.), *Prenatal exposure to toxicants* (pp. 148–183). The Johns Hopkins University Press: Baltimore MD.

Tygart, C.E. (1991). Juvenile delinquency and number of children in a family: Some empirical and theoretical updates. *Youth & Society, 22*, 525–536.

US Advisory Board on Child Abuse and Neglect. (1990). *Child abuse and neglect: Critical first steps in response to a national emergency.* Washington, DC: US Government Printing Office.

Wakschlag, L.S., Lahey, B.B., Loeber, R., Green, S.M., Gordon, R.A. & Leventhal, B.L. (1997). Maternal smoking during pregnancy and the risk of conduct disorder in boys. *Archives of General Psychiatry, 54*, 670–680.

11

TO OR FOR WHOM: A SOCIAL POLICY PERSPECTIVE ON CHILD ABUSE AND CHILD PROTECTION

David Gough

Institute of Education, University of London, UK

The last 30 years (and particularly the 14 years since the first edition of this book) have seen a vast increase in research, practice and policy developments, and an associated exponential growth in literature on child abuse and child protection. These new developments provide us all with additional understandings of how to respond to the problem of child abuse, but it also creates at least three types of difficulties.

First, this greater awareness results in the identification of previously hidden aspects of abuse that in themselves require the development of new research, public debate, and policy and practice development. For example, factitious abuse by proxy, ritual abuse, abuse allegations in divorce proceedings, and child perpetrators of sexual abuse.

Second, the greater awareness and sophistication about abuse may in itself lead to greater sophistication and development in the nature of child abuse. For example, the many publicly available writings on the nature of sexual abuse not only assist those wishing to prevent and stop such abuse but can also provide perpetrators of sexual offences with greater skills in identifying vulnerable victims and in avoiding detection. Also, although greater awareness of abuse can lead to increased identification and response to abuse in families this can also assist perpetrators to obsfucate allegations of abuse, for example, to claim that allegations of abuse within families are simply a weapon in acrimonious divorce battles (Brown et al., 2001).

Third, the mass of extra information and complexities of issues identified and newly created strains the individual and organisational resources in information

Early Prediction and Prevention of Child Abuse: A Handbook.
Edited by Kevin Browne, Helga Hanks, Peter Stratton and Catherine Hamilton. © 2002 John Wiley & Sons, Ltd.

management and interpretation. This can result in decisions being made with recourse to limited and thus probably non-representative information. It may also result in de-skilling when policy makers and practitioners feel that they are unable to use their professional abilities to the full because they do not have access to an unknown further range of information that might be relevant to their decision making.

The mass of information and issues may also result in an over-focus on micro issues of fact and a lack of sufficient consideration of the basic policy and practice aims of any decision. The aim of this chapter is to stand back from the academic and professional debates about child and family welfare and child protection services, to consider very basic questions of what services are being provided to what clients, what these services are attempting to achieve, whether these are being achieved, and the bases for these aims and services. In sum: who or what provides or does what, to or for whom, for what purposes, on what basis, and to what effect?

The purpose is not simply to list all the types of people or organizations that might be involved in this process but to help identify some of the issues that pertain to these different aspects of service provision for children and families. Issues that can be forgotten in the context of day to day pressures of being a child, parent, practitioner, or policy maker.

SERVICE PROVIDERS

Services for children and families can be provided direct by central and local government or by private commercial organisations on behalf of government. Many services are also provided by not for profit voluntary agencies and although these may have independent governance, the organisations have to work within the legal and procedural frameworks created by government. In addition, many of these organisations receive income from and provide services on behalf of central and local governments. Voluntary agencies thus vary in the extent that they are financially independent though they are usually much freer than statutory services in the organisational and service delivery frameworks within which they operate (Gibbons & Thorpe, 1989).

Services provided by government, commercial companies, and voluntary agencies are staffed by paid employees and volunteers with varying degrees of training and accreditation. Members of the public may be unaware of the training status of those providing them with direct or indirect services just as in many aspects of other public and commercial service provision. Many of the front line services are provided by staff without the full formal professional qualifications or licences of the discipline with which the service is commonly associated. In many countries residential social work staff, home supportive services, and even those specializing in child protection work may not have social work or other health or caring professional qualifications. In the USA, for example, the minimum qualification specified in many advertisements recruiting for child protection worker posts is a four year university degree in any subject. The onerous responsibilities of such child protection posts often include:

- investigating reports of abuse and neglect to children to assess current or future risk to children by interviewing parents, family members, and others; interviewing and examining children; assessing home environment; and gathering other information
- determining action to be taken to remove or lessen an immediate threat to the safety of a child
- providing evidence in Court to seek emergency removal of the child from the home and placing children in substitute care
- providing services to meet the specific needs of clients by identifying problem areas, developing treatment plans, using appropriate resources to minimize risk and provide for safety of the child
- documenting case records by completing forms, narratives, and reports to form a written record for each client
- developing and maintaining effective working relationships between CPS and other health and welfare and legal law enforcement agencies

Similarly, much work in lawyers' offices may be undertaken by non-legally qualified caseworkers and in England many magistrates (local judges) are not required to be legally qualified. In such cases, trust of the quality and commitment to both the user of the service and the wider community may depend upon the known status or obligations of the service provider rather than on the qualifications of individual staff.

Whatever the source of funding and the employment status or training of those providing the service the nature of the service is likely to be affected by the organisational context in which the work occurs. The context includes the roles, responsibilities, and rules of those organisations, which can differ substantially within, let, alone between, health, education, and welfare services. This context also includes the degree of local accountability of the service. The policy and procedural framework may, for example, be provided on the basis of a centrally decided national policy or procedure, may have developed though local consultation with the community, or be a grass roots local community initiative (Penn & Gough, 2002). Social services in countries like England work within a very precise statutory framework to provide particular kinds of provision. These services are based largely on individual behaviour change and may not fit with concepts of need held by members of the community such as Trivette and colleagues' (1997) list of income maintenance, healthcare, childcare, and leisure. In a recent study of an English local authority, child welfare services had very little focus on these four areas of need and were largely unaware of the very well developed leisure, personal growth, and educational services provided by the community services department of the same local government (Penn and Gough, 2002).

The various services provided by different types of organisation also need to be seen within a broader view of informal care that makes up the majority of material and psychological support for children and families. This role is largely undertaken by adult women but there are also many children who care for other children and adults (Becker et al., 2001).

Services also need to be seen within the broader international context of social policy development. In England, for example, recent child welfare policy such as the Quality Protects initiative to modernize social services for children has been strongly influenced by the Convention on the Rights of the Child (United Nations, 1990) and changing ideas about the nature of childhood and the needs of children (Mayall, 1999).

SERVICE PROVISION/ACTION

It is not always clear what services are provided by an organisation. The activities may be stated in such general terms that it is impossible to determine the content of the service unless research has been undertaken to provide a detailed and representative descriptive analysis of the content of the service. Words such as day care, home visiting and social casework can refer to a range of varied services and practices. The lack of specificity is partly because these are macro terms covering a range of specific activities or a place where such activities take place; for example "family centre work". However, this breadth may be misleading when terms such as social support cover a wide range of different actions undertaken for very different purposes (Thomson, 1995). Even if the service is described in detail in a manual or in case study reports, the actual service received by children and families may vary considerably. This can be seen positively in terms of adapting the service to the context of its implementation, but also negatively in terms of lack of fidelity of implementation.

Lack of specificity of terms may also have important social functions. The term casework, for example, is a broadly defined term used to cover work by many different types of practitioner on their cases. For social work, the term can describe highly therapeutic work, more general supportive services, the execution of agreed service plans, and, increasingly in Britain and the USA, to cover the management of services provided by others. The term is useful in distinguishing individual work from community based approaches. It is an activity often undertaken with only the caseworker and client present with the consequence that the monitoring of progress by managers and case conferences is highly dependent upon how the caseworker reports their work to colleagues and senior staff. Written and verbal accounts of casework provided for supervision or case conference meetings can be seen as a crucial dimension of casework. It is a medium for casework to be judged as competent and at which further casework planning takes place.

Non-specific macro terms may also do political work in allowing seeming agreement and shared purpose where there are differing conceptual or value positions. This may enable political compromise and progress where there is conflict. The danger is that "weasel words" with no specific meaning can hide important issues that require clarification and suggest agreement and coherent planning and action when there is none. Words like "need" and "prevention" have great potential in this regard (Gough, 1993a).

In addition, many practice activities are purposive actions. It is more communicative to describe an action in terms of purpose such as in "feed the cat" rather than as the actions of "put pieces of cooked meat in bowl on floor". Similarly, inherent within concepts such as assessment, monitoring, and treatment are the intended outcomes of such actions. These require interpretative information on the criteria and methods and timescales for meeting those goals and prompting or avoiding further actions. In child welfare work, purposive actions such as assessment and monitoring can imply potential consequences including state intervention in family life and removal of children into care. These activities might all be described as child protection which is a macro purpose defined activity that can include assessment, monitoring, enabling change, requiring change, and court enforced state intervention in family life.

It would not be practical to routinely make explicit all the assumptions involved in day to day work, but a failure to regularly consider such issues may lead to a lack of coherence of case management, specification of service objectives and monitoring of outcomes. On the other hand, such lack of clarity is an important component of the political process of practice and policy development and implementation.

Level of Intervention

Some services are provided universally, but many are provided selectively on the basis of demand, willingness and ability to pay, publicly stated criteria of provision, membership of some self or community generated initiative, professional decision making, or resource availability.

For child welfare and protection, most countries have three levels: of universal, selective, and court sanctioned service or intervention. Some countries have a further level of child protection between and overlapping with the selective service and court interventions levels. In England, for example, there are the following levels:

1. Universal services (provided for or required by all, such as community medical services and compulsory education)
2. Selective services (for example, provided for children defined as in need by the Children Act 1989)
3. Child protection system (government structures and procedural guidance for the investigation and case management of cases defined as at risk of significant harm)
4. Civil Court intervention to control care of child (child at risk of significant harm and better for child than not for there to be legal intervention)

In England, the child protection level of provision includes the responsibility of different agencies to work together to protect children including assessment, case conferences, and a child protection register (Department of Health, Home Office, are Department for Education and Employment, 2000). Children can only be placed on or removed from the register by a formal interdisciplinary case conference. The register is simply a list but has the important consequence of defining the case as one of child protection and thus invoking the child protection guidelines for how such cases should be managed including an action plan with assigned workers to achieve specified goals in order to reduce the risk of harm to the child. In other countries, the non-court level of child protection may be much more limited. It may be little more than an investigation service resulting in referral into the court system (level 4), referral to local support services but without ongoing child protection case management and monitoring (even if an intense service it is basically a level 2 selective service), or no further action.

The quantity, type, and quality of service provided at each level varies between countries and over time. Some countries have very extensive services at each level of provision, whereas others may have few services or concentrate what services there are on a particular level of intervention, such as the children receiving court sanctioned intervention.

In addition, the proportion of the population receiving each level of selective service will vary. In the USA, approximately 2.2% of children are referred to the third level of response and receive post-investigation preventive services (US Department Of Health And Human Services, 1999). In England, approximately 0.3% of children are at any one time receiving level 3 service of placement on the local child protection register (Department of Health, 2001). In the mid 1990s the government was concerned that too many children were being brought into the child protection system and decided that this child protection level of response should be narrowed on to a smaller proportion of the most serious cases (Department of Health, 1995). In practice, this meant requiring higher criteria (greater concern about the children) for the child protection level of response and thus reducing the numbers and thus the proportion of children in the population receiving child protection system services.

Similar discussions occur in the provision of support for children with disability. In England, children meeting certain criteria are provided with a statement of need that the local services should provide services to meet. More children deemed as meeting the criteria puts a greater pressure on service provision and can also change the social meaning of the categorisation. If all children where there was some concern about their welfare were put on some bureaucratic register to ensure adequate monitoring then there would be likely to be much less stigma associated with such registration. In contrast, the tightening of criteria to the "most serious cases" may increase negative labelling. Similarly, there may be labelling effects from the length of involvement with a level of service response such as child protection intervention.

Operational Definitions

The four levels of response previously described are in effect different levels of operational definition of need or risk of maltreatment for different levels of service response. Furthermore, a range of professional disciplines in the various agencies involved will have further or slightly different roles and responsibilities and so apply different operational definitions. The English child protection system of "working together" is planned as a uniform system across health, welfare, education, law enforcement, and civil law systems, but even a common statutory legal and procedural framework does not totally remove the effects that different roles, responsibilities, and accountabilities have on operational definitions within and between different agencies.

Operational definitions of child need and risk of maltreatment are good indicators of social policy in action. However, the application of these criteria is not only determined by a professional or other judgement about certain circumstances fitting the official criteria. Such judgements are also influenced by a range of other factors related to the purposes and consequences of applying an operational definition, including perceptions of (Gough, 1996):

- Quality of the information on which the criteria are judged
- Ways in which information is interpreted to assess the criteria
- Social psychological factors that influence decision making (such as group membership, bystander apathy, etc.)
- Structural, organisational, and resource factors affecting practices by people with different roles in different agencies
- Agreement with the supposed aim of the consequent actions
- Belief that the aims will not be achieved even if the criteria are applied
- Possible other consequences (such as affecting worker–user relationships)

Abstract Definitions

The English government guidance also includes descriptions of different types of abuse such as physical abuse, neglect, and sexual abuse. They emphasise abuse rather than criteria for child protection activity or other social intervention. There are very many examples of such descriptions of different types of maltreatment; often referred to as definitions of abuse even though such definition is usually stated in very broad terms. They all involve two basic concepts of some harm to the child and some responsibility for that harm (Gough, 1996). Ideas about what is or is not harmful to children vary, of course, between cultures and over time and harm includes the infringement of rights; sexual assault would still be considered abusive even if there were no physical or psychological effects (Finkelhor, 1979).

Not all adverse experiences of children are considered abuse. Normally this is restricted to the harm being considered the responsibility of certain groups of people as in familial or extra-familial abuse. Interestingly, the breadth of who could be responsible is often more broadly defined in sexual abuse with rape by a stranger seen as abuse, whereas homicide by a stranger is normally described as murder rather than as physical abuse. In addition to the breadth of who or what might be considered responsible is the assignment of responsibility based on a social interpretation of the actors and of their behaviour. The effects of what are perceived as accidents are not normally considered abuse unless there is perceived to have been lack of care and protection by normal caretakers. Typically accidents due to inappropriate care by an organisation or a member of the public are described as negligence, whereas extreme lack of care by a parent is neglect. In addition, the assessment is affected by the outcome for the child. A mother leaving a child alone at home whilst shopping is likely to receive much more social sanction if some accident befalls the child in the house whilst she is away. As the concept of child abuse is so dependent on responsibilities of care (except for sexual abuse) it is also linked to children's relationships with their carers (Stratton, 1988).

Finally, note also needs to be made of the political dimension of the development and use of concepts of child abuse in society. Not only do our understandings of the concept change over time but so also do the uses made of the concept in determining the needs and rights of different groups. This relates not only to the needs or rights of children, parents, and the state, but also to different socio-economic, racial, cultural, sexual orientation, professional, bureaucratic, and political groups (for example: Nelson, 1984; Parton, 1985). Culture and religious belief are particularly salient with contested views about male and female circumcision and the medical treatment of illness. Issues are also arising from the new genetics with children being born with the express purpose of treating their siblings medical condition.

Child Protection

By its very nature child protection has a controlling as well as a caring function. In order to protect a child it may be necessary to use power and this potential provides a background for any caring provision.

When children are referred to government services as potential child protection cases, the full picture of what did or did not occur may be unclear and so one component of the service provided is simply to monitor whether the situation in the family is stable and deserves concern.

When more active services are provided, this is normally to assist the child and family in some way and to enable change. If the concerns about the child are high there may be a requirement for, rather than simply the enabling of, change, with the threat of sanctions, and applications for legal powers of control of the care of the child.

These assessments and consequent service responses raise many issues about the bases of decision making. This could be on the basis of cases meeting specific criteria that could be provided by descriptive or scoring type technologies of child abuse risk or more broad based assessment. But this focus on the technology of assessment does not obviate the need for consideration of the ideological positions underpinning such assessment. Who owns such assessment criteria and the associated measurement systems, what is their evidence base, what other factors influence their application in practice, and what are the consequences of such decisions?

Much effort has been spent on attempting to devise technological methods of ascertaining risk. However, the lack of specificity of the tests (with many false positives and false negatives identified) means that they are better suited to identify general risk populations (for example, for research studies) than in identifying whether abuse has occurred or is likely to occur in a particular case (Dingwall, 1989).

The failure of the technological solution and the need to consider the child's needs and rights beyond risk of maltreatment has led several countries to develop batteries of measures to assess child and family functioning (Gough et al., 1999). The Framework for the Assessment of Children in Need and their Families (Department of Health, Department for Education and Employment, Home Office, 2000) developed in England is of particular interest for three reasons. Firstly, it provides a uniform structure with age specific recording forms to be used across different disciplines and agencies. Secondly, in addition to considering the dimensions of child and parental functioning, it also includes the wider social context in which the child and family are living. Thirdly, it provides a structure for considering what services are required to respond to any need identified in the environmental, parental or child domains. This move towards needs based assessment parallels earlier changes in English policy towards assessment of children with disabilities.

These recording systems should lead to more explicit decision making in terms of what is provided for or done to whom. Without such clarity, levels of intervention may be highly influenced by non-specified moral assessments of the parents. This was shown by Dingwall and colleagues' (1983) classic study of hospital outpatient reactions to different parents of children presenting with relatively mild injuries explained as accidents. The influence of other social factors is evident when countries with supposedly weak laws for intervening to protect children do manage to intervene strongly in particular types of cases (for example, high profile media cases) although these may not be the cases with the highest risk of abuse to the children.

CLIENT, PURPOSE, POWER AND CONSENSUS

Differential Clients

This book is concerned with child abuse and child protection, but children are not necessarily the only client. In England, the Children Act 1989, changed the language of the law from parental rights to parental responsibility to children, but parents do still have the normal rights of any adult in society to be treated equally and fairly and to be provided with different degrees of services and other forms of support. The legislation says that at home with their parents is the best place for most children unless it is in the best interests of the child for this not to be so. Even if the focus is only on the child, it may best fulfil the child's needs for the parent to receive services and thus be the intermediate client between the service providers and the primary client of the child. Research suggests that this is the case with many services such as home visiting for parents (See Daro, Chapter 7) but relatively few services being provided directly for children beyond child care (Gough, 1993b).

The problems arise when it is not clear that parental and children's interests are co-terminus. In these circumstances the state acts to protect the child. Thus child protection is defined negatively in terms of what is unacceptable for children rather in the more positive language of what children need or what would potentiate rather than limit their life opportunities and quality of life. As mothers are the most common carers of children, consideration of responsibility for lack of adequate care or protection from harm by others is likely to fall more frequently on mothers than other members of the community. In this way, child protection as with much of child welfare is not gender neutral (O'Hagan & Dillenburger, 1995).

The extent to which the state wishes to intervene will vary depending on its views of children's needs and rights, but these are likely to vary with views on the role of the state in terms of the rights of parents and children. Fox Harding (1996) describes seven models of the state's stance on this issue from *laissez-faire* policies which believes that it is not the state's role to intervene in family matters, to state paternalism where the state manages all aspects of children's welfare. The state, however, has a number of further agendas ranging from the use of families to manage individual roles in society (including work, sexuality, and child education and employability), maintenance of a stable moral order, and the avoidance of social exclusion which creates many direct and indirect costs including the economic effects from people not being involved in productive employment.

Furthermore, the focus on and thus the responsibility put on the family, whether this be in either the *laissez-faire* or paternalistic extremes of social policy, is at the expense of a focus on giving responsibility to or supporting local communities. The emphasis of services is typically on supporting or monitoring the functioning of parents rather than making communities more child friendly (Jordan, 2000). This individual and family focus is particularly problematic when child protection concerns arise from poverty (Garbarino & Kostelny, 1992) which is highly correlated with known incidence of physical abuse and neglect. There are also many issues about relativity of criteria for child protection responses in communities with different cultural beliefs about children and their needs and roles.

State Versus Community Control

It is beyond the scope of this chapter to consider all the factors that might influence government in developing and implementing a policy that is then applied as professional decision making in the community. Governments may come into power with certain political philosophies and mandates, but these will be affected by the availability of resources, the ideologies, skills and technologies of professional decision making, and the political debates played out in the media often involving high profile cases that can result in intense political pressure and policy change.

In countries with large variations in cultural and political views a centralized system can help define nationally what are acceptable situations for children and what are appropriate services and facilities for children and families. The problem is that local communities may not share these centralized views. Local variation can occur through fine tuning of professional decision making which in England is formalised through multi-agency child protection committees stipulated in national guidance. The courts can also adapt decisions to local sensitivities.

In some jurisdictions there have been attempts to create some local ownership of child protection within the local community (see Gough, 1993b, Chapter 3). In the USA, the 1996 amendments to the Child Abuse Prevention and Treatment Act (CAPTA) provides for federal funds for States meeting eligibility requirements including the establishment of citizen review panels to increase community awareness and accountability of child abuse and child protection.

In Scotland, evidence and legal actions in cases where children commit crimes, or legal action undertaken to protect children, are decided by the courts, but the disposal of the case is by panels of local members of the public. Although this ensures that local non-professionals have a central role, it is unclear how much the panel members are able to represent local interests and perspectives. However, in countries where there is a large sense of local community and community based governance, child welfare and protection action may be automatically part of such a local system. In France, for example, local judges have much power and become involved very early in child protection decision making and can require local government agencies to provide services for children. The judges are therefore a resource for members of the public rather than just a tool for local services. Commentators in England have suggested that the French system is less adversarial and more supportive to families than the English system (Baistow & Hetherington, 1998) but it is based on a different culture of local governance.

The adversarial aspects of legal processes can also be reduced with a more proactive supportive service rather than the residual responsive child protection service. Such a positive supportive approach requires the investment of considerable material and professional resources in the belief that this will have the desired preventive effect. Even if the belief is justified there will still be cases of child maltreatment that result in adversarial processes. Such adversity may be avoided if child protection is undertaken within a therapeutic context under control of health and welfare professionals. This may have many desirable effects including the involvement of families where there is not sufficient evidence for legal powers to be involved (King and Trowell, 1992). On the other hand, decision making by professionals does not have the explicit accountabilities of the legal process.

Another approach is to put more emphasis on the family finding its own solutions to its problems through family conferencing. This does not remove the responsibility of statutory services and the courts to ensure that any solution sufficiently protects the child. A potential criticism is that children may be pressured to accept a family solution that they are unhappy with, which is similar to some criticisms in the past of family therapy.

OUTCOMES

Criteria

Assessment of outcomes obviously depends upon criteria of success. These may be framed within narrow criteria related to individual services, to the outcome for the child in terms of protection from maltreatment, broader aspects of child outcome, outcome for other actors including the family, and community and societal outcomes.

Protecting children from maltreatment may be the most obvious criterion but such benefits may be outweighed by an abusive system response or disruption to the child's attachment relationships. Alternatively the best overall social psychological and economic outcome for a child might be long term fostering and adoption. This might also be true for large sections of the children in society who are not at risk of maltreatment but removing large numbers of children into care on the basis of optimising outcomes would not be a social policy that many would be happy with.

Social policy is also related to investment of resources and timescales. Spending much resource and time in helping a child remain at home may be a laudable aim but may simply be shoring up an untenable situation, prolonging a child's experience of an inappropriate environment, and delaying his or her adaptation to a new caring environment.

Society also has limits to what resources it is prepared to invest in different social policies and must balance different social and political agendas. Even within the relatively narrow limits of concern for child protection there is a distinction between individual and societal outcomes. In an individual case a child may suffer less if there is not a criminal prosecution of a sexual abuse perpetrator, but there may be a high cost to society of not enforcing criminal law in such cases; for example, the protection of other children who may be at risk from the offender and the social messages provided by such prosecution.

Social policy debates are often generated in the media in relation to high profile cases where children have suffered extreme harm and where services are accused of failing to protect children. In some cases the allegations are that agreed rules and procedures were not followed and the emotive and serious nature of the case results in calls for sanctions against such failures even though it was not the workers who caused the abuse to the child.

In other cases, the procedures may have been followed but the outcome was due to clinical decision making within the agreed social policy. There always is a balance between the risks of a child remaining in the family and the risks and other psychological and social costs of removing the child from those risks. If a child is subsequently seriously abused then the judgement may have only been wrong in retrospect. This does not however stop sections of society scapegoating professionals who make well informed decisions but where children have poor or abusive outcomes.

In other cases, the systems and procedures may be at fault. In England, for example, much of the community health services are organised around community doctors. This system may work well for the majority population but may miss children where the parents are not integrated into this system. Similarly, there are social benefits of living in a relatively liberal state where individuals are not required to carry identification or be officially known to government bodies, but this can result in children being missed and unknown to services that might protect their rights and intervene to reduce their vulnerability to abuse (Lynch and Gough, 2001).

Whatever the social or professional policy and criteria of service effectiveness, the problem is having access to the data to inform such decision making. In most cases there may not be access to the full facts nor a full knowledge of the effects of different actions or lack of action on the future life of a child.

Evidence Informed Policy and Practice

Policy and practice needs to be based on a whole range of factors, particularly societal values and ideology. However, knowledge of the effects of different policies and practices is necessary in order to understand how the aims of the particular value systems can be met.

The majority of research in this area has been on issues of case type and therapeutic intervention. The emphasis on the future life of a child has thus been on child abuse rather than child protection. Similarly, agency case statistics are typically in the form of the category of abuse, such as physical abuse and neglect. This is in contrast to child protection issues such as: type and degree of harm that the child is at risk of, the degree of risk, reasons for believing that the child is at such risk, and the broader aspects of the child's life (including the positive aspects). If agency data were collected in terms of child protection, they would be better able to act as a child protection management information system. Such systems can assist the management of individual cases as well as local area and national management, and thus also inform practice and policy development.

In terms of child abuse research, much emphasis has been on issues such as: short and long term outcomes of abuse; identification of risk; the processes by which children become vulnerable; interventions to protect children from harm; and interventions to repair the effects of any adversities experienced. To date the majority of published research studies are relatively small scale descriptive analytic or survey studies describing causal variables or treatment effects. Such methods are essential for hypothesis generation but there is also a need for much more large scale multivariate or experimental testing of causal theories and efficacy of interventions. The lack of experimental studies is probably due to a number of practical factors such as availability of funds for research, access to child protection cases, and ethical constraints. It is also probably due to a lack of understanding of experimental approaches with the common view that human social behaviour is too complex for such designs (rather than its strength being to control multiple variables) or is in some way ideologically incorrect (Oakley, 2000).

There has been an explosion in the amount of research undertaken on child abuse over the last two decades, but the field suffers from the common problem of fragmentation. This is not surprising considering the complexity and breadth of the topic where there are so many multiple interactions of variables concerned in the causes of maltreatment, the effects of maltreatment, the effects of health welfare and legal interventions, the nature of child development, and human social and political relations. One method for helping to develop coherence is to collate what is known and not known in relation to different policy and practice research questions.

In the health field the need for practice-led synthesis of research evidence was recognised in the early 1990s by the setting up of the Cochrane Collaboration as an international coordinating group to create systematic reviews of the evidence for the efficacy of different treatments. Cochrane reviews have found that many accepted medical treatments have either no proven effect or a negative effect. For example, until recently albumin was the accepted treatment for children suffering from extreme shock as in extensive body burns. There were theoretical reasons why it might be an effective treatment and there were a few studies supporting this view. A Cochrane review showed that administering albumin increased on average the chance of death from 8% to 14% (Bunn et al., 2000). Systematic research synthesis was necessary to show this effect as non-systematic syntheses, as in traditional literature reviews, can be biased in reporting only certain types of study. Systematic research synthesis was also necessary because individual clinicians did not have a broad enough view to disprove their assumption that the treatment worked. If the patient survived, the treatment had been successful. If not, then the patient had been too ill to recover despite the treatment. These issues are exactly paralleled in child abuse and protection services where there are few well designed primary studies showing the efficacy of services and little systematic syntheses of the research that has been undertaken.

The Cochrane Collaboration is concerned with health care interventions and has conducted a few systematic reviews related to child protection (for example, Hodnett and Roberts, 2000), and a related organisation, the Campbell

Collaboration, has started to coordinate reviews in the broader area of social interventions. Also, the Evidence for Policy and Practice Information and Coordinating (EPPI) Centre at the Social Science Research Unit is developing user-led systematic reviews in social interventions that answer a range of research questions including process issues rather than just pure effects of interventions. A user perspective ensures that the research is synthesized to address the issues most relevant to policy makers, professionals, and users of services rather than to address academic-led questions. Such a user-led approach should then feed through to affect the type of primary research undertaken to fill in the gaps to user-led systematic research syntheses and lead to a more coherent research agenda and a more evidence based approach to policy and practice in child protection.

Child protection is a complex issue in terms of ideology and social policy, human relations, human well being and development, knowledge of the effects of life experiences, and of our policies and practices. All policies have benefits and costs. Developing social policies with local communities should enable ownership and understanding of these policies and their implications. Similarly, greater democratic sharing of the research agenda and greater technological sophistication in primary research driven by better secondary research are important tools in helping us achieve the ideological and policy choices that we make.

REFERENCES

Baistow K, Hetherington R (1998) Parent's experiences of child welfare interventions: an Anglo-French comparison. *Children & Society*. **12** (2) 113–124.

Becker S, Dearden C, Aldridge J (2001) Children's labour of love? Young carers and care work, in Mizen P, Pole C, Bolton A (eds) *Hidden Hands: International Perspectives on Children's Work and Labour*. Brighton: Falmer Press.

Brown T, Frederico M, Hewitt L, Sheehan R (2001) *Child Abuse Review*, **10**, (2), 113–124.

Bunn F, Lefebvre C, Li Wan Po A, Li L, Roberts I, Schierhout G (2000) Human albumin solution for resuscitation and volume expansion in critically ill patients. The Albumin Reviewers. *Cochrane Database Systematic Review*, (2):CD001208.

Department of Health (1995) Messages from Research. London: Stationery Office.

Department of Health, Department for Education and Employment, Home Office (2000). *Framework for the assessment of children in need and their families*. London: Stationery Office.

Department of Health, Home Office, Department for Education and Employment (2000) *Working Together to Safeguard Children*. London: Stationery Office.

Department of Health (2001) *The Children Act Report 2000*. London: Stationery Office.

Dingwall R (1989) Problems of prediction in child abuse research, in Stevenson O (ed.) *Child Abuse: Public Policy and Professional Practice*. Brighton: Harvester Press.

Dingwall R, Eekalaar J, Murray T (1983) *The Protection of Children. State intervention and family life*. Oxford: Blackwell.

Finkelhor D (1979) What's wrong with sex between adults and children? *American Journal of Orthopsychiatry*, **49**, (4).

Fox Harding L (1996) *Family, State and Social Policy*. Basingstoke: MacMillan.

Garbarino J, Kostelny K (1992) Child maltreatment as a community problem, *Child Abuse and Neglect*, **16**, (4), 455–464.

Gibbons J, Thorpe S (1989) Can voluntary support projects help vulnerable families? The work of Home Start. *British Journal of Social Work*, **19**, (3), 189–201.

Gough DA (1993a). The case for and against prevention. In Waterhouse L (Ed.) *Child Abuse and Child Abusers: Protection and Prevention*. London: Jessica Kingsley.

Gough DA (1993b) *Child Abuse Interventions: A review of the research literature.* London: HMSO.

Gough DA (1996) Defining the Problem, Invited commentary. *Child Abuse and Neglect, The International Journal*, **20**, (11), 993–1002.

Gough DA, Waugh F, Wilkinson M (1999) *Options for Outcome Indicators for New South Wales Health Services for Children Who Have Been Physically Abused, Emotionally Abused or Neglected (Panoc).* Report Prepared For New South Wales Health, Sydney.

Hodnett ED, Roberts I (2000) Home-based social support for socially disadvantaged mothers. *Cochrane Database Systematic Review* (2).

Jordan B (2000) *Social Work and the Third Way. Tough love as social policy.* London: Sage.

King M, Trowell J (1992) *Children's Welfare and the Law.* London: Sage.

Lynch MA, Gough DA (2001) Reaching all children. Editorial. *BMJ*, **323**: 176–177.

Mayall B (1999) Children and Childhood. In Hood S, Mayall B, Oliver S (Eds) *Critical Issues in Sociology Research.* Buckingham: Open University Press.

Nelson BJ (1984) *Making an issue of Child Abuse. Political Agenda Setting for Social Problems.* Chicago: University of Chicago Press.

Oakley A (2000) *Experiments in Knowing: Gender and Method in the Social Sciences.* Cambridge: Polity Press.

O'Hagan K, Dillenburger K (1995) *The Abuse of Women within Childcare Work.* Buckingham: Open University Press.

Parton N (1985) *The Politics of Child Abuse.* Basingstoke: Macmillan.

Penn H, Gough DA (In press) The price of a loaf of bread: some conceptions of family support. *Children and Society.*

Stratton P (1988) Understanding and treating child abuse in the family: an overview. In Browne K, Davies C, Stratton P (Eds) *Early Prediction and Prevention of Child Abuse.* Chichester: John Wiley.

Thompson RA (1995) *Preventing Child Maltreatment Through Social Support. A Critical Analysis.* Thousand Oaks: Sage.

Trivette C, Dunst C, Deal A (1997) A Resource Based Approach to Early Intervention. In Thurman S, Cornwall J, Gottwald S (Eds) *Contexts of Early Intervention: Systems and Settings.* Baltimore: Paul H Brooks.

United Nations (1990) *Convention on the Rights of the Child.* Geneva: United Nations.

US Department Of Health And Human Services (1999) *Child Maltreatment 1999. Reports From the States to the National Child Abuse and Neglect Data System.* Washington: US Department Of Health And Human Services.

Section III

TERTIARY PREVENTION I: HELPING CHILDREN AND FAMILIES AFFECTED BY CHILD MALTREATMENT

EDITOR'S INTRODUCTION

Helga Hanks

This section points to therapy and interventions for individual children and families when abuse has occurred. While there is discussion of intergenerational issues here (see Egeland et al., Chapter 13) the treatment of perpetrators of child abuse appears in section IV.

Attachment theory in this section, as well as in many other chapters in this book, has rightly been the focus of attention. It is clearly thought to be one of the key concepts in human existence and develops from the early days and month of life well into adulthood. Relationships depend on attachment and provide as important a nourishment as food. Human beings, growth and development depend on it centrally. Understanding this concept is vital for interventions when the relationship between caregivers and children has been impaired and particularly when abuse has occurred. How attachment theory is used in therapy and research is described in this section, but for those who wish to understand its theoretical underpinning in detail, chapters like Pat Crittenden's (Chapter 7) provide a link to what is discussed in this section.

This section is opened by Lucy Berliner, who describes therapy for children who have been traumatised by the abuse inflicted on them and how one might help these children. Backed up by contemporary references and research, Trauma, Posttraumatic Stress Disorder (PTSD) and post-traumatic stress symptoms provide the base for her discussion Her immense clinical experience of working with abused children comes strongly through in her writing. She has such exceptional sense of what children's needs are and this chapter will be very valuable for practitioners. Research is cited to provide evidence-based work. Lucy acknowledges that in the present climate many abused children live within their families together with the perpetrator of the abuse. For some children this is not a problem. However, she observes that it is not surprising that children within many such families show aggressive behaviour which is hard to eliminate when aggression is modelled in the household. There is evidence that violent behaviour to children continues even when treatment is ongoing.

Egeland, Bosquet and Levi (Chapter 13) present us with an elegant search across the literature for evidence that it will be possible to break the cycle of abuse within the intergenerational patterns of families. At present there is more evidence that maltreatment does span the intergenerational divide and these authors analyse the various patterns. It is difficult to extract the most important aspect of this paper, because all of it is important, but what has struck me is the clear message that short-term interventions with abusing families do not bring about the desired effect. Egeland et al., as well as most of the authors in this section express the opinion, and give evidence to the fact, that interventions with maltreating families need to be both frequent and of sufficient length in order to be effective. Policy makers note.

Hanks and Stratton (Chapter 14) set out to describe what family therapy does and when it is thought to be effective in cases of child maltreatment. The chapter makes the case that the major consequences of abuse, and the route to tertiary protection, lies in the children's relationships. The great majority of abused children will continue to be cared for within their family. The implication is that the optimal context for treating the consequences of abuse and for preventing recurrence is the family itself. Treating the child or the parent in isolation is usually likely to be less effective. We propose systemic family therapy as a set of approaches which have been worked out in the context of serious family problems, and often with abuse itself. Research evidence of its effectiveness is reviewed, and the ways that family therapy would deal with common processes in families following the discovery of abuse are described.

Dorota Iwaniec, Alice Sluckin and Martin Herbert in Chapter 15 concentrate on parenting interventions particularly with children who fail to thrive and are emotionally abused within a family/caring setting. Their descriptions of the needs of parents and children are detailed and again guided by immense experience in the field. Responsive parenting, working with parents in treatment settings both at home and in specific places like nurseries, mother/parent group settings and individual counselling programmes are discussed. Bonding and attachment between carer and child and how this might come about are highlighted. The authors point out that "It could take three months of hard work to bring a mother and child closer together and to the point of beginning to enjoy (or stop disliking/fearing) each other" (p. 229). The descriptions of working with children who are failing to thrive are particularly important and I am very grateful that the authors have spent time discussing this in detail. Failure to thrive in children has always been an area that is underestimated and now there are even voices who wish to deny the concept of children not getting enough food and failing to thrive. Dorota Iwaniec and colleagues put this form of maltreatment into context and make a point of not excluding it from our concerns for children.

The next chapter in this section by Roger Bullock and Michael Little (Chapter 16) adds an invaluable understanding of the "contribution of children's services to the protection of children". Many of us who are rooted in research and clinical practice often have great difficulties in understanding the rules by which children's services are governed. The authors bring us right up to date with research, practice issues, outcome and evaluation studies. They also recount that the UK Department of Health estimations of children in need are—a staggeringly large number—"400 000 children are at any one time in need of some form of social services provisions" (p. 269). Their transparent analysis around this issue is a great credit to the authors who have managed to give a lucid account of children's services.

To mention just one point, Roger and Michael discuss under what circumstances parents should be part of the process of child protection. This is a continuing and major challenge. Closely linked are the fundamental aspects of inter-agency co-operation which is patchy and in great need of development and I think even possibly protection. With a world crises sparked off by the 11 September 2001 events and economic slow down there is a risk that resources and energy are being channelled away from child protection and children in need. The contribution of this chapter will help us to understand some of the process by which we can continue the development of services for these children.

12

THE TRAUMATIC IMPACT OF ABUSE EXPERIENCES: TREATMENT ISSUES

Lucy Berliner
University of Washington, USA

Children who have been maltreated may suffer a variety of adverse psychoso-cial consequences (Berliner & Elliott, 2002; Kolko, 2002a; Kendall-Tackett et al., Finkelhor, 1993; Wolfe, 1999). Some of these negative outcomes are the direct result of the traumatic impact of physical or sexual abuse experiences. Other effects derive from the familial context within which the abuse occurs. Unlike traumas inflicted by non-family members, child abuse threatens the fundamental assumption that parents and other relatives will protect and act in the best interests of their kin. In addition, families in which child abuse takes place frequently are dysfunctional, sometimes even despite an outward appearance of respectability or normalcy. They often contain family members who have psychiatric conditions or functional im-pairments that have a deleterious effect on children's growth and development (e.g., Kolko, 2002a). These factors combine with children's inherited capacities to produce the specific difficulties observed in individual children.

The treatment issues for abused children, therefore, will vary depending on the particular circumstances of the children and the potential sources of disturbance. This means that treatment plans must always evolve from an individualized assess-ment of the child and family. An abuse-informed assessment considers the nature of the experience, the child's attachment status, parental deficits and strengths, and the child's current functioning.

ABUSE IMPACT

One consequence of abuse experiences is the traumatic impact of the abusive acts—the physical or sexual assaults. Posttraumatic effects relate to the emotional, cognitive, and behavioral consequences of experiences that produce fear, horror,

Early Prediction and Prevention of Child Abuse: A Handbook.
Edited by Kevin Browne, Helga Hanks, Peter Stratton and Catherine Hamilton. © 2002 John Wiley & Sons, Ltd.

or extreme helplessness. Trauma is most specifically manifested as Posttraumatic Stress Disorder (PTSD) (American Psychiatric Association (APA), 2000) or posttraumatic stress symptoms. A large clinical and scientific literature has documented that child abuse can produce this condition in children (e.g., AACAP, 1998; Saigh et al., 1998). Studies with clinical populations of physically and sexually abused children reveal that more than a third of sexually abused children (McLeer et al., 1998) and physically abused children (McCloskey & Walker, 2000) meet diagnostic criteria for the disorder. Many abused children will have PTSD symptoms even if they do not develop the disorder. For example, a large majority of incestuously abused girls will have significant l PTSD symtpomatology (McLeer et al, 1998).

PTSD is unique among psychiatric disorders in that its etiology is specified as arising from an experience that qualifies as an extreme stressor and that the symptoms are directly linked to the trauma (APA, 2000). The symptoms include reexperiencing, avoidance, numbing, and hyperarousal. There are controversies surrounding the developmental appropriateness of current diagnostic criteria (AACAP, 1998). Although some adjustments have been made in recognition that children may manifest the trauma impact in different ways than adults (e.g., posttraumatic play as evidence of reexperiencing), many criteria require patients to report on internal states. Some commentators have argued that more changes are necessary to adequately capture young children's posttrauma responses (Scheeringa et al., 1995).

Some abused children will not develop posttraumatic stress symptoms. Not all abuse experiences contain the sudden, fear evoking qualities that make such experiences inherently traumatic (Carlson & Dalenberg, 2000). In some cases sexual abuse is carried out under the guise of normal behavior or involves non-forceful sexual touching that produces discomfort or confusion, but not fear or other intense negative affect. Physical abuse is often the result of ordinary discipline that goes too far. It may be experienced as aversive, but a normal part of family life. Attributions about the nature of the experience may be influential in determining symptom formation. For example, sexually abused children compared to physically abused children are more likely to perceive the experience as intentional, uncontrollable, and undeserved (Kolko, Brown & Berliner, 2002). This view of abuse as victimization may at least in part explain why sexually abused children are more likely to have PTSD.

Depression, anxiety, and shame are also common outcomes in abused children (Berliner & Elliott, 2002; Kolko, 2002a; Fiering et al., 1998). These symptoms may result from the negative attributions often observed in abused children (Spacerelli, 1996; Brown & Kolko, 1999). In the effort to explain why they have been subject to abusive behavior, children may develop a view of themselves as responsible for or deserving of mistreatment and a perception of others as untrustworthy. Negative attributional style, and maladaptive abuse-related or abuse-specific beliefs are associated with increased levels of emotional distress in sexually and physically abused children (Kolko et al., 2002a).

ATTACHMENT STATUS

Maltreatment is associated with attachment status. Children are thought to develop secure or insecure patterns of attachment based on their early experiences with caretakers and these patterns are believed to contribute to internal working models of relationships that can extend to other relationships. Parents who are consistently responsive to children's efforts to seek closeness or comforting engender secure attachment, while parents who are inconsistent, rejecting, or a source of harm can produce insecure attachment styles in children. Insecure attachment may be manifested in anxious, angry, aloof, disoriented, or manipulative behavior with caretakers. Not surprisingly, abused children are more likely to be insecurely attached than non-abused children (Barnett et al., 1999; Crittendon & Ainsworth, 1989; Morton & Browne, 1998).

Insecure attachment may precede or be the result of abuse experiences. Parents who are inconsistent or rejecting may be at higher risk to commit abuse or to fail to protect children from abuse experiences. Insecure attachment may also place children at greater risk to be abused by both family and non-family members. Physically abused children, for example, may behave in ways that elicit rejecting or inconsistent response that over time may erode secure attachment. Alexander (1992) has proposed a relationship between insecure attachment and sexual abuse in which children who have anxious ambivalent attachment styles may accept abusive behavior while avoidant children who are indiscriminate in their relationships with adults become vulnerable to exploitation by extrafamilial offenders. There is some evidence that sexually abused children suffer from disruptions in attachment behavior (Toth & Cicchetti, 1996).

Disturbed relating within primary caretaker relationships may set the stage for impaired social adjustment. Abused children, especially physically abused children, often, but not always, have poorer peer relationships compared to non-abused children (Bolger et al., 1999; Fantuzzo et al., 1998; Kinard & Milling, 1999). They may lack the requisite social skills to develop the peer relationships that are an important ingredient of normal developmental growth. In some cases abused children are withdrawn and have few peer interactions and in other cases they relate in aggressive, controlling, or incompetent ways.

FAMILY CONTEXT

Parental deficits and disorders often characterize families in which child maltreatment occurs. Both abusive and non-offending parents in families where there has been child abuse are frequently depressed, have substance abuse disorders, or have anti-social personality characteristics (e.g., Kolko, 1996; Wolfe, 1999). These conditions are implicated in abusive behavior and the failure to protect children from abuse experiences; they are also factors that increase the risk for recidivism. Domestic violence is common in these families and contributes to the risk for child abuse as well as interfering with the non-offending parent's ability to protect the children (Bowen, 2000; Edleson, 1999). In addition, these characteristics compromise the capacity of non-offending parents to respond supportively to their maltreated children after abuse is reported and intervention undertaken.

Some of abused children's emotional and behavioral problems are likely the result of living in a violent environment or with parents who are troubled, as opposed to direct consequences of abuse experiences *per se*. For example, Friedrich and Luecke (1988) compared sexually abused boys to sexually aggressive boys and found that while most of the sexually aggressive boys had been sexually abused as well, their parents were more likely to have mental health problems and criminal histories. The aggressive behavior often noted in physically abused children might constitute learned responses to coercive family environments.

TREATMENT CONSIDERATIONS

Abused children will usually have some emotional or behavioral problems as a result of their experiences or their family environment. The nature and severity of disturbance, however, will vary substantially. In some cases children will not exhibit any clinically significant distress. For example, in a review of clinical studies of sexually abused children, up to 40% of children, depending on the outcome, were apparently asymptomatic (Kendall-Tackett et al., 1993). These data do not prove that the children will never develop problems but they do argue for the importance of individualized assessment to determine the proper treatment focus for a particular child. A one-size fits all approach will lead to too much, too little, or the wrong type of intervention for many children.

ASSESSMENT

Systematic assessment prior to initiating treatment with children is a general principle that is widely viewed as the essential starting point for any type of therapy (Kazdin, 1993). The results of evaluations are used to match interventions to problems so that the impact of treatment is maximized. The era of generic therapy is long past now that there are treatments that have been found effective in scientifically rigorous studies for a variety of specific conditions and disorders in children (Weisz et al., 1995; Kazdin & Weisz, 1998). Many non-abuse focused proven treatments have application to abused children either as adaptations to abuse situations or when abuse-focused therapy does not produce improvement. Assessment should not only provide the basis for the treatment plan, but reassessment should occur at regular intervals to monitor responses to intervention (Kazdin, 1993).

Assessment of abused children should be abuse informed, although not exclusively abuse focused. This means that one component involves specific attention to determining the direct effects of the abusive events. Screening for posttrauma symptoms requires that the experience be explicitly acknowledged so that re-experiencing and avoidance symptoms can be elicited. Numbing and arousal symptoms may not be identified without specific inquiry. Similarly, the assessment should address whether abuse-specific (e.g., self-blame, guilt) and abuse-related (e.g., stigmatization attributions) are present since they may be important treatment targets.

There are standardized ways to assess posttrauma symptoms including structured diagnostic interviews for PTSD or the use of trauma specific symptom checklists. The Trauma Symptom Checklist for Children (Briere, 1996) and the Child

Sexual Behavior Inventory (Friedrich, 1998) are simple to use, have clinical norms established and are commercially available. A variety of other instruments have been used in research studies, mostly with sexually abused children to assess symptoms and attributions. Unfortunately there are no well-established measures of abuse perceptions and cognitive distortions with clinical application. At this time, practitioners must rely on clinical interviews to determine whether children have maladaptive beliefs about their experiences.

In addition to the abuse focus, children should be evaluated for the presence of emotional and behavioral problems that may or may not be the direct result of the abuse experience, but nonetheless impair functioning. Diagnostic interviews and standardized behavior checklists can be useful; at minimum evaluators should screen for the presence of depression, anxiety, and disruptive behavior disorders. Another approach is to assess for functional impairment or the degree to which children are having difficulties in role functioning at home, school, and in the community, and in their behavior with others. A useful standardized instrument in the Child and Adolescent Functional Impairment Scale (Hodges, 1997).

Assessment of attachment style in the clinical setting is generally based on the reports of children and parents, as well as observations of parent–child interactions because there are no standardized instruments designed for clinicians. There are a number of ways to make crude classifications. For example, one way to think about attachment style is children's valuations of self and others, with secure children evincing positive views of self and others, while insecure children tend to have either negative perceptions of themselves, others, or both. Parental responses to children can also be evaluated in terms of the degree to which they are responsive versus inconsistent, distant, or a source of danger. Classifying children into one of the attachment styles may be less important clinically than assessing the nature and quality of parent–child relationships more generally to identify problematic relationships that will need to be a treatment focus.

Screening for parental disorders or family characteristics that have important impacts on children's adjustment and parental capacity to cooperate with treatment is essential. For example, a priority should be placed on stopping or reducing violence between parents and toward children. This is especially relevant for physically abused children who will most often remain in the home with the parent who has abused them. Unfortunately, there is evidence that some violent behavior to children continues even when treatment is ongoing (Kolko, 1996a). However, treatment for the traumatic impact of abuse experiences is not only unlikely to be effective when violence continues, it might be iatrogenic. For example, it is adaptive for children to be hypervigilant when there is still danger present in the environment. Obviously aggressive behavior in children cannot be eliminated when aggression is modeled in the household.

Parental depression and substance abuse are specific disorders that when present will substantially undermine parents' ability to provide assistance to their children in the aftermath of abuse. Fortunately, especially in the case of depression, there are effective treatments available. Therapists treating abused children should refer parents to appropriate programs or be able to provide the services as part of treatment planning. Explaining the ways that these conditions interfere with helping children recover may be a helpful strategy to overcome parental resistance to a focus on their problems since most non-offending parents and some offending parents do have concern for their children's welfare.

Parental response to the abuse situation is also relevant. Level of parental support and their distress regarding abuse of the child in sexual abuse cases has been shown to be an important determinant of children's emotional and behavioral problems (Cohen & Mannarino, 1997). Therefore, the impact on the parent of learning about and coping with results of child maltreatment is important to address. The issue of acknowledgement and support has received less attention in cases of physical abuse, although presumably at the least a commitment to desist from physical abuse would be important to assess. Finally, there may be system interventions including investigations, legal proceedings, child placement, and disruption in living situations and arrangements that are a source of stress for the parents.

TREATMENT PLANS

The result of the assessment process should be an individualized treatment plan in which interventions are matched to identified problems or needs. There are many treatments now available that have been used with maltreated children and their families (Saunders et al., 2001).

TREATING THE TRAUMA

There is a large body of literature describing trauma-specific interventions for abused children (e.g., Cohen et al., 2000; Deblinger & Heflin, 1996; Friedrich, 1990; Saunders & Meinig, in press, National Crime Victims Research & Treatment Center, 2001). Some approaches have been subject to empirical investigation and have been proven effective (AACAP, 1998). At this time, abuse-focused cognitive behavioral (CBT) treatments should be considered first line for PTSD and other posttrauma effects in sexually abused children because there is substantial scientific support for their effectiveness. Abuse-informed CBT for physically abused children and their abusive parents has also been found effective, as has an abuse informed family systems approach (Kolko, 1996b).

Abuse-specific CBT is based on the principles of cognitive behavioral therapy (e.g., Brewin, 1996). The abuse experience produces intense and sometimes overwhelming negative emotions that are associated with memories or reminders of the events. Avoidance coping serves to reduce these affects, but may in some cases become maladaptive. Thoughts and perceptions about the abuse experience may be inaccurate or distorted. Treatment interventions should therefore address the source of the negative emotions and maladaptive attributions in order to reduce symptoms, decrease risk for problems in the future, and restore functioning. The components of abuse-specific treatment include standard cognitive-behavioral interventions: exposure, anxiety management, and correction of cognitive distortions.

Exposure refers to directly confronting the memories of the traumatic event in therapy. Gradual exposure is generally recommended with abused children as opposed to flooding or prolonged exposure (Deblinger & Heflin, 1996). Children are encouraged and supported in talking about, drawing, or playing out the experience as a means of deconditioning or reducing the intensity of negative emotional associations. They also learn to identify the cues that tend to evoke emotional abuse-related reactions. It is not yet established, however, how much exposure is necessary or that all children require systematic exposure treatment to decrease posttrauma symptoms. If children do not exhibit PTSD symptoms that are interfering with functioning, the extant evidence does not support a treatment regimen that insists that children repeatedly talk about the event.

Anxiety management training entails the teaching of a variety of relaxation and coping strategies (Cohen et al, 2000; Deblinger & Heflin, 1996). Deep muscle relaxation and controlled breathing address the physical sensations that mark states of nervousness or anxiety. Thought stopping, guided imagery, and reassuring self-statements are cognitive components designed to interrupt, replace, or counter excessive or irrational thoughts about danger. These skills may be applied to abuse related emotional reactions, worries, or apprehensions. They are also useful in dealing with everyday stressors and can serve to increase children's general competence.

Addressing cognitive distortions about abuse experiences begins with eliciting children's beliefs about why it happened, their role in the events, and their abuse-related perceptions of self, others, and the world. In some cases children are already accurate in their views about the abuse. For example, although some sexually abused children blame themselves, most hold offenders responsible (Hunter et al., 1992). In other cases psychoeducation about the nature of abuse, that it is wrong and harmful, that the offender is responsible legally and morally for the acts, will be sufficient clarification. Many children, however, will have distorted views that may exacerbate their distress and should be targets of intervention.

Recent investigations suggest that the relationship of cognitions to outcomes is complex and some degree of mixed perceptions may actually be accurate and are associated with better outcomes (Kolko et al., 2002a). For example, physically abused children are more likely to believe they had a part in causing the abusive events, which may be true, if the abuse occurred in the context of child misbehavior. One approach is to help children distinguish between their behaviors that may have contributed to the occurrence of sexual abuse (e.g., curiosity about sex, not reporting) or physical abuse (e.g., defiance and noncompliance) and the moral and legal responsibility for engaging in maltreatment. Abuse is likely to alter certain assumptions about others because a person who should be a source of security has committed abuse or has failed to protect; children have learned the hard way that all caretakers or adults are not safe. It is, however, a maladaptive over-accommodation to develop mistrust for all adults. Treatment can assist children in identifying risk factors and precursors that will enable them to make better judgments about others.

It is generally agreed that parents should be involved in some capacity in trauma-focused children's treatment. The way this is usually accomplished varies by type of abuse. In sexual abuse cases, non-offending parents often participate in therapy along with their children who are in treatment for the trauma impact. Therapy typically consists of parallel components to the children's trauma treatment including psychoeducation about abuse, exposure, anxiety management, and cognitive correction (Deblinger & Helfin, 1996). In addition, parental distress about their children's victimization is addressed. Many parents, especially those with their own history of abuse, are very upset to learn that they have not been able to protect their children from abuse or were not seen as a resource. Since this distress is associated with the level of children's emotional reactions, helping the parents is a necessary ingredient in children's recovery. Physically abused children are not ordinarily referred for trauma-focused treatment, but rather usually enter treatment as the result of behavior problems (Kolko, 2002a). Parental involvement may occur in this context but the emphasis is on parenting practices not on the parents understanding the impact of abuse experiences on their children or providing supportive responses.

One particularly difficult aspect of dealing with the impact of intrafamilial abuse is helping children come to some resolution with regard to the offender. In nonfamily cases, children will seldom have any continuing relationship with offenders so the issue is rarely salient. On the other hand, in most physical abuse situations children will not even be separated from offenders and in some incest situations children will live again with offenders. At minimum almost all of the children will be connected to offenders through biological ties or family relationships. Interestingly virtually no research exists that has explored how children resolve the competing views of parents or other family members as sources of danger and at the same time as attachment figures or significant relationships in children's lives. Considering the cognitive and emotional complexity of this task, it is not surprising that children will have difficulty simultaneously maintaining both of these conceptualizations but instead will adopt one over the other. The dependant status of children, their needs for family connections, and the potential pressures from other family members who have not suffered the victimization experience, will tend to result in forces favoring the resolution of the conflict in attributions that diminish the severity, intentionally, and wrongness of the abusive behavior.

Therapists may also be influenced in terms of how they address the clinical issue of helping children deal with feelings and beliefs about their offenders. There is a risk that they will encourage children to adopt their own views instead of carefully eliciting children's true feelings and perceptions and assisting children in tolerating competing emotions as well as developing a realistic view of their parents. It is especially important that therapists be fully aware of their own biases, that they create a treatment environment that promotes children's comfort in talking about this topic, and that they neither minimize nor exaggerate the nature of the abusive behavior and the concomitant parental characteristics.

An approach that takes these considerations into account has been explicated by Saunders and Meinig (2000) with reference to sexual abuse. Therapists are encouraged to think in terms of resolution instead of reconciliation; the importance of the relationship is acknowledged but there is no predetermined goal of restoring familial relationships. The future degree and nature of child–offender contact and relationship depends on the individual circumstances. For example, a situation involving biological parent offenders who admit their crimes and participate in treatment would be expected to result in very different outcomes than step-parent or paramour offenders, or situations in which offenders deny the abuse. Family resolution in incest cases involves a process that includes clarification, establishing family rules and supervision for risk reduction, and a gradual increase in contact. This model supposes that the offender admits the abusive behavior and receives treatment.

Acknowledgement of the abuse is associated with better outcomes for sexually abused children (Morris et al., 1996). Clarification is the process in which offenders take responsibility. With the help of their therapists, they write letters or make videotapes in which they explain why they committed abuse and absolve the victim and other family members of blame. These initial efforts are usually used as a treatment device to identify and correct cognitive distortions or self-serving beliefs before they are transmitted to victims. Subsequently in-person sessions may take place. In addition to what offenders may communicate, children are given the opportunity to ask questions and make statements about the abuse, their feelings, or any concerns about the future that they may have.

It has not been common practice to expect physically abusive parents to formally and publicly take responsibility for committing abuse. In fact, Wolfe (1999) recommends against confronting parents in less serious abuse cases so that an alliance may be formed and to mitigate parental resistance or defensiveness. On the other hand, Kolko (1996b) has demonstrated the effectiveness of both CBT and family therapy that directly addresses the issue of maltreatment and clarifies that such behavior is not acceptable. However, this model does not explicitly contain a component in which parents apologize or elicit children's feelings about what happened.

Parent–Child Treatments

Kolko and Swenson (2002b) has described two empirically tested approaches to treatment of children and abusing parents, which directly acknowledge the abuse experience and focus on changing beliefs about violence and teaching non-coercive discipline methods. Both the cognitive behavioral and family systems approaches were found more effective than routine community services.

Abused children may develop troubling or problem behaviors that require specific parental responses to be modified. They can range from posttrauma symptoms such as being afraid to sleep alone or withdrawal from usual activities to sexual and aggressive behavior. Cognitive behavioral treatments for sexual abuse usually contain a component in which parents learn effective behavior management techniques (e.g., Deblinger & Helfin, 1996). Interventions for physical abuse often include interventions for parents that are designed to alter maladaptive or coercive parenting (Kolko & Swenson, 2002b; Wolfe, 1999; Wolfe and Wekerle, 1993). Similarly, treatment approaches for children with sexual behavior problems routinely target parents as well as children in order to impart knowledge about appropriate and inappropriate sexual behavior in children, enhance positive parenting skills, and increase supervision (Gil & Johnson, 1993).

There is ample evidence that behavioral parent training programs are effective in reducing noncompliance and disruptive behavior (Brestan & Eyberg, 1998). These interventions generally teach the principles of social learning, how to use positive reinforcement, give effective instructions, and how and when to use various forms of non-physical punishment. Modeling, practice, and feedback of skills is typically part of the approach. Another intervention that has proven value with oppositional children, Parent Child Interaction Training (PCIT), has been advocated for abuse situations (Urquiza & McNeil, 1996). The intervention in currently being tested in abuse cases with promising results. PCIT has two main targets: increasing positive parent–child interactions and teaching discipline strategies.

Parents are coached to interact in more constructive ways in an *in vivo* practice and feedback context with their children.

Importantly, these programs focus on enhancing the quality of parent–child relationships, not simply teaching better parenting approaches. One result of increased positive interactions is that children are less defiant and misbehavior decreases. In situations where there is an insecure attachment relationship between parents and children, this circumstance may afford an opportunity to promote more sensitive and consistent parental responses to their children in general. While it has not yet been proven that these types of interventions can change insecure to secure attachment styles in children, it is the only currently available approach.

Role of the Therapist

Therapists have a variety of roles to play in responding to maltreated children. They provide assessments that determine the nature and extent of abuse impact, identify other child and family disorders and conditions that may require intervention, and make recommendations about the need for and type of treatment (e.g., Saywitz et al., 2000). When therapy is indicated they deliver treatments matched to identified problems and needs. Enhancing parental capacity is always a central consideration and is achieved by including parents, addressing their distress, increasing awareness and empathy, increasing skills, and promoting positive interactions. In some cases, parents will be unavailable, unwilling, or incapable of being a primary resource for their children. In this case, therapists should actively search for alternative attachment figures in children's lives and incorporate them into treatment. Occasionally, therapists will themselves become important attachment figures and treatment will become the context within which children may develop new working models for relationships with others.

Treating abused children also requires that therapists be prepared to work collaboratively with child protection/child welfare and even criminal justice professionals. Depending on the individual case situation, there may be legal proceedings, out-of-home-placement, or trials. These events affect children's emotional and behavioral functioning. Therapists may need to attend case staffings, communicate with other professionals, make recommendations about children's safety or treatment needs, or prepare children for impending events. Care must be taken not to compromise the therapeutic relationship, but therapist participation and cooperation is sometimes necessary to affect the best outcome.

CONCLUSION

Abuse experiences are a major risk factor for maladjustment, but many children will not suffer long-term psychological harm. The treatment issues for children who have experienced trauma depend on the specific impact of the abuse, the presence of pre-existing or other conditions that impair functioning, and the family context and parental response. An individualized assessment and treatment plan that matches interventions to identified child and family problems and needs is the most likely to result in positive outcomes. Therapists who are knowledgeable about potential consequences of abuse, comfortable talking directly with children and parents about the abuse experiences, and familiar with proven interventions can apply the type and intensity of interventions that will be most helpful.

REFERENCES

AACAP (1998). Practice and parameters for the assessment and treatment of children and adolescents with posttraumatic stress disorder. *Journal of the American Academy of Child and Adolescent Psychiatry*, **37**, 4s–26s.

Alexander, P. C. (1992). Application of attachment theory to the study of sexual abuse. *Journal of Consulting and Clinical Psychology*, **60**, 185–195.

American Psychiatric Association (2000). *Diagnostic and Statistical Manual of Mental Disorders* (4th edition text revision ed.). Washington, DC: American Psychiatric Association.

Barnett, D., Ganiban, J., & Cicchetti, D. (1999). Maltreatment, negative expressivity, and the development of Type D attachments from 12 to 24 months of age. *Monographs of the Society for Research in Child Development*, **64**, 97–118.

Berliner, L., & Elliott, D. M. (2002). Sexual abuse of children. In J. E. B. Myers, L. Berliner, J. Briere, C. T. Hendrix, C. Jenny & T. A. Reid (Eds.), *The APSAC handbook on child maltreatment* (pp. 55–78). Thousand Oaks: Sage.

Bolger, K. E., Patterson, C. J., & Kupersmidt, J. B. (1999). Peer relationships and self-esteem among children who have been maltreated. *Child Development*, **69**, 1171–1197.

Bowen, K. (2000). Child abuse and domestic violence in families of children seen for suspected sexual abuse. *Clinical Pediatrics*, **39**, 33–40.

Brestan, E., Eyeberg, S. (1998). Effective psychosocial treatments of conduct disordered children and adolescents: 29 years, 82 studies, and 5,272 kids. *Journal of Clinical Child Psychology*, 180–189.

Brewin, C. R. (1996). Theoretical foundations of cognitive-behavioral therapy for anxiety and depression. *Annual Review of Psychology*, **47**, 33–57.

Briere, J. N. (1996). *Trauma Symptom Checklist for Children (TSCC)*. Psychological Assessment Resources (PAR), Odessa, Florida.

Brown, E. J., & Kolko, D. J. (1999). Child victims' attributions about being physically abused: An examination of factors associated with symptom severity. *Journal of Abnormal Child Psychology*, **27**, 311–322.

Carlson, E. B., & Dalenberg, C. J. (2000). A conceptual framework for the impact of traumatic experiences. *Trauma Violence and Abuse*, **1**, 4–28.

Cicchetti, D., & Toth, S. L. (1995). A developmental psychopathology perspective on child abuse and neglect. *Journal of the American Academy of Child and Adolescent Psychiatry*, **34**, 541–565.

Cicchetti, D., & Toth, S. L. (1995). A developmental psychopathology perspective on the child abuse and neglect. *Journal of the American Academy of Child and Adolescent Psychiatry*, **34**, 541–565.

Cohen, J. A., & Mannarino, A. P. (1993). A treatment model for sexually abused preschoolers. *Journal of Interpersonal Violence*, **8**, 115–131.

Cohen, J. A., & Mannarino, A. P. (1996). Factors that mediate treatment outcome of sexually abused preschool children. *Child and Adolescent Pschiatry*, **34**, 1402–1410.

Cohen, J. A., & Mannarino, A. P. (1998). Factors that mediate treatment outcome of sexually abused preschool children: six-and 12-month follow-up. *Journal of the American Academy of Child and Adolescent Psychiatry*, **37**, 44–51.

Cohen, J. A., Berliner, L., & Mannarino, A. P. (2000). Treating traumatized children: A research review and synthesis. *Trauma, Violence, and Abuse*, **1**, 29–46.

Cohen, J. A., Mannarino, A. P., Berliner, L., & Deblinger, E. (2000). Trauma-focused cognitive behavioral therapy for children and adolescents: An empirical update. *Journal of Interpersonal Violence*, **15**, 1202–1223.

Crittenden, P., & Ainsworth, M. D. S. (1989). Child maltreatment and attachment theory. In Cicchetti & V. Carison (Eds.), *Child Maltreatment* (pp. 377–431). New York: Cambridge University Press.

Deblinger, E., & Heflin, A. H. (1996). *Cognitive behavioral interventions for treating sexually abused children*. Thousand Oaks, CA: Sage Publications.

Edleson, J. L. (1999). The overlap between child maltreatment and woman battering. *Violence Against Women*, **5**, 134–154.

Fantuzzo, J. W., Weiss, A. D., Atkins, M., Meyers, R., & Noone, M. (1998). A contextually relevant assessment of the impact of child maltreatment on the social competencies of low-income urban children. *Journal of the American Academy of Child and Adolescent Psychiatry*, **37**, 1201–1208.

Feiring, C., Taska, L., & Lewis, M. (1998). A process model for understanding adaptation to sexual abuse: The role of shame in defining stigmatization. *Child Abuse & Neglect*, **20**, 767–782.

Finzi, R., Cohen, O., Sapir, Y., & Weizman, A. (2000). Attachment styles in maltreated children: A comparative study. *Child Psychiatry and Human Development*, **31**, 113–128.

Friedich, W. N. (1998). *Child Sexual Behavior inventory: Professional Manual*. Odessa: Psychological Assessment Resources Inc.

Friedrich, W. N., & Luecke, W. J. (1988). Young school-age sexually aggressive children. *Professional Psychology: Research & Practice*, **19**, 155–164.

Friedrich, W. N. (1990). *Psychotherapy of sexually abused children and their families*. New York: Norton.

Gil, E., & Johnson, T. C. (1993). *Sexualized Children: Assessment & Treatment of Sexualized Children & Children Who Molest*. Rockville, MD: Launch Press.

Guidelines for the Psychosocial Treatment of Intrafamilial Child Physical and Sexual abuse. www.musc.edu/cvc.

Hodges, K. (1997). Child and Adolescent Functional Assessment Scale. In Functional Assessment Systems Ann Arbor, MI.

Hunter, J., Goodwin, D. W., & Wilson, R. J. (1992). Attributions of blame in child sexual abuse victims: An analysis of age and gender influences. *Journal of Child Sexual Abuse*, **1**, 75–90.

Kazdin, A. E. (1993). Evaluation in clinical practice: Clinically sensitive and systematic methods of treatment delivery. *Behavior Therapy*, **24**, 11–45.

Kazdin, A. E., & Weiss, J. R. (1998). Identifying and developing empirically supported child and adolescent treatments. *Journal of Consulting and Clinical Psychology*, **66**, 19–36.

Kendall-Tackett, K. A., Williams, L. M., & Finkelhor, D. (1993). Impact of sexual abuse on children: A review and synthesis of recent empirical studies. *Psychological Bulletin*, **113**, 164–180.

Kinard, E. M. (1999). Perceived social skills and social competence in maltreated children. *American Journal of Orthopsychiatry*, **69**, 465–481.

Kolko, D. J. (1996a). Clinical monitoring of treatment course in child physical abuse: Psychometric characteristics and treatment comparisons. *Child Abuse & Neglect*, **20**, 23–43.

Kolko, D. J. (1996b). Individual cognitive-behavioral treatment & family therapy for physically abused children & their offending parents: A comparison of clinical outcomes. *Child Maltreatment*, **1**, 322–342.

Kolko, D. J. (2002a). Child physical abuse. J. E. B. Myers, L. Berliner, J. Briere, C. T. Hendrix, C. Jenny., & T. A. Reid (Eds.). *The APSAC Handbook on Child Maltreatment* (pp. 24–54). Thousand OAKS, CA: Sage.

Kolko, D. J. & Swenson, C. C. (2002b). Assessing and Treating Physically abused Children and their Families: *A Cognitive-behavioral approach*. Thousand Oaks, CA: Sage.

McCloskey, L. A., & Walker, M. (2000). Posttraumatic stress in children exposed to family violence and single even trauma. *Journal of the American Academy of Child and Adolescent Psychiatry*, **39**, 108–115.

McLeer, S. V., Dixon, J. F., Henry, D., Ruggiero, K., & Escovitz, K. (1998). Psychopathology in non-clinically referred sexually abused children. *Journal of the American Academy of Child and Adolescent Psychiatry*, **37**, 1326–1333.

Meinig, M., & Bonner, B. L. (1990). Interfamilial sexual abuse: A structured approach to family intervention. *Violence Update*, 1–11.

Morris, T. L., Lipovsky, J. A., & Saunders, B. E. (1996). The role of perpetrator acknowledgement in mediating the impact of child sexual assault: An exploratory study. *Journal of Child Sexual Abuse, 5*, 95–102.

Saigh, P. A., Yasik, A. E., Sack, W. H., & Koplewicz, H. S. (1998). Child adolescent posttraumatic stress disorder: Prevalence, risk factors, and comorbidity. In P. Saigh & J. D. Bremner (Eds.), *Posttraumatic stress disorder: A comprehensive text* (pp. 18–43). Needham Heights, MA: Allyn and Bacon, Inc.

Saunders, B., Meinig, M. (2001). National Crime Victims Research & Treatment Center: Harbor view Center for Sexual Assault and Traumatic Stress (2001).

Saunders, B. E., & Meinig, M. B. (in press). Immediate issues affecting long term family resolution in cases of parent-child sexual abuse. In R. Reece (ed.), *The Treatment of Child Abuse*. Baltimore: The Johns Hopkins University Press.

Saywitz, K. J., Mannarino, A. P., Berliner, L., & Cohen, J. A. (2000). Treatment of sexually abused children and adolescents. *American Psychologist, 55*, 1040–1049.

Scheeringa, M. S., Zeanah, C. H., Drell, M. J., & Larrieu, J. A. (1995). Two approaches to the diagnosis of posttraumatic stress disorder in infancy and early childhood. *Journal of the American Academy of Child and Adolescent Psychiatry, 34*, 191–200.

Spaccarelli, S. (1995). Measuring abuse, stress and negative cognitive appraisals in child sexual abuse: Validity data on two new scales. *Journal of Abnormal Child Psychology, 23*, 703–727.

Spaccarelli, S., & Fuchs, C. (1997). Variability in symptom expression among sexually abused girls: Developing multivariate models. *Journal of Clinical Child Psychology, 26*, 34–35.

Toth, S. L., & Cicchetti, D. (1996). Patterns of relatedness, depressive symptomatology, and perceived competence in maltreated children. *Journal of Consulting and Clinical Psychology, 64*, 32–41.

Urquiza, A. J., & McNeil, C. B. (1996). Parent-child interaction therapy: An intensive dyadic intervention for physically abusive families. *Child Maltreatment, 1*, 134–144.

Wolfe, D. (1999). *Child abuse: Implications for child development and psychopathology.* Thousand Oaks, CA: Sage Publications.

Wolfe, D. A., & Wekerle, C. (1993). Treatment strategies for child physical abuse and neglect: A critical progress report. *Clinical Psychology Review, 13*, 473–500.

13

CONTINUITIES AND DISCONTINUITIES IN THE INTERGENERATIONAL TRANSMISSION OF CHILD MALTREATMENT: IMPLICATIONS FOR BREAKING THE CYCLE OF ABUSE

Byron Egeland
Michelle Bosquet
Alissa Levy Chung
University of Minnesota, USA

INTRODUCTION

Parents' own experience of abuse has long been hypothesized as a cause of abuse in the next generation. Evidence for the intergenerational hypothesis primarily comes from retrospective studies. This approach involves asking parents who have been identified as abusing their children to recall how they were raised. Results from retrospective studies indicate that a large majority of abusing parents were abused as children. In their classic study conducted shortly after Dr. C. Henry Kempe and colleagues (1962) identified the "battered child syndrome," Steele and Pollack (1968) found that all 60 abusing parents in their retrospective study were abused as children. However, Kaufman and Zigler (1987) critically reviewed the literature on the intergenerational cycle of abuse and concluded that serious methodological problems are inherent in the case study of abusing parents and that findings from

Early Prediction and Prevention of Child Abuse: A Handbook.
Edited by Kevin Browne, Helga Hanks, Peter Stratton and Catherine Hamilton. © 2002 John Wiley & Sons, Ltd.

retrospective investigations cannot be considered conclusive evidence in support of the intergenerational hypothesis.

Kaufman and Zigler (1987) have argued that the rate of transmission of maltreatment can only be determined through prospective studies in which a sample of individuals who were abused as children is followed and the care they provide for their children is assessed across time. They identified three prospective investigations (Hunter & Kilstrom, 1979; Egeland, Jacobvitz & Papatola, 1987; Straus, 1979) and from the findings estimated that approximately 30% of abused children are likely to become abusing parents. However, determining the true rate of transmission of maltreatment across generations on the basis of the findings of only three prospective investigations may be problematic.

We believe that the rates of transmission of 18% found in both the Straus (1979) and Hunter and Kilstrom (1979) studies are underestimates due to the nature of the samples and length of time the children were followed. For example, Straus included only two-parent families in his sample and restricted the history of abuse to adolescence (that is, parents who indicated that they were physically punished or abused in adolescence). However, abuse (with the exception of sexual abuse) is less likely to occur during adolescence than during other periods of development. Hunter and Kilstrom followed their sample from birth to only one year of age. Had they followed their children through at least age six, they likely would have found more cases of maltreatment and, consequently, a higher rate of transmission.

Using data from the Parent–Child Project, a longitudinal study of high-risk children and their families, we examined the rate of maltreatment across generations and attempted to identify factors associated with continuity and discontinuity in the cycle of maltreatment (Egeland et al., 1987). Detailed and comprehensive assessments of parent and child outcomes and of factors influencing these outcomes were conducted at regular intervals starting before the children's birth and continuing through their early adulthood. Using multiple sources of information, we identified 44 mothers who maltreated their children in the first two years of the children's lives. The 44 cases included instances of physical abuse, physical neglect, and emotional neglect by "psychologically unavailable" parents. Psychologically unavailable parents were emotionally unresponsive to their children, appearing detached and uninvolved. Independent of the identification of mothers who were maltreating their children, we determined the quality of parenting the mothers had received. On the basis of their responses, we found that 47 mothers had been neglected and/or sexually and/or physically abused as children.

As reported in an earlier publication (Egeland, 1988), our data support the hypothesis of intergenerational continuity of abuse. Of the 47 mothers who were abused as children, 16 (34%) maltreated their children, and 3 (6%) were in the "other problem" group, which consisted of mothers who gave up or lost custody of their children. Thus, 40% of the mothers who were abused as children were found to be maltreating their children. This rate underestimates the degree of continuity because maltreatment in the second generation was based upon parent and child data collected between birth and age two. As we have followed this sample over the years, we have identified additional cases of maltreatment. Including individuals who were maltreated between ages two and six increased the rate of transmission to 45%. Evidence for the intergenerational hypothesis was stronger when maltreatment was placed on a continuum, such as including cases of harsh physical punishment that did not meet the criteria for child protection intervention. With these extended criteria, 70% of parents who reported a history of abuse were having significant parenting problems. However, when estimating the rate of transmission based on the findings from the three prospective investigations, Kaufman and Zigler (1987) used the 40% rate reported in our 1987 article. Therefore, their estimate of a 30% rate may be low. On the other hand, the 70% rate is most likely an overestimate, reflecting the continuity of "poor quality parenting," not just abuse, across generations. The debate regarding the validity of the intergenerational hypothesis and the rate of transmission continues (Browne & Herbert, 1997).

In their 1987 review, Kaufman and Zigler recommended that further prospective study of the intergenerational hypothesis is needed. We are not aware of any longitudinal prospective investigations of caregiving practices of adults who were abused as children. In the past decade there have been a number of investigations (both retrospective and prospective) that have examined a variety of other parenting dimensions across generations, but surprisingly none of the recent studies have looked at maltreatment. There is evidence for the continuity of parental control and discipline across generations, including discipline strategies and behavior standards (Covell et al., 1995), harsh parenting (Simons et al., 1991), and "negative" parenting, including negative affect and authoritarian style (Chase-Lansdale et al., 1994). There is also evidence supporting continuity in the quality of parent–child attachment across generations (e.g., Fonagy et al., 1991; Benoit & Parker, 1994).

As continuity of certain aspects of parenting has been demonstrated, there has been an increasing effort to account for transmission across generations. The need to identify the mechanisms and environmental contexts that account for continuity has both theoretical as well as practical implications. In the area of child maltreatment, understanding the process would hopefully lead to interventions and preventions that result in breaking the cycle. Models have been proposed for explaining the complex causes of maltreatment (Belsky, 1993; Cicchetti & Lynch, 1993; Putallaz et al., 1998). Similar models need to be developed to explain the intergenerational transmission of maltreatment. Such models should be able to explain both continuity as well as discontinuity because all studies, particularly the prospective investigations, show a considerable degree of change in addition to the continuities. Discontinuity across generations should be explainable by the same kind of processes involved in continuities. In the remainder of this chapter we will propose possible processes responsible for continuity and discontinuity of maltreatment across generations.

CONTINUITY OF CHILD MALTREATMENT ACROSS GENERATIONS

Several mechanisms/models have been proposed to explain intergenerational continuity of child abuse, including social learning theory, attachment theory/inner working models, developmental psychopathology, genetic/biological factors, attribution theory, personality theory, and ecological models (Belsky, 1993; Caliso & Milner, 1992; Putallaz et al., 1998; Simons et al., 1991). These mechanisms/models are not mutually exclusive; we discuss each where applicable, with particular emphasis on the principles of developmental psychopathology and attachment theory within an ecological framework.

According to Cicchetti and Lynch's (1993) ecological model of the etiology of child abuse, risk (potentiating) and protective (compensatory) factors for abuse can exist at four levels of analysis: (1) ontogenic development—factors within the individual that influence the achievement of competence and adaptation; (2) microsystem—the family environment; (3) exosystem—formal and informal social structures that influence the individual's microsystem; and (4) macrosystem—the cultural values and beliefs within families and communities. These factors are thought to interact with each other within and across levels. Abuse is hypothesized to occur when risk factors outweigh protective ones (Cicchetti & Lynch, 1993). Here, we apply this model to the study of the intergenerational transmission of abuse, to understand why some parents with childhood histories of abuse maltreat their own children.

Ontogenic Development

Researchers have suggested factors at each level that may increase the probability that a parent with a childhood history of abuse will abuse her child. Much of the research and theorizing at the ontogenic level attributes intergenerational transmission of abuse to one of the following: (1) parent personality/psychopathology; (2) genetic/biological factors; (3) parental developmental history, including inner working models and history of adaptation; and (4) parental attributions/expectations.

PARENT PERSONALITY/PSYCHOPATHOLOGY

Research has not found a consistent pattern of personality attributes or psychopathology profiles that characterize parents who abuse their children (Eth, 1996). However, data suggest that, compared to controls, (physical) abusers are more immature, demanding, rigid, self-centered, angry, irritable, depressed, hyperreactive to negative stimuli, and fearful of external threat and control and less empathic and sensitive (Baumrind, 1995; Caliso & Milner, 1992; Eth, 1996; Putallaz et al., 1998; Zeanah & Zeanah, 1989). Abusive parents also appear to have poor impulse control, low self-esteem, and low ego strength and to have difficulty role taking and tolerating ambiguity (Baumrind, 1995; Belsky, 1993). These characteristics may increase the parents' risk for abuse by impeding their ability to monitor and be sensitive to their children's needs and by increasing the probability that they will react impulsively and negatively to the demands of their children. Some researchers have suggested that this irritable, explosive, harsh parenting style may train children to develop an aggressive interpersonal style with others, including their own children (Simons et al., 1991). Simons et al. found only weak support for the hypothesis that harsh parenting fosters a personality that is prone to the use of aggression, including abusive parenting practices. However, Patterson et al. (1989) found that explosive and irritable parenting was associated with an aggressive interpersonal style in children. Elder and colleagues' (Caspi & Elder, 1988; Elder et al., 1986) data suggest that explosive personalities are transmitted across generations via hostile parenting practices.

GENETIC/BIOLOGICAL FACTORS

A few researchers have suggested that genetic/biological factors may be involved in the intergenerational transmission of child abuse (DiLalla & Gottesman, 1991). For example, some of the characteristics noted in abusers, such as depression, have been found to be heritable (Belsky, 1993). Therefore, abuse may be transmitted across generations via inherited personality characteristics that decrease the parent's ability to parent sensitively and increase the parent's propensity toward poor impulse control and violence. Additionally, there is some speculation that children with difficult temperaments may be at increased risk for abuse (Putallaz et al., 1998). Children may inherit temperamental characteristics that make them more difficult to parent and therefore at heightened risk for abuse, particularly among parents who are at risk for abusing because of their own personality traits.

PARENTAL DEVELOPMENTAL HISTORY

Studying the effects that maltreatment has on individual development and adaptation may help us understand how a history of abuse can place an individual at risk for maltreating her own children. Cicchetti and Lynch (1993) described the importance of considering an individual's developmental history in order to understand her current functioning. According to Cicchetti and Lynch, maltreating parents frequently do not promote the child's successful adaptation of the major developmental tasks of childhood, including the formation of a secure attachment, the development of emotion regulatory abilities, the development of an autonomous self, the development of effective interpersonal relations, including peer relations, and the achievement of school/work competence. Failure at each of these tasks increases the risk for failure at subsequent developmental tasks and maladaptation at later points in development. Therefore, individuals with a history of childhood abuse are at risk for entering parenthood without having developed the skills necessary for creating and maintaining healthy relationships with others, including their own children. Lacking these skills, these parents may be at risk for maltreating their own children, continuing the cycle of abuse.

Researchers have focused significant attention on studying the quality of attachment in maltreating parent–child dyads and the influence of this relationship on the child's subsequent development. According to attachment theory, human beings have a tendency to develop strong affectional bonds to a few others in the environment (Bowlby, 1977; Sroufe, 1996). Bowlby (1969) suggested that these bonds act as a behavioral control system that allows the child to maintain an "environmental homeostasis" via behaviors that balance environmental exploration with attaining and/or maintaining caregiver proximity. The child is thought to develop "inner working models"—mental representations of the self and others—that reflect the quality of her repeated interactions with her primary attachment figures. These inner working models are thought to guide the child's behavior within these relationships. As new experiences tend to be integrated in a way consistent with prevailing, existing schemes, these models may also guide behavior in future relationships.

The child's primary attachment figure(s) has a crucial role in determining the quality of the attachment relationship. In a well-functioning attachment system, the caregiver is sensitive to the child's need for contact and comfort as well as environmental exploration and offers support that promotes the child's self emotional regulation (Sroufe, 1996). However, research suggests that, in the large majority of maltreating parent–child dyads, the quality of the attachment relationship is poor and promotes developmental maladaptation (Morton & Browne, 1998). Three different types of insecure attachment have been identified in the literature (Sroufe, 1996). The anxious/avoidant child has experienced chronic rebuffing by the caregiver during times of stress. The anxious/resistant child often has a history of inconsistent care. The disorganized/disoriented child may have a history marked by frightening or frightened caregiving behavior. All three types of insecure attachment have been found at increased rates among maltreated samples, particularly disorganized attachment (Cicchetti & Lynch, 1993; Morton & Browne, 1998).

Research has repeatedly demonstrated that an insecure attachment history is a risk factor for maladaptation in several areas of development. According to attachment theory, one of the mechanisms via which insecure attachment effects maladaptation is the inner working model, which reflects early caregiver–child interactions and guides future behavior. Though insecure children's inner working models may accurately reflect their attachment histories and lead them to behave in ways that are adaptive within those early relationships, these models are not adaptive for developing later positive relationships with other adults and peers, and may in fact lead to recreating negative relationships. Without corrective relationship experiences that may change their expectations and teach them interpersonal skills, these representations become further entrenched, and children may be at risk for developing maladaptive relationships into adulthood and parenthood.

Consistent with this model, DeLozier (1982) found that, compared to a control group, abusive mothers reported childhoods marked by more severe threats of abandonment and harm, role reversal, and uncertainty about caregivers' availability. DeLozier concluded that these mothers had not developed internal representations of others as available and reliable and that they consequently had difficulties as adults forming secure attachment relationships with others, including their own children.

Data also indicate that abused children are at risk for developing maladaptive approaches toward processing and regulating emotion. Helfer and Krugman (1997) noted that, early in development, abused children learn to cope with the pain in their environment by "muting" their senses. Eth (1996) related that some children employ defenses such as denial, psychic numbing, and dissociation; in extreme cases, some individuals may "forget" episodes of abuse or even portions of their childhood. Helfer and Krugman suggested that this approach toward managing painful stimuli becomes maladaptive when these individuals become parents, as responsive parenting requires parents' senses to be "open" and "aware." A number of other maladaptive patterns of emotion regulation may develop and interfere with the child's ability to establish positive, emotionally corrective relationships with others outside the home. Some abused children demonstrate excessive negativity, including unrelenting sadness and extreme rage (Cicchetti & Lynch, 1993; Eth, 1996). Some may become hypervigilant and suspicious to protect themselves from parental abuse. Data suggest that maltreated children also have difficulty processing and interpreting others' emotional displays (Cicchetti & Lynch, 1993).

Research suggests that the peer world supports many important issues of social and emotional development; peer relationships may be especially important for fostering positive adaptation in maltreated children because of their negative relationship histories (Cicchetti & Lynch, 1993). However, with histories of insecure attachment relationships and difficulties with emotion regulation, maltreated children are likely to have poor social relations with peers as well as adults. According to Helfer & Krugman (1997), maltreated children have been so consumed with trying to meet the needs of their parents, that they learn extreme, inappropriate, and maladaptive ways to meet their own needs. Research suggests that abused children over-attribute hostile intent to others and demonstrate high rates of aggressive, aversive, and avoidant behaviors and low levels of prosocial behaviors (Cicchetti & Lynch, 1993; Doumas et al., 1994; Eth, 1996). They also tend to respond to peers' distress with fear, withdrawal, threats, angry gestures, and a mix of comforting and angry behaviors (Putallaz et al., 1998). Such behaviors may lead the children's teachers and peers to label them "bad," confirming their internalization of their parents' feelings about them (Eth, 1996). Eth has suggested that abused children may confuse love with aggression and seek out physical contact at any cost, including harm to self and others. Children may find identifying with the aggressor a powerful antidote to feelings of victimization (Eth, 1996). Negative interactions with peers and teachers reinforce the lesson that maltreated children learned in their earliest attachment relationships: People hurt or disappoint, and asking others for help inevitably leads to pain (Helfer & Krugman, 1997). Consequently, these children may learn to isolate themselves, a pattern that could endure into adulthood.

Deficient in behavioral and emotional regulatory skills and lacking positive peer and teacher relationships, maltreated children are at heightened risk for school failure (Eth, 1996). Research indicates that abused children have worse grades and more discipline problems, are more dependent on teachers, score lower on tests of cognitive maturity, and are rated by parents and teachers as less ready to learn (Cicchetti & Lynch, 1993). Maltreated children may consequently be at increased risk for dropping out of school, putting them at risk for unemployment, substance abuse, delinquency, poverty, and teenage pregnancy (Eth, 1996).

Finally, from infancy through young adulthood, physical abuse disrupts and distorts maltreated children's development of a basic sense of self and maturation of autonomous ego functions (Eth, 1996). Data suggest that abusive parents discourage their children's autonomous development and that maltreated children have impaired self-esteem and self-concept and experience difficulty transitioning to autonomy in toddlerhood (Cicchetti & Lynch, 1993; Trickett & Susman, 1988). According to Helfer and Krugman (1997), maltreating parents expect their children to meet their emotional needs and fail to respond to their children's needs. Consequently, maltreated children do not learn that they have needs separate from their parents and that they are responsible for their own actions and not the actions of others. As parents, maltreated individuals are thus ill-prepared to see their infants as separate from themselves with needs of their own. They also may have difficulty acknowledging responsibility for their own abusive behaviors. At another level, maltreated children are taught that feelings and actions are the same, leading them to feel that they have little, if any, control over their lives (Helfer & Krugman, 1997). In later development, abused individuals are at risk for premature closure of identity formation in adolescence, desperate to enter adulthood (Eth, 1996). Such adolescents may believe they can assert their independence and have their unmet dependency needs met by having children. Unfortunately, such individuals will likely be disappointed by their children's neediness and inability to give the love and attention they crave, and they may react with overwhelming anger and abuse (Eth, 1996).

These findings have led some researchers to conclude that the physical acts of violence themselves may not be the only, or even the most important, factors that impact abused children's development (Trickett & Susman, 1988). Rather, the overall quality of parenting—the "world of abnormal rearing"—that maltreating parents provide may be the most critical determinants of abused individuals' adaptation, including their adaptation to parenthood (Helfer & Krugman, 1997).

PARENTAL ATTRIBUTIONS/EXPECTATIONS

Parental attributions and expectations may contribute to the intergenerational transmission of abuse. Abusive parents have been found to have unrealistic and rigid expectations of their children's development (Caliso & Milner, 1992; Putallaz et al., 1998). They were more likely to report problem behaviors in their children than trained observers and perceived their abused children as more difficult than their siblings (Zeanah & Zeanah, 1989).

Research also suggests that abusive parents have a tendency to make maladaptive attributions. They may attribute negative intentions to others (Belsky, 1993), and they have been found to attribute more malevolent intentions to their own children than to other children (Zeanah & Zeanah, 1989). Abusive parents have also been found to have an external locus of control, which allows them to deny responsibility for their children's injuries (Baumrind, 1995). Further, because they tend to presume little personal control, they interpret negative child behaviors as threatening and respond with heightened levels of arousal and negative affect (Belsky, 1993).

Maltreating parents' behavior may instill an external locus of control in their children. Trickett and Kuczynski (1986) compared the discipline strategies in abusive and non-abusive homes. They found that abusive parents used a greater total number of punishment techniques and were more likely to use severe physical punishment and less likely to use requests and reasoning. As abusive parents tend to be impulsive, punitive strategies may be more appealing because their effects on child non-compliance are immediate, though non-enduring. Trickett & Kuczynski noted that, from an attribution theory perspective, punitive strategies are less likely to promote internal motivations for compliance, but reinforce an external locus of control in children. Research has also found that maltreating parents are more likely to attribute failures and transgressions in their own children to stable, internal characteristics but other children's failures and transgressions and their own children's successes to unstable situational factors, a pattern opposite of control mothers (Zeanah & Zeanah, 1989). Therefore, maltreating parents may be transmitting to their children unrealistic expectations about others' behaviors, a tendency to attribute negative intentions to others, and an external locus of control. Such a constellation of expectations and attributions may increase the risk of later becoming abusive parents.

Microsystem

A number of qualities about a parent's microsystem, or immediate family environment, affect her risk for abusing her children. The following factors have received attention in the literature: (1) violence within the family/quality of the marital relationship; and (2) expectations/inner working models of the family.

VIOLENCE WITHIN THE FAMILY/QUALITY OF THE MARITAL RELATIONSHIP

Research suggests that men and women who were raised in violent homes are at extreme risk for abusing their spouses (Zeanah & Zeanah, 1989). Women with a childhood history of abuse are also at increased risk for being abused by their husbands. Individuals who were abused as children may be drawn to violent partners whose behaviors are consistent with their inner working models; and/or such individuals, because of poor interpersonal skills, may be severely limited in their choice of partners. Children born into families with spousal abuse are at greater risk for abuse themselves (Zeanah & Zeanah, 1989).

EXPECTATIONS/INNER WORKING MODELS OF THE FAMILY

Drawing from the work of Reiss (1981), Cicchetti and Lynch (1993) have hypothesized that families create representational models of their communities. These models are thought to evolve over the course of the family's development and to affect how the family processes information about and interacts with the larger community. The family's models may influence individual member's expectations about how the community will treat her and what her role and value in the community are. Cicchetti and Lynch suggested that the quality of the individual's inner working models of relationships and the family's representational models of the community likely interact. The authors hypothesized that families experiencing and being exposed to violence likely hold negative expectations that, like individual inner working models, may be transmitted across generations, increasing the risk for intergenerational transmission of child abuse.

Exosystem

Aspects of the parent's ontogenic development and microsystem are hypothesized to interact with qualities of her exosystem to influence her risk for continuing the cycle of abuse with her children. They include the following: (1) family's level of involvement in and support from the community; (2) poverty and the accompanying stressors; and (3) community violence.

FAMILY'S LEVEL OF INVOLVEMENT IN AND SUPPORT FROM THE COMMUNITY

As noted above, individuals with a history of child maltreatment are at risk for having poor interpersonal skills, inner working models that hold that others are not trustworthy or dependable and that the self is not worthy of others' help, and negative family representational models of the community. Not surprisingly, such individuals often isolate themselves and/or are isolated from neighborhood networks, support groups, and extended family (Belsky, 1993; Cicchetti & Lynch, 1993; Trickett & Susman, 1988). Research suggests that maltreating families actively isolate themselves from the community and fail to take advantage of available resources (Cicchetti & Lynch, 1993; Trickett & Susman, 1988). Trickett and Susman found that abusive parents encouraged their children to isolate themselves from the external world, such as intellectual and cultural pursuits and recreational activities. Characteristics of maltreating families, including their aggressive interactional styles and negative expectations, may also discourage others from interacting with them (Cicchetti & Lynch, 1993; Trickett & Susman, 1988). Consequently, maltreating families may not have access to emotional or material support when stressed (Cicchetti & Lynch, 1993).

Social learning theory suggests that maltreating families' tendency to be isolated from the community may contribute to the intergenerational transmission of abuse. Simons et al. (1991) found evidence for direct modeling as an avenue for the intergenerational transmission of abuse. They suggested that abused parents might use harsh techniques reflexively, with little awareness of alternatives or rationalization for their choices. Isolated parents are not exposed to new models of parenting that may challenge the practices that they learned from their abusive parents (Trickett & Susman, 1988). Maltreated children who are isolated are also prevented from interacting with the wider social environment, decreasing the probability that they will have positive experiences that could deter them from repeating the cycle of abuse (Trickett & Susman, 1988).

POVERTY

Several studies have indicated that the prevalence and severity of child maltreatment are correlated with poverty-related stressors, such as unemployment, overcrowded housing, geographic mobility, low levels of parental education, large family size, poor child spacing, and single parenting (Bittner & Newberger, 1982; Wilson & Saft, 1993). The abused child's poor developmental history increases the risk for school and work failure and subsequent poverty and the accompanying stressors. These stressors, combined with poor regulation skills and little support, may lead the formerly maltreated child to abuse her own children (Cicchetti & Lynch, 1993). In a study of three generations of families, Simons et al. (1991) found that low parental education was related to harsh parenting of adolescent males and education and economic hardship in grandparents. The authors concluded that cycles of harsh parenting of sons might be partly a function of socio-economic characteristics transmitted across generations.

COMMUNITY VIOLENCE

Cicchetti and Lynch (1993) noted that the frequent unemployment, low levels of education, and poverty found at increased rates among maltreating families may drive them to low-income neighborhoods where poverty, stress, and violence are concentrated. Community modeling and acceptance of violence further increase the risk for the intergenerational transmission of abuse.

Macrosystem

Researchers have identified a number of enduring factors at the macrosystem level that are hypothesized to influence the risk for abuse and its transmission. Corporal punishment is considered an appropriate form of discipline across social classes, and for some families the line between discipline and abuse is confusing (Bittner & Newberger, 1982; Pransky, 1991). In fact, a coherent, widely accepted definition of child abuse does not currently exist, further blurring the line between discipline and abuse (Zigler, 1983). Cicchetti and Lynch (1993) noted that society's tolerance of high levels of violence serves as a risk factor for child abuse. The risk for abuse in America also may be amplified by the glorification of the right to privacy, which may further isolate families at risk and reinforce the notion that children are ultimately the property of their parents, to be raised however the parents choose (Belsky, 1993; O'Brien, 1980).

APPLYING RESEARCH FINDINGS TO INTERVENTION

Discontinuity in the Intergenerational Transmission of Child Abuse: Implications for Treatment

Much can be learned about the risk and protective factors as well as the mechanisms that account for the transmission of maltreatment across generations by attempting to identify the factors that are associated with breaking the cycle of maltreatment. Though only a few investigations have attempted to identify such factors, evidence suggests that non-repeaters tend to have a history of an emotionally supportive relationship with a caring adult during childhood and/or are in an intact long-term stable relationship with a partner as an adult (Caliso & Milner, 1992; Egeland et al., 1988; Hunter & Kilstrom, 1979). Several studies have suggested that a supportive and satisfying marital relationship is important in helping individuals with a childhood history of abuse parent their own children competently. We interpreted these "relationship" differences between those mothers who broke the cycle and those who repeated it within the framework of contemporary attachment theory. As discussed earlier in this chapter, maltreated children develop a model of the world whereby their attachment figures may be seen as unavailable, unresponsive, and unloving (McCrone et al., 1994). According to Bowlby (1980), representational models of attachment relationships are difficult to change once they have been established. Despite this difficulty, it appears that mothers who broke the cycle were able to alter their existing representational models as a result of receiving emotionally responsive care from an alternative caregiver or emotional support from a spouse/mate. These findings, interpreted within an attachment framework, suggest that a major goal for breaking the cycle of maltreatment is to intervene early and intensively with maltreated children. Such early interventions need to be relationship-based and have as a primary goal altering the child's negative representational models of self and others.

Our finding that mothers who broke the cycle were more likely to have been in psychotherapy as adolescents or young adults also has implications for interventions (Egeland et al., 1988). Mothers who broke the cycle and who were in therapy were very aware of their history of having been abused, were able to recall the abuse in great detail, and appeared to have integrated their childhood experience of abuse into their views of self. Mothers who broke the cycle were aware of the effects of these experiences on their relationships with their children, whereas repeaters appeared to be unable to make these connections. Repeaters spoke in generalities without emotion and often gave idealized descriptions of their parents, suggesting that they coped with their childhood experiences by "splitting off" the abuse. Compared to mothers who broke the cycle, mothers who continued the cycle were rated higher on idealization and inconsistency in their description of their childhood and scored higher on the Dissociative Experience Scale, a self-report measure of dissociative symptoms (Egeland & Susman-Stillman, 1996). Dissociation is a coping strategy that involves a structural separation of psychological processes (that is, thoughts, emotions, memory, and identity) that are normally integrated (Spiegel & Cardena, 1991); a disturbance in memory and information processing results in a disruption in the integration of experiences. Not associating thoughts, feelings, and actions may make it more likely that parents could abuse their children without having empathy and feeling the pain. Our findings suggest that intervention/prevention aimed at breaking the cycle should include a mental health component, with an initial focus on integrating the abusive experiences and the memories associated with those experiences into a coherent sense of self for both the perpetrator and the child (Egeland & Susman-Stillman, 1996). A subsequent goal of intervention should be altering the maltreated individual's representational model of self in close relationships.

Further Implications: Lessons Learned
from the Continuity Literature

To understand the phenomena of intergenerational transmission requires complex models that take into account the many risk and protective factors and their inter-actions and transactions across time and different ecological levels. Unfortunately, in most instances the interventions available for victims and perpetrators of abuse do not address these needs.

Comprehensive programs are needed to meet the varied needs of the abusing family. Such programs should have available medical, social, and mental health services, including drug and alcohol rehabilitation services. Programs need to be flexible to meet the unique needs of each family. Most maltreating families are multi-problem families in which the parents are not able to provide adequate care for their children due to personal difficulties (such as depression or other forms of psychopathology, substance abuse, etc.), as well as adverse life circum-stances, including poverty and its associated problems of stress, isolation, and lack of resources. Unfortunately the majority of parent interventions do not focus on identifying and removing the obstacles to appropriate parenting before trying to teach new parenting behaviors. For the victim, maltreatment has been found to dis-rupt development and lead to behavior problems, peer incompetence, and school failure, greatly increasing the likelihood of maltreatment in the next generation. In order to break the cycle, these developmental problems also need to be addressed.

Maltreatment at a particular age is likely to lead to a predictable kind of de-velopmental maladaptation. For example, maltreatment in infancy is associated with insecure attachment between primary caregiver and child (Cicchetti & Lynch, 1993; Morton & Browne, 1998), which increases the probability of maladaptation at the next developmental stage (Egeland et al., in press). Interventions for children and adolescents need to be based on the developmental level of the child. Such in-terventions may include relationship-based interventions for insecurely attached children, play therapy for children with difficulties with emotional and behavioral self-regulation, social skills training for isolated and rejected children in elemen-tary school, and special education services for children with learning and academic problems.

The multi-problem crisis nature of maltreating families requires that intervention be of sufficient length to be effective. The parenting literature has shown that both the frequency and duration of intervention sessions are related to positive parenting outcomes (Liaw & Brooks-Gunn, 1994; Olds et al., 1997). Changing parents' repre-sentational models and the resulting behaviors requires time; parents must have new, positive emotional experiences to replace those that laid the foundations for insecure inner working models. To provide such experiences, the intervener must build a trusting relationship with the parent, which takes considerable time, espe-cially for parents who have histories of disappointing relationships. As people tend to fall back on their old patterns of coping under stress, the newer, more adaptive patterns must be firmly established during the intervention to increase the likeli-hood that parents will use them. In addition, long-term interventions are needed in order to deal with the personal as well as environmental crises in the lives of maltreating parents (Egeland et al., 2000). We recognize that comprehensive and intensive interventions as suggested are often not possible due to lack of resources to fund such a program. However, such an effort is necessary to break the cycle of maltreatment. Much is known about the course and consequences of maltreatment. This knowledge needs to be applied to the development of programs for maltreating families.

REFERENCES

Baumrind, D. (1995). Psychological characteristics of abusive parents. In *Child maltreatment and optimal caregiving in social contexts* (pp. 75–81). New York: Garland Publishing, Inc.

Belsky, J. (1993). Etiology of child maltreatment: A developmental-ecological analysis. *Psychological Bulletin*, **114**, 413–434.

Benoit, D., & Parker, K. (1994). Stability and transmission of attachment across three generations. *Child Development*, **65**, 1444–1456.

Bittner, S., & Newberger, E. H. (1982). Pediatric understanding of child abuse and neglect. In E. H. Newberger (Ed.), *Child abuse* (pp. 137–157). Boston: Little, Brown and Company.

Browne, K. D. & Herbert, M. (1997). *Preventing Family Violence*. Chicester, UK: John Wiley & Sons.

Bowlby, J. (1969). *Attachment and loss: Attachment* (2nd ed.). London: The Hogarth Press.

Bowlby, J. (1977). The making and breaking of affection bonds: Aetiology and psychopathology in the light of attachment theory. *British Journal of Psychiatry*, **130**, 201–210.

Bowlby, J. (1980). *Attachment and loss: Vol. 3. Loss, sadness and depression*. New York: Basic Books.

Caliso, J. A., & Milner, J. S. (1992). Childhood history of abuse and child abuse screening. *Child Abuse & Neglect*, **16**, 647–659.

Caspi, A., & Elder, G. H., Jr. (1988). Emergent family patterns: The intergenerational construction of problem behavior and relationships. In R. A. Hinde & J. Stevenson-Hinde (Eds.), *Relationships within families: Mutual influences* (pp. 218–240). New York: Oxford University Press.

Chase-Landsdale, P. L. Brooks-Gunn, J., & Zamsky, E. S. (1994). Young African-American multigenerational families in poverty: Quality of mothering and grandmothering. *Child Development*, **65**, 373–393.

Cicchetti, D., & Lynch, M. (1993). Toward an ecological/transactional model of community violence and child maltreatment: Consequences for children's development. *Psychiatry*, **56**, 96–118.

Covell, K., Grusec, J. E., & King, G. (1995). The intergenerational transmission of maternal discipline and standards for behavior. *Social Development*, **4**, 32–43.

DeLozier, P. P. (1982). Attachment theory and child abuse. In C. M. Parkes & J. Stevenson-Hinde (Eds.), *The place of attachment in human behavior* (pp. 95–117). New York: Basic Books.

DiLalla, L. F., & Gottesman, I. I. (1991). Biological and genetic contributors to violence—Widom's untold tale. *Psychological Bulletin*, **109**, 125–129.

Doumas, D., Margolin, G., & John, R. S. (1994). The intergenerational transmission of aggression across three generations. *Journal of Family Violence*, **9**, 157–175.

Egeland, B. (1988). Breaking the cycle of abuse: Implications for prediction and intervention. In K. D. Browne, C. Davies, & P. Stratton (Eds.), *Early prediction and prevention of child abuse* (pp. 87–99). Chichester: J. Wiley & Sons, Inc.

Egeland, B., Carlson, E. A., & Sroufe, L. A. (in press). Attachment theory and developmental psychopathology. In L. Atkinson (Ed.), *Attachment and Psychopathology*. Mahwah, NJ: Erlbaum.

Egeland, B., Jacobvitz, D., & Papatola, K. (1987). Intergenerational continuity of parental abuse. In R. Gelles & J. Lancaster (Eds.), *Child abuse and neglect: Biosocial dimensions* (pp. 255–276). New York: Aldine De Gruyter.

Egeland, B., Jacobvitz, D., & Sroufe, L. A. (1988). Breaking the cycle of abuse. *Child Development*, **59**, 1080–1088.

Egeland, B., & Susman-Stillman, A. (1996). Dissociation as a mediator of child abuse across generations. *Child Abuse & Neglect*, **20**, 1123–1132.

Egeland, B., Weinfield, N., Bosquet, M., & Cheng, V. (2000). Remembering, repeating, and working through: Lessons from attachment-based interventions. In J. Osofsky (Ed.), WHIMH *Handbook of Infant Mental Health* (Vol. **4.**, pp. 35–89). New York: John Wiley & Sons.

Elder, G. H., Jr., Caspi, A., & Downey, G. (1986). Problem behavior and family relationships: Life-course and intergenerational themes. In A. M. Sorensen, F. E. Weinert, & L. R. Sherrod (Eds.), *Human development and the life course: Multidisciplinary perspectives* (pp. 293–342). Hillsdale, New Jersey: Erlbaum.

Eth, S. (1996). A developmental-interactional model of child abuse. In C. R. Pfeffer (Ed.), *Severe stress and mental disturbance in children* (pp. 475–495). Washington, DC: American Psychiatric Press, Inc.

Fonagy, P., Steele, H., & Steele, M. (1991). Maternal representations of attachment during pregnancy predict the organization of infant–mother attachment at one year of age. *Child Development*, **62**, 891–905.

Helfer, R. E., & Krugman, R. D. (1997). A clinical and developmental approach to prevention. In M. E. Helfer, R. S. Kempe, & R. D. Krugman (Eds.), *The battered child* (pp. 594–614). Chicago: University of Chicago Press.

Hunter, R., & Kilstrom, N. (1979). Breaking the cycle in abusive families. *American Journal of Psychiatry*, **136**, 1320–1322.

Jacobvitz, D. B., Morgan, E., Kretchmar, M. D., & Morgan, Y. (1991). The transmission of mother–child boundary disturbances across three generations. *Development and Psychopathology*, **3**, 513–527.

Kaufman, J., & Zigler, E. (1987). Do abused children become abusive parents? *American Journal of Orthopsychiatry*, **57**, 186–192.

Kempe, C. H., Silverman, F. N., Steele, B. F., Droegemueller, W., & Silver, H. K. (1962). The battered-child syndrome. *Journal of the American Medical Association*, **181**, 17–24.

Liaw, F. & Brooks-Gunn, J. (1994). Cumulative familial risks and low-birthweight children's cognitive and behavioral development. *Journal of Clinical Child Psychology*, **23**, 360–372.

McCrone, E. R., Egeland, B., Kalkoske, M., & Carlson, E. A. (1994). Relations between early maltreatment and mental representations of relationships assessed with projective storytelling in middle childhood. *Development and Psychopathology*, **6**, 99–120.

Miller, L., Kramer, R., Warner, V., Wickramaratne, P., & Weissman, M. (1997). Intergenerational transmission of parental bonding among women. *Journal of the American Academy of Child and Adolescent Psychiatry*, **36**, 1134–1139.

Morton, N., & Browne, K. D. (1998). Theory and observation of attachment and its relation to child maltreatment: A review. *Child Abuse & Neglect*, **22**, 1093–1104.

O'Brien, S. (1980). *Child abuse: A crying shame*. Provo, Utah: Brigham Young University Press.

Olds, D., Eckenrode, J., Henderson, C. R., Jr., Kitzman, H., Powers, J., Cole, R., Sidora, K., Morris, P., Pettitt, L. M., & Luckey, D. (1997). Long-term effects of home visitation on maternal life course and child abuse and neglect. *The Journal of American Medical Association*, **278**(8), 637–643.

Patterson, G. R., DeBaryshe, B. D., & Ramsey, E. (1989). A developmental perspective on antisocial behavior. *American Psychologist*, **44**, 329–335.

Pransky, J. (1991). *Prevention: The critical need*. Springfield, Missouri: Burrell Foundation & Paradigm Press.

Putallaz, M., Costanzo, P. R., Grimes, C. L., & Sherman, D. M. (1998). Intergenerational continuities and their influences on children's social development. *Social Development*, **7**, 389–427.

Reiss, D. (1981). *The family's construction of reality*. Boston: Harvard University Press.

Simons, R. L., Whitbeck, L. B., Conger, R. D., & Chyi-In, W. (1991). Intergenerational transmission of harsh parenting. *Developmental Psychology, 27*, 159–171.

Spiegel, D., & Cardena, E. (1991). Disintegrated experience: The dissociative disorders revisited. *Journal of Abnormal Psychology, 100*, 366–378.

Sroufe, L. A. (1990). An organizational perspective on the self. In D. Cicchetti & M. Beeghly (Eds.), *The self in transition: Infancy to childhood* (pp. 281–307). Chicago: University of Chicago Press.

Sroufe, L. A. (1996). *Emotional development: The organization of emotional life in the early years.* New York: Cambridge University Press.

Steele, B., & Pollack, C. (1968). A psychiatric study of parents who abuse infants and small children. In R. Helfer & C. H. Kempe (Eds.), *The battered child* (pp. 89–133). Chicago: University of Chicago Press.

Straus, M. (1979). Family patterns and child abuse in a nationally representative sample. *International Journal of Child Abuse and Neglect, 3*, 213–225.

Trickett, P. K., & Kuczynski, L. (1986). Children's misbehaviors and parental discipline strategies in abusive and nonabusive families. *Developmental Psychology, 22*, 115–123.

Trickett, P. K., & Susman, E. J. (1988). Parental perceptions of child-rearing practices in physically abusive and nonabusive families. *Developmental Psychology, 24*, 270–276.

van IJzendoorn, M. H. (1992). Intergenerational transmission of parenting: A review of studies in nonclinical populations. *Developmental Review, 12*, 76–99.

Wilson, M. N., & Saft, E. W. (1993). Child maltreatment in the African-American community. In D. Cicchetti & S. L. Toth (Eds.), *Child abuse, child development, and social policy: Vol. 8. Advances in applied developmental psychology* (pp. 213–247). Norwood, NJ: Ablex Publishing Corporation.

Zeanah, C. H., & Zeanah, P. D. (1989). Intergenerational transmission of maltreatment: Insights from attachment theory and research. *Psychiatry, 52*, 177–196.

Zigler, E. (1983). Understanding child abuse: A dilemma for policy development. In E. Zigler, S. L. Kagan, & E. Klugman (Eds.), *Children, families and government: Perspectives on American social policy.* (pp. 331–352). New York: Cambridge University Press.

14

THE ROLE OF FAMILY THERAPY FOLLOWING PHYSICAL AND SEXUAL ABUSE

Helga Hanks
Peter Stratton
University of Leeds, UK

> *"Family therapy looks at problems within the system of relationships in which they occur, and aims to promote change by intervening in the broader system rather than in the individual alone."*
>
> (Burnham 1986)

Why does child abuse matter? The harm caused by the various forms of abuse is primarily due to their inappropriateness within relationships. Incidents of abuse, let alone sustained patterns of abusive interactions, cause major damage to the relationship in which they occur. But they are also likely to have a pervasive and corrosive effect on a much wider range of the child's relationships both present and future, and they sabotage the developmental processes that children's relationships normally underpin. Helping children and parents to overcome the consequences of abuse must therefore focus strongly on the ways they interact. We would claim that this work is usually most likely to be successful if it is conducted in the context of the relationships that have survived the abuse. That is, by working therapeutically with the (remaining) family. Our brief in this chapter has been to concentrate on physical and sexual abuse, but much of what we say applies also to neglect and emotional abuse.

In the previous edition of this book Stratton (1988) proposed a "heuristic" definition of abuse from which to explore the implications for societal definitions of the care that is owed to children by different people. The definition is simply: "Abuse occurs whenever there is a substantial failure of any person to act towards another with care appropriate to their relationship." (Stratton, 1988, p. 194).

Early Prediction and Prevention of Child Abuse: A Handbook.
Edited by Kevin Browne, Helga Hanks, Peter Stratton and Catherine Hamilton. © 2002 John Wiley & Sons, Ltd.

The exploration of this definition (Stratton & Hanks 1991) made it quite clear that it is intrafamilial abuse that is most likely to be damaging, and even extrafamilial abuse may have its major consequences within the child's own family. The more recent findings about the effects on children when they have been abused in institutions (Lindsay, 1999; Thomas, 2001; Hobbs et al., 1999), and the issues about children who have been coerced and/or forced into the area of pornography are stark reminders. If we take sexual abuse as an example we can observe that the developmental distortions, the secrecy and shame so often induced by sexual abuse have consequences for the child's ways of relating that are difficult to overcome. We would therefore argue that once abuse has occurred, most of the important tasks require helping to restore and enhance family relationships. Not just to help the child overcome the consequences, but also to create good relationships which are fundamental to future safety, and build a foundation for the future of the child as a potential parent.

If tertiary prevention is going to have relationships at its core, then attempts to treat the child in isolation are not going to be the easiest to make effective. Treatment will ideally involve all of those whose relationships will be crucial in future. In practice, this usually means the remaining members of the household whether or not this includes the perpetrator(s) and including, where possible, members of the wider family who will play a part in parenting. Individual work can, of course, effectively tackle relationships and we sometimes recommend that children have individual or group therapy alongside the therapy they receive with their families. Also, when a child is being treated in individual psychotherapy there is still a case for working with the parents (Pearce & Pezzot-Pearce, 1997). However, we believe there are good grounds for working with the whole family where possible (Furness & Bingley Miller, 1995; Bentovim, 2002). The value of working with the family is widely recognised in the current practice of social services and child psychiatric and psychological services. However, the majority of practitioners who work with families of abuse are not trained in family therapy. We believe that family therapy, using methods that have been developed largely in the process of dealing with the consequences of abuse, should be offered where possible. Where not, the methods should be made as available as possible to other family workers, which is an objective of this chapter. Therefore we propose and describe forms of family treatment that have been developed under the heading of systemic family therapy and which are specifically designed to mitigate the relational consequences of abuse.

WHY SYSTEMIC FAMILY THERAPY? EVIDENCE BASE AND RATIONALE

Although, as Jones (1997) states, treatment outcome in the area of abuse is a complex issue about which it is hard to make definitive statements, those studies that have attempted to evaluate family therapy have produced consistently positive findings (Shadish et al., 1993; Pinsoff & Wynne, 1995; Diamond et al., 1996). There is little direct evidence about how it compares with other approaches in the area of child abuse. However, the emphasis on changing the system at some fundamental level shows up in the facts that systemic family therapy is effective not just in changing the problem with which families present, but improves a wide range of their functioning, and that, unlike other therapies, the effects tend to increase rather than decrease after the end of therapy (Leff et al., 2000).

Some studies have examined specific forms of family therapy in relation to abuse. For example, Brunk et al., (1987) found that home-based multisystemic therapy was more effective than parent education alone, while Kolko (1996) reported that both family therapy and individual cognitive behaviour therapy were effective in treating physically abused children and their parents. The analysis of etiology by Belsky and Stratton (Chapter 6) indicates the multiple contexts involved in abuse and neglect. While all forms of systemic family therapy attempt to take account of the different levels of systemic context there are approaches which trace their roots to the ecological theory of Bronfenbrenner (1979) and which may be especially effective in cases of serious chronic maltreatment. Henggler (1999) has shown the multisystemic approach to be highly effective especially in terms of family engagement and staying in treatment. Sundelin and Hansson (1999) also report very positive results in a study of 109 Swedish families receiving "intensive family therapy". Although neither of these studies was specifically about abuse, all of the families involved were multi-problem and fairly representative of the families who would be referred for therapy following identification of abuse.

A different approach which was one of the earliest to be developed in the context of deprivation and abuse is the structural family therapy of Salvador Minuchin (1967). It works to establish appropriate boundaries and forms of communication, and sees the main task as being to re-establish functional structures within the family. While it has been criticised for prescribing conventional family forms, it is very effective with families whose circumstances have worked against their being able to develop effective organisation of their relationships. There can be no question of the relevance of Minuchin's work for the family with a high risk of parenting failure and abuse.

The issues and approaches relating to maltreatment of children described in this chapter draw on our experience of applying and developing a particular model of systemic family therapy: the Milan model (Stratton et al., 1990; Jones, 1993). However we have drawn freely on other approaches such as that of Minuchin and since all forms of family therapy have been developed in the context of working with difficult family relationships, the differences may be more in theoretical conceptualisation than in actual practice.

Families in which abuse has occurred may well have a long history of difficult interactions with each other, and will certainly be undergoing substantial re-evaluation and re-negotiation of their current relationships. We describe the general approaches that have been found useful with maltreating families but the approach taken in each individual case will vary considerably depending on the people attending therapy; their definition of current problems and hopes for the future; their resources; and the stage of dealing with the abuse. Some of the main contexts for family therapy are:

1. A family is being seen when a referring agency or the therapist comes to suspect that abuse is, or has been, taking place.
2. Parents are separated and one, or both, accuses the other of abuse during contact.

3. A family comes for therapy when a child has been abused by someone outside the family (extra-familial abuse).
4. A family in which one of the family members has abused one of the children comes to therapy as a condition of the perpetrator remaining in the family.
5. Sibling abuse.
6. Abuse by a family member has been identified and that person has left the family. The remaining family come to therapy.
7. Physical abuse by an extended family member has been identified and that person is not living in the family. The family come with the abuser to explore the possibility of their future contact with the child and family.
8. A family comes for family therapy when they are fostering or have adopted a child which has been maltreated in their biological, or previous family.

In each case the abuse may be manifold—physical, neglect, emotional, failure-to-thrive or sexual—and the issues are substantially different within and between the eight categories as well as depending on the nature and severity of the abuse (Crittenden & Claussen 1993; Department of Health, 1995; Stratton & Hanks, 1992; Hobbs et al., 1999, Chapter 5). At all stages of therapy Government guidelines need to be followed and incorporated in any treatment or consultation.

Browne (1995) shows that there is wide awareness among practitioners of the role of stress in abuse, but argues that too little attention is paid to the processes within families such as the models of parenting being followed; adverse patterns of family interaction; caregiver's misinterpretation of child behaviour, especially behaviour that can be construed as oppositional; and the quality of interactions. Section II of this Handbook is largely about the effectiveness of interventions to remove sources of stress, and parent education so that parents would become more skilled in parenting matters and feel more in control. The chapters in that section point to the need to use the simplest and most readily available interventions that will put the child and the family back on track. Family therapy should the considered, and in practice is usually only offered, when less intensive forms of support have proven inadequate. However, the methods can provide a basis for all forms of family work.

What is Systemic Family Therapy? What does it do?

Historical accounts of the development of systemic family therapy can be found in Stratton et al. (1990), Dallos & Draper (2000), and Carr (2000). Very briefly then; the roots of systemic family therapy can be traced to the engineering of guided systems during the Second World War. The principles were extended to general theories of goal directed machines and then applied to existing biological systems. The underlying phenomenon was that within a system of interacting parts, negative feedback provides the information and control by which all of the parts become mutually interacting and produce a systemic outcome that is not the product of the actions of any single individual. The next step occurred when these principles were applied to human systems. Scientists became also interested in the dysfunction of human systems and a group started to explore the application of systems ideas to psychiatric symptoms. Gregory Bateson was one of the leading figures in what is now known as the Palo Alto Group and their research into human communications in patients suffering from schizophrenia. Almost accidentally they happened to observe some of their patients with their families and discovered that behaviour which had appeared bizarre and incomprehensible in isolation now began to make sense. This was probably the point at which a systemic understanding of the family began.

From the pioneering work in Palo Alto (Bateson, 1972; Watslawick et al., 1967) a range of systemic approaches developed, but all with the basic premise that children's or adults' problems were not most usefully seen as dysfunctions that reside in the individual. Rather the symptomatic behaviour can be seen as the best adaptation that the person could manage at the time, and that these adaptations are most commonly generated through transactions within the family system (Stratton, in press; and see Chapter 6). It then makes much more sense to work with the family system so that future adaptations can be different, than to take the child out of the family and attempt to "cure" them.

CURRENT THERAPEUTIC APPROACHES TO CHILD ABUSE AND NEGLECT

With most therapies the individual becomes the focal point of assessment and treatment without necessarily including the wider family and context within which the child maltreatment has occurred. This is not to say that social workers were not undertaking family assessments and most often making good sense of what has taken place. However we believe that a systemic evaluation/assessment would have additional value in such cases. For example: when confronting a case of child abuse we tend to focus on the abuser and the child, and to intervene in their interactions. A specifically systemic approach to parental assessment is described by Stratton & Hanks (1995). Systemic thinking leads one to include the wider system (the family including siblings, social networks, professional systems, hospitals, social services, the Courts) and helps one to consider the effects interventions will need to have in order to achieve change, and for this change to be supported at all systemic levels.

The decision of whether family therapy is appropriate needs to be undertaken within a child abuse assessment. Furniss & Bingley Miller (1995) set out ways of working with families in an abusive setting. As Bentovim (1992) pointed out, including the perpetrator of sexual abuse in a family in family therapy sessions "... may be detrimental to victims because the approach implies that all members, including the victim, play a role in maintaining abusive interactions." (p. xviii) This concern has most certainly been strengthened by subsequent research which has produced no evidence that family therapy is being appropriate with the perpetrator of sexual abuse present. However, Swenson & Hanson (1997) review programmes that have worked with the perpetrator separately and seem to be effective in re-unifying the family.

It is probably worth mentioning here that the position of both male and female perpetrators of sexual abuse is the same. Their needs in treatment are different from those of the rest of the family (Hollin, 2000; Saradjian & Hanks, 1996; Hanks & Wynne, 2000; Calder, 2000). However, family therapy does seem to be helpful to families where the non-abusing parent, foster or adoptive families and siblings come together to understand what has been happening and to help each other to make changes in their behaviour, attitudes and thinking both towards themselves, towards each other (improving communication) and towards the systems (recognising the role social service, hospitals, legal and Court systems play) with which they may have to interact because of the abuse.

When children have been physically abused, neglected, emotionally maltreated or where they are failing to thrive the maltreating member of the family should be included. Even when the abuse is denied, and cannot be directly confronted in the sessions this denial is not always an indicator that family therapy will be ineffective. Robinson & Whitney (1999) described their systemic work with families following abuse and show how the work can be effective despite denial.

Jones (1997, Table 24.1, p. 528) provides an overview based on research of the situations in which therapy with families of abuse is, or is not, likely to succeed. There is however one specific type of family for whom, in our experience, family therapy will rarely be appropriate. These are parents who engage in what has been called Munchausen by proxy behaviour. These parents fabricate illness in their children (factitious illness by proxy), or may suffocate or poison them (Schreier & Libow, 1993; Hobbs et al. 1999). However, a systemic consultation to the professional systems involved in such cases may be very appropriate and beneficial. The difficulty of working therapeutically with these families is because the need to engage in this behaviour is overwhelming to such a parent and the concealment is highly skilled. Co-operation in achieving change away from such behaviour is not likely to be obtained in a family session. Here it is essential that the perpetrating parent receives help individually, the child is kept in a safe environment, and a thorough assessment is made of what has been happening.

In order to indicate what systemic family therapy is trying to achieve we describe a characteristic case.

A CASE EXAMPLE

A referral sent by a GP described a family situation in which a six-year-old child had made disclosures about having been sexually abused by a close male cousin 17 years of age. This had happened over a period of time before the child complained to her mother. The investigation by the authorities had revealed that she had indeed been abused and named the perpetrator correctly. It had been a difficult time for the family and six months after these investigations had taken place the mother presented to the GP in a distressed state explaining that she had now terribly negative thoughts about her daughter and in particular thinking that the child was somehow soiled, damaged, in a way that would never make her whole and loveable again. The mother was as much distraught about the fact of the abuse as of the state she found herself in *vis-à-vis* her child. She loved the little girl as much as her other child aged four years but had thoughts and feelings now which repulsed her. She was well aware of how doubly rejected her daughter must feel.

Both mother, father and the two children attended for family therapy. A story of confusion emerged as the family discussed the fact that the younger child was believed by the parents not to have any knowledge of what had happened. They requested that we did not mention the abuse while the younger child was in the room with them. We spent the first session discovering about their family and also learnt that the father's parents knew nothing about what had been happening, despite both children having been with them during the last six months.

We respected the parents' wishes and offered them either time to come without the children or that a member of the team could play with the children separately. The parents had no one they felt they could trust now but said they would be happy for the children to be in an adjacent room and supervised by a member of the team. The children seemed happy with that idea.

A discussion with the parents then revealed their own fears, shame and guilt of communicating what had happened, their feeling of having let their child down. Also their idea that if they did not talk about it time would somehow help them to forget what had happened. Not an unreasonable wish from their point of view however not a realistic one. The parents began to talk about what each of them had understood had happened and again many discrepancies emerged between their stories. An important part of their therapy was to have a shared story about the events. As they reached this stage they also recognised that their younger child must have known much of what had happened.

The children having joined their parents again turned out to be much more matter of fact about what had happened. When the father asked the younger child why s/he thought they had come to the clinic, the child said because of what had happened to the sister. The sister began to talk about her feelings and thinking and said that she thought her mummy and daddy did not love her any more. That they did not love her any more because of what had happened with the cousin. She said she did not know why mummy and daddy felt like this.

The parents acknowledged that they had been very upset and afraid that their family would never be the same again and that they could not be happy. Using age appropriate language, child friendly language, was an important part in this work though these children also showed just how much children understand of adult constructions of thoughts and feelings.

At one point the girl asked her mother "do you love me?" and the mother was able to give an unequivocal answer "yes". The girl looked puzzled and the therapist asked her what she was thinking. The child did not answer but kept looking at her mum. It was the father who said "I think you are right in thinking that there has not been much love about in our family for the last few months and we are here to make sure that we all get to feeling better again." "Was it my fault?" said the girl. "No" said the father "but it was about you and what had happened to you." "The abuse?" the child said. "Yes" said the father "and no, it was not your fault it was your cousin's fault." The child answered "Yes the social worker told me that too." Father: "And we agree." He then picked his daughter up and gave a her hug. The child snuggled in. There followed a period during which mum and daughter made very similar contact.

Looking back at a later stage the parents said they could not believe that they had become so distant from each other and that they found the method of all being together very helpful.

Of course the discussion also included the wider system. The father's parents, the extended family. The fact that the cousin ended up in prison, but not before he had disclosed abuse which he suffered as a child also from a family member.

THE OBJECTIVES OF SYSTEMIC FAMILY THERAPY

We would first distinguish therapy from assessment: the use of sessions to determine what has happened. Therapists may be drawn into assessment for a variety of reasons but we find it most productive to draw a clear distinction. In keeping with systemic principles, we have found it important to be clear with ourselves and with the family when our objectives change. Lang et al. (1990) suggest that we could think of operating in different domains, two of which are labelled "explanation" and "production". Therapists operate primarily in the domain of explanations in which they work to open up new possibilities. The domain of production being the world of objective fact and established truth. As we go on with our lives, encountering situations with different demands, one or another of the domains will naturally take precedence. In abuse work it is not enough to prioritise domains "naturally". It is suggested that the therapist must be alert to a need to switch out of their usual mode, with its strategy of neutrality and avoidance of blame, into the domain of production when they realise that a family member may be at risk.

McAdam and Hannah (1991) have developed the idea that a systemic therapist must be prepared to change from the domain of explanation to the domain of production when they encounter issues of child protection. This is a radical switch as shown by their list of the differences (Table 14.1).

So the therapist must be prepared to leave the stance developed within the current relativist version of systemic thinking when confronted by a need to protect a child. An example of being open about domains is when therapists inform families at the start of therapy that the confidentiality that is promised cannot be maintained if it would put someone at risk. They would then inform the family (using appropriate

TABLE 14.1   Alternative domains of action (based on McAdam & Hannah, 1991, page 222).

Domain of explanation	Domain of production
Create meaning and understanding	Something to be achieved
Consent essential	Consent preferable
Multiversa—multiple realities	A universe—objectivity and truth
Perpetrators and victims co-create causality	Perpetrators and victims with linear causality
Neutrality	No neutrality
Curiosity—explorer, discoverer	Curiosity—investigator
Archaeology metaphor – reconstructing civilisation	Mining metaphor – digging for truth

language) when they are switching domains so that the family does not think they are participating in therapy when in fact the process has become an investigation of abuse.

We now turn to consider the major functions to which systemic family therapy, primarily in the domain of explanation, is directed.

PROCESSES IN SYSTEMIC FAMILY THERAPY

Because the work with families in which a child has been abused can have such varied objectives, we now offer a brief general account of current thinking before moving to describe therapeutic work with specific aspects of abuse.

Systemic family therapy grew from a recognition that the symptoms of an individual family member are likely to be an essential component of a complexly interacting system. Whatever the contribution from some characteristic of an individual, the form and degree of distress experienced, and the prognosis, will be determined primarily by the meanings that the family create, and by the impact of their joint creation of meanings on the relationships between them. A powerful approach to this issue has been research into the attributions that family members make about each other (Munton et al., 1999, pp 97–104). We have found characteristic patterns among parents who have physically abused their children (Stratton & Swaffer, 1988; Silvester & Stratton, 1991) in that, for example, the child is perceived as having more control over bad events than the parent. The patterns for intrafamilial sexual abuse are less consistent but have been shown to predict the prognosis for the family (Silvester et al., 1995).

Working to try to understand the meanings that a family gives to their life and their difficulties, at the same time as engaging each member in the therapeutic process, is a complex business. Family therapists therefore, work where possible, with a team who are usually in an adjacent room but able to see and hear the family. The family is introduced to the team and the process of working. The therapist, assisted by ideas from the team, helps the family to "restory" the difficulties in ways that no longer push people into entrenched positions but leave them better able to choose a more acceptable life.

Systemic techniques have for many years been based on the recognition that asking questions can be the most powerful way of getting people to consider alternatives to their dominant narrative. Also that language can be gently shaped away from habitual patterns in which problems are all attributed to the character, or nature, of specific family members. A crucial aspect is that the therapist does not presume to know what family members believe, and avoids reinforcing existing negative stories. An example would be that, instead of explaining John's hitting as caused by his aggressiveness, it is talked of in terms of being *experienced* by others as an aggressive act. The shift is from a linear causal factual claim about John's nature (and his "nature" is anyway unobservable and unlikely to be changed by therapy) to a statement about the consequence in terms of the attributions that other family members will make. In order to bring a certain aspect into the open the therapist will talk of how it would affect him or her, and then see whether this enables the family members to say how it affects them. For example, John had hit his sister in the session and the parents had intervened. The therapist said: "John, when you hit Susan just then it made me feel concerned. I am concerned that you feel bad and that the only way you can think of to make you feel better is to make someone else feel bad. Am I right to be thinking like this?" Importantly, the second description opens up possibilities of considering how the reaction to his hitting feeds back to John, creating a cycle of repetitive and possibly escalating damage. Unlike the blaming which is only likely to provoke a denial from John, it can (with care) free John and other family members to consider alternative behaviours.

Onto this fundamental approach, which was most fully developed by a group of systemic therapists in Milan (Boscolo et al., 1987; Jones, 1993) three rather different orientations have been added during the last decade. While each has been proposed as a complete system of therapy, many systemic therapists have incorporated the three aspects into their own style of practice. The first involves reflexivity. It recognises that the therapist is part of the system (the family system as well as the therapeutic system) and therefore has an effect on and is affected by, what is happening in the session. This position makes it clear that the therapist does not control the session to produce a predetermined outcome, but that family and therapist co-construct a new position. A concrete example of the approach is the "reflecting team" (Friedman, 1995) where the family observe the therapists discussing how the family's difficulties or positives have affected them—their feelings and their attributions. It has also been found to be a process that helps the family to consider a variety of alternatives and explore them without feeling obliged to defend themselves or pass judgement on the idea too quickly.

The second development is of a "solution-focussed" approach (Berg, 1994) in which the discussion is moved away from "problem saturated descriptions" of the family and attention is directed to the partial solutions that the family has achieved so that these can be built upon. This orientation directs the therapist to focus on the sources of resilience within the family and to build on those aspects of their family life that are most positive. In cases of child maltreatment the approach has to be used with caution, a keen understanding of the complex difficulties these families are living through and a recognition that facts and behaviours have to be confronted. Therapists working in this way need to be very experienced with child protection systems as well as keeping family systems in mind.

The third movement, the narrative approach (White & Epston, 1990), gives precedence to the stories that the family has developed about itself. The process of therapy is to place the problem outside the family (as something that inflicts itself on them) and build up the alternative stories that all families have about themselves, so that these more optimistic narratives become the basis for how the family sees itself and operates. Family therapists working in the area of abuse need to be particularly vigilant to keep the abuse or maltreatment in focus and not diminish its often severe effects. Constructing alternative narratives, especially about the future, does not mean denying the stories about abuse.

The next section, on abuse-specific therapy draws on this brief general definition to show what may be done in practice.

SYSTEMIC THERAPY AND TYPICAL PROCESSES OF FAMILIES IN WHICH ABUSE HAS OCCURRED

In the previous edition of this book we described some of the issues which are central to family therapy and child abuse (Hanks & Stratton, 1988). Here we can only draw attention to a few of the most relevant aspects.

Cultural Contexts: Gender, Power and Poverty

In recent years systemic theory has paid greater attention to the wider social context of a family, the family dynamics and cultural issues. Feminist therapists have lead the way in thinking about the dominant cultural structures that exist in families and Goldner (1991) in particular highlights the place of gender roles in many societies. For instance working with couples who had shown patterns of violence and abuse revealed how these relationships could be legitimised on the basis of cultural norms about gender roles and male and female identities. Change in such thinking was needed and therapy was no exception. Child abuse cases also revealed that powerful and detrimental patriarchal assumptions operated in many cultures and were used to dominate families and to use violence to maintain compliance.

Of course it is vital that due attention is paid to the issues of power, gender and the social/political problems which are part of family settings (Bentovim, 1992). Nor can we ignore the strong links that child abuse has always had to poverty and social exclusion (see Section II). McCarthy (1994), in tackling the issues of poverty and social exclusion from a systemic perspective stated that:

> Working with clients who live in poverty is back on the agenda of systemic therapists and practitioners. This time around however, poverty is no longer viewed solely as a situation of material lack but also as a process of social exclusion. In this process, people are excluded from and deprived of a wide range of social, cultural and material resources due to their "race", gender, class, ability and/or sexual orientation (p. 127).

Closely linked to these issues is the high level of violence within so many families. There is now very strong evidence that supportive intervention to prevent child abuse will be ineffective if there is violence between the caregivers (see Olds et al., Chapter 10). Systemic practitioners have developed a variety of ways of reducing family violence (Vetere & Cooper, 2001). However, as with the related issues of substance abuse, family therapists need to employ all of their skills even to get these issues addressed. Because unacknowledged family processes are so central to working with families after abuse, it is these with which we conclude this chapter.

Family Secrets, Myths and Scripts

"Families develop complex and influential beliefs that may never be expressed, but which may dominate much of the life of the family and exist as internal representations of what they believe" (Hanks & Stratton 1988, p. 254). When we consider myths in relation to sexual abuse in the family we realise that much of what we encounter challenges our own myths. Many of the myths are so strong that they remain despite the facts that are now widely available. Many people still view child sexual abuse with disbelief and Roland Summit's comments from 1983 are still as valid today. He said: "Conspiracy of silence insulates adult society against confronting the terrifying discovery that large numbers of children are molested, assaulted, incestuously exploited, and raped by entrusted caregivers." Equally we have to abandon the myth that "good" families "nice" and "normal" adults do not abuse children (Hanks & Stratton, 1988). Child sexual abuse is found in all sections of society.

SECRETS

Families often have what are colloquially called "skeletons in the cupboard" and these topics must under no circumstances be discussed (Imber-Black, 1993). This tendency enables beliefs that seem quite bizarre when they are finally talked about to exist without being challenged. All forms of abuse may come under this heading. Sexual abuse and the strong beliefs in sexual taboos and laws, physical abuse and the issues of injuring children non-accidentally all are being hidden from view. Family therapy is able to offer ways of talking about these issues in the hearing of all family members in ways that do not provoke denial. As already indicated these discussions have to take place within the guidelines laid down by the Government such as, in the UK, the Children Act 1991.

MYTHS

Families, over the years, develop strong sets of beliefs which constitute a kind of "inner image" of family life. Myths may take generations to build up, and they may never be clearly stated, but they tend to have the following characteristics:

1. the whole family participate in them;
2. they exert an influence on all family members and on their relationships;
3. they go unchallenged despite the fact that they do not square with reality.

A very common myth in many families is "hitting him/her hard to teach them what is right never hurt anyone and is good for the kids and is how adults keep in control. All children are naughty". Everyone in the family knows that it is essential to maintain this belief. Neither parents nor children seek any other explanation and children get bruised or even more seriously injured. Parents become increasingly frustrated and try harder to control the children and achieve change by hitting harder. Whole family discussions can bring these beliefs into the open, focus discussion on the good things that all the family want (good behaviour, less conflict) and plan alternative means to achieve these goals.

In families where children fail to thrive a common myth prevails that "we were all thin and small in our family". The failure to thrive is explained by this myth, which many families state has been in the family for generations. Trying to change this pattern and feed the children more and different, calorie rich, enjoyable foods goes against the family myth. A powerful position not easily changed by therapy, and most certainly not changed if only mother and child are seen. It may be possible in a session to help the mother to see that her child needs more food and become "stronger" (a reframing of putting on weight) but when the mother gets home she will be confronted by other family members with the prevailing myth and may feel disloyal to continue with her new understanding about the need for her child to grow.

SCRIPTS

Closely connected to family myth is the family script (Byng-Hall, 1995; 1998). This powerful concept encapsulates the ways that family members have prescribed roles that lead the family to repeat even painful and damaging processes over and over again. Abusive behaviour is no exception.

Family members can be thought of as having acquired a script, primarily as it was jointly constructed within their family of origin, which tells them what their role is and how the family play should develop in its various functions. Not only is everyone casting the rest of the family in their personal inner world script, they are also simultaneously playing roles in everyone else's scripts. Families enter into transactions with each other, and in relation to wider systems, so that their scripts become compatible, and when a couple come together to set up a family, they often adopt one of the two commonest scripts: the replicative script, which aims to repeat the past, or the corrective script which attempts to alter past experience.

If a parent spent their childhood being subdued by violence, they may build this into their assumptions about how families work and create a family which incorporates this event in everyone's script. Or they may become determined to correct this script in their own parenting. Both kinds of script allow the past to determine the future, and therapy may be necessary to name the scripts so that they can free themselves from them.

PROSPECT AND CONCLUSION

There is both evidence and good reason to believe that tertiary treatment and prevention of child abuse and neglect will be best achieved by working therapeutically with the whole family. This will apply particularly to those of the more serious cases in which there is still a prospect that the abused child could remain in the family. It may however be necessary to work separately with the perpetrator.

While making the case for a family systems conceptualisation of child abuse and drawing on the approaches and techniques of systemic family therapy for treatment, we have only been able to give a small indication of the rich theoretical, research-based and clinical approaches available. Even so, systemic family therapy is at a comparatively early stage of development with a history only slightly longer than the current confrontation of child abuse. Both fields have much to learn from each other, and also from other well developed areas such as developmental psychology and feminist critical theory.

Our hope in this chapter has been to make systemic family therapy techniques and philosophy more widely available and to encourage all who work with families that have experienced abuse to draw on the resources that this approach has to offer. Adoption of a systemic stance, using current techniques and concepts, offers a direct route to the maintenance of realistically positive views by both professionals and clients of the attempts that family members are making, and of their untapped potential for change.

NOTE: The cases drawn on for this chapter have been altered to protect confidentiality.

REFERENCES

Bateson, G. 1972 *Steps to an Ecology of Mind*. London, Jason Aronson.

Bentovim, A. 1992 *Trauma-Organised Systems*. New York, Karnac Books.

Bentovim, A. 2002 Working with abusing families, In *The Child Protection Handbook, 2nd Edition*. K. Wilson, & A. James, Eds, London, Baillière Tindall.

Berk, I. K. 1994 *Family Based Services: A Solution-Focussed Approach*. New York, Norton.

Bosocolo, L., Cecchin, G., Hoffman, L., Penn, P. 1987 *Milan Systemic Therapy: Conversations In Theory And Practice*. New York, Basic Books.

Bronfenbrenner, U. 1979 *The ecology of human development*. Cambridge, MA: Harvard University Press.

Browne, K. D. 1995 Predicting Maltreatment. In P. Reder & C. Lucey Eds. *Assessment of Parenting*. Chichester, Wiley. pp. 118–135.

Brunk, M., Henggler, S. W., Whelan, J. P., 1987 Comparison of multisystem therapy and parent training in the brief treatment of child abuse and neglect. *Journal of Consulting and Clinical Psychology* **55**: 171–178.

Burnham J. 1986 *Family Therapy*. London, Tavistock Publications.

Byng-Hall, J. 1995 *Rewriting Family scripts: improvisation and systems change*, New York, Guilford Press.

Byng-Hall, J. 1998 Evolving ideas about narrative: re-editing the re-editing of family mythology *Journal of Family Therapy*, **20**, 2, pp. 133–43.

Calder M. 2000 *The Complete Guide To Sexual Abuse Assessments*. Lyme Regis, Russell House Publishing.

Carr, A. 2000 *Family Therapy: Concepts, Process and Practice*. Chichester, Wiley.

Children Act 1991, London, HMSO.

Crittenden, P., Claussen, A. 1993 Severity of maltreatment: assessment and policy. In C. Hobbs & J. Wynne Eds. *Baillière's Clinical Pediatrics, Vol 1, Child Abuse*. London, Baillière Tindall, pp. 87–100.

Dallos, R. & Draper, R. 2000 *An Introduction to Family Therapy*. Oxford, OUP.

Department of Health, 1995. *Child Protection: Messages From Research*. London, HMSO.

Diamond, G. S., Serrano, A., Dickey, M., and Sonis, W. 1996 Current status of family-based outcome and process research. *Journal of the Academy of Child and Adolescent Psychiatry*, **35**, 6–16.

Friedman, S. 1995 *The Reflecting Team in Action. Collaborative practice in family therapy*. New York, The Guilford Press.

Furniss T. & Bingley Miller L. 1995 Working with Abusing Families. In K. Wilson & A. James Eds *The Child Protection Handbook*. London, Baillière Tindall.

Goldner, V. 1991 Sex, power and gender: normative and covert hierarchies. *Family Process*, **27**, 217–231.

Hanks, H. G. I. & Stratton, P. 1988 Family perspectives on early sexual abuse. In K. Browne, C. Davies & P. Stratton Eds. *Early Prediction And Prevention Of Child Abuse*, pp. 245–266. Chichester, Wiley.

Hanks, H. & Stratton, P. 1995 The Effects of Child Abuse: Signs & Symptoms. In K. Wilson & A. James Eds *The Child Protection Handbook*. London, Baillière Tindall.

Hanks, H. & Stratton, P. 2002 Consequences and indicators of child abuse. In K. Wilson, & A. James Eds, *The Child Protection Handbook, 2nd Edition*. London, Baillière Tindall.

Hanks, H. & Wynne J., 2000 Females who sexually abuse: an approach to assessment. In M. Calder Ed. *The complete guide to sexual abuse assessments.* Lyme Regis, Russell House Publishing.

Henggeler, S. W. 1999 Multisystemic therapy: An overview of clinical procedures, outcomes, and policy implications. *Child Psychology & Psychiatry Review,* **4,** 2–10.

Hobbs, C., Hanks H., Wynne J. 1999 *Child Abuse and Neglect – A Clinicians Handbook.* London, Churchill Livingstone.

Hollin, C. 2000 Handbook of Offender Assessment and Treatment. Chichester, Wiley.

Imber-Black, E. 1993 *Secrets In Families And Family Therapy.* New York, Norton.

Jones, E. 1993 *Family Systems Therapy: Developments in the Milan – Systemic Therapies.* Chichester, Wiley.

Jones, D. 1997 Treatment of the child and the family where child abuse has occurred. In M. E. Helfer, R. S. Kempe & R. D Krugman Eds. *The Battered Child, 5ᵗʰEd.* Chicago, University of Chicago Press.

Kolko, D. J. 1996 Individual cognitive-behavioral treatment and family therapy for physically abused children and their offending parents: A comparison of clinical outcomes. *Child Maltreatment,* **1,** 322–342.

Lang P. Little, M., Cronen, V. 1990 The systemic professional: Domains of action and the question of neutrality. *Human Systems* **1,** 39–55.

Leff, J., Vearnals, S., Brewin, C. R., Wolff, G., Alexander, B., Asen, E., Dayson, D., Jonos, E., Chisholm, D. Everitt, B. 2000 The London Depression Intervention Trial. *British Journal of Psychiatry* **177,** 95–100.

Lindsay, M. 1999 The neglected priority: sexual abuse in the context of residential child care. *Child Abuse Review,* **8,** pp. 405–418.

McAdam, E. & Hannah, C. 1991 Violence – Part 2: Creating the best context to work with clients who have found themselves in violent situations. *Human Systems* **2.** 217–226.

McCarthy, I. C. 1994 Poverty and Social Exclusion. Special Issue of *Human Systems.* **5.** 127–336.

Minuchin, S. 1967 *Families of the Slums: An Exploration of their Structure and Treatment.* New York: Basic Books.

Munton, A., Silvester, J., Stratton, P., & Hanks, H. 1999 *Attributions in Action.* Chichester, Wiley.

Pearce J. W. & Pezzot-Pearce, T. D. 1997 *Psychotherapy of Abused and Neglected Children.* London, Guilford Press.

Pinsof, W. M. & Wynne, L. C. 1995 The effectiveness and efficacy of marital and family therapy: Introduction to the special issue. *Journal of Marital and Family Therapy,* **21,** 341–343.

Robinson, G. & Whitney, L. 1999 Working systemically following abuse: exploring safe uncertainty. *Child Abuse Review,* **8,** 4 pp. 264–274.

Saradjian, J. & Hanks, H. 1996 *Women Who Sexually Abuse Children.* Chichester, Wiley.

Schreier, H., & Libow, J. 1993 *Hurting For Love.* New York, Guildford Press.

Shadish, W. R., Montgomery, L. M., Wilson, P., Wilson, M. R., Bright, I., Okwumabua, T. 1993 Effects of family and marital psychotherapies: A meta-analysis. *Journal of Consulting and Clinical Psychology.* **61:** 992–1002.

Silvester, J., Bentovim, A., Stratton, P., Hanks, H. 1995 Using spoken attributions to classify abusive families. *Child Abuse and Neglect.* **19,** 1221–1232.

Silvester, J. & Stratton, P. 1991 Attributional discrepancy in abusive families. *Human Systems.* **2,** 279–296.

Stratton, P. 1977 Criteria for assessing the influence of obstetric circumstances on later development. In T. Chard and M. Richards Eds *Benefits and Hazards of the New Obstetrics.* pp. 139–156. London, SIMP.

Stratton, P. 1982 *Psychobiology of the Human Newborn.* Chichester, Wiley.

Stratton, P. 1988 Understanding and treating child abuse in the family context. In K. Browne, C. Davies & P. Stratton Eds *Early Prediction And Prevention Of Child Abuse,* pp. 193–202. Chichester, Wiley.

Stratton, P. in press Contemporary Families As Contexts For Development: Contributions From Systemic family therapy. In J. Valsiner & K. J. Connolly Eds *Handbook of Developmental Psychology*. New York, Sage.

Stratton, P. & Hanks, H. 1991 Incorporating circularity in defining and classifying child maltreatment *Human Systems*. 2, 181–200.

Stratton. P. & Hanks H. 1995 Assessing Family Functioning. In P. Reder & C. Lucy Eds *Assessment of Parenting*. pp. 21–38. London, Routledge.

Stratton, P., Preston-Shoot, M. Hanks, H. 1990 *Family Therapy: Training & Practice*. Birmingham, Venture Press.

Stratton, P. & Swaffer, R. 1988 Maternal causal beliefs for abused and handicapped children. *Journal of Reproductive and Infant Psychology*, 6, 201–216.

Summit, R. 1983 The child sexual abuse accommodation syndrome. *Child Abuse and Neglect*, 1, 177–193.

Sundelin, J. & Hansson, K. 1999 Intensive family therapy: a way to change family functioning in multi-problem families. *Journal of Family Therapy*, 21, 419–432.

Swenson C. C., & Hanson, R. F. 1998 Sexual abuse of chidlren: Assessment, research and treatment. In J. R. Lutzker Ed *Handbook of Child Abuse Research and Treatment*. New York, Plenum.

Thomas T. 2001 Preventing unsuitable people from working with children – the Criminal Justice and Court Services Bill, *Child Abuse Review*, 10, 1, 60–69.

Vetere, A. & Cooper, J. 2001 Working systemically with family violence: risk, responsibility and collaboration. *Journal of Family Therapy*. 23, 378–396.

Watzlawick, P., Beavin, J., Jackson, D. 1967 *Pragmatics Of Human Communication: A Study Of Interactional Patterns, Pathologies And Paradoxes*. New York, W.W. Norton.

White M. & Epston D. 1990 *Narrative means to therapeutic ends*, New York, Norton.

15

HELPING EMOTIONALLY ABUSED AND NEGLECTED CHILDREN AND ABUSIVE CARERS

Dorota Iwaniec
Queen's University of Belfast, UK

Martin Herbert
University of Exeter, UK

Alice Sluckin
University of Leicester, UK

INTRODUCTION

Of the four main types of maltreatment discussed in the literature—physical abuse, sexual abuse, neglect, and emotional maltreatment—the hardest to define and, hence, the most difficult to formulate for an intervention, is emotional abuse. It has been viewed as both central to all types of abuse and as occurring as a distinct problem. Emotionally abusive acts are ones that are psychologically damaging to the behavioural, cognitive, affective, or physical functioning of a child (Brassard et al., 1987; Iwaniec, 1999; Glaser & Prior, Chapter 4). Neglect involves the omission of activities that protect children from harm and ill-health; it includes a failure to provide minimal caregiving in the areas of emotional contact/responsiveness, supervision, nutrition, education, and safety, as well as providing inadequate environmental stimulation and structure (Wolfe, 1990). Emotional abuse and neglect affect some children's physical growth, cognitive and psycho-motor development, and can trigger off serious emotional and behavioural problems.

   Non-organic failure-to-thrive, in many cases, is the result of combinations of emotional abuse and neglect, poor parenting style, inadequate food intake, feeding difficulties, problematic relationship and interaction between parents and child,

Early Prediction and Prevention of Child Abuse: A Handbook.
Edited by Kevin Browne, Helga Hanks, Peter Stratton and Catherine Hamilton. © 2002 John Wiley & Sons, Ltd.

insecure attachment, and weak bonding. This chapter will discuss a range of treatment and intervention strategies to help emotionally abused and neglected children and their parents generally, and those who fail-to-thrive specifically. Further discussion of emotionally abused children without growth-failure is provided in Glaser and Prior, Chapter 4. The use of family therapy in relation to failure-to-thrive is discussed by Stratton and Hanks in Chapter 14.

NON-ORGANIC FAILURE-TO-THRIVE

There is a strong association between emotional abuse and neglect *per se* and non-organic failure-to-thrive. Failure-to-thrive is seen as a relationship problem between mother and child and interaction difficulties experienced generally but, in particular, during the act of feeding. (Iwaniec, 1983; Skuse, 1989; Hanks & Hobbs, 1993; Raynor & Rudolf, 1996; Batchelor, 1999). Failure-to-thrive is a term used to describe infants and children whose growth and development are significantly below age-related norms, and in whom no physical causes can be detected. These children are frequently presented psychologically as depressed, tearful, whiney, withdrawn, lethargic, anxious, apprehensive, physically small, thin, of starved appearance, and looking ill (Iwaniec et al., 1985a).

Failure-to-thrive is generally defined in terms of growth. When children are undernourished they fail to gain weight; after a while their growth in height also falters, and their growth often drops below the third percentile in weight and height. Most children are diagnosed when their weight or height percentiles are low; others are diagnosed when their growth drops down across percentile lines, including head circumference. Interpretation of weight-loss needs to be viewed in an informed way taking into consideration the child's motor development and natural slimming down due to increased activities. These abnormalities in growth and development are linked to inadequate food intake, feeding difficulties, insecure attachment of children to their mothers, and weak bonding of mothers to their children (Crittenden, 1987; Hobbs & Hanks, 1999; Iwaniec & Sneddon, 2001). The relationship between parents (notably mothers) and their children often seems to be fraught and unhappy. Many studies have found that the mothers of non-organic failure-to-thrive children are socially isolated and lack social support (Drotar, 1991; Iwaniec, 1995; Hanks & Hobbs, 1996). In addition family life is often seen to be filled with conflict and tension, rather than being a source of emotional support. Mothers were found to be less emotionally available to their children and enjoyed their children's company less (Iwaniec, 1991).

The consequences of failure-to-thrive are quite serious if not attended to early in a child's life. Sustained failure-to-thrive throughout early childhood (which often leads to stunting of growth) is associated with an exceptionally poor outcome of mental abilities. These children are thought to be at risk of poor cognitive development, show emotional instability, and have poor academic attainments (Skuse et al., 1992; Iwaniec, 2000). The majority of children who fail to thrive present feeding difficulties and insufficient intake of food for their chronological age. Furthermore, interaction, general management, and understanding of children's nutritional and emotional needs are found to be poor in many cases. Taking into consideration a wide range of problems associated with non-organic failure-to-thrive we shall illustrate approaches and methods used by us and others to help these children and their families. The major therapeutic task in many failure-to-thrive cases is changing unresponsive (often emotionally abusive or neglectful) parenting into better informed and sensitive care-giving. It is worth pausing to look briefly at these issues.

RESPONSIVE PARENTING

The interactions between parents and children (particularly the early ones involving communication between mother and baby) are of crucial significance in a child's development. What a baby needs is a close, confident, and caring physical and emotional contact with the parent, (be it mother, mother surrogate, or father, or both) in order to be healthy and vigorously develop. The absence of such continuing nurturance and physical intimacy can bring about anxiety in a child, fretting, and disruption of biological functions. One of the indices of basic trust and security in an infant (in Erik Erikson's sense) is stable feeding behaviour. In order for eating to be nutritionally beneficial and enjoyable it requires conditions that denote a relatively benign and calm state of psychosomatic harmony. If the eating time is fraught and tense, the intake of food will be insufficient resulting in poor physical growth and psychomotor development.

Parental responsiveness is a complex and many-sided phenomenon, but there are at least three different elements that make for what one might assess to be *sensitive* responsiveness: these are tendencies to react *promptly*, *consistently*, and *appropriately* in response to a child's crying or other communications and actions. Personal factors can interfere with these intricate processes. To take an extreme case, a mother suffering from depression is unlikely to "tune in" to the child in a sufficiently sensitive manner to be able to construct with him/her a mutually beneficial and stimulating sequence of interaction (see Schaffer & Collins, 1986, for a review of the literature). Equally, mothers who abuse alcohol or other substances are not able to attend to children's physical and emotional needs in a consistent and responsive manner. Being under the influence of drugs or alcohol disables them in providing the quality of care that promotes adequate development and well-being. These children are often both physically and emotionally neglected to the point of significant harm, and in need of care and protection outside the family unit (Iwaniec, 2001, in press). Cousins and Monteith (2002), in a study of 395 foster children under five years, reported that in 75% of families there was a history of alcohol abuse, and in 41% of families a history of substance abuse. In 26% of families, both parents had abused alcohol, while in a further 29% of families the mother abused alcohol, and in 11% of cases the father abused alcohol. In some families there was a generation link with a history of grandparents also abusing alcohol. These authors stated that actual or potential global neglect (50%) was the biggest main reason for referral of younger children to social services, followed by the inability of carers to cope due to various cognitive and personality limitations (31%) and potential abuse especially of emotional kind (28%). It is of concern that intervention strategies regarding alcohol-abusing families are haphazard and poorly planned. More often than not children are returned home before adequate treatment for alcohol abuse takes place, and before there is evidence that consumption of alcohol or substances of a different kind have been eliminated (Iwaniec, in press).

PARENT–CHILD BONDING

The question of sensitive or insensitive responsiveness has been linked (in part) with the quality of the emotional bond or "attachment" that forms between the parent and baby. The emotional bond between mother and child is defined as the extent to which a mother feels her child occupies an essential position in her life and that the interest of a child will take precedence over her own interests in life. Components of mothers bonding to a child or children include feelings of warmth, love, sacrifice, a sense of possession and belonging, devotion, protection and concern for the child's well-being, positive anticipation of prolonged contact, and a need for and pleasure in being together. Mothers who are strongly attached/bonded to their children respond to signals of distress (such as pain, hunger, discomfort, or boredom) promptly and consistently. They show empathy and concern when a child looks sad, withdrawn, and unwell. Obviously the infant's survival depends upon a loving and long-term commitment by adult caregivers (Sluckin et al., 1983); assessment of parental bonding and attachment to and with children is considered as essential when dealing with children at risk of abuse.

PLANNING INTERVENTION AND TREATMENT

Emotional abuse and neglect resulting in failure-to-thrive seldom arise as a consequence of a single factor, but rather as a combination adversely affecting child development and well-being. Neglect and abuse tend to be multi-dimensional and it is crucial to examine each of these dimensions in order to devise appropriate and successful interventions. Intervention strategies can take many forms, follow different routes, and may require several methods and approaches to deal effectively and suitably with the presenting problems. Several studies, (eg., Wasik; et al., 1990; Wolfe et al., 1993; Iwaniec, 1995) confirmed that a combination of interventions and use of different therapeutic methods produced better results in the longer term than a single approach. For example, the use of a day-nursery or family centre to help a child with developmental retardation, training of parents to deal with child-rearing deficit, and informal and formal group-work to reduce social isolation and to provide emotional support for the parents in their own rights may be helpful. It is now generally recognised that child-maltreatment more often than not is the result of child-rearing deficit, rather than deliberate parental action, (Azar et al., 1998; Wolfe et al., 1993). Helping parents in more effective child-rearing practices, and raising their awareness about children's developmental needs, should dominate intervention strategies. The available evidence suggests that support and monitoring of these types of neglect cases alone is insufficient to achieve long-lasting improvements in children's and their parents' lives (Garbarino, et al., 1986; Crittenden, 1988; Wolfe, 1990; Iwaniec, 2000). More pro-active skill-teaching approaches and methods are advocated, where parents can be actively involved in problem solving, which would in turn generate a sense of achievement and competence (Herbert, 1993; Iwaniec, 1995). However, there is not a single or simple way to deal with many and complex problems, neither is there an identified single approach or method that could claim an all-embracing success. Helping strategies need to be tailored to the specific requirements of the individual families in their special circumstances. For example, if non-organic failure-to-thrive is due to ill-informed parenting, then parent-training would appear to be the most suitable approach to adopt. If, on the other hand, it is due to parental rejection, then a step-by-step approach of reducing hostile feelings towards the child will be required using various methods of attachment work and modelling of anxiety and fear-reducing interaction on the part of the child, and hostility and anger on the part of the parent.

INTERVENTION AND TREATMENT OF NON-ORGANIC FAILURE-TO-THRIVE

Intervention with non-organic failure-to-thrive cases usually falls into two basic categories: immediate (crisis intervention) and longer-term therapeutic work. Immediate intervention focuses on the child's safety, neglected developmental attainments, and urgent family needs. In cases of severe emotional neglect and abuse (whatever the reason) the child's development might be seriously retarded, so the provision of day-care, (in a day-nursery, family centre, using a daily-minder, or, in more serious cases, placement in a foster home or extended family) might be necessary to give a child much needed social stimulation, safety, and opportunity to developmentally catch up.

Many families might need assistance with welfare rights, housing, health problems, employment, or financial difficulties, and these should be dealt with early on to reduce stress and to create an atmosphere where further intervention could take place. Equally, in cases of substance and alcohol abuse or maternal depression, treatment should start in resolving maternal problems before embarking on addressing relationships and interactional issues. Unfortunately intervention often stops here these days, especially in social services, yet this is where it should begin in earnest. Providing day-care services for a child does not necessarily resolve his or her problems at home. Even if the child has learned new skills and new ways of behaving this is not going to be reinforced and encouraged if parents are not going to change their attitudes and behaviour, improve their functioning on an individual and family level, enhance their parenting skills, and increase their awareness of their children's needs. No amount of help is going to be effective if an alcoholic mother is not going to stop drinking, or a depressed mother does not get treatment. Azar et al. (1998) are of the opinion that, given the immediate risks to children, interventions with families in which child abuse is taking place may initially target parenting skill defects, aggressive and rejecting behaviours (e.g. by increasing

TABLE 15.1   Potential interventions

Systemic Level	Dyadic Level (Interactions/relationships)	Individual Level
Family group discussion/therapy Written contracts Negotiation training Settling differences Contingency contracting (exchange theory) Communication enhancement Clarification of roles and rules Improvement of physical/ environment resources (e.g. child-minding/day care) Cognitive restructuring (reframing) Ecological consideration	Enhancing positive interaction Operant programmes Positive reinforcement— "catching the child out in good behaviour" Decreasing threats, criticism Encouraging play with children (including demonstrations/ modelling) Increasing consistency Negotiating fair/ few/clear rules Marital work	*Parent/caregiver* Training in more effective child-care practice (e.g. use of appropriate sanctions; setting limits; praising Developmental counselling to enhance knowledge/ decrease faulty perceptions/ptattributions Cognitive restructuring (reframing) Reducing inappropriate anxiety/anger/cynicism Relaxation Self-talk Self-control training *Child* Improving life skills Play therapy Systematic desensitization Skills training

responsiveness, using positive management strategies, and improving communication), stress management, and cognitively based strategies (e.g. problem solving, reframing/cognitively restructuring children's behaviour). Although the child's family is always a major concern in an intervention, the focus of therapy may range (or shift) over several levels (see Table 15.1).

The treatment programme for failure-to-thrive developed by the authors and positively evaluated by them is presented as an example of effective treatment.

The therapist dealing with the family made it a practice to discuss in specific detail the assessment and later the plan for intervention with the mother—and with the father if the parents lived together. The intervention plan usually had five stages (stages 4 and 5 were optional):

1. resolve feeding difficulties and improve feeding style, i.e. modify maternal behaviour and responses during the act of feeding (by means of counselling, modelling, and carefully structured feeding situations);
2. deliberately, and in a planned and graduated fashion, create positive interactions and reduce negative interactions (e.g. hostile actions, avoidance tendencies) between mother and child, and, indeed, other members of the family. We would usually attempt to desensitise the child's anxiety and fear of the mother's feeding and other caregiving activities. This intervention might also involve systematic desensitisation of the mother's tension, anger, and resentment when in

the child's company by means of relaxation training, graduated exposure training, etc., and by cognitive restructuring;
3. intensify and increase positive mother–child interactions;
4. some older children with a longer history of failure-to-thrive presented behaviour problems. These were dealt with when the extreme "emotional arousal"
in the family (associated with the crisis of having an undernourished child) had
subsided. It was generally thought unwise and also unproductive to attempt to
deal with all presenting problems at the same time. The majority of children did
not require further treatment, once emotional parental responsiveness to them
improved;
5. self-help mothers' group.

No cases were exactly alike. Nevertheless a description of a fairly "typical"
intervention sequence is as follows:

Stage 1

Feeding is tackled in a highly structured (and thus directive) manner. Meal-times
are made more relaxed. Mothers are asked (behaviour being rehearsed) to desist
from screaming, shouting, and threatening the child over meals. The period of
eating is made quiet and calm. The mother is asked to talk soothingly and pleas-
antly to the child. It is usually difficult for her to achieve and maintain this pattern
of behaviour: the therapist therefore assists, role-plays, and also directly models
the feeding. She may feed the child a few times, where necessary providing reas-
surance. She observes the mother at work and prompts her (where necessary) to
help the child to eat—in a gentle manner—when she is in difficulties. The mother
is encouraged to look at, smile, and touch the infant. If the child refuses food,
the mother leaves the room for a while; this she does only if she cannot encourage or coax him or her by means of play and soft words. Fathers are encouraged to play a part in the child's care generally, and in feeding activities more
specifically.
   Where meals are thought to be too rigidly ritualistic, parents are encouraged to
be more flexible or, alternatively, to be rather more regular when routines are absent
and family eating patterns are chaotic;

Stage 2

This phase is discussed in detail with parents: rationale and methods are explained
carefully and sometimes written down. In most cases a contract is drawn up spec-
ifying the mutual obligations and rules for the family and therapist. What might
happen in situations where parent–child interactions are highly (and sometimes
mutually) aversive—a common finding—is that each evening after her partner returns from work, the mother is encouraged to play exclusively with her child for
10 to 15 minutes during the first week, and for 15 to 20 minutes during the fourth
and subsequent weeks. After the mother's session with the child the rest of the
family might join in for a family play session. The way the mother plays and the

toys she uses may have to be demonstrated and rehearsed with her (some parents did not know how to play with their children). She is encouraged to talk to her child in a soft, reassuring manner and to encourage him or her to participate in the play.

Mothers are encouraged—as a general principle—to smile at their children, look at them, hold their hands, stroke their hair, and praise them for each response they give. This may require careful programming if their behaviour is very timid. The mothers' approaches are shaped by a series of successive approximations; they are encouraged to initiate as well as react. After a few days or even weeks, mothers are guided to seek proximity by hugging their children briefly and holding them on their lap for increasing intervals of time, eventually holding them close but gently, while reading to them, looking at and describing pictures, etc.

There were several "rejecting" mothers in our sample and they usually found this very difficult and, at times, distasteful. This aversion gradually lessened when the child began to smile back, seek her presence, and in other ways respond to her overtures. This period of therapy requires a lot of support for the mother and the whole family. Frequent visits and telephone calls were made to monitor the programme (reinforcing the reinforcer is critical in this work). It could take three months of hard work to bring a mother and child closer together and to the point of beginning to enjoy (or stop disliking/fearing) each other;

Stage 3

The third stage is planned to include two weeks of deliberately intensified mother–child interaction. The mother is to take the child with her almost everywhere she goes and whatever she does—within reason. She is asked to chat to him/her as much as possible, regardless of whether or not he/she fully understands what she is doing or saying. She is told to make a lot of eye contact, smile, cuddle, and hug the infant as often as possible.

These requirements of a tired mother—particularly a single parent—could be counterproductive if "demanded" insensitively. Discussions are important, as are child-minding arrangements which give the mother "a break". During the period of intervention at the home the children and their families routinely attended outpatient clinics for purposes of monitoring weight and other indices;

Stage 4

Children also still presenting behavioural problems at this stage of treatment are helped by the introduction of systematic positive reinforcement on a large scale: they are praised for good conduct or for even attempting to behave in a pro-social manner. They are rewarded by favourable activities, e.g. story-reading, favourite foods, or special play. Parents are guided through the process in order to create a warm anxiety-free atmosphere, so children can begin to feel that they are liked and wanted;

Stage 5

Mothers of children with failure-to-thrive tend to be socially isolated and generally have little support. They also suffer from low self-esteem and lack of confidence. In order to boost their morale, and create an opportunity to acquire a social network, self-help parents' groups, and more structured parent-training in groups have been set up and have proved to be highly beneficial. These methods of treatment are fully discussed in Iwaniec (1995).

The formal programme is faded out gradually (over a period of several weeks, depending on the particular case). The case is terminated when there is evidence of the child's continued satisfactory growth and evidence of improved family inter-actions, maternal feeding, and attitudes towards the child (as carefully monitored in terms of explicit behavioural criteria [see Sluckin et al., 1983]).

WORKING WITH PARENTS

There are many routes in helping parents to become more effective in child-rearing practices and to enjoy their children. Some of the methods used which proved to be helpful (see Iwaniec et al., 1985, and Iwaniec & Sneddon, 2001) are discussed below.

Personal Counselling

The main task of counselling is to help parents reflect on the problems they are experiencing and to direct them to a better understanding of themselves and their behaviour. Counselling involves rigorous exploration of difficulties, clarifying con-flicting issues, and searching for alternative ways to understand and to deal with the problems. The emphasis is put on self-help, calling on the inner resources of the person who is in difficulties, promoting personal growth and more mature ways of acting and reacting, thinking first and responding in a thought-through way. These parents are often themselves emotionally deprived, and they have nobody to turn to for help; they might be reluctant to approach child-welfare agencies for fear of losing their children. It "opens a door" to more sincere, anxiety-free sharing of true feelings and difficulties. Counselling, however, is not sufficient or even appropriate to use with very chaotic dysfunctional families riddled with violence, alcoholism, or drug abuse, who have little insight, and are unable to see or to accept their faults and the point of view of others.

Developmental Counselling

One of the most important and necessary aspects of intervention is developmental counselling, which is educational and informative in the sense of disseminating the knowledge we have of child-development (for example, what is normal or appropriate to the child's age, sex, and level of ability, and suggesting to parents what are reasonable expectations for their child). The transmission of information about normal child-development and basic child-needs for "optimal" development is often as important as suggestions about ways of dealing with worrying behaviours. Unrealistic expectations on the part of parents as to what the child should (or should not) do often leads to parent–child relationship problems and maltreatment. When pressure is put on a child to perform certain tasks which he is not developmentally ready to perform, then the child will get anxious, confused, and nervous which, in turn, may bring about behavioural and emotional problems and a sense of helplessness. Abusive parents often perceive a child as lazy and disobedient, and punish it for non-compliance with their requests: abuse can start here, when parents, dissatisfied with a child's performance, constantly criticise, rebuke, or deprive it of affection and treats, or call it stupid, thick, ignorant, or good for nothing.

Parents often compare their children, or a child, with those of friends and neighbours, so it is essential to counsel them about individual differences in speed of development and how to encourage a child to learn different skills. In the case of emotional and physical neglect, where a child's development might be delayed due to lack of stimulation, attention, and proper care, parents need to be guided and instructed on what to do and why. This is often the case with toddlers, when temper tantrums and oppositional behaviour are interpreted as sheer naughtiness and wickedness, and not as inner frustration when striving to master a skill. Bowel- and bladder- control is another example of often unrealistic expectations and faulty perceptions on the part of the parents.

Not infrequently those difficulties between parent and children have contributed to the child's behaviour problems in the first place and get in the way of the parent's practical efforts to implement a programme. We know that some children seem temperamentally resistant to socialisation and nuturing from birth (Herbert, 1994). Parents may have special sensitivities or anxieties with regard to this particular child which make it impossible or difficult for them to be firm or consistent when he behaves in a certain manner. High levels of arousal (anger, anxiety) on the part of the parents plus a common non-compliance in the child interact so as to disrupt his routines or even his socialisation. Parents often have fixed ideas about rearing children, which represents the standard of their parents or reactions against them. These matters may require discussion and a sympathetic hearing before the parents can sustain the modification of their own behaviour which (inter alia) is being required of them.

USE OF COGNITIVE METHODS OF INTERVENTION

Common characteristics of neglectful parents are their self-defeating thoughts and beliefs about their abilities to cope effectively with different life-tasks. These dysfunctional thoughts lead to dysfunctional feelings, and consequently to negative outcomes for the parents and for the child. A change in cognition needs to occur when a person says *"I can do it"*, *"I will find a way to stand up for myself and my children"*, *"I will make an effort to do more things with my children"*. Cognitive work

TABLE 15.2a Cognitive beliefs

Event	Belief	Feeding	Behaviour	Outcome
Child fails to thrive.	He/she does not want to eat, this is not my fault, prefers to be left alone, dislikes to be fussed about.	Anger, frustration, not knowing what the fuss is all about. There is nothing wrong with him.	Do nothing.	Serious developmental delays, due to physical and emotional neglect.

with neglectful parents should also address attitudes and perceptions of parental duties and responsibilities in order to raise their awareness of children's developmental needs and to work out caring strategies which would facilitate the child's healthy, vigorous, and happy development. If parents believe that children should amuse themselves, or that playing with children is childish and stupid, or that the way to make children behave is to tell them off, scream, and shout at them, or that there is nothing wrong if they are not attended to, properly supervised, and guided, then those beliefs have to be challenged, explored, and changed. Little can be achieved if cognitive change does not take place. When choosing the cognitive methods of working, the first task is to accurately identify such damaging thoughts, and to demonstrate their link with the child's negative outcomes. Chains of dysfunctional thoughts and beliefs, leading to emotional neglect, can be graphically demonstrated to parents (see Table 15.2a and b).

Parents are asked to record unhelpful thoughts that seem to recur frequently, and to link them to the feelings accompanying those thoughts in order to create a realisation of how such thoughts can influence behaviour and well-being, and how exaggerated they are at times. These statements and associated feelings are not just ordinary negative thoughts: they are unhealthy, distorted, and damaging to both parents and child; they contain elements of chronic emotional discomfort and maladaptive behaviour; and they are self-defeating in nature. Help is needed to generate different ways of thinking and functioning. This is particularly useful when working with depressed parents of low esteem, for example, with mothers whose children fail-to-thrive.

TABLE 15.2b What are the alternative ways of thinking and understanding—cognitive change?

Event	Belief	Feeling	Behaviour	Outcome
Child fails to thrive.	I must be doing something wrong. I must pay more attention to the child.	Hope, commitment, and determination.	Attends to child's nutrition, is more stimulating and encouraging.	Child puts on weight, becomes more alert and active; makes progress developmentally.

STRESS MANAGEMENT TRAINING

Most maltreating parents have difficulties in controlling frustration and anger, so they lash out physically or verbally, not only at their children, but at anyone who happens to be around. This sort of behaviour is self-reinforcing because it brings immediate (though not long-lasting) relief. When things do not go the way parents expect them to go, they hit harder and more frequently, scream, and use degrading language with greater passion, believing that this is the only way to make things happen (when dealing with different authorities, neighbours, extended families, and so on). Self-control training is designed to teach a person how to manage and to regulate anger arousal in order to achieve a greater degree of behaviour-control (for example, learning to control verbal aggression, drinking, or outbursts of violence). The first task in self-control training is to examine what leads to an item of behaviour and what are the consequences of that behaviour and, secondly, to explore alternative ways of behaving by devising self-control techniques. Coping strategies include the use of self-instructions to reduce arousal when this is identified, (e.g. dealing with difficult issues or tasks [such as feeding difficulties] or frustrations [such as those regarding housing or benefits]). The client is taught how to prepare for possible provocation by using self-instruction in how to behave, (e.g. *"I am going to talk quietly, I am not going to lose my temper, I will not swear, scream, and shout I will just try to coax him to eat"*). It is very useful to role-play possible scenarios, to acquire stress-management skills in various life situations. Such self-talk helps the person to feel in control and it helps to reduce stress.

MATERNAL POSTNATAL DEPRESSION AS A PRECIPITANT OF EMOTIONAL ABUSE AND NEGLECT

The negative effects on an infant's development as a result of postnatal depression is now widely accepted (Murray et al., 1991). Such a mother can be unresponsive to infant cues as she withdraws from contact with her baby. Relative cognitive delay in the infant may be significantly related to the quality of the mother–infant relationship in the post-partum period. Murray & Cooper (1991) maintain that, in order to treat insecurity in the mother–infant relationship, it is necessary to explore in depth the mother's own attachment history. They describe the case of a mother who had become depressed in the early post-partum period despite good support from her husband and family. At 18 months her daughter was clearly avoidantly attached and the mother was offered brief therapy to deal with a problem. It transpired that the mother had an emotionally very distant relationship with her own mother, something she was at pains to avoid repeating with her own daughter. Much of the treatment focused on remembering episodes and angry feelings during the mother's childhood. Gradually the treatment focus shifted to the here and now and the mother was able to admit that she felt devastated by the child's lack of affection for her as demonstrated at reunion in the "Strange Situation". The duration of treatment was two months at the end of which the mother was no longer depressed and the child showed "clear signs of secure attachment". Reflecting on the treatment six months later the mother said she had for the first time begun to understand herself, her present and past relationship with her parents, and she was able to see now that she had no "intrinsic personality defect", as she had feared when finding herself unable to bond with her baby.

A very different approach is adopted by Andrew Sluckin (1998) in his treatment of postnatal depression and bonding failure. His therapeutic focus is in the "here and now" and combines ideas from Video Interaction Guidance encompassing the impact of the meaning, Systems Therapy, and Art Therapy. The focus for therapeutic work with "failure to bond", he stresses, has progressively broadened from an individual (the mother) to a family and systems perspective. If the treatment is to be successful both the needs of the mother as well as the needs of the child need to be accommodated in a society where there is a lot of pressure on a mother to live up to a stereotype.

ATTACHMENT WORK

There are numerous ways in which children with attachment disorders can be helped, and in which parent–child bonding can be strengthened. Iwaniec (1999) pointed out that in infancy it would involve proactive and sensitive maternal behaviour during feeding, bathing, changing, and responding to the child's signals of distress promptly, consistently, and appropriately. To increase secure attachment between children and mothers, the latter are asked to hold the children gently while being fed, and to talk to them softly, establish eye contact, and smile at them upon eye-contact.

With older children parents are advised to sit a child on their lap holding him gently and closely, and being warm and reassuring when talking to the child, reading a story, describing pictures in the book, or simply watching television together. These deliberate "increasing in time physical and emotional togetherness" exercises should be done three to four times a day and lasting a few minutes each time. As time goes on, children begin to feel more relaxed, at ease, gradually seeking contact and affection spontaneously and quite frequently.

VIDEO RECORDING AND FEEDBACK

A variety of techniques can be used to increase parents' awareness and understanding of what is happening and how to correct inappropriate parental responses to their children. Very effective work has been done videoing the interaction of parents who persistently criticise, rebuke, humiliate, ridicule, and react with hostility to their children as well as during aversive feeding interaction of failure-to-thrive children (Iwaniec, 1995; Hanks & Hobbs, 1996; Hampton, 1996). Examples of aversive parental behaviour is videoed and then played back to parents, so they can see and hear for themselves how they behaved and what they said. They are asked to pay particular attention to their tone of voice, eye contact, facial expression, and general body language when they speak to the child. They are also asked to observe their child's anxious and fearful reaction to them, and their apprehension when in the parents' company. The impact of parental emotionally abusive behaviour on the child is discussed in terms of immediate pain and long-term consequences (such as prevention of developing strong self-esteem and self-confidence, a sense of belonging and security, and a general feeling of being loved and wanted).

Parents are asked to imagine how they would feel and how they would react if they were treated in the same way as they were treating their child. By asking them to reflect on their harsh and hostile behaviour it is hoped that they will be able to get in touch with their own and the child's feelings, which in turn will help them to empathise and recognise pain and hurt inflicted by them on the child. Parents are asked to observe the role-play conducted by a therapist demonstrating warm, encouraging, and caring behaviour when doing things with the child. In turn they are asked to play with the child, which is videoed, played back, and discussed.

WORKING WITH CHILDREN

Therapeutic work with children who are the victims of emotional maltreatment is seldom conducted on a dyadic basis alone, although there is a subgroup of children (with anxiety and insecurity problems) whose emotional disturbance may require individual play therapy or psychotherapy (see Kazdin, 1987; Herbert, 1993, Knell, 1998; for a discussion of these methods). More commonly the social or mental-health worker is faced with problems which (in many instances) are strategies for gaining attention or proximity of caregivers who are unresponsive to the child's pro-social communications. These are aimed at encouraging caring parenting as operationalised in Table 15.3.

TABLE **15.3** Qualities of caring parenting

Emotional Needs	Some defining criteria
1. Affection	Affection includes physical contact, admiration, touching, holding, comforting, making allowances, being tender, showing concern, communicating.
2. Security	Security means continuity of care, a predictable environment, consistent controls, settled patterns of care and daily routines, fair and understandable rules, harmonious family relationships, the feeling that one's home and family are always there.
3. Responsibility	Responsibility involves discipline appropriate to the child's stage of development, providing a model to emulate/imitate, indicating limits, insisting on concern for others.
4. Independence	Independence implies making opportunities for the child to do more unaided tasks and make decisions, first about small things but gradually about larger matters.
5. Responsiveness	Responsiveness means prompt, consistent, appropriate actions to meet child's needs.
6. Stimulation	Stimulation means encouraging curiosity and exploratory behaviour, by praising, by responding to questions and play, by promoting training/educational opportunities and new experiences.

Azar et al. (1998) caution that to monitor child-safety, it is crucial that some individual work with children and/or the family as a whole occurs concurrently with group treatment (e.g. adjacent home, existing careful child protective agency monitoring).

Emotionally abused and neglected children show very low self-esteem. Their behaviour and reactions are marked by apprehension, withdrawal, shyness, and fearful avoidance of initiating conversation or other activities: they seem to be in constant doubt of their ability to do anything right. This is not surprising if we take into consideration aversive parent–child interaction. Persistent criticism, rebukes, and lack of guidance and supervision to acquire appropriate behaviour bring about painful feelings of confusion and helplessness. Such children are seldom praised, and their good behaviour and task-accomplishment are rarely acknowledged or even noticed: their attempts to please parents by attending to different task or behaving in a pleasing manner are generally ignored or dismissed. All this creates apprehension and a general reluctance to try new tasks. Change can be achieved by encouraging and teaching parents how to play with children, and how to create opportunities for learning in an anxiety-free atmosphere. Behavioural methods are very effective here. Parents are shown and advised how to use various forms of reinforcements (like praise, smiles, kisses, touching, activities that are liberal, and so on) to show their children how pleased they are with their behaviour and performance. These increased (in quality and quantity) interactions do not only improve care and attention, but also tend to improve mutual attachment, affection, and a sense of belonging. Sometimes it is necessary to provide alternative care to stop hurtful and emotionally damaging interaction and to create opportunity for the child to be compensated for emotional harm. Iwaniec's 20-year follow-up study of children who failed to thrive indicated that those removed from parental care after attempts to resolve problems at home had failed did much better long term than those who remained at home when there was only marginal improvement. In addition, children referred during the first year of life for assessment and treatment (that is before extensive damage occurred in the parent–child relationship) did much better than those referred between three to five years of life.

SUMMARY

Emotional abuse and neglect is difficult to define, and the extent of the harmful effects on the child are hard to quantify. Emotional abuse can occur on its own, but it is always associated with other forms of child maltreatment. Treatment of emotional abuse *per se* is, as yet, not well developed, and methods used to resolve, or to ease, the problems are poorly evaluated. There are very few validated studies dealing with the effectiveness of chosen methodologies. This chapter outlines a multi-dimensional approach to helping strategies for parents whose children fail-to-thrive due to emotional abuse and neglect, and suggests some techniques to help the children. It is argued that treatment of emotional abuse lends itself to al-ready well-established and verified therapeutic methods, such as: family therapies, cognitive-behavioural methods and techniques, attachment work, and reflective counselling.

REFERENCES

Azar, S.T., Ferrare, M.M. and Breton, S.J. (1998) Intraglamical Child Maltreatment. In T.H. Allendick and M. Hersen (Eds) *Handbook of Child Psychopathology* (3ʳᵈ Edn).

Azar, S.T. and Wolfe, D. (1989) Child Abuse and Neglect. In F. J. Marsh and R.A. Barkley (Eds) *Treatment of Childhood Disorders*. New York: Guilford Press.

Batchelor, J.A. (1999). Failure-to-thrive in young children. Research & Practice Evaluated. The Children's Society, London.

Brassard, M.R., Germain, R. and Hart, S.N. (1987) *Psychological Maltreatment of Children and Youth*. New York: Pergamon.

Cousins, W. & Monteith, M. (2002). The lives of younger looked after children: preliminery findings from the Multiple Placements Project Belfast: beutie for Child Care Research, Queen's University.

Crittenden, P.M. (1988) Family and Dyadic Patterns of Functioning in Maltreating Families. In K. Browne, C. Davies, and P. Stratton (Eds), *Early prediction and Prevention of Child Abuse* (pp. 162–189). New York: John Wiley.

Crittenden, P.M. (1987) Non-organic failure to thrive: deprivation or distortion? *Infant Mental Health Journal*, **8**: 51–64.

Drotar, D. (1991) The family context of non-organic failure-to-thrive. *American Journal of Orthopsychiatry*, **6**(1): 23–24.

Garbarino, J., Guttman, E. and Seeley, J.A. (1986) *The Psychologically Battered Child*. San Francisco: Jossey-Bass.

Hampton, D. (1996) Resolving the feeding difficulties associated with nonorganic failure to thrive. *Child: Care, Health and Development*, **22**(4): 273–284.

Hanks, H.G.I. and Hobbs, C. (1996) A multi-disciplinary approach for the treatment of children with failure-to-thrive. *Child: Care, Health and Development*, **22**(4), 273–284.

Hanks, H.G.I. and Hobbs, C. (1993) Failure-to-thrive: a model for treatment. *Baillière's Clinical Paediatrics*, **1**(1), 101–119.

Herbert, M. (1994) Behavioural methods. In M. Rutter, E Taylor and L.Hersov (Eds) *Child and Adolescent Psychiatry: Modern Approaches* (3ʳᵈ edn). Oxford: Blackwell Scientific.

Herbert, M. (1993) *Working with Children and the Children Act*. Leicester: BPS Books (British Psychological Society).

Hobbs, C. Hanks, H. and Wynne J. (1999) *Child Abuse and Neglect – A Clinician's Handbook*. Edinburgh: Churchill Livingstone.

Iwaniec, D. and Sneddon, H. (2001) Attachment style in adults who failed-to-thrive as children: outcomes of a 20-Year follow-up study of factors influencing maintenance or change in attachment style. *The British Journal of Social Work*, **31**(2), 179–195.

Iwaniec, D. (2000) From childhood to adulthood: the outcomes of a twenty-year follow-up of children who failed to thrive. In D. Iwaniec and M. Hill (Eds) *Child Welfare, Policy and Practice: Issues and Lessons Emerging from Current Research*, London: Jessica Kingsley Publishers.

Iwaniec, D. (1999). Child abuse, parenting, identification and treatment. In D. Messer and F. Jones (Eds) *Psychology and Social Care*, London: Jessica Kingsley.

Iwaniec, D. and Herbert, M. (1999) Multi-dimensional approach to helping emotionally abused and neglected children and abusive parents. *Children and Society*, **13**, 365–379.

Iwaniec, D. (1995) *The Emotionally Abused and Neglected Child. Identification, Assessment and Intervention*. Chichester: Wiley.

Iwaniec, D. (1991) Treatment of children who fail to grow in the light of the new Children Act. *Association for Child Psychology and Psychiatric Newsletter*, **13**(3), 21–27.

Iwaniec, D., Herbert, M. and McNeish, A.S. (1985b) Social work with failure-to-thrive children and their families, Part II: Behavioural social work intervention. *The British Journal of Social Work*, **15**, 375–389.

Iwaniec, D., Herbert, M. and McNeish, A.S. (1985a) Social work with failure-to-thrive children and their families, Part I: Psychosocial factors. *The British Journal of Social Work*, **15**, 243–259.

Iwaniec, D. (1983) *Social and psychological factors to the aetiology and management of children who fail to thrive*, Leicester University, PhD thesis.

Kazdin, A.E. (1987) Treatment of anti-social behaviour in children: current status and future directions. *Psychological Bulletin*, **102**, 1897–203.

Knell, S.M. (1998). Cognitive-behavioural play therapy. *Journal of Clinical Child Psychology*, **27**, 28–33.

Murray, L. and Cooper, P.J. (1991a) Clinical application of attachment theory and research: change in infant attachment with brief psychotherapy in the clinical application of ethology and Attachment Theory. *Child Psychology & Psychiatry, Occasional Papers*, No. 9, pp. 15–24.

Murray, L., Copper, P.J. and Stein, A. (1991b) The impact of post natal depression on infant development. *British Medical Journal* No 678327, 978–979.

Raynor, P. and Rudolf, M.C.J. (1996) What do we know about children who fail-to-thrive? *Child: Care, Health & Development*, **22**(4), 241–250.

Schaffer, H.R. and Collis, G.M. (1986). Parental responsiveness and child behaviour. In W. Sluckin and M. Herbert (Eds), *Parental Behaviour*, Oxford: Blackwell.

Skuse, D. (1989) Emotional abuse and delay in growth. In R. Meadow (Ed) *AMB of Child Abuse*. London: British Medical Association.

Skuse, D., Wolke, D. and Reilly, S. (1992) Failure-to-thrive: clinical and developmental aspects. In H. Remschmidt and M.H. Schmidt (Eds) *Developmental Psychopathology*. Lewiston, NY: Hogrefe and Hubber.

Sluckin, A. (1998) Bonding Failure: "I don't know this baby, she is nothing to do with me" *Clinical Child Psychology and Psychiatry*, vol. 3, no. 1 January 1998.

Sluckin, A., and Dolan, P. (1989) Tackling child abuse in the EC. *Social Work Today*, 31.8.89, 14–15.

Sluckin, W., Herbert, M. and Sluckin, A. (1983) *Maternal Bonding*, Oxford: Blackwell.

Wasik, B.H., Ramey, C.T., Bryant, D.M. and Sparling, J.J. (1990) A longitudinal study of two early intervention strategies: project CARE. *Child Development*, **61**, 1682–1696.

Wolfe, D.A. (1990) Preventing child abuse means enhancing family functioning. *Canada's Mental Health*, **38**, 27–29.

Wolfe, D.A. and Wekerle, C. (1993) Treatment strategies for child physical abuse and neglect – a critical progress report. *Clinical Psychology Review*, vol. 13, no. 6, 473–500.

16

THE CONTRIBUTION OF CHILDREN'S SERVICES TO THE PROTECTION OF CHILDREN

Roger Bullock
Dartington Social Research Unit, UK

Michael Little
Dartington Social Research Unit, and University of Chicago, USA

Had this chapter been commissioned a decade ago, its title would have contained the words social services. It is increasingly recognised, however, that much social intervention on behalf of children in need, whatever their circumstances, is provided not only by social workers but also by health, education and police professionals or by services that they organise. Increasingly, therefore, the term children's services is used to encapsulate a series of activities on behalf of children in need. They are defined as services organised by but not necessarily provided by health, education, social and police services on behalf of children with the intention of addressing an identified social need. One fundamental need for children is to be protected from maltreatment.

That said, the majority of research on child protection in the context of children's services is still attributable to social services. The balance in this summary of current knowledge is, therefore, somewhat skewed. More is said about children looked after away from home than about the contribution of primary physicians or health visitors because there have been more studies about the former.

The chapter begins with some definitions of intervention, since the changing pattern of children's services has invalidated previously held assumptions. It next reviews aspects of the process dealing with referrals to children's services since the handling of a case can have a bearing on outcomes for children. A section on inter-agency co-operation is also included. Consideration is then given to research on the

Early Prediction and Prevention of Child Abuse: A Handbook.
Edited by Kevin Browne, Helga Hanks, Peter Stratton and Catherine Hamilton. © 2002 John Wiley & Sons, Ltd.

contribution of services that look after abused and neglected children away from home. The chapter ends by drawing attention to the growing body of knowledge about effective practice that rests on carefully planned controlled trials and with a review of future problems and challenges in child protection.

DEFINING INTERVENTION

Children who are maltreated are at risk of a range of poor outcomes. For some the risk is literally grave. How should society respond? Sociologically, responses have varied and sometimes competed. There have been times when the care of children has been viewed as the concern of parents rather than the state (Eekelaar, 2001). At other times, there has been a mood of child rescue to protect the maltreated from the excesses of their families (Pinchbeck & Hewitt, 1973). At other moments the trend has been to reduce stress on parents as a mechanism for increasing protection afforded to the child (Department of Health, 1995). Fox Harding (1991) has summarised the different forces that shape a society's services for children at risk or victims of maltreatment.

Much more attention has been given to the social forces influencing child protection activity than to the organising principle of clinical work. Very often practitioners know they have to intervene (with different levels of compulsion, depending on the particular historical and national context) without a strong theory about how that intervention will help.

Elsewhere (Little & Mount, 1999) we have argued that good outcomes across children's services result from a combination of prevention (with the entire population to stop the identified problem from emerging), early intervention (to stop an existing problem getting worse), treatment (to help those who have succumbed to the problem), social prevention (to minimize the social sequelae for those who have succumbed to the problem) and better diagnosis. This model encourages practitioners to view their activity in the context of the development of the child and any psycho-pathology consequent upon his or her previous experiences. Other models exist, including some reviewed elsewhere in this book.

To our knowledge, clinical practice in children's services or the child protection process has never been organised around this or any other set of organising principles. This has several consequences. First, services tend to carry general descriptions, such as family support, that encompass a range of objectives (e.g. to prevent or treat), agencies (e.g. health or social services), activities (e.g. home visits or family centres) and length of involvement (short or long) (Manalo & Meezan, 2000; Bullock et al., 2001). Second, children with similar needs and backgrounds can receive widely different interventions, some of which carry the same descriptor (Axford et al., 2001). Third, hardly any activity is mounted on the basis of rigorous evidence of its value with a particular category of case (MacDonald & Winkley, 1999). Fourth, there has been relatively little innovation in activity on behalf of children in need although child protection has been better served in this respect than other areas of work in the child welfare field (Bullock et al., 2001).

What has changed is the amount of activity on behalf of children in need, although the result may be that a large number of children are getting a small amount of help with few apparent indications of success. The UK Department of Health (2000) estimates that at any one time in England (with a child population of circa 11 million) there are nearly 400 000 children in need known to be requiring some form of social services provision, nearly three-quarters (73%) of whom can be categorised into groups signalling some form of maltreatment. This calculation is based on figures in three categories used in the survey, (1) abuse or neglect, (2) family dysfunction and (3) absent parenting. But the true figure may be higher than this as some children in the other six categories used to classify children will also be victims of maltreatment. This is certainly suggested in the research by Hamilton and Browne (1999), who found that over a 27-month period, one in four children in a community were referred to a child protection unit each year, and by Little and Madge (1998) who found that in a rural area (with relatively little deprivation) one in four children were referred each year to health, education, social or police services for a social need, 9% of whom were processed through child protection processes and 24% were known to have suffered some maltreatment.

In the absence of organising principles of clinical practice, there is an imperfect correlation between the seriousness of the referred child's situation and the type, level and intensity of activity. For example, Axford et al. (2001) made individual assessments of the seriousness of need for 668 children in a deprived inner-city urban area in England. They used an instrument being developed for use in research and practice contexts to develop the language of the Children Act 1989 for England and Wales in a way that makes it applicable across orthodox administrative boundaries. They found that the development of 38% of the children was impaired and that in 11% of cases that impairment was significant. As would be hoped, they found that a case identified by researchers to be suffering significant impairment was more likely to receive an intervention than one where the impairment was not significant or where there were no apparent needs. However, one in seven (15%) of the significantly impaired children were not in contact with children's services while 39% of the cases where there was negligible or no need for receiving an intervention (appropriately so in some cases) were. It may be appropriate for children's services to intervene with a case where there is no apparent need, for example, to forestall emerging need. Whether these cases should be prioritised ahead of those where there is significant impairment is another matter. For the record, 30% of the cases where non-significant impairment was found received an intervention. Similar patterns were found when intensity and duration of service were evaluated.

This type of finding relating to clinical assessment is relatively new to child care research and has rarely been used in the organisation of children's services. Instead, there has been much discussion of a sociological or ideological nature and much consideration of the competing rights of children and families (e.g. Little, 2002).

The result can be captured in the varying amount of compulsion used to protect children in different jurisdictions and over time. For example, in the USA there is much less intervention sanctioned outside of the Court than is found in most European countries. However, there are considerable variations across US and EU states and aggregate figures should be treated with caution. For example, New York City (pop. 10 million) has as many children in state care as England (pop. 50 million) but France (pop. 57 million) probably has a similar rate of children in state care as the USA as a whole. Nevertheless, it is reasonable to conclude that most of the US states have much higher rates of children in state care than EU countries and the proportion of children in state care who are subsequently adopted is 40% greater in the USA than in the UK, which has a higher rate of adoptions from care than all other EU states (Parker, 2000; Selwyn, 2000).

The research completed for the UK Prime Minister's review of adoption confirms these patterns (Selwyn, 2000). The USA has high rates of children in state care and high rates of adoption from state care. The UK has comparatively low rates of children in state care but high rates of adoption from state care. Australia has low rates on both criteria. The net result is a rate of 462 per 100 000 children going into care and being adopted in the USA, compared with 15.2 in the UK and 2.4 in Australia. Whether children are better protected in any one of these countries compared to the others remains a moot point. There is no evidence that greater compulsion leads to better protection of children from maltreatment and it could be posited (on the basis of evidence summarised below) that higher rates of state care and adoption may ultimately be counter-productive for the children so affected. We simply do not know.

EFFECTIVE CHILD PROTECTION PROCESSES

There is now a consensus that inter-agency co-operation is fundamental to effective child protection processes. The evidence on this matter is set out in more detail below. In most jurisdictions there has been considerable progress towards effective co-operation, although there remains further scope for development. The requirement to involve the broad array of agencies that comprise children's services continues to pose challenges.

Few jurisdictions have a common language to summarise the seriousness of a child's situation. In the context of child protection, the fundamental assessments must be the risk of future impairment to development and the level of impairment consequent upon previous maltreatment. Within this will be several assessments of the child's psycho-social well-being, educational performance and behaviour at home and in the community. Several disciplines contribute to these assessments and each will apply different criteria and use differing levels of rigour. There has been some work on how the assessments of some disciplines take primacy over those of others (e.g. Hallett, 1995) but little on how to develop summary assessments that will suit all disciplines and agencies.

Child protection processes are hampered if there is not an effective balance between discovering what has happened to a referred child and deciding on how best to protect and enhance his or her development. As an illustration, Farmer and Owen (1995) found that case conferences focused mostly on the establishing that abuse had occurred and the likelihood of the situation deteriorating or of an incident being repeated. Family dynamics were frequently ignored and on average only nine minutes in every hour was devoted to decisions about how to intervene. The issues of risk and intervention are both important but a failure properly to plan the service could leave children for whom the extent of previous maltreatment remains doubtful at risk of future maltreatment.

This leads to the thorny issue of parental involvement in the protection process that re-emerges several times in this chapter. The discussion is best prefaced with the statement of fact that there are a small population of parents for whom participation in the professional process to decide on a child's well-being will be dangerous for that child. Some work exists on how to identify and proceed with such cases (Dent & Hagell, 1998; Hagell, 1998).

For the majority of cases, however, parental involvement in the process of investigation is likely to be advantageous. This can be looked at in two ways. First, from the practical point of view, most child protection enquiries concern children who will stay at home throughout that enquiry (Department of Health, 1995) or return to live with relatives within a short period of separation (Bullock et al., 1998). Since children are so likely to continue to live with relatives, it makes sense to avoid aggravating any sense of injury carers may feel by virtue of professionals enquiring into their parenting practices. Second, from the point of view of child outcomes, although the evidence is equivocal, it generally leans towards keeping parents involved (e.g. Thoburn, 1991; 1995; Sharland et al., 1995).

We recognise the difficulty for professionals implicit in the message "exclude the dangerous parents, involve the others", since getting it right can literally be a life or death issue. This continues to be one of the major challenges of child protection work.

If an argument in favour of inclusiveness holds, then so too does one in favour of professionals taking a wide perspective on child protection issues. This cuts a number of ways. First, parents are likely to be responsive to an interest in the possible causes of child maltreatment, such as poor housing conditions, unemployment or illness. Second, where child maltreatment is the product of social stressors, there are likely to be other products to consider, for example domestic violence. Providing help in several areas is likely to encourage parental involvement. Third, the sequelae of child maltreatment are varied, including behaviour problems, psychological disorders, educational difficulty and strained family relationships, so a child-centred approach also demands a broad view of the child's needs.

An effective child protection process also depends upon professionals having a good knowledge of ordinary patterns of child development. There is no systematic evidence on the extent to which this situation prevails but our development work in several countries does not lead us to be optimistic. For example, Dartington-i, the development arm of the research organisation in which we work, currently operates in England, Wales, two US states, Canada, Italy, Spain and Ireland and in each of these countries there is little indication among professionals of good knowledge of either child development theory or empirical evidence, although there is of course much variation. The UK Department of Health (1995) overview of research on child protection, for example, contains a contribution on normative patterns of control (Smith et al., 1995) and sexual behaviour ordinarily experienced within families (Smith & Groeke, 1995) both of which can help professionals judge the significance of reported events, such as a child bathing or sleeping with a parent. Concomitant to a requirement to take a wide perspective on child protection is a need to look for strengths and weaknesses in all areas of the child's life. This necessity implies some understanding of child development theory and empirical evidence on normative patterns of development.

ASPECTS OF INTER-AGENCY CO-OPERATION

Child protection demands the attention of all agencies working with children. Empirical evidence on how agencies come together to protect children in different jurisdictions remains sketchy. One conclusion is that in some countries—England for example—the situation is greatly improved on that which existed a quarter of a century ago when woeful failures were directly attributable for child deaths. However, in general, improvements have focused on ensuring that agencies report to one other important facts.

There has been less concentration on inter-agency co-operation at the point of service delivery, despite overwhelming evidence (in this book alone) that victims of maltreatment have multiple needs that seldom fit within the administrative boundaries of any one agency. Little and Madge (1998) found that health (generally primary care physicians) and education (school and education welfare specialists) picked up over four times as many referrals for children's social needs as did social services and that the police (dealing with referred abandonment, parental mental health problems and domestic violence) were as important a point of first referral as social workers. However, the longer the case remained open, the more likely it was that health, education and police would drop out of the picture and that social services became the sole provider for children with multiple needs (see also Axford et al., 2001).

The fact that many agencies are involved in the process of referral leads to another challenge in child protection, namely finding an effective balance between the effective transmission of knowledge about children at risk of maltreatment and avoiding unnecessary delay in supporting identified victims of maltreatment. To the lay observer, the process takes an inordinate amount of time (see Gibbons et al., 1995), especially if the courts are involved (Parker, 2000).

One reason for delay is the variable knowledge about child protection possessed by children's services professionals. As Hallett et al. (1995) discovered, some professionals are fully employed with questions of maltreatment but others, for example some primary care physicians, will come across a case only rarely. Unfortunately, policy makers have tended to respond to this dilemma with procedural guidance, a fundamental part of the workings of an effective protection process but not the only part. For example, it is evident from accumulated research that there is potential for professionals to do more in providing practical help at the point of referral, since this can be an effective way of protecting the child.

That said, procedure is important and in most jurisdictions is generally much improved in the last decade. Problems occur when the functions of the procedure are lost. Hallett et al. (1995) refer to the three pillars of the English and Welsh child protection process: a register of names of children most at risk of maltreatment available for checking to professionals working with children; conferences to bring together professionals who may have information on the child's circumstances and, where appropriate, family members; and national and local guidance to professionals endorsed by committees comprising the hierarchy of children's services agencies. Each pillar serves specific functions that are undermined by misinterpretation. For example, Gibbons et al. (1995) found that some professionals interpreted the placing of the child's name on the register as an intervention (which it clearly is not) or perceived the overall rate of children on the register (an indicator recorded by UK Department of Health) as suggesting a rate of maltreatment in a locality (which again it does not). As Little and Gibbons (1993) show, the rate is at best an indication of (1) social deprivation in the locality together with (2) the way in which the register is operated in that locality (there are considerable variations from one authority to another). In the worst instances, professional behaviour, for example a decision to recommend registration, can be influenced by these misinterpretations.

WHEN CHILDREN ARE LOOKED AFTER AWAY FROM HOME

Some victims of maltreatment known to children's services will eventually be looked after away from home. Very little has been written about the experiences of maltreated children once they enter care or accommodation. This is a serious gap in the evidence base consequent upon the tendency to view children accommodated by or in the care of the state as a homogeneous group.

There is a body of evidence on the experiences of children looked after by the state and some of this is relevant to work with victims of maltreatment. Much research has attempted retrospectively to decipher the function of substitute care in meeting the child's needs. Unfortunately, clinical practice and, arguably, legal sanction have tended to view the decision to use state care as a single service and, at worst, as the only response to the needs of child abuse victims. Care or accommodation can be used to provide a safe haven for children at risk. It can also be used to provide a stable environment to permit wider treatment goals or to enhance education. Alternatively, substitute care can be used to replace a gap in the social and family network of the child's immediate family, for example by providing respite to an exhausted parent.

Most children in state care or accommodation return home to live with relatives (Bullock et al., 1998) and most reunions take place within a few weeks of the separa-tion (Department of Health, 1991). These are empirical facts not recommendations. The facts do not suggest that most children should go home. There is hardly any evidence on outcomes for these rapid reunions. It is known that three-quarters of those returning to relatives are not again looked after, an output measure and a crude proxy for child outcomes. This evidence does emphasise the varying func-tion achieved by looking after a child away from home and the powerful role of relatives in situations where the care of the child has been found to be deficient.

For those children who return home from care quickly, effective outcomes tend to follow from voluntary arrangements agreed with parents that permit high levels of contact during the separation although there is danger of tautology here since levels of contact with relatives during separation is the strongest single predictor of the reunion. But the evidence is convincing (Bullock et al., 1998). Just as we know that most children do go home not that they should, we know that contact correlates with return from care but not that it correlates with good outcomes. The evidence on this matter is mixed and no strong conclusion can be drawn one way or the other (Ryburn, 1994; Quinton et al., 1997; Quinton & Selwyn 1998).

Some children will not safely be able to return to relatives and for them the state or another family sanctioned by the state effectively becomes the parent.

In programme jurisdictions, for example in England and Wales and Norway, the powerful role of relatives is acknowledged by legislation that encourages voluntary arrangements and effectively shares care between the state and birth parents even in court sanctioned separations (Ryan, 1999). In other jurisdictions, even those with a strong emphasis upon parental rights, like those in most of the US states, the state assumes all rights when the child is separated (Little, 2001). In England, about 8% of all children entering care are looked after for a long period by the state. Conservatively, this represents about one in 40 of all child protection enquiries. Half of those children will be long supported by social services (usually in foster placements), the other half will eventually be adopted (Bullock et al., 1998). While the outputs from the two alternatives are broadly similar, outcomes are unknown. Thoburn found that 22% of children with "special needs", a definition intended to capture children looked after by social services and other children in need, with the exception of babies given up by birth parents to adoptive parents, in long-term foster or adoptive placements broke down. The breakdown rate varied with age from less than 5% for those placed before their fifth birthday to 49% for those placed at 10 years of age (Thoburn, 1991). Combining this evidence, it can be said that only a small proportion of children do not return to live with relatives, but that three-quarters of those long separated (about 6% of all separations) have enduring placements.

Several commentators (e.g. Parker, 1980) have summarised the above evidence by asking the question "can the state parent and can it do it better than an errant parent?" The evidence is mixed but it would seem safe to conclude that the answer is "yes" in some cases but "no" in others. A social worker can use substitute care to protect a child but in some cases that course of action can be damaging to the child (Department of Health, 1998; 2001). Decision-making can be enhanced by careful analysis of the functions of substitute care. Practitioners would also benefit from better evidence on outcomes for children looked after; most of that currently available deals with outputs like breakdown, reunification and recidivism rates. With such evidence, practitioners would be better placed to balance practical considerations, such as the fact that most children do go home and that contact is beneficial to return processes, with clinical considerations about which children should go home and for whom contact should be used to further the child's development.

THE BROADER "WHAT WORKS" LITERATURE

The evidence described so far in this chapter has played an important part in the development of child protection policy and practice, in the UK at least. For the most part it is what might be termed applied policy research, focusing at least as much on the process of responding to children's needs as on the children themselves.

In recent years this perspective has been challenged by a complementary paradigm that focuses on "what works" in children's services interventions. The challenge, however, is largely theoretical because of the current poor state of knowledge in children's services and at the moment they can be perceived as complementary (Little, 1998). There is no need to review the "what works" evidence here since it is covered elsewhere in this book and has been summarised in several publications (e.g. MacDonald & Winkley, 1999) that form part of a Barnardos series looking at different aspects of children's services. It is, however, worth drawing attention to certain salient features of this literature.

The "what works" approach is rooted in research that explores the aetiology of childhood disturbance. The approach evaluates interventions aimed at specific categories of children and designed to respond to evidence about aetiology. The interventions also reflect hypotheses about what will happen to the child with and without the intervention. They tend, therefore, to be realistic about what can and cannot be achieved. As MacDonald and Winkley (1999: 146) observe "child protection workers cannot eliminate child abuse any more than the police service can eliminate crime". The "what works" paradigm then demands a rigourous evaluation of the intervention, the incorporation of control groups and, where possible, random allocation of cases to the intervention or a placebo. The aspiration is for the same standards of evidence as are applied in the field of medicine.

This is a very different approach from most children's services as described so far in this chapter. Most orthodox interventions have emerged as a reaction to scandal about the failings of a system (Parton, 1985; 1991; 1997). Much intervention is, therefore, actually a process not the service. Rather curiously, there has been a tendency for commentators and even for some professionals within children's services to see child protection processes and broad responses like taking the child into state care as a solution to the problem of maltreatment when, at the very most, they represent part of the solution or the context in which interventions with modest objectives are provided.

OTHER PROBLEMS AND CHALLENGES FOR THE FUTURE

The evidence just reviewed produces several challenges for research on child protection in the context of services offered under the auspices of health, education, social and police services, or children's services to use the collective label. That evidence also poses several dilemmas for policy and practice. In this final part of the chapter, consideration is given to other challenges consequent on what remains unknown in this field of study.

First, very little is known about the timing and onset of childhood problems consequent upon maltreatment. Nothing at all has been written about timing and onset of children's services designed to respond to those problems. This represents a significant challenge to policy, practice and research. It is possible to hypothesise that many services fail to have an impact not because they are irrelevant to a child's specified needs but because they are delivered at the wrong moment. For example, it is evident that at least some victims of sexual maltreatment can benefit from psycho-therapeutic work designed to give insight into behaviours consequent upon maltreatment. But some of those who could benefit in this way may require several years of support before they can handle the therapeutic input (Little & Kelly, 1995). Services seldom recognise those temporal issues.

Second, more could be done to recognise the impact of delayed development upon the maltreated child. There has been a tendency in children's services research and practice to treat all victims of maltreatment as if they experienced ordinary patterns of development. This is appropriate in all cases prior to assessment and will be appropriate for many cases beyond assessment, but not all. To take one finding from basic research, if children's cognitive functioning is adversely affected by maltreatment (Skuse & Bentovim, 1994), what adjustments should be made to research and clinical assessments resting on the child's perspective?

Third, for all the improvements in inter-agency co-operation in the child protection arena, few assessments are truly holistic in the sense that they concentrate on the whole child. It is for this reason that some commentators, ourselves included, have encouraged a perspective that looks at child protection in the context of children's wider needs (e.g. Department of Health, 1995). Unfortunately, there have been occasions when our perspective has been viewed as being weak on child protection when the message is that the best way to protect a child from future maltreatment and the effects of previous abuse is to look at all needs. Healthy physical and psychological development, good schooling, optimal family and social relationships as well as reasonable standards of behaviour are as important to victims of abuse as they are to any other child.

Fourth, as improvements in research on child development come on stream, children's services and research therein will be encouraged to move away from the crude administrative categories that were initially necessary to construct a state response to child maltreatment. It makes increasingly less sense to refer to children as "child protection" cases since child protection extends to all children and most victims of maltreatment are unknown to the processes designed to protect them. Other labels like "family support", "child in care" or "other child in need" (all common in the UK context) are likely to become redundant if the central focus of research and practice is on child development.

Fifth, more consideration could be given to thinking about what can be considered a good outcome in the context of children who have suffered different types and levels of maltreatment (see Department of Health, 1998). This issue can be tackled in several ways. At the aggregate level, for example, no matter how effective child protection policies and practices become, there will always be children who die at the hands of their carers. But what mortality rate can be considered optimal in any one jurisdiction? Or, put another way, what rate of improvement each year should any jurisdiction be looking for? This sort of question is likely to come more into focus as international comparisons improve (see Pritchard, 1992). At the clinical level, what can a practitioner reasonably be expected to achieve with different categories of case? We have followed into adulthood individual cases originally studied as children: Siobahn Kelly provides an example (Little et al., 1995). These generally show strengths (educational and social development in the case of Kelly) and weaknesses (high levels of movement and continuing patterns of depression). At present, there is little to guide practitioners on when they had done well and where they have failed.

CONCLUSIONS

Questions of child protection as they play out in the context of children's services have traditionally focused as much on ideology as evidence. As a consequence, too little is known about the effectiveness of the sector. Most of the empirical evidence would suggest that a major problem is inconsistency, that there are pockets of excellence and poor practice and variations in policy. Recent evidence on patterns of referral introduced in this chapter indicates the possibility that too little is being done for too many. But we cannot be sure of this.

The imperative is for more and better evidence. As ideological battles are won, for example that the state must protect children from maltreatment, so the balance between ideology and evidence must tip towards the latter. Empirical evidence can help. There is also potential to apply research perspectives to clinical practice, particularly if there is a requirement for greater consistency.

This book, like so many others is in the child protection sphere, is a reminder not only of how much has been learned in this field over the last 30 years (and even since the previous edition of the book) but also how much more we must discover. Research has only scratched the surface of the child protection plain. The children's services component of the child protection field remains less well served by evidence than possibly any other of the components.

REFERENCES

Axford N, Little M, Madge J, Morpeth L (2001) *Children Supported and Unsupported in the Community: Analysis of the Descriptive Data and Implications for Policy and Practice.* Dartington: Dartington Social Research Unit.

Birchall E, Hallett C (1995) *Working Together in Child Protection.* London: HMSO.

Bullock R, Gooch D, Little M (1998) *Children Going Home: The Reunification of Families.* Aldershot: Ashgate.

Bullock R, Randall J, Weyts A (2001) *Social Work Effectiveness: Evaluating the Contribution of Social Work to Interventions with Children in Need.* Dartington: Dartington Social Research Unit.

Dent R, Hagell A (1998) *Dangerous Care: Working to Protect Children.* London: The Bridge Child Care Development Service.

Department of Health (1991) *Patterns and Outcomes in Child Placement.* London: HMSO.

Department of Health (1995) *Child Protection: Messages from Research.* London: HMSO.

Department of Health (1998) *Caring for Children Away from Home: Messages from Research.* Chichester: Wiley and Son.

Department of Health (2000) Children in Need in England: A Survey of Activity and Expenditure as Reported by Local Authority Social Services Children and Families' Teams for a Survey Week in February 2000.

Department of Health (2001) *The Children Act Now: Messages from Research.* London: Stationery Office.

Eekelaar J (2001) Child Welfare and Child Protection in England and Wales. In M. Rosenheim (ed) *A Century of Juvenile Justice.* Chicago: University of Chicago Press.

Farmer E, Owen M (1995) *Child Protection Practice: Private Risks and Public Remedies – Decision Making, Intervention and Outcome in Child Protection Work.* London: HMSO.

Fox Harding L (1991) *Perspectives in Child Care.* London: Longmans.

Gibbons J, Conroy S, Bell C (1995) *Operating the Child Protection System: A Study of Child Protection Practices in English Local Authorities.* London: HMSO.

Hagell A (1998) *Dangerous Care: Reviewing the Risks to Children from their Carers.* London: Policy Studies Institute.

Hallett C (1995) *Inter-agency Co-ordination in Child Protection.* London: HMSO.

Hallett C, Birchall E (1995) *Coordination and Child Protection.* London: HMSO.

Hamilton C, Browne, K (1999) Recurrent maltreatment during childhood: a survey of referrals to police child protection units in England. *Child Maltreatment* 4:275–86.

Little M (1998) Whispers in the library: a response to Liz Trinder's article on the state of social work research. *Child and Family Social Work* **3**:49–56.

Little M, Gibbons J (1993) Predicting the rate of children on the child protection register, *Research, Policy and Planning* **10**:15–18.

Little M, Kelly S (1995) *A Life without Problems? The Achievements of a Therapeutic Community.* Aldershot: Arena.

Little M, Madge J (1998) *Inter-agency Assessment of Need in Child Protection.* Dartington: Dartington Social Research Unit.

Little M, Mount K (1999) *Prevention and Early Intervention with Children in Need.* Aldershot: Ashgate.

Little M (2002) The law concerning services for children with social and psychological problems. In M. Rutter, E. Taylor and L. Hersov (eds) *Child and Adolescent Psychiatry: Modern Approaches.* Oxford: Blackwell Scientific Publications.

MacDonald G, Winkley A (1999) *What Works in Child Protection?* Ilford: Barnardos.

Manalo V, Meezan W (2000) Toward building a typology for the evaluation of services in family support programs. *Child Welfare* **74**:405–429.

Parker R (1980) *Caring for Separated Children.* London: National Children's Bureau.

Parker R (2000) *Adoption Now.* Chichester: Wiley and Son.

Parton N (1985) *The Politics of Child Abuse.* Basingstoke: Macmillan.

Parton N (1991) *Governing the Family: Child Care, Child Protection and the State.* Basingstoke: Macmillan.

Parton N, Thorpe D, Whattam C (1997) *Child Protection: Risk and the Moral Order.* Basingstoke: Macmillan.

Pinchbeck I, Hewitt M (1973) *Children in English Society.* London: Routledge and Kegan Paul.

Pritchard C (1992) Children's homicide as an indicator of effective child protection: a comparative study of Western European statistics. *British Journal of Social Work* **22**:663–84.

Quinton D, Rushton A, Dance C, Mayes D (1997) Contact between children placed away from home and their birth parents: research issues and evidence. *Clinical Child Psychology and Psychiatry* **2**:393–413.

Quinton D, Selwyn J (1998) Contact with birth families in adoption: a response to Ryburn. *Child and Family Law Quarterly* **10**:349–61.

Ryan M (1999) *The Children Act 1989: Putting it into Practice.* Aldershot: Ashgate.

Ryburn M (1994) *Open Adoption: Theory, Research and Practice.* Aldershot: Gower.

Selwyn J (2000) *Evidence to the Prime Minister's Review of Adoption.* Bristol University: School for Policy Studies.

Sharland E, Jones D, Aldgate J, Seal H, Croucher M (1995) *Professional Intervention in Child Sexual Abuse.* London: HMSO.

Skuse D, Bentovim A (1994) Physical and emotional maltreatment. In M. Rutter, E. Taylor and L. Hersov (eds.) *Child and Adolescent Psychiatry: Modern Approaches.* Oxford: Blackwell Scientific Publications, pp. 209–229.

Smith M, Grocke M (1995) *Normal Family Sexuality and Sexual Knowledge in Children.* London: Royal College of Psychiatrists/Gorkhill Press.

Smith M, Bee, P, Heverin A, Nobes G (1995) *Parental Control within the Family: The Nature and Extent of Parental Violence to Children.* London: Thomas Coram Research Unit.

Thoburn J (1991) Evaluating Placement: An Overview of 1165 Placements and Some Methodological Issues. In Fratter J, Rowe J, Sapsford J, Thoburn J (eds) *Permanent Family Placement: A Decade of Experience.* London: BAAF, pp. 34–57.

Thoburn J, Lewis A, Shemmings D (1995) *Paternalism or Partnership? Family Involvement in the Child Protection Process.* London: HMSO.

Section IV

TERTIARY PREVENTION II: WORKING WITH OFFENDERS

EDITOR'S INTRODUCTION

Catherine Hamilton

Some people might question the purpose of a section on "working with offenders" in a book aimed at the early prediction and prevention of child abuse. Indeed this was not addressed in the earlier edition of this book (Browne, Davies and Stratton, 1988) or in other books concerned with the prevention of child maltreatment. Therefore, it is helpful to spend a moment considering this issue and why it was felt important to include. The simple answer is that the treatment of offenders is perhaps the most effective way of protecting children on a long-term basis. Without treatment, offenders are likely to re-offend and place other children at risk, as well as previous victims. By working with offenders, the number of victims will hopefully be reduced.

Extensive offender treatment programmes have been introduced in several countries (i.e., Canada, USA, UK, Australia). There is also a recent decline in physical and sexual abuse referrals (see Chapter 1). Although this reduction is a complex issue with many contributing factors, such as changes in reporting and registration procedures, it is also possible that these treatment programmes may have contributed. Indeed, Jones and Finkelhor (2001) argue that when the complex factors (e.g., reporting/registration) are taken into account, a "real" downward trend is still observed. In other parts of the world where interventions with child abuse and neglect are still primarily aimed at victims (taking a "reactive" stance), such downward trends have not been observed. This may be related to the fact that even after extensive child protection work with children and/or victims, these individuals still require protection in the absence of work with offenders.

Finkelhor and associates (1986) presented a well-known four-stage process through which an individual becomes a sexual offender against children. The first two stages require the individual to both be motivated to offend and to overcome his or her internal inhibitions to do so. The third requirement is that the offender is able to overcome the external inhibitors or obstacles to offending (e.g., appropriate guardianship), whilst only the final requirement relates to overcoming the child's resistance. Thus it can be seen that working with a child and his/her family can assist in terms of prevention at stage 3 and 4 (reducing vulnerability through appropriate guardianship and defense mechanisms in a child). Only by working with the offender can prevention be aimed at stages 1 and 2 of this model. Therefore, it could be argued that by changing the focus of intervention from victims to offenders, we are moving from a reactive to a proactive approach to prevention.

In the long-term, treating offenders can also help to break the victim to offender cycle. In Chapter 17, Arnon Bentovim reviews the literature on preventing the victim to offender cycle and outlines the pioneering work he and his team have undertaken at Great Ormond Street. This research is aimed at identifying risk and protection factors in this cycle to establish those victims more or less likely to go on to victimise others sexually. Most importantly, it included a long-term prospective study to test out earlier hypotheses. The study highlighted predictive factors, behavioural indicators and protective factors in the victim to offender cycle. Bentovim has discussed the implications for therapeutic intervention with adolescent victims of abuse who are at risk of sexually offending. This is based on four levels: phase of disclosure, decisions about care in the context of initial assessments (with indicators for hopeful, doubtful and hopeless prognosis), treatment in a context of safety, and stage of rehabilitation to family life.

Looking at adult offenders, assessing the risk of further offending behaviour using assessment tools is a relatively new area, developed mainly in the late 1990's. To date, much of this work is primarily related to sexual offending. Friendship and Thornton (Chapter 18) have reviewed this area, considering the purpose of risk assessment, rates of sexual reconviction, methodological issues, and current risk assessment instruments for sexual offenders. This chapter also presents a new method of assessment for alleged sexual offenders devised by David Thornton in collaboration with the Lucy Faithfull Foundation (Faithfull Classification Scheme, FACS). This is an important development in the area of risk assessment and the development of this tool is fully described.

Having identified those individuals at risk of re-offending, what forms of treatment have been most effective in reducing this risk? Chapters 19 and 20 address this issue: Browne, Falshaw and Dixon considering adult one teenage violent offenders, whilst Fisher and Beech address the issue of treatment of adult sexual offenders.

Browne, Falshaw and Dixon emphasise the need to take an holistic approach to domestic violence and child abuse by intervening and treating all members of the family (ie: both the offender and the victims). The importance of therapy for young violent offenders is also highlighted to prevent the victim to offender cycle.

Fisher and Beech begin by reviewing the classification of sexual offenders against children and the aetiology of child abuse in order to outline influences in the development of treatment programmes. They make the point that, if they are to be effective, programmes must account for the differences between sexual abusers of children. This chapter then goes on to review the cognitive-behavioural approach to treatment and outlines a model of treatment devised by the authors in 1988. This provides a clear and helpful description of the content and methods of delivery. It should be noted that this chapter relates to adult child abusers and does not review the treatment needs of adolescent sexual offenders given the different needs of this group (see instead Bentovim, Chapter 17).

In conclusion, this section of the book provides information about the assessment of the risk of adolescent boys to become sexual offenders, as well as the re-offending risk of adult sexual offenders against children or alleged sexual offenders. Having assessed risk, Section IV also addresses issues of engaging with adult and adolescent offenders therapeutically.

REFERENCES

Browne, K.D., Davis, C., and Stratton, P. (1988). *Early Prediction and Prevention of Child Abuse.* Chichester: Wiley.

Finkelhor, D., Araji, S., Baron, L., Browne, A., Peters, S.D., and Wyatt, G.E. (1986). *A Sourcebook of Child Sexual Abuse.* Beverly Hills, CA: Sage.

Jones, L., and Finkelhor, D. (2001). The decline in child sexual abuse cases. *Juvenile Justice Bulletin,* January 2001.

17

PREVENTING THE VICTIM TO OFFENDER CYCLE: RISK AND PROTECTION FACTORS, AND THE IMPLICATION FOR THERAPEUTIC INTERVENTION

Arnon Bentovim

Great Ormond Street Hospital, London, UK

INTRODUCTION

There is increasing awareness of the connection between childhood maltreatment and subsequent offending behaviour (e.g. Rivera & Widom, 1990; Widom, 1989; Widom & Ames, 1994). There are however a number of suggestions about how maltreatment connects with such behaviour. Farrington (1995) highlighted the fact that a variety of adverse experiences, e.g. poverty, poor parental child rearing, and family criminality predisposed to delinquent behaviour, whilst Patterson et al. (1989) adopting a developmental approach noted the links between poor parenting, antisocial behaviour, academic failure, rejection, association with deviant peers and the subsequent initiation of delinquent behaviour. This model was supported in Falshaw and Browne's (1997) study of the adverse childhood experiences of young people who subsequently form such violent acts that they are placed in secure accommodation.

This chapter will look in some detail at sexual offending behaviour, and how this can be prevented, taking note of Kaufman and Zigler's (1987) cautionary note not to place too much emphasis on retrospective analysis of factors, compared to

Early Prediction and Prevention of Child Abuse: A Handbook.
Edited by Kevin Browne, Helga Hanks, Peter Stratton and Catherine Hamilton. © 2002 John Wiley & Sons, Ltd.

a prospective analysis which may give a very different impression of the factors which need to be focussed on in therapeutic intervention.

There is a widespread assumption that male victims of sexual abuse go on to become offenders. It is acknowledged that the majority of sexual abuse is perpetrated by males. Consistently referrals to the Great Ormond Street Sexual Abuse Treatment Service were 90% abuse perpetrated by males with 10% of abuse perpetrated by females. At least half of abuse perpetrated by females was perpetrated jointly with male partners, so that even in this instance the predominance of abuse is perpetrated by males. The supposition is made therefore that if the victim of abuse is a male, that the risks of that child or young person going on to abuse others is high.

If a young person or an adult abuses a child, an assumption tends to be made that he must have been abused himself, even if victimisation is denied. The myth that males who abuse sexually must have been abused themselves is therefore perpetuated. Such a construction will inevitably have an impact on males who have been abused and will lead young people to believe that they are themselves at risk of going on to abuse others. The fact that a considerable proportion of sexual offenders against children state they have been sexually abused perpetuates the myth, although it is possible that claiming to have been sexually abused is a way of pleading victimisation as a way of lessening the feared consequences of having to own a sexual interest in children. The popularity of the earlier intergenerational cycle explanation of abuse maintains the notion of inevitability. The parent who abused was abused themselves, violent patterns of parenting are transmitted from generation to generation.

REVIEW OF RESEARCH

Finkelhor (1986) has argued cogently about the dangers of a single factor theory whereby victims become victimisers, and he too is concerned that it could become a self-fulfilling prophesy. However the victim to abuser cycle has been noted to be relevant in those working with both adolescent and adult offenders. Becker (1998) noted that adolescent sex offenders reported more histories of maltreatment—both physical and sexual—compared to generally conduct disordered young people. Samples of adult child molesters have reported significant experiences of sexual trauma. Groth and Burgess (1979) reported 32% in their sample, Faller (1988) reported 27%. Freeman-Longo (1986) noted that factors such as long duration, or multiple abusers, were more influential, indicating that sexual abuse itself may be an important contributory, but not a necessary, factor in the development of perpetrating behaviour.

Current approaches to research are refining such notions. It is beginning to be possible to devise a more sophisticated pathway approach to understand what are the risks of an abused individual abusing others, and what are the protective factors which will mitigate against such repeating patterns, and what other sort of interventions can help prevent such a process (e.g. Bentovim, 1995). The aim of this chapter is to look at ways of understanding risk factors, and consider what protective factors may prevent such a process. The account will draw on recent research at the Institute of Child Health/Great Ormond Street Hospital research on factors which lead to the onset of sexually abusive behaviour amongst male victims of sexual abuse.

Cross-Sectional Study (Skuse et al., 1998)

This took the form of an intensive hypothesis generating study on a relatively small number of young people. A series of young people and their families were studied intensively. There were four groups recruited including:

1. boys between 11 and 16 who had been victims of sexual abuse who showed no evidence of perpetrating abuse against others, that is there was no evidence of the victim to offender cycle being evident
2. boys who had been victims of sexual abuse who were showing evidence of having begun to perpetrate against other children, that is a group who were showing the victim to offender cycle
3. a group of boys with no evidence of sexual abuse, but who nevertheless were offending against other children
4. a group of young people who were showing antisocial behavioural problems, but with no evidence of sexual abuse in their history, nor of abuse of others. This group acted as a control population.

It was therefore possible to carry out a variety of assessments on each group of these young people, to understand what were the specific factors which increased the risk of a young person who had been abused in childhood beginning to offend against other children. Awareness of such factors form the focus for prevention of the victim to offender cycle.

In total 78 boys were referred to the study, of whom 32 had abused other children and young people. There was a phase of general assessment and a socio-metric study carried out in the schools the young people attended to understand peers' perceptions of the boys.

The second stage consisted of three months of individual weekly psychoanalytic psychotherapy sessions. Sessions were both semi-structured and there were measures of attachment and hostility analysed using a grounded theory approach to derive childhood themes relating to history of care and maltreatment.

There were also less structured sessions covering the boys' life history, their pattern of sexually abusive behaviour, and sexual fantasies. Birth mothers were interviewed about their own life history, their experience of maltreatment, and aspects of family life.

It was therefore possible to carry out a variety of comparisons and derive hypotheses to assist in understanding the processes which could lead from victim to offender cycles.

The important factors which emerged from the analyses were as follows:

1. There were no differences found between the groups who suffered abuse in terms of their experience of sexual victimisation, based on personal accounts and contemporaneous records, e.g. severity of abuse ascertained from evidence of penetration, the number of perpetrators involved, or whether abuse was within

or outside the family. This lack of difference was unexpected; however numbers assessed were small, therefore there may have been a referral bias.

2. A number of other factors were looked at which seemed to be relevant during the assessment process. These included:

- experiencing intrafamilial violence
- witnessing intrafamilial violence
- rejection by the family
- discontinuity of care
- rejection by peers
- experiencing a generalised sense of grievance
- poor identification with father figures
- absence of a non-abusive male attachment figure
- having a mother who was sexually abused in childhood
- maternal depression
- poor sibling relationships
- having a mother who was physically abused in childhood
- low levels of guilt concerning abusive action

Many of these factors emerge when working with young people who have abused sexually, and therefore may well seem to be a natural focus of concern in preventing the victim to offender cycle. In this cross-sectional study the most significant factors however were those relating to:

- experiencing intrafamilial violence
- witnessing intrafamilial violence
- discontinuity of care

These experiences preceded the sexually abusive behaviour which led to referral. We conceptualised the factors which differentiated the group who went on to abuse as living in a climate of intrafamilial violence which may or may not have directly involved the boys as a victim. It was felt that discontinuity of care and rejection amplified the effects of witnessing and being subject to violence.

There were many similarities in the lives of boys who abused sexually, without a history of sexual abuse themselves, indicating that sexual abuse is likely to be a risk factor amongst others. They also grew up in a family context where they were exposed to a climate of violence in the home. In addition the mothers of boys who abused other children had themselves been subject to extensive sexual and physical abuse not only in their own childhood, but in adult life. So these boys were exposed not only to a climate of physical violence, but also a sexual violence which may have had a similar effect to being sexually abused themselves.

Experiencing physical violence directly or being exposed to a climate of violence subjects a child to prolonged fear, stress, often for long periods of childhood development. This will adversely affect key developmental tasks and personality development through early childhood, middle childhood, adolescence, and adult life (Pynoos et al., 1996).

Discontinuity of care, living in turn briefly with various parents and step-parents, or being in local authority care could lead to a profound feeling of rejection. This had a bearing on the formation of attachments, and may result in the lack of a secure relationship with an adult. Severe, unpredictable stresses have links with psychopathology in both adolescence and adulthood. We felt that these boys were having the worst of both worlds, suffering both disruption of care and violence. They were missing confiding relationships that could have a protective effect.

We also felt that directly traumatic and traumagenic effects of pervasive violence led to subjected helplessness, the evacuation of defensive aggressive fantasies and traumatic visualisation of abusive experiences. Later sexualisation of aggressive fantasies led to the "eroticisation" of aggression, which leads in turn to abusive behaviour. We felt that such aggressive behaviour may well be a fight response, taking the form of revenge fantasies acted out in adolescence to reverse a sense of powerlessness and project such feelings on other young people as a way of feeling less burdened themselves.

Prospective Study (Skuse et al., 1999)

These findings were further tested in a prospective manner. All males referred to Great Ormond Street for reasons relating to sexual abuse from 1980 were studied. A sample of 284 male subjects were studied, with a subset of 107 subjects who were subjected to more intensive studies. Demographic data and information about sexual victimisation of the sample was collected from clinic, and social services files when these were available. Evidence of the victim to offender cycle was obtained by further scrutiny of social services files when they were available in the years which followed original victimisation. In addition criminal record data were studied from a range of sources, national police conviction records, and local police caution records to ascertain which of the young people had gone on to abuse.

We were therefore able to address the following questions:

1. What proportion of sexually victimised subjects would become sexual perpetrators in later life? What is the risk of victims following the victim to offender cycle?
2. What proportion of such victims are dealt with subsequently through criminal procedures?
3. What proportion of those individuals who perpetrated during adolescence continue to offend in later life?
4. The more intensive study directly addressed the issues concerned with prevention of the victim to offender cycle, by asking what experiences would increase the risk of a sexually victimised young person becoming a perpetrator, and what experiences would decrease this risk. Which risk factors should alert professionals to the danger of a young person going on to abuse others, and what are the factors which can be brought into play to prevent this process occurring?

Young people who had been abused sexually were investigated intensively by both Social Services Department and at Great Ormond Street who referred young people for treatment. There was considerable information available which throws light on any subsequent perpetration which became evident through tracking the young person's subsequent history. Of the 284 boys originally referred as victims, a; little over 10% of the sample became sexual perpetrators. About a third of these received either a caution or conviction for a sexual offence. The prospective design will also demonstrate whether those young people who had been abused and went on to abuse other children also committed crimes of violence. The question can be answered whether factors which lead to the sexual abuse of others may also lead to other forms of violence against others suggesting a generally antisocial picture.

Looking at the group of young people who perpetrated during adolescence, it was possible to asses how many of them continued beyond the age of 16 into adult life. Results will be reported in detail shortly.

RISK FACTORS

The prospective study will be able to determine whether the originally defined risk factors which distinguished those young people who had been victims of sexual abuse who went on to become offenders were operating in the longitudinal study, i.e. had they experienced physical abuse, witnessed family violence, and experienced disruption of care.

Other factors which had not differentiated the risk population in the cross-sectional study could be studied, including:

- Being abused by a female.
- A general pattern of neglect, either of failure to provide adequate care or to provide adequate supervision.
- Rejection by carers.

The prospective design will clarify the importance, not only of a climate of violence, but also other factors such as neglect (remains), failure of supervision, a female care figure who sexualises the mother–child relationship as well as a paternal figure who provides a violent role model for identification.

BEHAVIOURAL INDICATORS

It was also possible to investigate the rôles of other behavioural indicators which clinically appear to be important in predicting which young person was more likely to go onto follow an abusive track. These included:

- Cruelty to animals.
- Soiling behaviour.

Such responses may represent the mode of response to an already existing climate of violence, rejection, and neglect, which may then be amplified through an experience of sexual abuse.

PROTECTIVE FACTORS

A number of protective factors were also tested to see whether the above risk effects could be modified:

1. having one good relationship with an adult in the child's life
2. having a good relationship with a sibling
3. having a good relationship with a peer

4. spending a significant period in foster care, with non-abusive male carers and non-abusive female carers
5. having a significant period of time cared for by the same carer

These factors were selected not on the basis of a previous finding, but in terms of the general information obtainable from the general literature on protection. It will be necessary to test the protective capacity of individual factors, and an overall the protective index, and whether there is an interactional effect.

Overall the prospective research will demonstrate whether a potential for positive attachments and adequate care, can neutralise the impact of living in a climate of violence, and the cumulative effects of abuse and neglect.

IMPLICATIONS FOR PRACTICE

To avoid the victim to abuser cycle it is necessary to develop appropriate intervention strategies:

1. At the time when abuse has been disclosed.
2. During the phase of work when the child or young person is protected from abuse.
3. Careful consideration needs to be given about rehabilitation of children abused within their family context to their family.
4. Alternative family placements need to be found for those children who will continue to be exposed to a climate of violence, neglect, and rejection.

The remainder of this chapter is focussed on the issue of working with boys who show a potential to be involved in the victim to offender cycle. It seems likely from the work of Saradjian (1996) that female abusers may well share many of the factors which lead to the abusive pattern shown by boys. But there is a lesser likelihood of girls becoming abusers and many of the factors which lead to explosive violent behaviour on the part of boys may well lead to explosive violent behaviour against themselves, noted in girls who are self-mutilating, show anorectic or self-harming patterns of behaviour. Boys may also show similar patterns. In the treatment of girls who have been sexually abused, many of the approaches described have relevance.

PREVENTING THE VICTIM TO OFFENDER CYCLE

Level 1: Work during the Phase of Disclosure

Disclosure that sexual abuse has occurred is always an intense crisis because of the effect of breaking the web of secrecy and silencing. The Descriptive and Treatment Outcome Research at Great Ormond Street (Monck et al., 1996) demonstrated that denial that abuse had occurred was the most frequent response by perpetrators in a series of 99 children. Only a small proportion (9% of abusers) took full responsibility for their actions, 15% took some responsibility, whilst the largest proportion

(74%) continued to state they were not responsible, accusing the child of lying, or professionals of constructing abuse falsely. Watkins and Bentovim (2000) noted the difficulties for boys in being able to state they had been abused at all. Boys are more likely to be abused outside the family, and there may well be denial on the part of boys because of fears that their freedom will be restricted if they report abuse. In addition boys often experience intense fears that abuse occurred because their abuser has seen something "homosexual" in their bearing, and therefore have picked them out. Therefore considerable denial on the part of boys is a common process as well as denial by abusers.

Often maternal responses fitted in with the father's perception: 36% of mothers were perceived as negative and disbelieving, whilst only 44% supported the child unequivocally. By the time the children were referred for therapeutic work it was not surprising that 60% of the children were living in alternative contexts, and a third of children continued to be disbelieved by both parents by the time the children were referred for treatment. It was striking that children's mental health as measured by levels of anxiety, depressive symptoms, post-traumatic symptoms, and self esteem was influenced in part by the extensiveness of abuse, e.g. when penetrative abuse had occurred over a significant period of time. But mental health status was also significantly related to whether the child was believed and supported by their mother, or whether they were criticised and therefore felt a negative sense of esteem. It was noted in the series that if the child was younger, if he was a boy, it was more likely that he would be believed and supported than if the victims were older girls.

It is therefore essential during this phase of disclosure to ensure that there is an assessment of the extent of abuse, its nature, length, severity, extensiveness, and who is responsible. This work often takes a period of time to overcome the reluctance, anxiety, denial, and fear of consequences of disclosure.

To assess the risk of abusive behaviour occurring it is necessary to explore the impact of abuse on the regulation of emotional life of the child, on attachment style, and sense of self. Of particular concern are emotional responses which are externalising rather than internalising. Externalising responses include hyper-arousal, intrusive actions, violent fantasies, explosive outbursts, the development of an intimidating frightening style, a sense of anger and grievance, sexualisation of closeness, and sexual aggression.

There is also concern if attachments are dismissive, indiscriminate, controlling, or disorganised in form. The sense of self may well be of concern if there is a fragmented self, identity with the aggressor, evidence of the beginning of the imposition of sexual and aggressive behaviour on others, a blaming punitive style, or an aggressive bullying response.

These patterns are all indicative of a style that is potentially dangerous, threatening, and evidence that the child or young person is moving from victim to perpetrator mode.

An assessment of the family context is an essential counterweight to the behavioural pattern shown by the young person. It is essential to assess whether the pattern of risk already referred to is present. Whether the child or the young person has been exposed to physical violence, domestic violence, a history of abuse perpetrated against parents, particularly the mother, the presence of neglect, failure of supervision, absence of non-abusive carers within the family context are all an essential aspect of the initial assessment following disclosure. The assessment also needs to find out whether there are protective factors present.

Taking appropriate responsibility for abuse and maternal support are essential factors leading to judgements about placement for children both short- and long-term. Motivation for help both by and for the victim, and motivation for help as far as parents are concerned, taking responsibility, acknowledging the need for treatment of perpetrating behaviour, are further factors. Determining care and criminal issues are part of a complex assessment often deeply affected by an extensive denial, and blaming of professionals for being involved in the assessment, particularly if the abuse is intrafamilial.

Level 2: Decisions about Care in the Context of Initial Assessments

The research on factors which trigger abuse emphasise the climate of family violence, and the need to ensure the abused child lives in a supportive context. The decision about care depends on the making of a prognosis for change within the family context, the extensiveness of needs of children and their timeframe, the capacities of the parents to acknowledge their role in direct or cumulative family violence effects, and the potential for change.

HOPEFUL PROGNOSIS

It is possible to make a hopeful prognosis, and to maintain children within the family context if:

1. Family members acknowledge their roles and responsibilities; an abusive parent accepts that he or she needs to live separately to seek help in their own right; and protective parents are firm in their belief that the child has been abused and able to maintain the relationship with the child despite the pressure brought against them by an abusive partner.
2. The child is not blamed for having spoken.
3. The parents are willing to work on personal and family issues; to confront personal experiences of violence; to deal with past and present domestic violence to which children have been exposed; and to demonstrate a capacity to work with professionals.
4. Boys show predominantly internalising responses, anxiety, fearfulness, clinging, depressed responses, and their sense of self is not pervaded with guilt or self blame.

DOUBTFUL PROGNOSIS

These are situations where it seems necessary to use the care process because there is far more uncertainty about outcome, doubt about the capacities of parents to work with professionals, or to achieve positive outcome within the child's timeframe.

In these situations there is often a high level of uncertainty whether the child or adult is responsible for the state of the child, the child is tentative, unsure of support from caretakers. There may be a limited perception for the need to change on individual or marital basis, or a degree of uncertainty about the capacity of the parent to be able to change, to manage to extricate themselves from a seriously violent relationship. There may be the presence of individual parental problems which are unlikely to change, e.g. presence of addiction/alcoholism. There may be a pervasive multi-generation pattern of abuse which seems extremely difficult to confront or to change. These are situations of considerable doubt and often need the use of statutory proceedings together with appropriate testing of work to assess a prognosis and the needs of the children. Boys may show both internalising responses—anxiety, fearfulness, explosive responses, some disorganisation of attachments, and guilt mixed with anger.

HOPELESS PROGNOSIS

These are situations where there is an absolute failure to acknowledge the child's state, his or her statements of abuse are absolutely rejected, or it is imputed that the professional has been putting ideas in the child's mind. Therefore the child or professionals are scapegoated, there is no capacity to protect the caretaking parent. Serious problems of violence, neglect, or rejection are not acknowledged, or not amenable to treatment, there are few resources available to deal with the often extensive nature of problems, and maturation is non-existent. Boys may already be displaying externalising responses, are dismissive of relationships and care, and are developing an explosive blaming style.

It can be seen from the outcome of the Great Ormond Street Therapeutic Project that about half the children who were in care at the time of referral were able to return to a family member, that is approximately 63% of children at the end of a 12-month period were living with a family member (10% including the abuser). But 37% were still living in care or needing therapeutic community help because of persisting rejection of failure to accept responsibility for abuse, parents holding together in a context of denial, children continuing to be doubly rejected. These are children who are at significant risk for whom it is essential that appropriate care be provided, so that a context is provided for the repair of attachments, the neutralisation of grievance, rejection, and anger.

Level 3: Treatment in a Context of Safety

Once the initial assessment has been carried through with a decision made about where the child should live and with whom, it then becomes essential to work during the context of safety to reverse the effects of abuse. Providing a positive context of care is the essential first step, and any therapeutic work which does not have a background of adequate care will be ineffective. Therapeutic work can assist in the process of a child or young person becoming reattached or re-parented, although therapeutic work cannot be a substitute for good care but can only facilitate the process.

REPAIR OF ATTACHMENTS

Disruptive disorganised attachments which result from living in a climate of violence and abuse needs work not only in the family context, but also in individual and group contexts. Individual work with children and young people who have been abused focus on building a positive attachment between the therapist and the child as one of the elements to repair avoidant or disorganised attachments. There needs to be the fostering of acceptance between the therapist and the child, and a sensitivity to the attachment style of the child, rather than expecting a uniform response. There should be a reasonable degree of warmth and responsiveness, but not too intense, otherwise the child may be reminded of an abusive context which groomed him or her to accept inappropriate sexual activity. Therapeutic work needs to be rewarding, developing relatedness, finding solutions in a collaborative fashion rather than leaving the initiative to the child. A working alliance needs to be created which develops connectedness, availability, and safety.

Group work can help a young person gain a sense of belonging and identity, and find a healing family context in a group with other young people and therapists, preferably of both sexes. There needs to be the fostering of boundaries, safety, and confronting the re-enactment of abusive models occurring between group members and the therapists with constant confrontation and finding alternative ways of relating.

Work needs to take place between family members who accept that abuse has occurred in the child in the first instance. The possibility of family work including the perpetrator can be considered at a later date to foster understanding of what led to abusive action, and the intergenerational effects which may be re-enacted. There needs to be a process of externalising problems so that family members can work together to deal with an abusive experience, and reattach in the fight against abuse. Small or rapid treatment gains are necessary using activities to enhance shared affiliation, pleasure, and achievement.

MANAGEMENT OF EMOTIONAL DYSREGULATION

The essential core of helping children and young people regulate their emotions is through sharing of abusive experiences, so that the emotional negative impacts of abuse and externalising responses, post-traumatic stress symptoms, can be exposed, and processed. It is essential to explain that the aim is to reduce anxiety, that children are given a training in coping skills, and in the expression of emotion by developing a vocabulary for emotions, identifying their own and others' emotions, coping with anger/arousal/anxiety, being able to describe emotions associated with abuse, and to develop relaxation skills.

It is essential that coping strategies are developed before there is exposure and attempts to describe the extensiveness of abusive experiences. The cognitive behavioural approach (Deblinger et al., 1996) has been demonstrated as being a highly effective way of dealing with emotional dysregulation. It is important for the child to find ways of being able to deal with re-enactment, visualisations, explosive feelings and responses. Children need to start by describing non-abusive experiences, the initial disclosure, first episodes of abuse, additional episodes of abuse, specific episodes, most disturbing and embarrassing event. The use of play, creative productions in vivo visiting contexts, visualisation of episodes are all methods of exposing and sharing. There needs to be considerable care in how experiences are shared, limiting the amount shared in each session, structuring sessions to limit exposure time, using creative psychoeducational approaches, diagrams, pictures charts, games as ways of separating the experience from self during the process of working through, and reducing emotional arousal. There needs to be a collaborative/problem solving solution focussed approach to the work with careful monitoring of responses.

Protective parents require coping skills training themselves, identifying their own feelings related to the abuse of their child, and then gradually being exposed to a discussion of their children's experiences and activities. They need to enter discussions about sex education, personal safety, and coping with post-traumatic symptoms, sexualised behaviour, and emotional outburst. Group and family work can reinforce ways of sharing, particularly by children of similar ages and stages of development (Monck et al., 1996; Bentovim et al., 1988). Group work for parents has been shown to have a particularly useful impact on both the mother's mental health and their capacity to provide adequate care (Monck et al., 1996) in developing a positive sense of self both for themselves and their children.

DEVELOPING A POSITIVE SENSE OF SELF

The treatment aims of helping children and young people develop a positive sense of self which will prevent the victim offender cycle include:

1. developing a correct attribution for events
2. creating a healing alternative story
3. becoming safe from re-traumatisation and the abuse of others

Both individual and group work approaches need to confront the cognitive/affective processes evoked by abuse. Adequate motivation is required to explore and understand the attributions of self-blame, guilt, and responsibility for having been vulnerable, for having allowed oneself to be targeted and groomed into abusive activities. There needs to be the development of a cognitive skill to dispute the nature and origin of beliefs which blame the self rather than the other. An alternative healing belief story needs to develop. What may seem to be frightening—flashbacks, intense angry outbursts, abusive revenge, fantasies—are connoted as pathways to autonomy and strength, turning powerlessness to power. Even though they may appear to be dangerous, at the same time they need to be seen as part of a healing process.

There needs to be extensive explanation given for the process by which the child or young person has become abused; the silencing and rationalisation used to entrap and silence. Sexual feelings evoked and beliefs need to be corrected. There needs to be openness and acceptance of all communications, and a full history of experiences obtained including victimisation and victimising experiences. Boys who are in the process of becoming offenders find their sexual lives filled with confusing images of themselves, their abuser, feelings about other children which create a considerable sense of shame and guilt. An assumptive therapeutic style which names such processes with familiarity and comfort will enable boys who are extremely uncomfortable about such experiences being able to share them.

Dysfunctional thoughts about body image, body change, and gender orientation is also an essential accompaniment of such experiences. For instance, one of the common defensive processes that boys have described is imagining that hetero-sexual activities were going on when they were being abused by a male. When confronted with who is the female partner this often helps gain an understanding of why boys may feel confused about their identity, about their bodies, about them-selves, whether they are homosexual, whether they have abnormal sexual feelings.

There needs to be working with guilt and responsibility for the inevitable sex-ual arousal which needs careful explanation. Education about healthy sexuality, gender, and the law is necessary. Young people need to understand the process of healthy and unhealthy cycles of relationships. The notion of a dating cycle which helps young people learn how relationships are made with peers can be helpful in contrast to an abusive cycle which may very well be part of the victim to offender cycle, including fantasies, masturbatory activities including their own abuse and abuse of others, a sense of grievance. They need to understand that it is possible to blame young people who evoke sexual arousal in themselves rather than own responsibility, and take control of their own actions and response.

It becomes essential to develop personal safety skills, notions of ownership boundaries, safe space. Social skills need to develop to deal with powerlessness in a more effective way, without using aggressive or intimidating behavioural approaches.

It becomes essential to develop a positive sense of self as survivor, to construct a script of competence and understand what may seem negative as survivor strate-gies, and to understand the link between powerlessness, grievance, and revenge. It is essential to identify potentially dangerous situations and to recognise the justi-fication/distortions of thinking which confuse sexuality and affection. There need to be teaching modes of interrupting and challenging such cycles, and to find safe ways of finding support within the community. Such issues need to be tracked within groups and family contexts, particularly when a family member has been able to acknowledge abusive action, take part in appropriate therapeutic work, and take responsibility and truly apologise to the victim of abuse. In the Great Ormond Street research less than 10% of families were able to achieve the rehabilitation of the child who had been abused with the abuser, although as already indicated many children were able to live within the family context with a protective parent or family member. Denial of abuse by an adult perpetrator gives a negative mes-sage to a young person who may have been abused, and who begins to experience abusive feelings themselves.

Level 4: Stage of Rehabilitation to Family Life

(A) TO THEIR OWN FAMILIES

The ideal is for children who have been abused to be able to be restored to their own family, for the relationship with their caring parent to be strengthened. Where abusive family members can take responsibility there should be thorough work on reversing abusive patterns, and a process of apology and reconciliation and understanding of processes which led to violent behaviours, freeing the victim of a sense of guilt and grievance, and considering the possibility of rehabilitation of the abuser to the family. A number of areas need to be worked with in families.

Working on a climate of violence – exposure and experience of physical abuse A key factor which leads to the promotion of a victim to offender cycle is the exposure to physical violence, both between parents, and perpetrated against the young person themselves. In the phase of assessment the possibility of therapeutic work with families focussed on this issue needs to be evaluated. Where there is acknowledgement that such factors are relevant, and that a child has been subject to sexual abuse within a family context, and accompanying physical abuse, then involving the family either as a whole, or parallel work with the young person and the family on this theme, needs to be considered. As far as approaches are concerned Kolko (1996) contrasted cognitive behavioural treatment with family therapy against a community care control group. Both therapeutic approaches were more successful than control, and if there is a potential for rehabilitation of boys who have been abused to family contexts, it is essential that as well as individual work with the child and young person, there need to be parallel approaches to the issues of family violence, as well as sexual abuse potential.

Cognitive behavioural treatment of family violence addresses cognitive, affective, and behavioural repertoires, clarifies family stresses, develops coping and self-control skills, training and safety, support, planning, and relaxation. Training in assertion rather than the use of inappropriate punitive models are provided, views of violence and physical punishment clarified, self-control, anger management, and time out reinforcement were all part of the approaches used following well known cognitive behavioural approaches.

The family therapy approach used an interactional/ecological model to enhance family functioning and relationships. This was obtained by promoting and helping to understand the nature of coercive behaviour, teaching positive communication skills, and helping develop problem solving skills together as a family. There was a phase of engagement which assessed structural roles and interactions, a middle phase which reviewed the effects of physical force, and develop a no violence contract for each family member. There was training in problem solving skills and communication skills, building the capacities and skills of each family member. The termination phase included the establishment of problem solving skills, and developing family routines as an alternative to coercion or physical punishment.

Both therapeutic approaches had a significant impact on reducing parental violence towards children, on reducing children's externalising/aggressive behaviour, lessening the transmission of an aggressive style, improving family cohesion, and the reduction of conflicts. Parents felt less angry, and parental depression was very much lower. Such work, whether with the family as a whole, or with individuals within the family to reduce violence between parents and to reduce the overall climate of violence in the family, is going to be an essential component to prevent the victim to offender cycle. Such approaches need to be included in a multi-systemic approach (Henggeler, 1999) which stresses the need for collaborative work with all family members, the utilisation of evidence based approaches, and an active approach which can demonstrate tangible gains.

Specific work with the family which can impact on the victim to offender cycle includes:

- extensive work on clarifying exactly what abusive action has been perpetrated, by whom, and attempting to ensure that full responsibility is taken, blame reduced, and appropriate apologies given;
- constant work on denial, minimisation, and projection of blame so that children who are abused do not take on inappropriate responsibility with a sense of guilt and perpetuation of externalising responses;
- the issue of power, powerlessness, and appropriate empowerment constantly focussed on within the family context to redress the inappropriate use of power, and to ensure that appropriate assertion replaces intimidation;
- blurred and confused role boundaries corrected so that inappropriate role modelling and identification with the aggressor is not amplified within the family context;
- loss and bereavement appropriately focussed on to assist young people who cannot live with their families of origin to deal with the "identification with the aggressor" which is a process of dealing with such losses.

(B) NEW FAMILIES

There are considerable difficulties for foster families and alternative placements caring adequately for children who have been extensively abused, and there is a risk of re-enactment of abusive behaviour within foster families.

CONCLUSIONS

To prevent the cycle of victim to offending behaviour in boys who have been abused requires us to identify those children who have grown up in family contexts where they have been subject to the cumulative family violence, neglect, and rejection which puts them at particular risk of re-enacting their own experiences with other children and young people.

There needs to be an extensive assessment of whether such family contexts can change and whether parents will involve themselves with effective individual and family approaches to change their patterns of behaviour. There is a considerable pressure against accepting responsibility for such actions, and a significant number of young people who have been sexually abused will be rejected by family members, disbelieved and unsupported, and will require alternative family placements who can protect against the development of abusive behaviour.

Whatever the context children are living in, whether within their own family contexts or in alternative care, it is essential that abuse focussed work is provided to: repair disrupted attachments by providing reparenting and therapeutic relationship; rebalance the dysregulation of emotional life caused by being subject to cumulative trauma and stress, by dealing with traumatic effects, and externalising behaviour through exposure of experiences in a context of safety; reverse the pervasive negative sense of self guilt and attribution of responsibility to the self by creating a healing story of survival.

These changes are achieved through a combination of individual, group, and family work whether with the family who is accepting responsibility for abuse and who are prepared to undertake appropriate remedial help, or with an alternative family/carers who are willing to meet the very considerable challenge of such young people who have grown up in a context of violence.

Research on boys who are abused who are also subject to a context of family violence reveals the extent of their dangerousness to other children and young people, the risk of perpetrating sexual abuse in adult life, and violent actions against other individuals. Professionals' response to abused boys demonstrates that in many cases adequate care was provided for abused children who grow up in a context of high risk. A systematic application of therapeutic interventions can further reduce the incidence of abusive behaviour, and begin to reduce the numbers of children caught in the cycle.

Although the focus of this chapter has been sexual abuse, the overall approach holds for children who have been subjected to other forms of maltreatment. Sexual abuse is a risk factor alongside others, not a cause. Indeed much of the therapeutic approach described here is focussed on other forms of childhood adversity which occur along with sexual abuse. Therefore when other forms of abuse are present, e.g. physical abuse, emotional abuse, neglect, or exposure to violence, then a similar therapeutic approach is essential to prevent the cycle of victims becoming offenders.

ACKNOWLEDGMENTS

The support of the Department of Health is acknowledged who funded the cross-sectional and prospective study of risk factors for the development of sexually abusive behaviour in sexually victimised males.

REFERENCES

Becker J. (1998). What we know about the characteristics and treatment of adolescents who have committed sexual offenses. *Child Maltreatment* **3**: 317–329.

Bentovim A. (1995). *Trauma Organised Systems: physical and sexual abuse in families*. London and New York: Karnac.

Bentovim A., Elton A., Hildebrand J., Tranter M., Vizard E. (eds) (1988). *Child Sexual Abuse within the Family*. London: Wright.

Deblinger E., Lippman J., Steer L. (1996). Sexually abused children suffering post traumatic stress symptoms: initial treatment outcome findings. *Child Maltreatment* **1**: 310–21.

Faller KC. (1988). Why sexual abuse? An exploration of the intergenerational hypothosis. *Child Abuse and Neglect* **13**: 543–8.

Finklehor D. (1986). Abusers: Special Topics. In *A Source book on child sexual abuse* (ed D Finkelhorn). Beverly Hills: Sage.

Freeman-Longo R. (1986). The impact of sexual victimisation on males. *Child Abuse and Neglect* **10**: 411–14.

Groth N. and Burgess A. (1979). *Sexual Trauma in the Life Histories of Rapists and Child Molesters*. New York: Wiley.

Henggeler SW. (1999). Multi-systemic therapy: an overview of clinical procedures, outcomes and policy implications. *Child Psychology Psychiatry Review* **4**: 2–10

Kaufman J. and Zigler E. (1987). Do abused children become abusive parents? *American Journal of Orthopsychiatry* **57**, 186–92.

Kolko D.J. (1996). Individual cognitive behavioural treatment and family therapy for physically abused children and their offending parents: the comparison of clinical outcomes. *Journal of Child Maltreatment* Vol 1: No 4 322–342.

Monck E., Bentovim A., Goodall G., Hyde C., Lewin R., Sharland E., Elton A. (1996). *Child Sexual Abuse – a descriptive and treatment study*. Studies in Child Protection. London: HMSO.

Patterson G.R., DeBaryshe, B.D., Ramsey E. (1989). A developmental perspective on antisocial behaviour. *American Psychologist*, **44**, 329–335.

Pynoos R.S. Sorensen S.B., and Steinberg A.M. (1996). Interpersonal violence and traumatic stress reactions. In Goldberger, L. and Breznitz (eds) *Handbook of Stress: Theoretic and Clinical Aspects*, Second Edition, New York Free Press pp. 573–590.

Rivera B., Widom C.S. (1990). Childhood victimisation and violent offending. *Violence and Victims* **5**, 19–35.

Saradjian J. (1996). *Women who Sexually Abuse Children – From Research to Clinical Practice*. Chichester: John Wiley and Sons.

Skuse D., Bentovim A., Hodges J., Stevenson J., Andreou C., Lanyardo M., New M., Williams B., McMillan D. (1998). Risk factors for development of sexually abusive behaviour in sexually victimised adolescent boys: cross-sectional study. *British Medical Journal* **317**: 175–179.

Skuse D., Stevenson J., Hodges J., Bentovim A., Richards M., McMillan D., Salter D., Moore T. (1999). *Risk Factors for the Development of Sexually Abusive Behaviour in Sexually Victimised Males*. Institute of Child Health London. Submitted to the Department of Health.

Watkins B., Bentovim A. (2000). Male children and adolescents as victims: a review of current knowledge. In G Mezey (ed) *Male Victims of Sexual Assault*. Second Edition. Oxford: Oxford University Press.

Widom, C.S. (1989). Does violence beget violence? A critical examination of the literature. *Psychological Bulletin*, **106**, 3–28.

Widom, C.S., Ames, M.A. (1994). Criminal consequences of childhood sexual victimisation. *Child Abuse and Neglect* **18**, 303–318.

18

RISK ASSESSMENT FOR OFFENDERS

Caroline Friendship
David Thornton
HM Prison Service, UK

The primary benefit of effective risk assessment of offenders is public protection. Risk assessment is an essential element in the effective management of sexual and violent offenders in prison, in other secure environments and in the community. The recent formation of public protection systems in the UK (often referred to as Public Protection Panels) highlights joint working practices across government agencies, including probation services, the National Health Service, housing departments, social services and the police. Standardised and validated risk assessment tools for sexual and violent offenders aids accountable decision-making at the same time as protecting the public. This chapter focuses on sexual offending as an illustrative example of risk assessment in action. However, the issues raised are equally applicable to risk assessment of violent offenders. For a review of the risk assessment of violent offenders see Douglas et al. (1999). In addition, Browne and Falshaw (Chapter 19) examine the treatment of violent offenders.

INTRODUCTION

A study of the prevalence of convictions for sexual offending in England and Wales estimated that one in 60 men born in 1953 had a conviction by age 40 for some type of sexual offence (Marshall, 1997). This study also suggested that at least 110 000 men in the 1993 population had a conviction for an offence against a child. National Statistics for England and Wales (Povey, 2000) reported that 37 400 sexual offences were recorded by the police in the 12 months prior to September 2000. This figure represents less then 1% of all offences recorded in the same period. Whilst sexual offending appears to be a minority behaviour in terms of overall recorded crime,

Early Prediction and Prevention of Child Abuse: A Handbook.
Edited by Kevin Browne, Helga Hanks, Peter Stratton and Catherine Hamilton. © 2002 John Wiley & Sons, Ltd.

the consequences for the victim are profound, as are the consequences to family and friends (e.g., Finkelhor & Browne, 1985; Beitchman et al., 1991; Prentky & Burgess, 2000).

Offence categories used in official statistics for sexual offenders often fail to record the age of the victim and this makes it difficult to estimate the incidence of child sexual offending *per se*. Where offence categories can discriminate victim age, the most commonly recorded sexual offences against children in 1995 were: indecent assault on a female under 16; unlawful sexual intercourse (USI) with a girl under 16; indecent assault on a male under 16; USI with a girl under 13; rape of a girl under 13; and gross indecency with a boy under 14 (Grubin, 1998). Evidence from victim surveys has highlighted the under-reporting of criminal offences to the police e.g., the British Crime Survey (Hough & Mayhew, 1983). For sexual offending it is estimated that only 20% of sexual offences are reported to the police (Mayhew et al., 1989). The British Crime Survey, however, has been criticised for not being a sensitive tool for identifying the prevalence of sexual offending with few people reporting sexual crimes. Special surveys of women have found much higher reports of sexual violence than is reflected in official figures (e.g. Russell, 1984).

Recorded crime provides a measure of the volume of sexual crime committed during a specified time-period but it reveals little information regarding the perpetrators of such crime. However, the sexual offender literature predominately focuses on the characteristics of sexual offenders (e.g., Marshall et al., 1999) and, in particular, sexual offenders' past and subsequent behaviour. This longitudinal investigation of sexual offenders requires data that include recorded behaviour for an individual (or named offender) in a consistent way over time. In many jurisdictions, the government routinely records criminal conviction data often referred to as "official records". These provide researchers with a valuable data source for assessing the criminal histories of offenders. In England and Wales there are two sources of official data; police data (Police National Computer) and Home Office data (the Offenders Index) (Friendship et al., 2001). The Offenders Index, at present, is the most accessible to researchers. This can be used to assess past sexual criminal history and subsequent sexual reconviction. Most publications in England and Wales focus on sexual reconviction as an outcome measure and it is commonly defined as the conviction of another sexual offence during a specified follow-up period (Furby et al., 1989). It is recognised that sexual reconviction data is an underestimate of the true level of re-offending. A conviction for a sexual offence is contingent on the victim reporting the crime to the police, the police proceeding with the charges and the offence being proven in court.

North American longitudinal studies tend to focus on recidivism as the outcome measure. Recidivism in the field of offender rehabilitation refers to relapsing into previous patterns of criminal behaviour (Maltz, 1984). There is, however, little consistency across studies in the operational definition of recidivism, and a review of 90 studies in the USA, Maltz (1984) identified nine definition categories of recidivism i.e. arrest, reconviction, incarceration, parole violation, parole suspension, parole revocation, re-offence, absconding and probation violation. As the specificity/generality of definitions also varied considerably, Maltz proposed a move away from a single operational definition of recidivism in favour of a number of definitions for specific recidivating events. Recidivism, therefore, covers a broad range of criminal behaviour including reconviction.

RATES OF SEXUAL RECONVICTION

The low base rate of sexual reconviction or recidivism has been documented in England and Wales (Friendship & Thornton, 2001), Denmark (Christansen et al., 1965) and North American studies (Marques et al., 1994; Hanson & Bussière, 1998). Christansen et al. (1965) found that 11% of Danish sexual offenders were convicted of a subsequent sexual offence during a 12- to 24-year follow-up ($N = 2900$). In California the volunteer and non-volunteer control group of a treatment impact study had a 13.8% sexual recidivism rate, although this included non-official data to supplement reconviction information (Marques et al., 1994). The average follow-up period for the sample was four years. Finally, Hanson and Bussière (1998) found an average sexual recidivism rate of 13.4% for a 4- to 5-year period in a meta-analysis of 61 follow-up studies ($N = 23\,393$). In an earlier study, however, Marshall and Barbaree (1988) assessed unofficial sources of information on re-offences for child sexual offenders and this included credible allegations of abuse which did not lead to conviction. The authors estimated that the actual sexual recidivism rate was 2.7 times greater than that indicated by the official records.

The low base rate of sexual reconviction in England and Wales is compounded by a phenomenon unique to this jurisdiction, an actual decline in the sexual reconviction base rate over time (Friendship & Thornton, 2001). This illustrates the fact that base rates are not static and may fluctuate. Variation in base rate data could alter the predictive performance of a risk assessment tool over time. Thornton and Travers (1992) reported the low base rate of sexual conviction for sexual offenders (serving four years or more) discharged from prison in England and Wales. For a 1980 discharge sample ($N = 313$), 12% had been reconvicted of a sexual offence. This rate is similar to the rates expressed in Europe and North America. Marshall (1994) followed-up a later sample of 1987 sexual offenders discharged from Her Majesty's Prison Service. He found the four-year sexual reconviction rate was only 7% ($N = 402$) and proposed that the reduced likelihood of a reported sexual offence resulting in conviction was one possible explanation for this decline. An analysis of the attrition of sexual offences from reporting to conviction led Marshall to conclude that the proportion of sexual offences resulting in conviction/caution had dropped from 38% to 25% in the decade 1981 to 1991. Friendship and Thornton (2001) extended this analysis to the end of 1997 and found that over a 16-year period, the proportion of sexual offences resulting in conviction/caution had halved to 17%. They also reported on two 1990 prison discharge cohorts of sexual offenders ($N = 555$ and 535 respectively) as sexually reconvicting at just 5% within four years of release.

Further research is required to examine the process of attrition for reported sexual offences in order to understand why the Criminal Justice System is becoming less efficient at securing a conviction for sexual offences. A recent Home Office study (Harris & Grace, 1999) examined the attrition process for rape in 1997 with only

9% ($N = 360$) of reported rapes resulting in conviction. Whilst sexual reconviction data underestimates the true level of sexual offending, they are the best proxy for re-offending available for large samples of offenders (Lloyd et al., 1994).

Actuarial Risk Prediction

There has been little evidence to support the accuracy of clinical or human judgement when making decisions as to whether an offender will sexually re-offend. For example, Hanson and Bussière (1998) found that the predictive accuracy of professional judgement was only slightly better than chance when predicting sexual recidivism. Statistical prediction models have been used to predict various outcomes in a number of criminal justice settings (Farrington & Tarling, 1985). These have included: predicting parole failure; absconding from prison; and reconviction following discharge from prison. The use of statistical prediction models is commonly referred to as actuarial risk prediction. The development of such models has been widespread and the results of the predictive reliability and validity of these instruments has been encouraging (Quinsey et al., 1998). Actuarial risk scales are not designed to replace human judgement but to aid the decision-making process. The construction of a risk assessment schedule requires a body of information that systematically records the outcome to be predicted (the dependent variable) and variables potentially related to that outcome (independent variables) (Quinsey et al., 1998). Longitudinal outcome studies of sexual reconviction or recidivism have mainly relied on existing official data. In England and Wales this is due to the accessibility of such records and the fact that the data are computerised (Friendship et al., 2001). Official data tend to cover demographic and past criminal history variables only and this is why most risk assessment tools for offenders have predominately been based upon static risk factors.

Variables which are related to recidivism but are fixed and unchangeable are known as static risk factors (Bonta, 1996) e.g., demographic factors and past conviction history. The predictive power of instruments that rely solely on static factors is reasonably high, as illustrated by a static risk assessment tool for sexual offenders, Static-99 (Hanson & Thornton, 2000). Recently, dynamic risk factors have been given more prominence in the development of risk assessment tools. Dynamic risk factors are considered to be changeable or open to intervention. Hanson and Harris (1998) viewed dynamic risk as having two components. Stable dynamic refers to factors that have the potential to be changed but are relatively stable over time, e.g. deviant sexual preferences and personality factors. Acute dynamic refers to rapidly changing factors, e.g. alcohol or drug intoxication and mood. These acute factors can be indicators or triggers for re-offending. The systematic recording of dynamic risk variables is not common. Recently in North America, research has attempted to understand the role of dynamic risk variables in the prediction of recidivism. Gendreau et al. (1996) argued from a meta-analytical study of general recidivism that dynamic factors perform as well or better than static risk factors. In relation to sexual offenders in England and Wales, it has been demonstrated that the predictive value of a static risk procedure increased when an offender's psychological profiles were taken into account (Beech et al., 2001).

TABLE 18.1 2 × 2 Contingency table of predicted and Actual outcomes in risk

		Actual Outcomes	
		Yes	No
Predicted Outcomes	Yes	True Positives (TP) "*hits*"	False Positives (FP) "*false alarms*"
	No	False Negatives (FN) "*misses*"	True Negatives (TN)

RISK ASSESSMENT METHODOLOGY

The majority of risk assessment techniques are based on the simplest probability distribution where there are only two options, whether an outcome will or will not occur (also known as success or failure) e.g. heads or tails when tossing a coin (Prentky & Burgess, 2000). In England and Wales sexual reconviction data define success or failure whilst in North America this decision is based upon specific operational definitions of recidivism (which may vary from study to study). Prentky and Burgess (2000) described prediction as the estimation of the likelihood (or probability) that an offender will succeed or fail. Risk prediction involves estimating which offenders will succeed or fail and comparing this estimate with what was actually observed. This is illustrated in 2 × 2 contingency tables (based on Bayes Theorem) and it is this model that underpins risk classification methods (Table 18.1).

The proportion of recidivists correctly predicted is known as the "hit rate", or in technical terms the sensitivity of a risk predictor. The proportion of "false alarms", or offenders incorrectly predicted to be sexual recidivists, is subtracted from the proportion of hits to give the specificity of an instrument (Quinsey et al., 1998). Receiver Operating Characteristic analysis (ROC) is used to evaluate the predictive accuracy of a risk assessment tool using the area under the ROC curve statistic. This is the most commonly used technique in the predictions field (Mossman, 1994). A ROC curve plots the hits (accurate prediction of sexual recidivism) and false alarms (predicted as sexually recidivating but no recidivism was observed). An area under the ROC curve of 1.0 indicates perfect prediction (ROC area can range from 0.50 to 1.0, with 0.50 indicative of predictions no better than chance). Prentky and Burgess (2000) described in technical detail the science of prediction including the methodological problems associated with 2 × 2 contingency tables and the problems of over-prediction i.e. false positives or false alarms.

A low base rate of reconviction or recidivism is raised as one of the primary factors associated with over-prediction (Monahan, 1981). Prentky and Burgess (2000) concisely summarise the implications of the low base rate as follows: "when the base rate is as low as 10%, the best prediction is that no one will re-offend. We will be wrong 10% of the time. A risk assessment scale would have to be accurate 91% of the time to do better than the simple conclusion that no one will re-offend" (p. 108). A low base rate also limits the researcher's ability to develop a risk assessment instrument unless they have a very large sample of offenders. ROC analysis as a measure of predictive accuracy, however, is not dependent on the base rate. Sexual reconviction data as the actuarial basis for predicting sexual re-offence may also lead to prediction error. It has been established in this chapter that these data underestimates true levels of sexual re-offending. These data sources, therefore, can be considered as incomplete histories of actual re-offending (Moore, 1996).

Quinsey et al. (1998) described in detail the construction and validation process used in the development of the Violence Risk Appraisal Guide (VRAG) which is a tool used for both sexual and violent offender populations. This illustrated the typical stages of analysis used to develop an assessment tool. The specific analytical strategy may, however, vary between researchers. In the development of VRAG, the first stage involved studying the relationships between the independent variables and dependent variable (violent recidivism) using a data set sometimes referred to as the construction sample. Only variables with a significant univariate relationship with outcome were included in the subsequent analysis. Outcome (success or failure) is a dichotomous variable, and so stage two, a multivariate analysis to explore the significant relationships of the independent variables with violent recidivism, consisted of logistic regression analysis. In some studies other appropriate methods have been used e.g., discriminant function analysis. Logistic regression analysis was used to assess the relative contribution of the independent variables in the model and this was then used to develop the scoring or weighting of items in the tool (stage three). ROC techniques were then used to assess the predictive accuracy of the developed tool in terms of predicting outcome for the original sample data, i.e. the construction sample. The final step of the process was the validation (sometimes referred to as cross-validation) of the instrument on a new sample of data by assessing its predictive accuracy using ROC analysis.

RISK ASSESSMENT INSTRUMENTS FOR SEXUAL OFFENDERS

The development of risk assessment tools for sexual offenders has been informed by empirically based evidence which has supported various single factors as being related to sexual recidivism. An excellent summary of the literature can be found in Prentky and Burgess (2000). Factors that have consistently been associated with sexual recidivism have included sex of the victim, strength of sexual preoccupation with children, social competence and prior sexual offences. In recent years there has been an emergence of risk assessment tools that use combinations of variables to formulate scales. The most commonly used risk assessment tools are presented below.

Rapid Risk Assessment for Sexual Offence Recidivism (RRASOR)

RRASOR was developed by Karl Hanson (Hanson, 1997). It was constructed using a sub-sample ($N = 2592$) of a large meta-analysis of follow-up studies of sexual recidivism conducted by Hanson and Bussière (1998). The scale contains four items, variables that have consistently been demonstrated to be related to sexual recidivism. These were past sexual offences, age at commencement of risk (less than 25 years old), extra-familial victims (i.e. unrelated victim) and any male victims. Offenders can score between 0 and 6 points. The predictive accuracy of RRASOR was identical for the development and validation samples ($r = 0.27$, area under the ROC curve $= 0.71$). The cross-validation of the tool used a sample of sexual offenders discharged from prison in England and Wales in 1979 ($N = 531$).

Structured Anchored Clinical Judgement (SACJ)

Thornton (in Grubin, 1998) developed a scale to assess both sexual and violent recidivism. This tool was developed from criminal conviction history data for sexual offenders discharged from HM Prison Service in the context of the national Sex Offender Treatment Programme (SOTP). SACJ is a three-step process. Step one relates to static risk factors and five items assess current and past criminal history. Unlike RRASOR it also assesses non-sexual crime. Risk is calculated on a point system and the offender is categorised into one of three risk levels (low, medium or high). Step two assesses what are called aggravating factors and eight items cover both static and dynamic factors, e.g., stranger victims, substance abuse, never been married, deviant sexual arousal and Psychopathy Checklist- Revised (PCL-R) score (Hare, 1991). If two or more aggravating factors are present the individual offender is moved up by one risk level. The final step to SACJ assesses an offender's progress in prison, e.g. prison behaviour or participation in offending behaviour programmes. These factors are considered to mediate risk and an offender's risk level may be reduced by one level. A brief version of SACJ has also been developed. This can be scored on a minimum set of items as its name suggests (SACJ-Min). SACJ-Min was validated on a sample of sexual offenders discharged from prison in England and Wales in 1979; it correlated with sexual recidivism ($r = 0.33$) and the ROC area under the curve $= 0.74$ (Hanson & Thornton, 2000).

Minnesota Sex Offender Screening Tool-Revised (MnSOST-R)

MnSOST-R, formerly the Sex Offender Screening Tool (SOST) was developed by Epperson et al. (1995) of the Minnesota Department of Corrections. It was developed to identify which level of community notification and supervision was required for sexual offenders following release from correctional institutions. Originally it was a 21-item classification, which covered static and dynamic factors including institutional behaviour and treatment. A revised tool of 17 items correlated with sexual recidivism ($r = 0.27$) and had an area under the ROC curve of 0.77 (D. Epperson, personal communication in Hanson, 2001). A validation study of MnSOST-R used a Canadian offender population (Barbaree et al., 2001). The area statistic was 0.65, much lower than for the Minnesota population. This highlights the need to validate prediction scales in the jurisdiction where they are going to be used.

Static-99

This risk assessment instrument for sexual offenders pooled the findings from the validation studies from SACJ-Min and RRASOR (Hanson & Thornton, 2000). The tool is based on static risk variables only (demographic variables combined with criminal history factors). The 10 items in the instrument are:

1. prior sex offences
2. prior sentencing dates
3. any conviction for non-contact sex offences
4. index non-sexual violence
5. prior non-sexual violence
6. any unrelated victims
7. any stranger victims
8. any male victims
9. young (under 25)
10. single

The validation sample ($N = 1208$) combined UK sexual reconviction data with Canadian sexual recidivism data in four diverse samples. Cross-validation results demonstrated moderate predictive accuracy for sexual recidivism ($r = 0.27$, area under the ROC curve $= 0.71$) and violent recidivism (area under the ROC curve $= 0.69$).

A copy of the assessment tools described in this chapter can be found in Prentky and Burgess (2000). Other risk assessment tools for sexual offenders are also described in some detail. These tools were constructed and used mainly with North American sexual offenders.

APPLYING RISK ASSESSMENT TO ALLEGED OFFENDERS

People working in a child protection context often have to assess the risk posed by men who are alleged to have committed a sexual offence but have not been convicted for it. This kind of work is fraught with difficulties. Assessors have to make two distinct judgements. Firstly, they have to judge the credibility of the allegation(s) against a civil standard of proof, and secondly, if they judge the person has offended, they need to determine the likelihood of re-offending in various circumstances. In particular, they have to assess the likelihood of re-offending against specified children if the offender lives in the same household as them. The first judgement ("did the accused do it?") is a police matter and relies on the available evidence. No psychological test or statistical risk assessment procedure can determine whether a person committed an offence. In principle research-based assessment processes can be used to assist professionals with the second judgement: "how likely is the offender to do it again?"

There are some practical difficulties in applying existing risk assessment procedures to alleged offenders. The difficulties include:

- Past and current sexual conviction are key items in existing prediction instruments

- Existing prediction instruments were designed to discriminate levels of risk amongst heterogeneous groups of sex offenders while child protection issues normally relate to sexual offending committed by immediate family or close relatives
- Existing instruments relate to risk of offending against any victim whereas in a child protection context the issue is often whether a particular child is likely to be at risk
- Existing instruments are designed primarily to discriminate at higher levels of risk whereas in child-protection the concern is whether it is safe enough for the alleged offender to go into a very high risk situation (living with a potential victim)

David Thornton in collaboration with the Lucy Faithfull Foundation has undertaken a project to develop a classification tool that could be used to assist professionals in risk assessments in a child protection context. The Faithfull Classification Scheme (FACS) has adapted an existing risk assessment instrument (Static-99) to make it more applicable for use with alleged offenders. The various stages of its development used data from the English cross-validation of Static-99 (Hanson & Thornton, 2000). Step one examined whether existing instruments predict sexual recidivism as effectively with familial offenders as they do with other types of sex offenders. Offenders were classified as familial (at least one victim was a related child); extra-familial child-molesters (at least one victim was a child; no victim was a related child); or rapist (meaning all victims were adults). The correlation between offender's score using Static-99 and sexual recidivism was calculated for each group of offenders. The correlations were 0.30 for familial offenders, 0.34 for extra-familial offenders and 0.31 for rapists. These correlations are similar in magnitude and suggest Static-99 is equally predictive for the three offender groups. The factors used in Static-99 appear to be as relevant to familial abusers as they are to other sex offenders.

Step two identified whether information on the items contained in Static-99 is available for alleged offenders. Examination of child protection information suggested that there would be sufficient data to score the following five items: age, relationship status, male victims in alleged offence, prior record of non-sexual criminality and non-sexual violence in alleged offence. In order to examine whether this reduced set of items would be predictive, a count was made of how many of these factors applied to the offenders in the cross-validation sample and then relating this to rates of sexual reconviction over the following 16 years. Table 18.2 shows the result.

It appears that these items are reasonably predictive of risk. Number of risk factors could be equated with level of risk i.e. none = low risk, one or two = medium risk, three or more = high risk.

TABLE 18.2   16-year sexual reconviction rates

Number of Risk Factors	% Reconvicted
0	3
1	22
2	26
3 or more	55

TABLE 18.3 Estimated re-offence rates

Number of Risk Factors	Estimated Re-offence Rate
None (low risk)	$3 \times 3\% = 1$ in 10
One or two (medium risk)	$3 \times 24\% = 3$ in 4
Three or more (high risk)	$3 \times 55\% =$ virtually all

The gap between reconviction and re-offending prompted step three. This builds upon the work of Marshall and Barbaree (1988) who found that adding credible allegations to child protection agencies to police data multiplied the sexual recidivism rate by 2.7. Within their sample the multiplier for incest was actually three times higher. If that multiplier is applied to our reconviction statistics we then get estimated re-offence rates as shown in Table 18.3.

There is a stark difference between offenders with some of the risk factors present as opposed to offenders where none of the risk factors apply. The latter group appear to be reasonably safe in the sense that the great majority are estimated not to re-offend. In contrast the majority of the medium risk level are estimated to re-offend and virtually all the high-risk level.

Although a 1-in-10 re-offence rate might be deemed relatively low it is desirable to further discriminate risk within the low risk group. Step four (the final study), examined whether psychological information about the alleged offender (not used in Static-99) can distinguish between incest offenders who had multiple victims from those who had just one known victim. This study was based on psychological assessment data from imprisoned sex offenders taking part in the national sex offender treatment programme. Statistical analysis of this psychological assessment data identified two factors associated with having multiple incest victims: impulsiveness and cognitive distortions. The multi-victim incest offenders were statistically significantly more likely to have a general tendency to act without thinking through the consequences of their actions and more likely to endorse (or fail to reject) beliefs that can be used to give permission to abuse children. Table 18.4 shows the proportion of incest offenders who have multiple (three or more) victims according to levels of impulsiveness and cognitive distortions. The pattern observed in the table could indicate that the presence of either of these features suggests a raised level of risk. Firestone et al. (1999) have recently published findings which reinforces the centrality of these features for recidivism amongst incest offenders. This follow-up study of convicted incest offenders found that those who

TABLE 18.4 Multiple victimisation by impulsiveness and distortions

Impulsive?	Distorted?	% with Multiple Victims
No	No	9
No	Yes	19
Yes	No	35
Yes	Yes	36

went on to be reconvicted scored one standard deviation higher on a measure of cognitive distortions and half a standard deviation higher on a measure of lifestyle impulsiveness.

Two features, which are well documented in the research literature but were not covered in this particular project, also need to be considered in the effective assessment of alleged offenders. A sexual preference for children and any (alleged) offence against an unrelated victim have been established as predictors of sexual recidivism (Hanson & Bussière, 1998). These items were also added into the checklist developed and this can be found in the Appendix. The checklist has been piloted by the Lucy Faithfull Foundation using the child protection cases referred to the Foundation. As a result of this pilot, the checklist has been revised so the items can be easily scored and are based on the information typically available in these cases. The checklist results correspond well to the conclusions reached through an extensive clinical assessment.

In addition to the development of this checklist, the other tool that has been developed relates to the issue of risk for a particular child. The question of offence specialisation is widely debated in this area but research has typically been based on past offending, rather than examining the critical issue of whether the nature of past victims predicts the kind of victim chosen in the future. A recent study by the second author examined sexual reconviction for offenders categorised into three broad groups (child victim, teenage victim and adult victim) according to the age of their youngest victim in the index offence. The results are found in Table 18.5. This study also used data from the cross-validation of Static-99 (Hanson & Thornton, 2000). It is important to remember that re-offence rates are higher than reconviction rates in the interpretation of this table; 0% in a cell does not mean "no risk". Two conclusions may be made from the table. Firstly, offenders with male victims are riskier than those with female victims. Secondly, there is a marked specialisation by victim gender. Essentially, victimisation in the re-offence is overwhelmingly against the same gender as the victimisation in the original offence, with one exception, men who had abused male children (under 13) posed nearly the same risk to female children as men who had initially abused female children.

From the above studies, it can be seen that the safest configuration would be an alleged offender who had none of the checklist risk factors, whose alleged victim was a teenage female, and where the child who was potentially

TABLE 18.5 Gender of victims in past and future offences

Victim in the Index Offence	Rate of Reconviction for a Sexual Offence against a Male (%)	Rate of Reconviction for a Sexual Offence against a Female (%)
Male, aged 0–12	35	12
Female, aged 0–12	3	16
Male, aged 13–17	43	0
Female, aged 13–17	1	10
Male, aged 18+	23	0
Female, aged 18+	1	19

living in the same household as them was a male. The development of FACS is work in progress. Professionals may find it useful when forming their judgements. It is important to emphasise that FACS is intended to assist professional judgement, not be a substitute for it. A full risk assessment will need to consider other factors such as the presence or absence of a strong protective adult figure in the household, a well-developed protection plan, the alleged offender's participation in treatment and the personal resources of the child concerned.

PROTECTING THE PUBLIC

The benefit of risk assessment is the effective management of offenders in prison, in other secure settings, e.g. special hospitals, and whilst in the community (and thereby protecting the public). In HM Prison Service, risk assessment of sexual and violent offenders is a key part of management and is used to develop a sentence plan for offenders, match offenders to the appropriate treatment programmes and facilitate balanced decisions relating to release from prison, e.g. parole decisions. Plotnikoff and Woolfson (2000) recommended that the police used sex offender registration information governed by the Sex Offenders Act 1997 in order to prevent and investigate sexual crime. Risk assessment of registered sexual offenders would be one important part of this approach. A recent Home Office report (Maguire et al., 2001) described the practices of six multi-agency risk management groups for police force areas, these are usually known as Public Protection Panels (PPPs). They play a key role in bringing together representatives of police, probation services and other local agencies, including housing, in order to exchange information and formulate risk management plans for individual sexual and violent offenders. Risk assessment tools, mainly Thornton's SACJ, are commonly used by police forces for sexual offenders subject to registration procedures but their outcomes vary widely between areas and are often inconsistent in quality. Standardisation and consistency in the application of risk assessment procedures are needed. The report's conclusion, however, highlights the widespread benefits of using standardised risk assessment measures for sexual offenders: "such an approach [the promotion of defensible decision making] offers the best chance of simultaneously providing effective protection to the public, safeguarding the rights of offenders, and protecting decision-makers from unfair recriminations when new crimes are committed despite their best efforts" (Maguire et al., 2001).

REFERENCES

Barbaree, H.E., Seto, M.C., Langton, C. & Peacock, E. (2001). Evaluating the predictive accuracy of six risk assessment instruments for adult sex offenders. *Criminal Justice and Behaviour*, **28**, 490–521.

Beech, A.R., Erikson, E., Friendship, C. & Ditchfield, J. (2001). A follow-up of men going through representative probation based sex offender treatment programmes. *Home Office Research, Development and Statistics Directorate, Research Findings No. 144*. London: Home Office.

Beitchman, J.H., Zucker, K.J., Hood, J.E., DaCosta, G.A., Ackman, D. & Cassavia, E. (1991). A review of the long-term effects of child abuse. *Child Abuse and Neglect*, **16**, 101–118.

Bonta, J. (1996). Risk-needs assessment and treatment. In A.T. Harland (Ed.), *Choosing correctional options that work* (pp. 18–32). Thousand Oaks, California: Sage.

Christiansen, K.O., Elers-Nielsen, M., Le Marie, L. & Sturup, G.K. (1965). Recidivism among sexual offenders. In K.O. Christiansen (Ed.), *Scandanavian Studies in Criminology* (pp. 55–85). London: Tavistock.

Douglas, K.S., Cox, D.N. & Webster, C.D. (1999). Violence risk assessment: Science and practice. *Legal and Criminological Psychology*, **4**, 149–184.

Epperson, D.L., Kaul, J.D. & Huot, S.J. (1995). *Predicting risk of recidivism for incarcerated sex offenders: Updated developments on the sex offender screening tool (SOST)*. Poster presentation at the fourteenth annual Research and Treatment Conference of the Association for the Treatment of Sexual Abusers. 11–14 October 1995, New Orleans, Louisiana.

Farrington, D. & Tarling R (Eds.) (1985). *Prediction in Criminology*. Albany: State of New York Press.

Finkelhor, D. & Browne, A. (1985). The traumatic impact of child sexual abuse: A conceptualization. *American Journal of Orthopsychiatry*, **59**, 328–245.

Firestone, P., Bradford, J.M., McCoy, M., Greenberg, D.M., Lerose, M.R. & Curry, S. (1999). Prediction of recidivism in incest offenders. *Journal of Interpersonal Violence* **14**, 511–531.

Friendship, C., Erikson, M., Thornton, D. & Beech, A.R. (2001). Reconviction: a critique and comparison of two main data sources in England and Wales. *Legal and Criminological Psychology*, **6**, 121–129.

Friendship, C. & Thornton, D. (2001). Sexual reconviction for sexual offenders discharged from prison in England and Wales: Implications for evaluating treatment. *British Journal of Criminology*, **41**, 285–292.

Furby, L., Weinrott, M.R. & Blackshaw, L. (1989). Sex offender recidivism: A review. *Psychological Bulletin*, **105**, 3–30.

Gendreau, P., Little, T. & Goggin, C. (1996). A meta-analysis of the predictors of adult offender recidivism: what works! *Criminology*, **34**, 575–607.

Grubin, D. (1998). Sex offending against children: understanding the risk. *Home Office Research, Development and Statistics Directorate, Police Research Series Paper 99*. London: Home Office.

Hare, R.D. (1991). *Manual for Hare Psychopathy Checklist – Revised*. Toronto, Ontario: Multi-Health Systems.

Hanson, R.K. (1997). *The development of a brief actuarial risk scale for sexual offence recidivism* (User Report No. 1997-04). Ottawa, Canada: Department of the Solicitor General of Canada.

Hanson, R.K. (2001). Sex offender risk assessment. In C. Hollin (Ed.), *Handbook of offender assessment and treatment* (pp. 85–96). Chichester: Wiley.

Hanson, R.K. & Bussière, M.T. (1998). Predicting relapse: a meta-analysis of sexual offender recidivism studies. *Journal of Consulting and Clinical Psychology*, **66**, 348–362.

Hanson, R.K. & Harris, A.J.R. (1998). *Dynamic predictors of sexual recidivism*. (User Report 1998–01). Ottawa, Canada: Department of the Solicitor General Canada.

Hanson, R.K. & Thornton, D. (2000). Improving risk assessments for sexual offenders: a comparison of three actuarial scales. *Law and Human Behaviour*, **24**, 119–136.

Harris, J. & Grace, S. (1999). A question of evidence? Investigating and prosecuting rape in the 1990s. *Home Office Research, Development and Statistics Directorate No. 196*. London: Home Office.

Hough, J.M. & Mayhew, P. (1983). The British Crime Survey. *Home Office Research, Development and Statistics Directorate, Research Study No. 76*. London: Home Office.

Lloyd, C., Mair, G. & Hough, M. (1994). Explaining reconviction rates: a critical analysis. *Home Office Research, Development and Statistics Directorate, Research Study, No. 136*. London: Home Office.

Maguire, M., Kemshall, H., Noaks, L. & Wincup, E. (2001). Risk management of sexual and violent offenders: The work of Public Protection Panels. *Home Office Research, Development and Statistics Directorate, Police Research Series Paper 139*. London: Home Office.

Maltz, M. (1984). *Recidivism*. London: Academic Press.

Marques, J.K., Day, D.M., Nelson, C. & West, M.A. (1994). Effects of cognitive-behavioural treatment on sex offender recidivism: preliminary results of a longitudinal study. *Criminal Justice and Behaviour*, **21**, 10–27.

Marshall, P. (1994). Reconviction of imprisoned sexual offenders. *Research Bulletin*, **36**, 23–29. London: Home Office.

Marshall, P. (1997). The prevalence of convictions for sexual offending. *Home Office Research, Development and Statistics Directorate, Research Findings No. 55*. London: Home Office.

Marshall, W.L., Anderson, D., Fernandez, Y. (1999). *Cognitive behavioural treatment of sexual offenders*. Chichester: Wiley.

Marshall, W.L. & Barbaree, H.E. (1988). The long-term evaluation of a behavioural treatment program for child molesters. *Behaviour Research and Therapy*, **6**, 499–511.

Mayhew, P., Elliott, D. & Dowds, L. (1989). The British Crime Survey. *Home Office Research, Development and Statistics Directorate, Research Study No. 111*. London: Home Office.

Monahan, J. (1981). *Predicting violent behaviour: An assessment of clinical techniques*. Beverly Hills, CA: Sage.

Moore, B. (1996). *Risk assessment: A practitioner's guide to predicting harmful behaviour*. London: Whiting Birch Ltd.

Mossman, D. (1994). Assessing predictions of violence: being accurate about accuracy. *Journal of Consulting and Clinical Psychology*, **62**, 783–792.

Plontnikoff, J. & Woolfson, R. (2000). Where are they now? An evaluation of sex offender registration in England and Wales. *Home Office Research, Development and Statistics Directorate, Police Research Series Paper No. 126*. London: Home Office.

Povey, D. (2000). Recorded Crime: England and Wales, 12 Months to September 2000. *Home Office Statistical Bulletin, National Statistics, No. 1/01*. London: Home Office.

Prentky, R.A. & Burgess, W.A. (2000). *Forensic management of sexual offenders*. New York: Kluer Academic/Plenum Publishers.

Quinsey, V.L., Harris, G.T., Rice, M.E. & Cormier, C.A. (1998). *Violent offenders: Appraising and managing risk*. Washington DC: American Psychological Association.

Russell, D. (1984). *Sexual exploitation: Rape, child sexual abuse and sexual harassment*. Beverly Hills: Sage.

Thornton, D. & Travers, R. (1992). A Longitudinal Study of the Criminal Behaviour of Convicted Sexual Offenders. *Proceedings of the Prison Service Psychology Conference, 16–18 October 1991*, 13-22. London: HM Prison Service.

APPENDIX: FAITHFULL CLASSIFICATION SCHEME (FACS)

This scheme is intended for adult males who are alleged to have committed a sexual offence against a related child. Before applying it, assessors must determine the alleged offences that are credible (in the judgement of the assessor, probably true). The scheme is only applicable if there is at least one credible allegation. This is a determination of fact that can only be resolved on the basis of the balance of evidence. Once this determination has been made the scheme provides a framework which focuses the assessor on factors that have been associated with repeated offending by familial sex offenders.

CLASSIFY "RAISED RISK FOR NEW VICTIMS" IF ANY OF THE FOLLOWING APPLY:-

1.   3 + victims?
Are there credible allegations of sexual offences against at least three persons aged under 16 at the time they were first offended against?

2.   Any extra-familial victims?
Are there credible allegations of sexual offences against any child who is not a relative (count step-children as relatives if lived with the offender as a dependent child for at least two years before offending began; "child" = under 16)

3.   Young (18 to 30)?
The age offender will be when he next has the opportunity to offend (age now if in the community; age when offender is to be released if currently in prison or hospital).

4.   Criminal (non-sexual offences)?
Any convictions for non-sexual offences? Count only offences for which he could have been given a probation order or a custodial sentence. Do not count offences for which he was only cautioned.

5.   Lack of Stable adult relationships?
After the age of 18, has never lived with an adult sexual partner for at least 2 years.

6. Violent (convictable)

Any credible allegations of non-sexual assaults sufficiently severe that if proved in court they could result in a criminal conviction for violence? Threatening behaviour short of physical violence does not count for this item.

7. Distortions

When assessed, does the offender express beliefs of the kind that might be used to "give permission" for the sexual abuse of children? To count for this item these beliefs must be generalised i.e. not be specifically limited to just one child. Typical examples of "permission giving" beliefs are: "children are interested in sex with adults"; "children are seductive to adults"; "children can enjoy sex with adults so long as the adult is nice/gentle/kind"; "men suffer when they are deprived of sex and are entitled to seek gratification where they can find it" etc.

8. Impulsiveness

Apart from the sexual offending itself, does the offender show evidence of any of the following: a) repeated poor problem-solving; b) repeatedly acting without thinking about the consequences of his behaviour; c) a lifestyle that is disorganised and chaotic, d) a general tendency to make irresponsible choices. A lifestyle disrupted by serious alcohol abuse or drug problems would count as an example of "disorganised lifestyle".

9. Sexual Preference

Is there evidence of a sexual interest in children below the age of 13? Score this item as present if there is a credible allegation of a sexual offence against any male under the age of 16. Score this item as present if there is a credible allegation of a sexual offence against three or more female children aged under 13. Also score it as present on the basis of finding child pornography, of specialist assessment (e.g. PPG), the finding of a diary recording fantasies, or admissions by the offender.

Reproduced by permission of the Lucy Faithfull Foundation.

19

TREATING DOMESTIC VIOLENT OFFENDERS

Kevin Browne[1], Louise Falshaw[2] and Louise Dixon[1]

[1]School of Psychology, University of Birmingham, UK

[2]HM Prison Service, UK

INTRODUCTION

In the past 20 years there has been much debate about what services can be delivered in order to minimise both domestic violence and child abuse (Edleson, 1999; Edleson & Eisikovits, 1996; Peled, Jaffe & Edleson, 1995). Reviews on the causes of aggression in the family have emphasised the growing recognition that there are extensive overlaps between all forms of domestic violence and child maltreatment, as both are products of impoverished family relationships (Browne & Herbert, 1997). Nevertheless, violence in the home has been only recently highlighted as an issue that needs addressing within the context of public health care (British Medical Association, 1998; Chief Medical Officer, 1997; Gondolf, 1998; World Health Assembly, 1999). This chapter looks at the advances in interventions with domestic violent offenders from the perspective of assessment and treatment.

Within each community, domestic violence and child maltreatment occur in the context of complex interactions between institutional, social and individual factors (Peled, Jaffe & Edleson, 1995). Hence, effective intervention must involve cooperation at all levels between and within health, social welfare, educational, legal and law enforcement systems (Office of the Tanaiste, 1997; World Health Organization, 1998). Shared community values that underpin this cooperation are that:

- Everyone has the right to live in a safe environment.
- Violence in any form is unacceptable.
- Perpetrators of domestic violence need to be held accountable for their actions.

Early Prediction and Prevention of Child Abuse: A Handbook.
Edited by Kevin Browne, Helga Hanks, Peter Stratton and Catherine Hamilton. © 2002 John Wiley & Sons, Ltd.

TABLE 19.1   Forms of family violence and child abuse (from Browne & Herbert, 1997, with permission. Adapted from Stratton, Davies & Browne, 1988)

	Physical violence	Psychological violence	Sexual violence
Active abuse	Non-accidental injury Forced coercion and restraint	Intimidation Emotional abuse Material abuse	Incest Sexual assault and rape
Passive neglect	Poor health care Physical neglect	Lack of affection Emotional neglect Material neglect	Failure to protect Prostitution

Many definitions of domestic violence have been developed for different settings (e.g. legal, medical, welfare, educational). Whilst there is a lack of specific agreement among the various perspectives, most definitions refer to physical, psychological and sexual damage to the victim, consistent with that described for child maltreatment (see Table 19.1). As domestic violence is predominantly, but not exclusively, perpetrated by men against women (Gelles, 1987; Browne, 1989; Browne & Herbert, 1997; Dobash & Dobash, 1998; Renzetti, Edleson & Bergen, 2001), the perpetrators are generally described as partners, spouses and boyfriends or ex-partners, ex-spouses and ex-boyfriends.

EXTENT OF DOMESTIC VIOLENCE

Domestic violence findings from the Home Office British Crime Survey (Mirrlees-Black, 1999) indicate that 23% of women and 15% of men aged 16–59 say they had been physically assaulted by a current or a former partner at some time. The survey also stated that 12% of the women and 5% of men report that they had been assaulted on three or more occasions. In 1995, it was estimated that 6.6 million incidents of domestic physical assault had occurred and that 2.9 million of these had involved injury. Although these figures provide evidence for the interactive nature of spouse abuse within coercive family relationships (see Frude, 1991, 1994; Browne & Herbert, 1997), most agree that, "When men hit women and women hit men, the real victims are almost certainly going to be the women" (Gelles, 1981, p. 128).

At "any one time 10% of women are experiencing domestic violence, and it affects one in four women at some time in their lives". Further research identifies that more than one in two women had been in psychologically abusive relationships during their lives, and that one in three women had suffered physical and sexual abuse serious enough to have required medical attention (Mooney, 1993; Morley & Mullender, 1994; Stanko, 1998). Hence, considerable time and resources are spent, by a range of government and non-government agencies, in dealing with the aftermath. Indeed, domestic violence has profound psychological and emotional effects on both perpetrators and victims. This places demands on social, health, welfare and other services over long periods of time. Children who witness their parents fighting experience adverse health and development, with poor psychological and emotional outcomes. These conditions are unlikely to come to the attention of health and welfare agencies, except perhaps as "conduct disorder problems" in the school environment (Browne & Herbert, 1997; Falshaw, Browne & Hollin, 1996). Unfortunately, in a significant proportion of violent families, the father assaults the children as well as the mother.

LINKS BETWEEN SPOUSE ABUSE AND CHILD MALTREATMENT

It is estimated that 3.3 million children in the USA live with violent parents (Carlson, 1984) and that children are present for at least two-thirds of wife assaults (Pahl, 1985). Furthermore, research in the UK on women in shelters report that four out of five battered women recall witnessing their mother being assaulted by their father during their childhood (Gayford, 1975).

Regardless of whether children are victims of aggression themselves, witnessing family violence can be regarded as "emotional abuse", as it will still have a very profound effect on children's development and attitudes to social relationships (Carroll, 1994). According to research, the effects of witnessing wife assault can result in childhood conduct and personality disorders (Jouriles et al., 1989; Grych and Fincham, 1990).

In their book *Children of Battered Women*, Jaffe et al. (1990) explain that boys and girls learn that violence is an acceptable way to resolve conflict with an intimate partner after witnessing their mother and father fighting. Boys and girls also learn about victimisation and the extent to which males can use aggression and fear to gain power and control over other family members. This learning results in a change of their own behaviour. However, many children are the victims of physical and sexual assaults in the same way as their mother.

For over 20 years, authors have reported a link between spouse abuse and child physical abuse (Browne, 1993; Gayford, 1975; Merrick & Michelsen, 1985; Milner & Gold, 1986), as well as between spouse abuse and child sexual abuse (Dietz & Craft, 1980; Goddard & Hiller, 1993; Stanley & Goddard, 1993). Evidence for a close link between spouse abuse and child maltreatment is now well established, with child abuse and neglect occurring in approximately half of those families where there is violence between parents. For example, Straus, Gelles & Steinmetz (1988) estimated that 40% of those families experiencing wife assault also showed child (physical and sexual) assault; this compares to 53% of spouse abuse cases in a study by Walker (1984).

From the opposite perspective, Browne & Saqi (1988) found that spouse abuse was occurring in 52% of families where child abuse and neglect was identified by health visitors. Browne & Hamilton (1999) also confirmed an overlap of 46% a decade later from police records. However, the implication of this overlap for child care proceedings have not been fully realised (Peled, Jaffe & Edleson, 1995; Schechter & Edleson, 1995).

Where both spouse abuse and child maltreatment are occurring in the family, the severity of the violence is greater, and mental health problems, alcohol and drug dependency appear to be the most significant risk factors (Browne & Hamilton, 1999). In the USA, surveys of battered women typically show that 60% of their partners have an alcohol problem and 21% have a drug problem (Roberts, 1987), and the majority of female victims suffer from mental health problems as a result (Stark &

Flitcraft, 1996). Some authors propose that these are the major causes of family violence (Pernanen, 1991). However, it is more likely that alcohol and drug dependency relieves the man of the responsibility for his behaviour and gives the wife justification for remaining in the relationship in the hope that he will control his addiction and end his aggression to her and her children.

It is true that alcohol and drugs appear to exacerbate pre-existing emotional problems, which increases the likelihood of violence. However, the majority of individuals who abuse drugs and alcohol admit that they have been violent to their dependants while not under the influence of alcohol and drugs (Sonkin, Martin & Walker, 1985). Indeed, mental health problems, alcohol and drug dependency are not the causes of family violence, but rather conditions that coexist with it, along with many other factors. Nevertheless, they are often used as excuses for violent behaviour—personally, socially and legally.

Interventions aimed at the protection of women and children must first address these associated factors, as individuals addicted to alcohol and drugs or suffering from mental illness can rarely benefit from social services interventions. The inter-agency cooperation between health and social services is a necessary prerequisite in such cases, especially in relation to the assessment of families and the potential harm to children. This is very important during pregnancy, as the abuse of pregnant women has potentially dangerous consequences for the unborn child (McFarlane, 1991; Newberger et al., 1992). In a study of 290 pregnant women, Helton (1986) found that 15.2% reported battering before their current pregnancies and 8.3% reported battering during their current pregnancy.

LEGAL ISSUES

Children, including unborn children, are sometimes taken into public care with the view of fostering and adoption on the basis of the mother failing to protect her children (see Hilton, 1993). It is claimed that the mother places the children at the risk of harm by associating with a violent and/or sex offender. However, the mother is often a victim of physical and/or sexual assault by the same offender and is not in a position to protect her unborn or newborn child(ren).

One of the difficulties the courts face in care proceedings is to assess whether it is in the best interest of the child(ren) to separate their mother, permanently or temporarily, while she seeks treatment for her victim experiences, mental health difficulties and low self-esteem. Sometimes this decision depends on the speed with which the mother can respond to therapy and demonstrate change towards appropriately protecting and parenting her children. This is because of the urgency to provide a stable and stimulating environment for the child(ren). Young children are particularly regarded as urgent cases because of their developmental needs. Mothers who have mental health and addiction problems (frequently as a consequence of spouse abuse) may not recover in the time frame required to avoid damaging the development of their infants (Gondolf, 1998; see Glaser & Prior, chapter 4).

In the UK, law may dictate that an assessment must be funded, resourced and carried out on offenders, their victims or the family as a whole (Assessment Orders). However, no such legal provision is available for treatment (Treatment Orders) so that violent fathers and abused mothers only attend treatment voluntarily, if it is available, and often at their own expense. Just those violent offenders who are convicted of assault may be diverted into treatment programmes or offered therapy while in prison.

As a consequence, most domestic violent offenders do not receive treatment, as they are rarely convicted "beyond all reasonable doubt". The children are more often taken into public care on the "balance of probability", a level of proof easier to establish. The estranged violent father often moves on to another family to create more havoc and in some cases returns to victimise the original family once again. Hence, the burden of family violence legally rests with the victims, rather than the offender, with the mother sometimes being separated or losing her children without ever offending against them (see Buzawa & Buzawa, 1996a).

It is important to establish, therefore, whether both the mother and the father are at risk of harming their child(ren) or just one of them, usually the father. Unfortunately, family typologies in relation to domestic violence are poorly developed, and consequently so are the assessment and treatment strategies for dealing with domestic violence at a more holistic family system level. It is essential to take a broader perspective in legal proceedings, and to determine whether or not the mother wishes to separate from her violent partner, in order to assess what is in the best interest of the children.

FAMILY TYPOLOGIES IN RELATION TO DOMESTIC VIOLENCE

Typology research may be criticised for its narrow focus on the offender without considering other factors, such as the context and behavioural actions of the victim. The literature has mainly classified domestic violent men utilising individual characteristics of the offender, such as personality, psychopathology or physiological response. By contrast, some researchers have stipulated that aggression in the family is a product of the person–environment interaction (Frude, 1991; Browne & Herbert, 1997). Therefore, a more holistic family-focused typology, based on the interpersonal characteristics of the offender and victim, together with those situational factors that triggered the violent act, may be a more fruitful approach. Research suggests that spouse abusers are not a homogenous group. Holtzworth-Munroe & Stuart (1994) propose three types of domestic violent men; family only, generally violent/antisocial, and dysphoric/borderline personality. A review of nine empirical research studies (Dixon and Browne, 2002) showed an average prevalence for the three types as 50%, 30% and 20% of violent men, respectively.

Bartholomew, Henderson & Dutton (2001) assert that relationship abuse is best understood within a dyadic context, with both persons being considered in relation to one another. Bartholomew et al. (2001) report different patterns of violence between couples (reciprocal, or one-way violence), depending on the interacting attachment styles of the two individuals involved in the relationship. Family typologies should be considered, given the high association between different forms of family violence, especially spouse abuse and child abuse. The patterns of violence in the family have implications for both assessment and treatment, and therefore typologies of violent families are in desperate need of development.

(a)

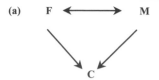

Reciprocal family violence

(b)

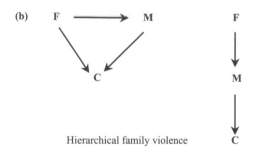

Hierarchical family violence

(c)

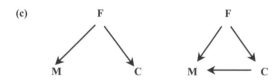

Paternal family violence

FIGURE 19.1   Abuse patterns within domestic violent families. *F = father or step-father. M = mother or step-mother. C = child/children or step-child/children.* (From Dixon & Browne, 2002, with permission)

Taking a family system approach, some common forms of violent patterns observed in families can be broadly classified into reciprocal, hierarchical and paternal family violence (see Figure 19.1).

- *Reciprocal family violence.* This involves the mother retaliating violently to the abusive father. Where children are present, both parents have the potential to be violent towards their children, and if not, the children may still suffer emotional abuse through witnessing the reciprocal violence of their parents (see Figure 19.1a). In these families both the father and the mother may be seen as offenders in terms of treatment.
- *Hierarchical family violence.* This involves a hierarchy where the father is violent to the mother, and the mother is violent to the children but does not retaliate violently to the abusive father. In some cases the father may also be violent to the children (see Figure 19.1b). In terms of treatment, the father is the main perpetrator of violence and the mother may be considered to be both a victim and an offender.

• *Paternal family violence.* This involves the mother being regarded by the father as another vulnerable dependant with no more status than the children in the family. In fact, the children may observe the mother to be as powerless as them, and in some circumstances also become violent to their mother (see Figure 19.1c). In these families, the mother is very much in need of support and treatment as a victim, with the father being the main perpetrator of violence.

In all the above scenarios, the children require support and treatment as victims of family violence, whether they are directly victimised physically or sexually or indirectly victimised through witnessing violence between their parents (Peled & Davis, 1995). Children who do not receive such help have a higher probability of aggressing toward both their mothers and their fathers as teenagers and young adults (Browne & Hamilton, 1998).

DOMESTIC VIOLENCE INTERVENTIONS

Reviews on the causes of family violence have emphasised that domestic violence is a product of poor family relationships (see Figure 19.2). This interactive perspective places less emphasis on the inherent problems of individuals that lead to aggressive outbursts, such as, neurological, hormonal and mental illness explanations. Therefore, interventions by health and social workers with violent families that strengthen family relationships are considered to be more promising for prevention than those aimed at individual psychopathology (Cahn, 1996).

Given the complex nature of human aggression, together with the possible triggers and potential reinforcers, the modification of violent behaviour faces obvious difficulties. Nonetheless, recent years have seen considerable advances in

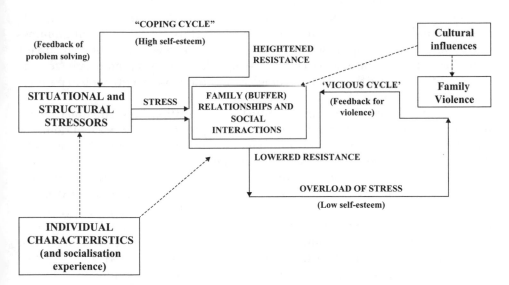

FIGURE 19.2   Causes of family violence and child abuse (from Browne & Herbert, 1997, with permission)

intervention with violent individuals in terms of both assessment and treatment (Browne & Howells, 1996; Watt & Howells, 1999). The safety of potential victims takes precedence and factors that trigger the perpetrator's violent behaviour are the focus of assessment. Problems such as mental illness, psychological problems and chemical dependencies may also need to be addressed (Rosenbaum & O'Leary, 1986).

The treatment of spouse abuse involves multiple strategies (Browne & Herbert, 1997) but most approaches to violent offenders address the following components of aggressive behaviour (adapted from Goldstein and Keller, 1987):

- Interpretation of situations as irritating or threatening (e.g. self-talk).
- Strategies and methods of conflict resolution.
- Causes of heightened affective arousal (e.g. anger).
- Patterns of poor communication.
- Mismanagement of contingencies.
- Prosocial skill deficiencies.
- Prosocial value deficiencies.

However, offenders are often reluctant to attend group counselling sessions and voluntary attendance is often variable, with significant drop-out rates. Once men drop out, they are rarely followed up and the consequences for other family members may go unnoticed (Edleson & Tolman, 1992). Often treatment is offered to different members of the family (i.e. men, women and children), with little attention to a holistic approach that takes into account the different needs of family members.

Until recently, help for abused women concentrated on removing the immediate threat of violence by providing shelters, safe homes and refuges, followed by help in leaving the violent relationship (Buzawa & Buzawa, 1996a). However, some women choose to remain in the relationship and see the violence as being only one of a number of stressful events in their lives. Thus, intervention programmes that focus on a single approach to violence in the home will have limited success with these families (Browne & Herbert, 1997). However, programmes have been developed to increase the safety of women who choose to stay with violent partners (Goodman & Fallon, 1995).

The Family Safety Programme conducted by Relationships Australia (Shaw, Bouris & Pye, 1996) is designed as an integrated programme to prevent domestic violence. This programme offers group and individual therapy to help women reduce feelings of personal responsibility and emotional dependency, and to explore the possibility of separation. An educational programme is offered to volunteer men, focusing on behaviour and attitudinal change. Other services are also utilised when appropriate (e.g. alcohol services, child protection services). On a 12 month follow-up of the programme, women were more likely to take a restraining order or separate if the violence continued. For the men attending the programme, their female partners reported that the physical violence had stopped in all but two cases, although verbal aggression and emotional abuse often continued.

A recent study by Dobash, Dobash, Cavanagh & Lewis (1996, 2000) report similar findings, that one third of "treated men" continue to engage in coercive and verbally violent interactions when the physical violence stops. Nevertheless, the study does provide evidence that treatment programmes are more effective than other forms of criminal interventions at reducing physically violent offending. Further research is required to determine the characteristics of men resistant to change and still at risk of psychological violence to women and children. There is a need for systematic evaluation of the apparent shift from physical to verbal violence shown by some abusive men in treatment.

With many offender programmes, the assessment procedure and structure of the treatment package lack consistency. Problems in defining goals and lack of a clear step-by-step structure reduces the treatment integrity and relative effectiveness of the programme (see Hollin, 1996). The success of each component of the treatment package cannot be easily determined or consistently examined. Thus, evidence-based programme evaluation and development may prove impossible.

The promotion of safety for women and children in the family can only be guaranteed by clear evidence of positive change in those men attending treatment. Whether such positive change is reliable and permanent is of paramount importance, yet few projects follow up men with a history of violent offending after they have left their treatment programme. Recent developments in London, Birmingham and Liverpool have aimed at producing an integrated interagency approach to intervention with domestic violent offenders and their victims. This is based on the Duluth educational model and tied in with the Criminal Justice response (see Pence & Paymar, 1993; Shepard & Pence, 1999).

Example of Good Practice

The West Midlands Domestic Violence Project (DVP) provides a range of services, based around a group treatment programme for violent men, to families affected by domestic violence. Through interagency cooperation, families are identified by the judicial system. The court is asked to consider requiring violent offenders to enter a group treatment programme. The goal of the interagency work is to coordinate, with the full cooperation of the correctional services, the health and social services, a holistic approach to the assessment and treatment of family violence. Thus, the victims, both women and children, receive help in parallel to the male offender.

The West Midlands Domestic Violence Project has been jointly developed by staff in the West Midlands Probation, Women's Aid, The Children's Society, Police and Psychologists at the University of Birmingham. The main objectives of the Project are to:

1. Increase the level of safety of women and children affected by domestic violence.
2. Reduce violent behaviour in men by increasing the options available to them.
3. Develop a coordinated and consistent interagency response.
4. Evaluate the effectiveness of the project.

The Domestic Violence Project (DVP) ensures treatment integrity and offers a 20 week group treatment programme for violent men, who will attend a $2^1/_2$ hour group session once a week. Each week, groups run with 10 men in the group. The programme is structured on a modular system and topics are covered in sequence

TABLE **19.2** Example of a core treatment programme for domestic violent offenders

Module A	*Non-violent and non-threatening behaviour:* Analysing use of violence (including role play reversal) Understanding and ending violence as a means of control Examining the effects of violence on relationships Defining intimidation/planning non-abusive alternatives
Module B	*Community response to domestic violence* *(inter-agency reponses):* Drama/portrayals of domestic violence in the media Social constructs of gender Health and social services Role of the police and probation Women's Aid, shelters and support groups Stories, songs and poems from victims
Module C	*Respect, trust and support:* Humiliation Emotional abuse Trust and support Establishing trust and support
Module D	*Honesty, accountability and sexual respect:* Defining honesty and accountability Denial, minimisation and blame Defining sexual respect and consent Analysing use of sexual coercion and ending it
Module E	*The effects of domestic violence on children:* Children's experience of domestic violence Effects of domestic violence on children Seven ages of childhood and pathological learning Responsible and consistent parenting Positive parenting skills

(see Table 19.2). The groups are run by experienced probation officers who have received specialist training from the London Domestic Violence Intervention Project. All sessions are video-filmed. It is the responsibility of the group to ensure that core topics are included in the group discussion process.

Evaluation

Each man entering group therapy should be assessed one week before the group sessions commence. Social, demographic and criminal record information is collected. The initial assessment examines attitudes, expectations and self-esteem, together with current levels of physical, sexual and psychological violence. The men may be also assessed using psychometric instruments to measure responses to:

- Anger-provoking situations (eg: Novaco, 1975).
- Levels of hostility (eg: Buss & Durkee, 1957).
- Conflict tactics (eg: Straus, 1979).
- The potential for spouse abuse (eg: O'Leary & Curley, 1986).

The men's female partners may be appropriately assessed using the Women Abuse Scale (Saunders, 1992) and the Index of Spouse Abuse (Hudson & McIntosh, 1981). If children are present in the family, both parents also may be assessed using the Parenting Stress Index (Abidin, 1990) and the Child Abuse Potential Inventory (Milner, 1986; Milner & Gold, 1986).

The psychometric instruments are administered best to each man, on a one-to-one basis, the week before the group sessions begin and again on completion of the programme (20 weeks later), or earlier if the man drops out. Follow-up assessments should occur for all men who start the programme at 6 months post-completion of the programme and, if possible, at 12 months post-completion.

An integral part of DVP projects is to evaluate the effectiveness of the group treatment programme for violent men, in particular how the men change in relation to:

- Physical and verbal aggression.
- Distorted beliefs and perceptions of family interactions.
- Violent strategies to conflict resolution.

Reasons for any drop-out and risk assessment of these violent men before and after the 20 week group programme identifies factors and characteristics that inhibit or facilitate positive change. Current levels of emotional, sexual and physical assault of family members can be also determined, together with any previous offences. Differences in the characteristics and progress of male offenders who have been maltreated themselves in childhood, in comparison to those in the programme who have no such history, may be established. This establishes the need for additional therapy for adverse childhood experiences.

The projects identify characteristics of men most suitable for the group treatment programme in terms of a subsequent reduction of their violent behaviour. The success of treatment is measured by assessing both the perpetrator and the victim of domestic violence. Performance indicators are as follows:

- Reductions in violent and aggressive behaviour.
- Reductions in power and coercion to control family members.
- Improved positive interactions and relations with family members.
- Improved attitude with regard to the safety and well-being of women and children.
- Increased self-esteem and personal feelings of self-worth.

The outcome of such projects is to increase the level of safety in families by reducing the number of violent incidents in the family home. Interagency cooperation on domestic violence interventions can maximise the use of limited resources and minimise the costs of violence in the family.

LAW ENFORCEMENT RESPONSES

West Midlands Police patrols attend domestic violence disputes as part of their normal protocol and establish the safety of any children present. Addresses are checked against the Child Protection Register to determine whether children are already considered to be at risk of harm. All incidents of domestic violence are communicated to social services. Surveys of victims show that 14–27% of domestic assaults are reported to the police (Dutton, 1988; Jones et al., 1986) but only a small minority are recorded (Edwards, 1989). Dutton (1987) estimated that the probability of "wife assault" being detected by the criminal justice system in Canada is about 6.5%. If detected, the probability of arrest is 21.2%. Overall, the offender has a 0.38% chance of being punished by the courts.

In the English West Midlands, a representative of the probation service attends when domestic violent offenders are being processed by the courts. If an offender pleads guilty or is found guilty, the court has a number of options; a custodial sentence, probation on order with conditions, or community service. The court is alerted to the possibility of the offender attending a group treatment pro-gramme for domestic violence and encouraged to ask for presentence reports, to assess the man's suitability for treatment in the community. Offenders are consid-ered suitable for a community treatment programme when the following exclusion criteria are absent:

- In breach of a current bond.
- Has a psychiatric condition.
- Is chemically dependent on drugs or alcohol.
- Is transitory and/or itinerant.
- Unable to speak English adequately.

When the offender is found to be unsuitable, the court is notified and sentencing will proceed in its usual manner. The use of community treatment programmes for domestic violent offenders is preferred to the exclusive use of arrests and restraining orders. Such restricted approaches to the control of family violence have met limited success (see Buzawa & Buzawa, 1996b; Sherman, 1992). However, relying on the court process is also limited in its effectiveness, as West Midlands police statistics show that the offender is cautioned or charged in only 13% of child maltreatment cases and 8% of spouse abuse cases. Arrests occurred in 4% and 16% of cases, respectively, with no further action for the vast majority of incidents (64% and 72%, respectively). This is despite the fact that 27% of child abuse and neglect cases and 47% of spouse abuse cases have been previously referred to the police (Browne & Hamilton, 1999).

In light of the above figures, it could be argued that a more fruitful approach to the prevention of family violence is to intervene with aggressive children and violent teenagers prior to their involvement as a partner and parent to others in adulthood.

INTERVENTION WITH VIOLENT YOUNG OFFENDERS

Adverse childhood experiences are common in young people placed in secure accommodation. Indeed, research has highlighted the link between childhood ad-verse experiences and later antisocial behaviour (e.g. Browne, 1994; Boswell, 1995; Browne, Falshaw & Hamilton, 1995; Falshaw & Browne, 1997; Farrington, 1995;

TABLE 19.3 Known history of child maltreatment and registration amongst Glenthorne residents (from Falshaw & Browne, 1997, with permission)

Maltreatment Type*	Residents (%) (n = 77)	Males (%) (n = 59)	Females (%) (n = 18)
Within family			
Physically abused	53	52	58
Neglected	32	32	32
Severe emotional abuse	28	30	21
Sexually abused	14	5	42
Outside family			
Sexually abused	29	23	47
Physically abused	14	12	21
Placed on Child Protection Register	34	32	42

* Residents may have suffered more than one type of abuse.

Rivera & Widom, 1990; Scudder, Blount, Heide & Silverman, 1993; Widom, 1989a, b, 1991; Widom & Ames, 1994). According to this research, delinquent and disturbed children are significantly more likely to have been referred for child abuse and neglect than non-delinquents (Falshaw, Browne & Hollin, 1996). In fact, it has been suggested that childhood maltreatment and/or witnessing violence as a child may be a primary cause of delinquency and violent offending in adolescence (Jaffe, Wolfe & Wilson, 1990; Widom, 1991; Hamilton, Falshaw & Browne, 2002), although the majority of maltreated children do not become delinquent (O'Connell-Higgins, 1994).

The findings of two British studies, Boswell (1995) and Falshaw & Browne (1997), demonstrate that 72% of young offenders in security have experienced some kind of maltreatment (see Table 19.3). Similar findings have been reported by Stein & Lewis (1992) for incarcerated youths in the USA. They found that four out of five residents admitted that severe abuse had taken place during their childhood.

The above research provides support for a developmental model of delinquency, such as that proposed by Patterson, DeBaryshe & Ramsey (1989). They suggested that, firstly, inept parenting encourages the adoption of antisocial behaviour by the child. This conduct disorder then produces academic failings and rejection by peers. This rejection and failure, in turn, forces association with deviant peers, who provide the necessary encouragement and reinforcement for the maintenance of delinquent behaviour (see Figure 19.3). The predisposition to delinquency and criminal behaviour, therefore, is a complex interplay of dysfunctional child-rearing practices and detrimental childhood experiences (Lake, 1993; Lauritsen, Sampson & Laub, 1991; Simons, Whitbeck, Conger & Conger, 1991; Simons, Chyi-In, Conger & Lorenz, 1994).

Youth offending has become an increasing focus of government with the introduction of the Crime and Disorder Act 1998 in England and Wales, which attributes full criminal responsibility to children as young as 10 years. The government considers that secure provision provides safety for absconding delinquent children who place themselves and others at risk and gives an ideal opportunity to offer violent young people early intervention.

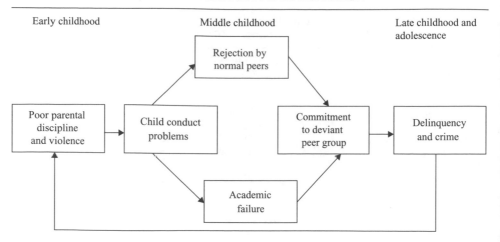

FIGURE 19.3   The cycle of violence and delinquency (adapted from Patterson et al., 1989; from Browne & Herbert, 1997, with permission)

Maltreatment within the family home may result in a young person running away or absconding from a number of care placements (see Falshaw & Browne, 1999). Some end up living on the streets (Browne & Falshaw, 1998a). This, in turn, may lead to the misuse of drugs/alcohol (Dembo, Williams, Fagan & Schmeidler, 1993) and/or to sexualised behaviour and involvement in prostitution and sexual offences (Watkins & Bentovim, 1992).

The opportunity to encourage these young delinquents to learn new skills at the expense of those they have so far acquired, cannot be wasted. Secure care placements must be long enough to provide sufficient stability and support to overcome the detrimental effects of prior childhood experiences, but also be effective in preparing the young person to lead a successful, law-abiding existence upon release, as soon as possible. Only then will secure provision be fulfilling its duty to both young people and the general public.

TREATMENT OBJECTIVES

According to research (Falshaw & Browne, 1997; Browne & Falshaw, 1998b), when a young person is admitted to secure accomodation, he/she will often present with a childhood history of the following:

- Serious and/or persistent involvement in criminal activity.
- Extreme maltreatment both inside and outside the family.
- Medical complaints.
- Educational problems.
- Dysfunctional family environments characterised by domestic violence and criminality and/or a string of foster and institutional placements due to disruptive behaviour and habitual absconding.

Assessment of Need

The first part of a young person's stay in security should be devoted to a thorough assessment of his/her individual needs. Information can be collected from background files, through interviews with the young person, his/her family and agencies responsible for his/her welfare, as well as observation of his/her behaviour in the institution. From this, a 'personal programme plan' may be constructed to meet the young person's short-term and long-term needs. This plan may be reviewed and updated in relation to a local authority's overall care plan.

Behavioural Management

Behavioural management of the young person can be employed in order to promote the necessary stability required to engage the individual in treatment. Some centres adopt a grading system, based on social learning principles, which enforces strict behavioural limits on the residents' everyday behaviour according to their achieved grade. This behavioural management system gives "young people a structured and graded access to increasingly higher levels of privileges contingent upon their behaviour" (Hollin, Epps & Kendrick, 1995, p. 116).

THERAPY

According to Winnicott (1956), "it is the environment that plays the essential role in the natural healing of the anti-social tendency". Severely emotionally disturbed adolescents and young offenders need a safe healing environment, which provides them with experiences which they can live through positively and thereby rework earlier difficulties.

Treatment objectives for disturbed adolescents and young offenders need to consider the whole person and not merely be focused on the violent behaviour that is a symptom of their disturbance (Bemak & Keys, 2000). When the care staff are trained appropriately, the structured environment of a secure therapeutic setting can compensate to some extent for an inadequate and disorganised domestic environment.

Disturbed adolescents need to establish relationships with care staff who are capable of imposing meaningful limits, as well as coping with anger (Flavingy, 1988). When the young person acts out intense feelings belonging to an earlier stage of life, the care staff may be provoked into reacting as an inadequate parent would have done, so therapeutic skills training is essential for residential care workers.

To achieve change with damaged children is to contain their anxiety by providing a safe forum for exploration and shouldering their feelings of inadequacy (Mawson, 1994). Because of earlier maltreatment, damaged children often mistrust others and form insecure attachments. Indeed, psychological and behavioural problems related to an insecure attachment often emerge in the relationship between a child and his/her carer. The skilled carer can intervene, in the context of the relationship, to enable the child to modify negative and pessimistic beliefs and expectations of others and of him/herself (Pearce & Pezzot-Pearce, 1994). Details of clinical approaches to working with young offenders and successful interventions to prevent violence can be found in Hollin & Howells (1996) and Loeber & Farrington (1998), respectively.

CONCLUSION

The aim of all those involved in work with violent offenders must be the prevention of physical and sexual violence in the family. This means being available, with suitable resources, to help families with serious problems before violence, abuse and neglect occurs. Even for individuals who were maltreated as children, the prognosis may be good with effective intervention and therapy.

In their book *Preventing Family Violence*, Browne & Herbert (1997) take a holistic approach to family violence. They indicate that it is not sufficient to evaluate intervention on the basis of occurrence or non-occurrence of physically violent behaviour, as many other forms of maltreatment coexist or replace aggression. Helping family members to inhibit physical violence towards each other and their dependants may still leave unchanged the emotionally harmful environment in which the initial abuse occurred. Therefore, work on interpersonal relationships is essential if prevention of family violence is to be achieved, both in this generation and the next.

REFERENCES

Abdin, R. (1990). *Manual of the Parenting Stress Index (PSI)*, 3rd edn. Charlottesville, VA: Psychology Press.

Bartholomew, K., Henderson, A.J.Z. & Dutton, D.G. (2001). Insecure attachment and partner abuse. In Clulow, C. (ed.), *Attachment and Couple Work: Applying the "Secure Base" Concept in Research and Practice*. London: Routledge.

Bemak, F. & Keys, S. (2000). *Violent and Aggressive Youth: Intervention and Prevention Strategies for Changing Times*. New York: Corwin.

Boswell, G. (1995). *The Prevalence of Abuse and Loss in the Lives of Section 53 Offenders*. School of Social Work, University of East Anglia: March.

British Medical Association (1998). *Domestic Violence: A Health Care Issue?*. London: British Medical Association Science Department and Board of Science and Education.

Browne, K.D. (1989). Family violence: spouse and elder abuse. In Howells, K. & Hollin, C. (eds), *Clinical Approaches to Violence*. Wiley: Chichester; 119–154.

Browne, K.D. (1993). Violence in the family and its links to child abuse. *Ballière's Clinical Paediatrics*, **1**(1): 149–164 [Special Issue on Child Abuse, Hobbs, C. & Wynne, J. (eds)].

Browne, K.D. (1994). Child sexual abuse. In Archer, J. (ed.), *Male Violence*. London: Routledge; 210–230.

Browne, K.D. & Falshaw, L. (1998a). Street children and crime in the UK: a case of child abuse and neglect. *Child Abuse Review*, **7**(4): 241–243.

Browne, K.D. & Falshaw, L. (1998b). Treatment work with young people in secure care. *Irish Journal of Psychology*, **19**(1): 208–225.

Browne, K.D., Falshaw, L. & Hamilton, C. (1995). The characteristics of young persons resident at the Glenthorne Centre during the first half of 1995. *Youth Treatment Service Journal*, **1**(2): 52–71.

Browne, K.D. & Hamilton, C. (1998). Physical violence between young adults and their parents: associations with a history of child maltreatment. *Journal of Family Violence*, **13**(1): 57–79.

Browne, K.D. & Hamilton C.E. (1999). Police recognition of links between spouse abuse and child abuse. *Child Maltreatment*, **4**(2): 136–147.

Browne, K.D. & Herbert, M. (1997). *Preventing Family Violence*. Chichester: Wiley.

Browne, K.D. & Howells, K. (1996). Violent offenders. In Hollin C.R. (ed.), *Working with Offenders: Psychological Practice in Offender Rehabilitation*. Chichester: Wiley; 188–210.

Browne, K.D. & Saqi, S. (1988). Approaches to screening for families high-risk child abuse. In Browne, K.D., Davies, C. & Stratton, P. (eds), *Early Prediction and Prevention of Child Abuse*. Wiley: Chichester; 57–85.

Buss, A.H. & Dukee, A. (1957). An inventory for assessing different types of hostility. *Journal of Consulting Psychology*, **21**: 343–349.

Buzawa, E.S. & Buzawa, C.G. (1996a). *Domestic Violence: the Criminal Justice Response*, 2nd edn. Beverley Hills, CA: Sage.

Buzawa, E.S. & Buzawa, C.G. (1996b). *Do Arrests and Restraining Orders Work?* Beverley Hills, CA: Sage.

Carlson, B.E. (1984). Children's observations of interparental violence. In Roberts A.R. (ed.) *Battered Women and Their Families*, New York: Springer; 147–167.

Carroll, J. (1994). The protection of children exposed to marital violence. *Child Abuse Review*, **3**(1), 6–14.

Cahn, D. (1996). Family violence from a communication perspective. In Cahn, D. & Lloyd, S. (eds), *Family Violence from a Communication Perspective*. Beverley Hills, CA: Sage.

Chief Medical Officer (1997). *Report on the State of Public Health*. London: Department of Health.

Dembo, R., Williams, L., Fagan, J. & Schmeidler, J. (1993). The relationships of substance abuse and other delinquency over time in a sample of juvenile detainees. *Criminal Behaviour and Mental Health*, **3**: 158–179.

Dietz, C.A. & Craft, J.L. (1980). Family dynamics of incest: a new perspective. *Social Casework*, **61**: 602–609.

Dixon, L. & Browne, K.D. (2002). Heterogeneity of spouse abusers: a review. *Aggression and Violent Behaviour*, 8 (in press).

Dobash, R.E. & Dobash, R.P. (eds) (1998). *Rethinking Violence Against Women*. Beverley Hills, CA: Sage.

Dobash, R., Dobash, R.E., Cavanagh, K. & Lewis, R. (1996). *Re-Education Programmes for Violent Men—An Evaluation*. Home Office Research and Statistics Directorate Research Findings, No. 46. London: HMSO; 1–4.

Dobash, R.E., Dobash, R.P., Cavanagh, K. & Lewis, R. (2000). *Changing Violent Men*. Beverley Hills, CA: Sage.

Dutton, D.G. (1987). The criminal justice response to wife assault. *Law and Human Behaviour*, **11**(3): 189–206.

Dutton, D.G. (1988). *The Domestic Assault of Women: Psychological and Criminal Justice Perspectives*. Boston, MA: Allyn and Bacon.

Edleson, J.L. (1999). The overlap between child maltreatment and woman battering. *Violence Against Women*, **5**: 134–154.

Edleson, J.L. & Eisikovits, Z.C. (1996). *Future Interventions with Battered Women and Their Families*. Thousand Oaks, CA: Sage.

Edleson, J.L. & Tolman, R.M. (1992). *Intervention for Men Who Batter: An Ecological Approach*. Newbury Park, CA: Sage.

Edwards, S.S.M. (1989). *Policing 'Domestic' Violence: Women, the Law and the State*. London: Sage.

Falshaw, L. & Browne, K.D. (1997). Adverse childhood experiences and violent acts of young people in secure accommodation. *Journal of Mental Health*, **6**: 443–455.

Falshaw, L. & Browne, K.D. (1999). A young man referred to specialist secure accommodation. *Child Abuse Review*, **8**: 419–432.

Falshaw, L., Browne, K.D. & Hollin, C.R. (1996). Victim to offender: a review. *Aggression and Violent Behavior*, **1**(4): 389–404.

Farrington, D.P. (1995). The development of offending and antisocial behaviour from childhood: key findings from the Cambridge study in delinquent development. *Journal of Child Psychology and Psychiatry*, **36**: 929–964.

Flavigny, M.H. (1988). Violence in adolescents: organisation expressed by psychopathic means. In Esman, A.H. (ed.), *International Annals of Adolescent Psychiatry*, vol 1, Chicago: University Press.

Frude, N. (1991). *Understanding Family Problems: A Psychological Approach*. Chichester: Wiley.

Frude, N. (1994). Marital violence: an interactional perspective. In Archer, J. (ed.), *Male Violence*. London: Routledge; 153–169.

Gayford, J.J. (1975). Wife battering: a preliminary survey of 100 cases. *British Medical Journal*, **25**(1): 94–97.

Gelles, R.J. (1987). *Family Violence*, 2nd edn. Beverley Hills, CA: Sage.

Gelles, R.J. (1981). The myth of the battered husband. In Walsh, R. & Procs, O. (eds), *Marriage and Family*. Guildford, Surrey: Dustkin; 81–82.

Goddard, C. & Hiller, P. (1993). Child sexual abuse: assault in a violent context. *Australian Journal of Social Issues*, **28**: 20–33.

Goldstein, A.C. & Keller, H. (1987). *Aggressive Behaviour: Assessment and Intervention*. New York: Pergamon.

Gondolf, E.W. (1998). *Assessing Woman Battering in Mental Health Services*. Beverley Hills, CA: Sage.

Goodman, M.S. & Fallon, B.C. (1995). *Pattern Changing for Abused Women: An Educational Program*. Beverley Hills, CA: Sage.

Grych, J.H. & Fincham, F.D. (1990). Marital conflict and children's adjustment: a cognitive-contextual framework. *Psychological Bulletin*, **108**(2): 267–290.

Hamilton, C.E., Falshaw, L. & Browne, K.D. (2002). The link between recurrent maltreatment and offending behaviour. *Legal and Criminological Psychology*, **46**(1): 75–94.

Helton, A. (1986). The pregnant battered female. *Response to the Victimisation of Women and Children*, **1**:22–23.

Hilton, N.Z. (1993). *Legal Responses to Wife Assault: Current Trends and Evaluation*. Beverley Hills, CA: Sage.

Hollin, C.R. (1996). The meanings and implications of programme integrity. In McGuire, J. (ed.), *What Works: Reducing Reoffending: Guidelines from Research and Practice*. Chichester: Wiley.

Hollin, C.R. & Howells, K. (eds)(1996). *Clinical Approaches to Working with Young Offenders*. Chichester: Wiley.

Hollin, C.R., Epps, K. J. & Kendrick, D.J. (1995). *Managing Behavioural Treatment: Policy and Practice with Delinquent Adolescents*. London: Routledge.

Holtzworth-Munroe, A. & Stuart, G.L. (1994). Typologies of male batterers: three subtypes and the differences among them. *Psychological Bulletin*, **116**(3): 476–497.

Hudson, W. & McIntosh, S. (1981). The assessment of spouse abuse: two quantifiable dimensions. *Journal of Marriage and Family*, **42**: 873–885.

Jaffe, P.G., Wolfe, D.A. & Wilson, S.K. (1990). *Children of Battered Women*. Beverley Hills, CA: Sage.

Jones, T., MacLean, B. & Young, J. (1986). *The Islington Crime Survey: Crime, Victimization and Policing in Inner-city London*. Aldershot, Hants: Gower.

Jouriles, E.N., Murphy, C.M. & O'Leary, K.D. (1989). Interspousal aggression, marital discord, and child problems. *Journal of Consulting and Clinical Psychology*, **57**: 453–455.

Lake, E. S. (1993). An exploration of the violent victim experiences of female offenders. *Violence and Victims*, **8**: 41–51.

Lauritsen, J. L., Sampson, R. J. & Laub, J. H. (1991). The link between offending and victimization among adolescents. *Criminology*, **29**: 265–291.

Loeber, R. & Farrington, D.P. (eds)(1998). *Serious and Violent Juvenile Offenders: Risk Factors and Successful Interventions*. Beverley Hills, CA: Sage.

Mawson, C. (1994). Conforming anxiety in work with damaged children. In A. Obholzer, A. & Roberts, V.Z. (eds), *The Unconscious at Work*. London: Routledge.

McFarlane, J. (1991). Violence during teen pregnancy: health consequences for mother and child. In Levy, B. (ed.), *Dating Violence: Young Women in Danger*. Seattle, WA: Seal; 136–141.

Merrick, J. & Michelsen, N. (1985). Child at risk: child abuse in Denmark. *International Journal of Rehabilitation Research*, **8**(2): 181–188.

Milner, J.S. (1986). *The Child Abuse Potential Inventory Manual*, 2nd edn. Minniapolis, MN: National Computer Systems.

Milner, S. & Gold, R.G. (1986). Screening spouse abusers for child abuse potential. *Journal of Clinical Psychology*, **42**(1): 169–172.

Mirrlees-Black, C. (1999). Domestic Violence: Findings from a New British Crime Survey Self-completion Questionnaire. Research, Development and Statistics Directorate Report, Home Office Research Study 191. London: Home Office.

Mooney, J. (1993). *The Hidden Figure: Domestic Violence in North London* [the findings of a survey conducted on domestic violence in the North London Borough of Islington]. London: Islington Council (cited in Morley & Mullender, 1994).

Morley, R. & Mullender, A. (1994). *Preventing Domestic Violence to Women*. Police Research Group—Crime Prevention Unit Series, Paper 48. London: Home Office.

Newberger, E.H. Barkan, S., Lieberman, E., McCormick, M., Yllo, K., Gary, L. & Schechter, S. (1992). Abuse of pregnant women and adverse birth outcome: current knowledge and implications for practice. *Journal of the American Medical Association*, **267**(17).

Novaco, R.W. (1975). *Anger Control: The Development and Evaluation of an Experimental Treatment*. Lexington, MA: Health.

O'Connell Higgins, G. (1994). *Resilient Adults: Overcoming a Cruel Past*. New York: Jossey-Bass.

Office of the Tanaiste (1997). *Report of the Task Force on Violence against Women*. Dublin: Government of Ireland.

O'Leary, K.D. & Curley, A.D. (1986). Assertion and family violence: correlates of spouse abuse (and the Spouse Specific Aggression Scale). *Journal of Marital and Family Therapy*, **12**: 284–289.

Pahl, J. (1985). Violent husbands and abused wives: a longitudinal study. In Pahl, J. (ed.), *Private Violence and Public Policy: The Needs of Battered Women and the Responses of the Public Services*. London: Routledge and Kegan Paul; 23–94.

Pahl, J. (1995). Health professionals and violence against women. In Kingston, P. & Penale, B. (eds), *Family Violence and the Caring Professions*. Malaysia: Macmillan; 127–148.

Patterson, G.R., DeBaryshe, B.D. & Ramsey, E. (1989). A developmental perspective on antisocial behaviour. *American Psychologist*, **44**: 329–335.

Pearce, J.W. & Pezzot-Pearce, T.D. (1994). Attachment theory and its implications for psychotherapy with maltreated children. *Child Abuse & Neglect*, **18**(5): 425–438.

Peled, E. & Davis, D. (1995). *Groupwork with Children of Battered Women: A Practitioner's Manual*. Beverley Hills, CA: Sage.

Peled, E., Jaffe, P.G. & Edleson, J.L. (1995). *Ending the Cycle of Violence: Community Responses to Children of Battered Women*. Thousand Oaks, CA: Sage.

Pence, E. & Paymar, M. (1993). *Education Groups for Men Who Batter: The Duluth Model*. New York: Springer.

Pernanen, K. (1991). *Alcohol in Human Violence*. London: Guilford.

Renzetti, C.M., Edleson, J.L. & Bergen, R.K. (eds) (2001). *Sourcebook on Violence Against Women*. Beverley Hills, CA: Sage.

Rivera, B. & Widom, C.S. (1990). Childhood victimization and violent offending. *Violence and Victims*, 5: 19–35.

Roberts, A.R. (1987). Psychosocial characteristics of batterers: a study of 234 men charged with domestic violence offenders. *Journal of Family Violence*, **2**(1): 81–84.

Rosenbaum, A. & O'Leary, K.D. (1986). The treatment of marital violence. In Jacobson, N. & Gurman, A. (eds), *Clinical Handbook of Marital Therapy*. New York: Guilford.

Saunders, D.G. (1992). woman battering. In Ammerman, R.T. & Hersen, M. (eds), *Assessment of Family Violence: A Clinical and Legal Sourcebook*. New York: Wiley; 208–235 (Appendix: Woman Abuse Scale, p. 235).

Schechter, S. and Edleson, J.L. (1995). In the best interest of women and children: a call for collaboration between child welfare and domestic violence constituencies. *Protecting Children*, **11**(3): 6–11.

Scudder, R.G., Blount, W.R., Heide, K.M. & Silverman, I.J. (1993). Important links between child abuse, neglect and delinquency. *International Journal of Offender Therapy and Comparative Criminology*, **37**: 315–323.

Shaw, E., Bouris, A. & Pye, S. (1996). The family safety model: a comprehensive strategy for working with domestic violence. *Australian and New Zealand Journal of Family Therapy*, **17**(3): 126–136.

Shepard, M.F. & Pence, E.L. (Eds) (1999). *Coordinating Community Responses to Domestic Violence: Lessons from Duluth and Beyond*. Beverley Hills, CA: Sage.

Sherman, L.W. (1992). The influence of criminology on criminal law: evaluating arrests for misdemeanour domestic violence. *Journal of Law and Criminology*, **83**(1): 1–45.

Simons, R.L., Chyi-In, W., Conger, R.D. & Lorenz, F.O. (1994). Two routes to delinquency: differences between early and late starters in the impact of parenting and deviant peers. *Criminology*, **32**: 247–276.

Simons, R.L., Whitbeck, L.B., Conger, R.D. & Conger, K.J. (1991). Parenting factors, social skills, and value commitments as precursors to school failure, involvement with deviant peers, and delinquent behaviour. *Journal of Youth and Adolescence*, **20**: 645–664.

Sonkin, D., Martin, D. & Walker, L. (1985). *The Male Batterer: A Treatment Approach*. New York: Springer.

Stanko, B. (1998). *Research on Domestic Violence*. AUT Woman, Issue 44. London: Association of University Teachers.

Stanley, J. & Goddard, C. (1993). The association between child abuse and other family violence. *Australian Social Work*, **46**: 3–8.

Stark, E. & Flitcraft, A. (1996). *Women at Risk: Domestic Violence and Women's Health*. Beverley Hills, CA: Sage.

Straus, M.A. (1979). Measuring family conflict and violence: the Conflict Tactics Scales. *Journal of Marriage and the Family*, **41**: 75–88.

Straus, M.A., Gelles, R.J. & Steinmetz, S.K. (1988). *Behind Closed Doors: Violence in the American Family*, revised edn. Newbury Park, CA: Sage.

Stein, A. & Lewis, D.O. (1992). Discovering physical abuse: insights from a follow-up study of delinquents. *Child Abuse & Neglect*, **16**: 523–531.

Walker, L.E. (1984). *The Battered Woman Syndrome*. New York: Springer.

Watkins, B. & Bentovim, A. (1992). The sexual abuse of male children and adolescents: a review of current research. *Journal of Child Psychology and Psychiatry*, **33**(1): 97–248.

Watt, B.D. & Howells, K. (1999). Skills training for aggression control: evaluation of an anger management programme for violent offenders. *Legal and Criminological Psychology*, **4**(2): 285–300.

Widom, C. S. (1989a). Does violence beget violence? A critical examination of the literature. *Psychological Bulletin*, **106**, 3–28.

Widom, C. S. (1989b). The cycle of violence. *Science*, **244**: 160–166.

Widom, C. S. (1991). Avoidance of criminality in abused and neglected children. *Psychiatry*, **54**: 162–174.

Widom, C. S. & Ames, M. A. (1994). Criminal consequences of childhood sexual victimization. *Child Abuse and Neglect*, **18**, 303–318.

Winnicott, D.W. (1956/1984). The anti-social tendency. In Winnicott, C., Shepherd, R, & Davis, M. (eds), *Deprivation and Delinquency: Selected Papers*. London: Tavistock.

World Health Organization (1998). *European Strategies to Combat Violence against Women*. Copenhagen: WHO Regional Office for Europe.

World Health Assembly (1999). *Resolution WHA 50.19*. New York: United Nations.

20

TREATING ADULT SEXUAL OFFENDERS

Dawn Fisher
Llanarth Court Psychiatric Hospital, UK
Anthony Beech
University of Birmingham, UK

It is now generally acknowledged that men who sexually offend against children are not a homogeneous group and hence may have different treatment needs. Therefore coming up with a reasonable classification of child abusers has important implications for treatment. Methods employed in the classification of child molesters can be broadly divided using four approaches (adapted from Blackburn, 1993 by Bickley & Beech, 2001):

- use of clinical descriptions which represent the prototypical features of group members
- pragmatic combination of a number of variables of immediate interest (e.g., the victim's age or sex)
- psychometric profiles derived through the use of statistical analysis
- classification by attributes of central concern to a particular theory

Some of the better known classification systems of child abusers are illustrated in Table 20.1.

However there are a number of problems with these schemes. In particular classification by clinical or pragmatic description does not say very much about treatment need. Classification by psychometric profile and by attributes driven by a specific theory therefore can be seen to have more to offer. We will now consider the usefulness of the psychometric approach.

Early Prediction and Prevention of Child Abuse: A Handbook.
Edited by Kevin Browne, Helga Hanks, Peter Stratton and Catherine Hamilton. © 2002 John Wiley & Sons, Ltd.

TABLE 20.1 Summary of the suggested methods of classification for child molesters

Classification method		Examples	Studies
I. Clinical descriptions	Psychiatric diagnosis	DSM-IV "pedophilia"	APA (1994)
	Sexual preference	"fixated/regressed" or "situational/preferential"	Groth (1978) Howells (1981)
II. Demographic clusters	Univariate	Sex-of-victim/ relationship-to-victim	Grubin & Kennedy (1991)
	Multivariate	Risk assessment tools	Hanson & Thornton (2000)
III. Psychometric profiles	Single measure	MMPI or MSI	Schlank (1995)
	Multiple measures	STEP battery	Beech (1998)
IV. Theory-driven groups	Degree of fixation/type of contact	MTC:CM3	Knight & Prentky (1990)
	Offence pathway description	Self-regulation model	Ward & Hudson (1998)

Adopted from table originally reported by Bickley and Beech (2001).

PSYCHOMETRIC PROFILES AND ITS RELATIONSHIP TO TREATMENT NEED

Beech (1998) has developed a method of classifying child abusers according to their level of problems on a battery of psychological measures. He identified two main types of child abusers, which he termed "High/Low Deviancy".

High Deviancy Child Abusers

In terms of their psychological profiles this type of offenders is identified as having a high level of treatment need as measured by high levels of pro-offending attitudes and social adequacy problems. In terms of pro-offending attitudes, Fisher et al. (1999) found that High Deviancy men had significantly higher levels of distorted attitudes about children and sex (cognitive distortions) than non-offender controls. Here they perceived children as sexually sophisticated and proactive with adults and being unharmed by such contact. This group was also found to have significantly poorer empathy for victims of sexual abuse than non-offenders. Other significant differences between High Deviancy men and non-offenders indicated that they reported difficulty in forming intimate adult attachments, while perceiving that their emotional needs (emotional identification) could be better met by interacting with children than adults. High Deviancy men were also found to be significantly more underassertive and to have significantly lower levels of self-esteem than non-offenders.

Low Deviancy Child Abusers

These offenders appear to have a lower level of treatment need than High Deviancy men in that although they again (like High Deviancy men) show poor empathy for victims of sexual assault, they did not evidence globalised cognitive distortions about children. Also they did not show the high levels of emotional identification with children seen in High Deviancy men. On the contrary, emotional identification with children in this group was found to be significantly lower than non-offender controls (Fisher et al., 1999), this result probably being a part of their denial about future risk to children. Fisher et al. found that this group again showed significantly higher levels of social adequacy problems than non-offenders but this was not as marked as that found in High Deviancy men.

Not only did the psychometric responses differ between the two deviancy groups; the groups also differed in terms of offence history. Beech (1998) found that High Deviancy group, compared to the Low Deviancy group, had significantly more victims, were more likely to have a previous conviction for a sexual offence, were more likely to have committed offences outside the family, and were more likely to have committed offences against boys. Compared to High Deviancy offenders, Low Deviancy offenders were more likely to have committed offences against girls within the family.

It could be argued that the High Deviancy/Low Deviancy distinction is simply a renaming of distinctions previously articulated in the literature; e.g., fixated versus regressed (Groth, 1978); preferential versus situational (Howells, 1981); or high and low fixation (Knight & Prentky, 1990). In response to such concerns, it should be noted that nearly a third of the men that would be identified as regressed/situational perpetrators in such classifications (and would by definition be treated as low risk) were found to be classified as High Deviancy in the Beech system.

Such a classification has been an influence in the development of treatment programmes, in the UK as these two categories of offender obviously have different treatment needs. Beech et al. (1999) report that High Deviancy child abusers require twice as many more hours of treatment (160 hours) than do Low Deviancy child abusers (80 hours) to show a "treatment effect". Such a finding obviously has implications for treatment, as it is important not to waste resources by either providing offenders with more input than they need or not having sufficient impact because treatment is too short. Thus, treatment providers need to consider carefully the needs of offenders before assigning them to programmes.

CURRENT THEORY REGARDING THE AETIOLOGY OF CHILD ABUSE

Due to the fact that sex offenders are a heterogeneous group it would not be expected that a single model of sex offending would be sufficient to cover the range of different sex offenders. Indeed, general theories of criminal behaviour emphasise that offending is not caused by a single factor but rather is the culmination of multiple factors that influence the individual's personality and functioning (Andrews & Bonta, 1994). With regard to sex offenders, multi-factorial models have come more to the fore in the last decade (Marshall & Barbaree, 1990; Marshall & Marshall, 2000).

Marshall's current thinking on the aetiology of offending goes something like this. The root of the offender's problem is in the poor quality of the relationship in his childhood with his primary caregivers. This may be due to a number of reasons, including: sexual, emotional, physical abuse, rejection, lack of support, emotional coldness, disruptive experiences. This may leave the individual more open to suffer sexual abuse from others and/or to lack self-confidence to initiate relationships with appropriate others. High levels of masturbation in adolescence coupled with this lack of self-confidence may lead to fantasies incorporating elements of power and control. These fantasies may become more deviant over time. Such fantasies and low levels of social competence lead to a "disposition to offend". Such a disposition may be acted upon if the right circumstances to offend occur coupled with "disinhibiting factors" such cognitive distortions. Here it should be noted that this explanation more closely fits the extrafamilial/High Deviancy perpetrator than the incestuous/Low Deviancy abuser.

THE COGNITIVE-BEHAVIOURAL GROUP-WORK APPROACH TO TREATMENT

The method of treatment most commonly used in the UK is best described as cognitive behavioural. This approach has developed from the combining of two separate schools of psychology, cognitive and behaviour therapy. Detailed descriptions of the development and methodology of cognitive behavioural approaches can be found elsewhere (Marshall et al., 1999), but to briefly summarise:

Behaviour therapy concerns the overt and covert behaviour of an individual and the principles of learning theory. Originally this was confined to the use of procedures to alter behaviour, i.e. rewarding desired behaviours and punishing unwanted behaviours, but has since broadened out to include modelling (demonstrating a desired behaviour) and skills training (teaching specific skills through behavioural rehearsal).

Cognitive therapy concerns the thoughts or cognitions that individuals experience and which are known to affect their mood state and determine their behaviour. Cognitive therapy therefore aims to encourage an individual to think differently about events, thus giving rise to different affect and behaviour. The use of self-instruction and self-monitoring, in addition to developing an awareness of how one thinks affects how one feels and behaves, are vital components in cognitive therapy.

By combining these approaches, cognitive behavioural therapy (CBT) provides a comprehensive approach to treating sex offenders which now has research evidence to support its efficacy (Alexander, 1999).

Group work is the usual method of CBT as it is generally seen as the most effective method. Beech and Fordham (1997) outlined the benefits of group work as including an environment that can offer both support and challenge to the individual. Group work also provides the opportunity for discussion with peers, provides opportunities for increasing self-esteem and empathic responding. In addition, having male and female therapists can act as appropriate role models.

The style by which treatment is delivered is also important. Beech and Fordham (1997) report that therapists who adopted a confrontational, hostile and punitive attitude were less effective than those who showed respect, were task orientated and engendered cohesiveness in their groups. These findings suggest that group facilitators should focus on the positive aspects of an individual and his behaviour: this helps to boost the self-esteem of group members as their strengths are continually being remarked upon. When needing to give constructive criticism it is important to highlight the positive aspects first before pointing out ways in which there could be improvement.

Andrews and Bonta (1994) suggest that for positive reinforcement to be effective it needs to include the following elements:

* An immediate statement of approval of what has been said. This can be verbal or non-verbal. Non-verbal statements can be communicated via eye contact or smiling;
* An elaboration of the reason why approval is being offered;
* The expression of approval should be sufficiently intense to distinguish it from the baseline level of support and interest usually offered by therapists.

It should also be mentioned that individual work could also be undertaken. This can often take place prior to the offender joining the group to prepare them for the group. In addition, if an individual requires fantasy modification work he can be referred for individual work.

A MODEL OF TREATMENT

Programmes for sexual offenders have generally been developed to address the factors shown by research as being either contributory or characteristic factors in child abuse. Given that sex offenders are not a homogeneous group it is not expected that all factors apply to everyone.

A model, which describes a generic model of treatment, has been outlined by Fisher and Beech (1998). An updated version of the model is shown in Figure 20.1.

This model covers the range of areas in which child abusers have been shown by research to have problems and therefore need to be addressed in treatment. The model is divided into four main sections: denial and minimisation, offence specific problems, social adequacy problems and relapse prevention. A further group of factors called mediators to treatment effects are also included. Each of these areas are described in detail below.

Denial and Minimisation

Sex offenders are well known for their high levels of denial and minimisation (Maletzky, 1991; Barbaree, 1991). Here, denial is used in the broad sense to include

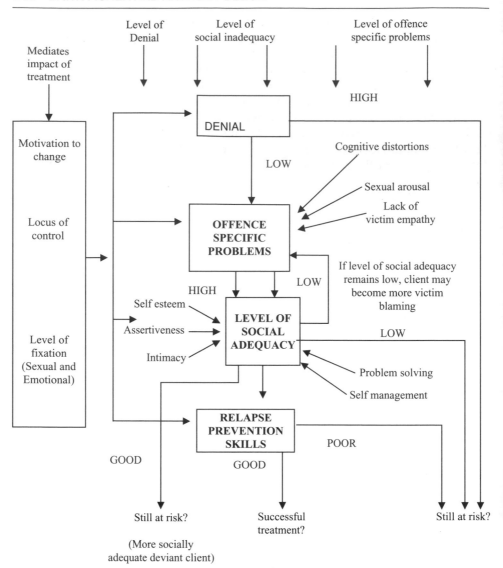

FIGURE 20.1 Model of CBT treatment

total denial where the individual refuses to acknowledge any part of the offence through to denying specific aspects of the offence, i.e. admits one piece of behaviour but not another. Minimisation refers to the lessening of the offence in some way, i.e. lessening frequency, duration or severity.

While it is acknowledged that level of denial is not a predictor of recidivism (Hanson & Bussière, 1998), and reducing the level of denial does not equate with changes in other areas such as attitude towards the offence(s) and victim(s) (Beckett et al., 1994), it is nonetheless the first area that is addressed in treatment, as it is difficult to work on any offence related problems if the offender is denying such an offence(s) even took place.

The finding that denial does not predict risk appears to have been interpreted by some (e.g., Marshall et al., 1999) to mean that working on denial is irrelevant. We would argue, however, that it seems more likely that it is simply illustrating that because an individual admits the offence it does not mean that they are less risky than someone who denies the offence. Many offenders use denial partly because they feel guilty and ashamed of what they have done. Such individuals may be at less risk of re-offending than an individual who does not care about what he has done and openly admits to it. Indeed, Beech (1998) reports that High Deviancy offenders are generally more open about their offending behaviours than Low Deviancy men. Research by Beckett et al. (1994) showed that reduction in denial did not equate with changes in other areas and highlights that admitting offence level is clearly not enough.

The individual then needs to go on to work on the factors that led to the offending and it is changes in these areas that equate with successful treatment outcome (Beech et al., 1999). However, this does not mean that working on denial is not important. In fact, working on denial, even though it is not, in itself, a criminogenic need, would seem to be vital when working with sex offenders for the following reasons:

- Lessening denial allows the individual to talk openly about himself, his thoughts, attitudes, feelings and behaviours. This means that he can identify the factors which contributed to his offending and the areas he needs to work on;
- Admitting his role in the offending enables the individual to take responsibility for his behaviour (having an internal locus of control). He is then in a position to look at the choices and decisions he made and see that he could do things differently in the future. Fisher et al. (1998) found that internal locus of control prior to treatment was a predictor of treatment success.
- For those individuals who remain in total denial it is usual to find that they refuse to participate in treatment programmes and therefore are unlikely to have addressed any of the factors that contributed to their offending. For that reason they tend to be viewed as remaining at risk of re-offending.

Offence Specific Problems

Once the individual has acknowledged that he did commit an offence he is then more receptive to considering the factors that may have contributed to the development of the offence behaviour and so work can then begin on the "offence specific" problems. The next section of the model concerns those factors directly relevant to sexual offending. These include the individual's beliefs and attitudes towards sex, offending behaviour and also their pattern of sexual arousal.

DISTORTED THINKING

It has been well documented that sex offenders typically hold beliefs about their offending which allow them to justify and rationalise their behaviour (Murphy, 1990; Abel et al., 1984). Work on raising awareness of these thinking errors (cognitive distortions) and enabling individuals to recognise and challenge their own distorted thinking forms an important part of many treatment programmes.

LACK OF VICTIM EMPATHY

Work on increasing victim empathy also forms a major part of treatment programmes, although it is more probable that apparent lack of empathy is a specific form of cognitive distortion rather than a deficit in empathic responding (Fisher, 1998; Marshall et al., 1999). A number of studies have described sex offenders' lack of empathy for their own victims (Fisher, 1998; Pithers, 1994; Scully, 1988).

DEVIANT SEXUAL AROUSAL

The other area contained within the offence specific section concerns sexual arousal. While the majority of sex offenders will not show deviant sexual preferences as their primary preference (Freund, 1991) the experience of being sexually aroused to the victim or the offending behaviour is an issue that needs to be addressed in some. For those individuals it may be necessary to refer them for individual work using fantasy modification techniques, despite there being poor evidence for their efficacy (Marshall et al., 1999). In some instances it may also be necessary to refer the individual to a psychiatrist for anti-libidinal medication. Here, offenders would still be expected to continue with the programme whilst on such medication.

Social Adequacy Problems

The third section of the model is labelled "social adequacy". This covers a wide range of areas that relate to the efficacy of an individual's social functioning. There is a large body of evidence highlighting various deficits in sex offenders, which are grouped together under this heading as they refer to how well an individual relates to others and feels about themselves. How they feel about themselves is also related to how well they cope generally in life. The range of factors included within the social adequacy heading are outlined below.

SELF-ESTEEM

Sex offenders are generally regarded as having low self-esteem, which it is believed may contribute to their offending and hinder their progress in therapy. Finkelhor (1984) and Groth (1979) have suggested that low self-esteem and sex offending are related, while Marshall et al. (1997) found that enhancement of self-esteem facilitated the attainment of a number of specific treatment goals and was associated with reductions in deviant arousal. Fisher et al. (1999) found significantly lower levels of self-esteem in child abusers compared to non-offenders. Because self-esteem is so linked with how the individual relates to others and copes with life it is likely that improvements in these areas will lead to a corresponding increase in self-esteem. It is for these reasons that self-esteem is regarded as important to assess and target in treatment even though it is not, in itself, a criminogenic need.

EMOTIONAL LONELINESS/LACK OF INTIMACY

Evidence suggests that sex offenders report high levels of emotional loneliness and have difficulty in developing intimacy with adults (Fisher et al., 1999; Garlick et al., 1996; Seidman et al., 1994). Bumby and Hansen (1997) found that fear of intimacy/emotional loneliness and isolation was characteristic of child abusers. There is also evidence that lack of intimacy can lead to sexual offending (Proulx et al., 1996). Marshall (1989) has proposed that deficits in intimacy cause sex offenders to seek sexual satisfaction with either children or non-consenting adults. Marshall believes that sex offenders identify intimacy with sex and thus think that sexual behaviour of any kind will meet their intimacy needs.

Marshall's work on intimacy has highlighted the influence of childhood attachments to later sexual offending. There is evidence that many sex offenders do indeed have histories of poor parental attachments. Smallbone and Dadds (1998) found that poor relationships with mothers was a predictor of general antisocial behaviour and poor paternal attachments predicted sexual coercion in adulthood. Awad et al. (1984) reported the parents of adolescent sex offenders as being either rejecting, abusive or emotionally detached. Grossman and Grossman (1990) suggest that insecure parent–child bonding results in a child who is unfriendly, dependent, moody, low in self-esteem and who has social competency problems.

POOR SELF-MANAGEMENT

It is known that for many sex offenders, emotional disturbance is a precursor to offending (Pithers et al., 1987) and to deviant fantasy (Proulx et al., 1996). Cortoni et al. (1996) reported that sex offenders tend to use sexual thoughts and behaviour as a comfort strategy when distressed. It would therefore seem that many sex offenders do not cope effectively with negative mood states (e.g. anger, boredom, humiliation, resentment, anxiety, depression) and use sexual thoughts and behaviours to cope. Thus, it is important that treatment includes work on teaching more effective coping strategies. However, not all sexual offending is preceded by a negative mood state, for some it is a positive mood state that precedes offending, especially in those who see offending as a positive goal (Ward & Hudson, 1998).

In addition to poor coping strategies, disorganised, irresponsible life-style and poor impulse control has also been found to be a characteristic of some sex offenders and one which is predictive of re-offending (Thornton, in press).

ASSERTIVENESS DIFFICULTIES

Child abusers are also frequently regarded as lacking in assertion skills. However, research evidence for this is somewhat mixed. A number of studies report child abusers as being underassertive (Abel et al., 1984; Pithers et al., 1987). Other studies however, have failed to find differences in assertiveness between sex offenders and others (Overholser & Beck, 1986), while Fisher et al. (1999) reported that it was only High Deviancy child abusers who were underassertive and so this may only be a problem for this group.

PROBLEM SOLVING DEFICITS

Problem solving concerns the ability to effectively identify problems, generate possible solutions, choose the most effective solution and put it into practice. Effective problem solving is beneficial to all aspects of an individual's life including his ability to relate well to others and deal with the inevitable interpersonal problems that arise in all types of relationships. Problem solving can therefore be beneficial to sex offenders who have interpersonal difficulties.

Barbaree et al. (1988) examined the problem-solving abilities of sex offenders and reported that while they could identify as many potential solutions to problems as did non-offenders they typically chose an inadequate solution. Barbaree et al. concluded that sex offenders may have poor general problem-solving skills and have developed inadequate generic coping styles, rather than simply being deficient in specific skills. They recommended that treatment should include training in problem-solving and the development of a problem-focussed coping style. Robinson (1995) also reported that cognitive skills training (which includes problem solving) had a significant impact on sex offenders, reducing recidivism by 57% in programme completers. He concluded that of all offenders, "sex offenders appeared to derive the greatest benefits from the programme".

Social adequacy appears to be an important element of treatment for many sex offenders and it could be argued that despite working successfully on denial and offence specific problems an individual may remain at risk of offending if he also remains socially inadequate and unable to form appropriate relationships.

Relapse Prevention

The final section of the model is labelled relapse prevention. This concerns the ability of an individual to identify risk situations and to have developed effective coping strategies to deal with such situations. Although it may be that if an individual has successfully addressed the deficits he has had in the offence specific and social adequacy areas his risk of recidivism is very low, the reality for most offenders is that their progress is not sufficient in these areas for them not to benefit from relapse prevention work. Relapse prevention raises an individual's awareness of the variety of situations, thoughts and feelings which are risky for them and could act as "warning signs" for future problems and teaches them the skills to deal appropriately with these risky situations. Recent work on relapse prevention has highlighted the different pathways (approach and avoidance) to relapse for different individuals which have implications for treatment (Ward & Hudson, 1998). The approach pathway concerns individuals who are motivated to offend and require work on the negative consequences to themselves of offending, while the avoidant pathways concern individuals who are motivated not to offend but do so because they lack the skills to successfully avoid and cope safely with risk situations. For this group treatment should be about teaching appropriate skills. Bickley and Beech (2002) have found that the approach pathway offenders are High Deviancy men while avoidant goal offenders are Low Deviancy men.

Mediators to Treatment Effectiveness

There are three factors which could be regarded as mediators to treatment effectiveness: motivation to change, locus of control and level of fixation.

MOTIVATION TO CHANGE

This is the key factor in the success of a treatment programme. Unless an individual is motivated to use what he has learned from treatment he will not apply his new skills and knowledge to changing his lifestyle and his likelihood of recidivism will not be reduced. It is therefore vital that treatment encourages motivation to change.

It is likely that most offenders enter treatment with an ambivalent attitude towards changing their offending behaviour. Many will have enjoyed the offence but not the negative consequences for themselves. Others may be reluctant to change because they have little else in their lives. Some may be unmotivated because they do not believe they have the ability to change and may be very fearful of what change will involve. By demonstrating that change is possible, that there are alternatives to offending, and by understanding that an abuse-free life will ultimately be more rewarding than continuing to offend, it is possible to develop a motivation to change in offenders. The delivery style of group facilitators will be a key element in this, if they are supportive, encouraging, praising and respectful.

LOCUS OF CONTROL

This concerns the extent to which an individual regards himself as having little influence over his life and therefore regards things that happen as being due to others. Such individuals are less likely to benefit from treatment unless they can be encouraged to take responsibility for their behaviour and become more internally controlled (Fisher et al., 1998). Analysing an individual's offence(s) in detail and getting him to identify the decisions he made is an important element in treatment. This would seem to link strongly to denial in that unless the individual is able to admit the offence behaviour and detail the processes which led to the offence he is not in a position to take responsibility for his actions.

LEVEL OF FIXATION

Here the term refers to both sexual and emotional fixation. Individuals are described as being sexual fixated when they have strong deviant sexual interests and a lack of appropriate sexual arousal such that they only appear to be aroused to deviant sexual activity. Individuals who are only aroused by deviant activity and have no interest in appropriate sexual activity will remain strongly motivated to offend. Given the paucity of evidence for the efficacy of fantasy modification techniques (Laws & Marshall, 1991) it is likely that such individuals will remain at high risk of recidivism. The use of anti-libidinal medication may be of benefit to such individuals.

Emotional fixation describes those individuals who can only meet their emotional needs through relationships with children and are unable to relate to adults, either because they are fearful of them or have no interest in them. Such individuals can be described as being emotionally congruent with children. Unless this emotional congruence can be addressed, they too will remain at risk of recidivism.

We should also make clear that this model of treatment may not be directly applicable to work with adolescent sexual offenders and space precludes any coverage of work with this group. Several books (Barabaree et al., 1993; Erooga & Masson, 1999; O'Reilly et al., in press) make a useful starting point in consideration of the assessment and treatment with adolescents.

HOW THERAPY IS ACTUALLY CARRIED OUT

The following approaches are often used in CBT groups.

Group Discussion

Group discussions allow individuals to state their views and receive feedback from a range of other people. This can help build self-esteem in having others listen and treat their opinions with respect but can also challenge distorted thinking. This can be a useful method to encourage discussion between group members rather than always addressing the group facilitators. It can be a less threatening method of asking questions of group members as opposed to asking individual group members directly. However, quieter group members can sometimes end up saying nothing and more forceful members can dominate the group. It is up to facilitators to ensure that quieter members are encouraged and supported and dominant members kept under control, particularly so that the latter not intimidate other group members.

Open Questioning

Open questioning techniques should be used to encourage individuals to have to say more and think more about what they are saying, rather than the use of closed questions which enable an individual to say the minimum and be defensive. Open questioning can be valuable when asking an individual to talk about his offence and explain what was going on for him at the time.

Socratic Questioning

Socratic questioning involves asking a series of questions which lead an individual to the appropriate answer for themselves. This form of questioning enables the individual to achieve insights themselves rather than being told what is right by the therapist (Beck, 1976). Socratic questioning is particularly helpful in challenging distorted thinking.

Cognitive Restructuring

Cognitive restructuring involves challenging the way an individual thinks which then leads the individual to change his way of thinking. In the case of sex offenders this involves identifying the pro-offending beliefs and then using Socratic questioning, discussion and the provision of information to help the individual challenge his own thinking. The goal is for the individual to develop anti-offending beliefs.

Modelling

Group facilitators should involve themselves in two types of modelling, formal and informal. Formal modelling involves demonstrating a particular skill or piece of behaviour as an example to the group members during an exercise within a session. Informal modelling concerns attitudes, values and behaviours shown by facilitators. Here they should behave in a respectful manner, take responsibility for their actions, demonstrate effective problem solving, admit mistakes and give praise to others where appropriate. It is important to be consistent and to remember that the group members take a lot of notice of how facilitators behave. Good modelling of appropriate behaviours and attitudes can therefore have a profound impact upon the group.

Role-Play

Giving the group members the opportunity to take on the roles of different people involved in the offence, such as the victim, greatly enables perspective taking and thus can enhance victim empathy. Role-play is also invaluable to allow individuals to rehearse new skills that they are taught in group. Observing others in role-plays can also help achieve insights into both the errors that people make and how others are affected by events.

Behavioural Rehearsal

Behavioural rehearsal involves the opportunity to practise skills and behaviours taught during the programme. This is vital to the success of treatment, as simply teaching someone the concept is likely to be insufficient for them to develop the skill themselves. Members have to practise the skill and also observe others before they become proficient. However, the skill only develops with sufficient practice and it is therefore important to stress to group members that they need to keep practising outside of sessions.

Word-Storming

This involves the whole group suggesting ideas about a particular topic. They are asked to think of as many different things as they can. Once a list has been compiled the individual ideas can be examined in more detail. Word-storming is an effective method for encouraging group members to come up with their ideas about a particular topic because it is less threatening than other types of questioning. This is due to the fact that the individual is suggesting an idea rather than saying that the idea relates specifically to him. Once a list has been compiled group members can then identify which ideas relate to them.

Education

At times throughout the programme it is necessary to provide information about a topic. As far as possible methods are used to elicit the information from the group themselves but this is not always possible. Time spent in straightforward didactic education should be kept to a minimum to avoid group members becoming disengaged from therapy.

Self-Instruction

Self-instruction involves the individual being aware of his own self-talk (the things he says to himself in his head) and using this self-talk to plan how to carry out a behaviour or deal with a problem. The individual should be taught to break each behaviour down into stages and work through each stage giving himself feedback on his performance.

Self-Monitoring

Group members should be encouraged to view self-monitoring as an important part of leading an abuse-free life in the future. Although a network of external monitors is encouraged the value of being able to self-monitor should be highlighted. Group members are required to self-monitor particular aspects of their thoughts and behaviours throughout the programme with a particular emphasis during Relapse Prevention. Diary sheets are used to record thoughts, behaviours and coping strategies at various points throughout the programme.

TREATING THE PSYCHOPATHIC SEX OFFENDER

Clark (2000), reporting data from men who had been through short social skills or educational programmes, found that highly psychopathic offenders were more likely to be reconvicted if they have been through such therapy compared to matched controls who had not been through treatment. This finding is perhaps the latest to indicate that structured therapy does not help this type of offender.

Our own observations (Beech et al., 1999) suggests that the presence of such individuals can disrupt groups, therefore having a negative effect upon other men in the group. The presence of such men in a group can also potentially lead to tutor burn-out. Therefore it would seem essential to assess the level of psychopathy and give careful thought given to including very psychopathic individuals in any group treatment programme.

SUMMARY

The aim of this chapter has been to give a brief account of the main classification systems of adults who offend against children and describe why it is important to know the level of problems that an offender has in order to match the individual with the right amount of treatment. We have then given a broad overview of the CBT approach to work with adult sexual offenders, and its relationship to theory and research. The chapter then went on to describe a model of CBT treatment. Finally, we have described some of the methods of delivery of CBT treatment for adult child abusers. We have not attempted to cover assessment and treatment of adolescent sexual offenders as these present different problems in both assessment and treatment.

REFERENCES

Abel, G.G., Becker, J.V. & Cunningham-Rathner, J. (1984). Complications, consent and cognitions in sex between children and adults. *International Journal of Law and Psychiatry*, **7**, 89–103.

Alexander, (1999). Sexual offender treatment efficacy revisited. *Sexual Abuse: A Journal of Research and Treatment*, **11**, 101–116.

American Psychiatric Association. (1994). *Diagnostic and statistical manual of mental disorders: Fourth Edition*. Washington, DC: American Psychiatric Association.

Andrews, D. & Bonta, J. (1994). *The psychology of criminal conduct*. Cincinatti, OH: Anderson Publishing Co.

Awad, G., Saunders, E. & Levene, J. (1984). A clinical study of male adolescent sex offenders. *International Journal of Offender Therapy and Comparative Criminology*, **28**, 105–115.

Barbaree, H.E. (1991). Denial and minimization among sex offenders: Assessment and treatment outcome. *Forum on Corrections Research*, **3**, 30–33.

Barbaree, H.E., Marshall, W.L. & Connor, J. (1988). The social problem-solving of child molesters. Unpublished manuscript, Queen's University, Kingston, Ontario, Canada.

Barbaree, H.E., Marshall, W.L. & Hudson, S. (1993). *The juvenile sex offender*. New York: Guilford Press.

Beck, A.T. (1976). *Cognitive therapy and the emotional disorders*. New York: International Universities Press.

Beckett, R.C., Beech, A.R., Fisher, D. & Fordham, A.S. (1994). *Community-based treatment for sex offenders: An evaluation of seven treatment programmes*. London: HMSO.

Beech, A.R. (1998). A psychometric typology of child abusers.*International Journal of Offender Therapy and Comparative Criminology*, **42**, 319–339.

Beech, A.R. & Fordham, A. (1997). Therapeutic climate of sexual offender treatment programmes. *Sexual Abuse: A Journal of Research and Therapy*, **9** , 219–237.

Beech, A.R., Fisher, D. & Beckett, R.C. (1999). *STEP 3: An evaluation of the prison sex offender treatment programme*. London: HMSO.

Bickley, J.A. & Beech, A.R. (2001). Classifying child abusers: Its relevance to theory and clinical practice. *International Journal of Offender Therapy*, **45**, 51–69.

Bickley, J.A. & Beech, A.R. (2002). An empirical investigation of the Ward and Hudson self-regulation model of the sexual offence process with child abusers. *Journal of Interpersonal Violence*, **71**, 371–393.

Blackburn, R. (1993). *The psychology of criminal conduct: Theory, research and practice*. London: Wiley.

Bumby, K.M. & Hansen, D.J. (1997). Intimacy deficits, fear of intimacy and loneliness among sexual offenders. *Criminal Justice and Behaviour*, **24**, 315–331.

Clark, D. (2000). The use of the Hare PCL-R to predict offending and institutional misconduct in the English Prison System. *Prison Research and Development Bulletin*, **9**, 10–14.

Cortoni, F. & Marshall, W.L. (1995). Childhood attachments, juvenile sexual history and adult coping skills in sex offenders. Paper presented at the 14th Annual Research and Treatment Conference of the Association for the Treatment of Sexual Abusers, New Orleans.

Erooga, M & Masson, H. (1999). *Children and young people who sexually abuse others*. London: Routledge.

Finkelhor, D. (1984). *Child Sexual Abuse: New Theory and Research*. London: Macmillan.

Fisher, D. (1998). Assessing victim empathy. Unpublished PhD. Thesis. University of Birmingham, England.

Fisher, D. & Beech, A.R. (1998). Reconstituting families after sexual abuse: The offender's perspective. *Child Abuse Review*, **7**, 420–434.

Fisher, D., Beech, A.R. & Browne, K. (1998). Locus of control and its relationship to treatment change and abuse history in child sexual abusers. *Legal and Criminological Psychology*, **3**, 1–12.

Fisher, D., Beech, A.R. & Browne, K.D. (1999). Comparison of sex offenders to non-sex offenders on selected psychological measures. *International Journal of Offender Therapy and Comparative Criminology*. **43**, 473–491.

Freund, K. (1991). Reflections on the development of the phallometric method of assessing sexual preferences. *Annals of Sex Research*, **4**, 221–228.

Garlick, Y., Marshall, W.L. & Thornton, D. (1996). Intimacy deficits and attribution of blame among sexual offenders. *Legal and Criminological Psychology*, **1**, 251–258.

Grossman, K.E. & Grossman, K. (1990). The wider concept of attachment in cross-cultural research. *Human Development*, **33**, 31–47.

Groth, A.N. (1978). Patterns of sexual assault against children and adolescents. In A.W. Burgess, A.N. Groth, L.L. Holstrom, & S.M. Groi (Eds.), *Sexual assault of children and adolescents* (pp 3–24). Boston: Heath.

Groth, A.N. (1979). *Men Who Rape: The Psychology of the Offender*. New York: Plenum Press.

Grubin, D. & Kennedy, H. (1991). The classification of sexual offenders. *Criminal Behavior and Mental Health*, **1**, 123–129.

Hanson, R.K. & Bussière, M.T. (1998). Predicting relapse: A meta-analysis of sexual offender recidivisim studies. *Journal of Consulting and Clinical Psychology*, **66**, 348–362.

Hanson, R. K. & Thornton, D. (2000). Improving risk assessments for sex offenders: A comparison of three actuarial scales. *Law and Human Behavior*, **24**, 119–136.

Howells, K. (1981). Adult sexual interest in children: Considerations relevant to theories of etiology. In M. Cook & K. Howells (Eds.), *Adult sexual interest in children* (pp. 55–94). London: Academic Press.

Knight, R.A. & Prentky, R.A. (1990). Classifying sexual offenders: The development and corroboration of taxonomic models. In W.L. Marshall, D.R. Laws & H.E. Barbaree (Eds.) *Handbook of sexual assault: Issues, theories and treatment of the offender*. New York: Plenum Press.

Laws, D.R. & Marshall, W.L. (1991). Masturbatory reconditioning with sexual deviates: An evaluative review. *Advances in Behaviour Research and Therapy*, **13**, 13–25.

Maletzky, B.M. (1991). *Treating the sexual offender*. Newbury Park, CA: Sage.

Marshall, W.L. (1989). Intimacy, loneliness and sexual offenders. *Behavior Research and Therapy*, **27**, 491–503.

Marshall, W.L., Anderson, D. & Fernandez, Y. (1999). *Cognitive-behavioural treatment of sexual offenders*. Chichester: Wiley.

Marshall, W.L. & Barbaree, H. E. (1990). An integrated theory of sexual offending. In W.L. Marshall, D.R. Laws & H.E. Barbaree (Eds.) *Handbook of sexual assault: Issues, theories and treatment of the offender*. New York: Plenum Press.

Marshall, W.L., Champagne, F., Sturgeon, C. & Bryce, P. (1997). Increasing the self-esteem of child molesters. *Sexual Abuse: A Journal of Research and Treatment*, **9**, 321–333.

Marshall, W.L. and Marshall, L. (2000). The origins of sexual offending. *Trauma, Violence and Abuse*, **1**, 250–263.

Murphy, W. (1990). Assessment and modification of cognitive distortions in sex offenders. In W.L. Marshall, D.R. Laws & H.E. Barbaree (Eds.) *Handbook of sexual assault: Issues, theories and treatment of the offender*. New York: Plenum Press.

O'Reilly, G, Marshall, W.L., Beckett, R.C & Carr, A. (in press). *The handbook of clinical intervention with juvenile sexual offenders*. London: Routledge.

Overholser, C. & Beck, S. (1986). Multimethod assessment of rapists, child molesters, and three control groups on behavioural and psychological measures. *Journal of Consulting and Clinical Psychology*, **54**, 682–687.

Pithers, W.D. (1994). Process evaluation of a group therapy component designed to enhance sex offenders' empathy for sexual abuse survivors. *Behavior Research and Therapy*, **32**, 565–570.

Pithers, W.D., Buell, M.M., Kashima, K.M., Cumming, G.F. & Beal, L.S. (1987). Precursors to relapse of sexual offenders. Paper presented at the 7th Annual Conference of the Association for the Behavioural Treatment of Sexual Abusers, Newport, Oregon.

Proulx, J., McKibben, A. & Lusignan, R. (1996). Relationship between affective components and sexual behaviours in sexual aggressors. *Sexual Abuse: A Journal of Research and Treatment*, **8**, 279–289.

Robinson, D. (1995). The impact of cognitive skills training on post-release recidivism among Canadian federal offenders. Correctional Service of Canada, Research Division: Canada.

Schlank, A.M. (1995). The utility of the MMPI and the MSI for identifying a sexual offender typology. *Sexual Abuse: A Journal of Research and Treatment*, **7**, 185–194.

Scully, D. (1988). Convicted rapists' perceptions of self and victim: Role taking and emotions. *Gender and Society*, **2**, 200–213.

Seidman, B.T., Marshall, W.L., Hudson, S.M. & Robertson, P.J. (1994). An examination of intimacy and loneliness in sex offenders. *Journal of Interpersonal Violence*, **9**, 518–534.

Smallbone, S.W. & Dadds, M.R. (1998). Childhood attachment and adult attachment in incarcerated adult male sex offenders. *Journal of Interpersonal Violence*, **13**, 555–573.

Thornton, D. (in press). Constructing and testing a framework for dynamic risk assessment. *Sexual Abuse: A Journal of Research and Treatment*.

Ward, T. & Hudson, S.M. (1998). A model of the relapse process in sexual offenders. *Journal of Interpersonal Violence*, **13**, 700–725.

CONCLUSION: FUTURE CHALLENGES IN CHILD PROTECTION

Margaret A. Lynch
Guy's, King's and St Thomas' School of Medicine, London UK

Kevin Browne
University of Birmingham, UK

This book has looked in detail at the approaches that are available to prevent child abuse and neglect, focusing predominantly on industrialised society. The main focus has been the prevention of abuse and neglect that occurs within families (see Chapter 1). The influence of environmental and social factors on families has also been considered (see Chapter 6). Indeed, the new Assessment Framework for Children in Need (Department of Health et al., 2000) considers environmental and social factors to significantly influence the capacity for parents to meet the needs of their children (see Chapter 3). Hence, the Framework assesses three domains: the developmental needs of the child, the parenting abilities of the parents, and social, environmental and extended family influences. This holistic approach is applied throughout Britain to families and children who come into contact with health and social services. However, it will become increasingly important to place abuse and neglect in a much wider context. The aim of this final chapter is to highlight those sections of society that have identifiable needs but may be outside, and/or excluded from, the routine assessment and intervention process. These groups will present the greatest challenge to child protection work in future.

In the UK, initiatives to improve the well-being of children are operating against the backdrop of a National Health Service plan committed to reducing health inequalities and improving access, the setting up of a Children's Task Force and the promise of a National Service Framework for Children's services. Ensuring, however, the right of all children to have equal access to services, in line with the United Nations Convention on the Rights of the Child (1989) is likely to remain a significant challenge. This will not just in resource terms but because of the difficulties

Early Prediction and Prevention of Child Abuse: A Handbook.
Edited by Kevin Browne, Helga Hanks, Peter Stratton and Catherine Hamilton. © 2002 John Wiley & Sons, Ltd.

of ensuring that universal services really do reach all children (Lynch & Gough, 2001) and that those children and young people already disturbed or distressed are identified and offered acceptable support.

ETHNIC MINORITY FAMILIES

Most developed countries are multicultural societies. If services are to be truly accessible to ethnic minority families, this must be acknowledged and welcomed by those planning and delivering services. Whilst no-one should use "culture" as an excuse to ignore anything that causes a child harm, there is also the risk that harm may result from inappropriate intervention by ill-informed ethnocentric professionals. Staff require training and support in working with populations with diverse child-rearing practices. Professionals may need help in distinguishing between cultural practices that cause harm, either intentionally or unintentionally, and those that are harmless or indeed beneficial. While no one professional can be expected to know everything about all the cultures he/she may encounter, efforts should be made to learn something of the predominant cultures in any society and to know how to access reliable information on other minority cultures.

For those involved in child protection, such background knowledge is essential if appropriate assessments and decisions about interventions are to be made. As Lau (1991) pointed out, an emergency assessment of an ethnic minority family, who may or may not be behaving in a harmful manner, is not the ideal time to be learning about their specific cultural practices in child rearing. Commitment to such a multicultural approach will also require investment in well-trained and supported interpreters. This is no less essential when dealing with parents caring for disabled children, because of the varying attitudes and expectations of children with disabilities across different cultures.

DISABLED CHILDREN

Disabled children have been shown to be at increased risk of abuse (Morris, 1999; Sullivan & Knutson, 1998, 2000) and therefore it is essential that they receive special consideration when the prevention of abuse is being considered. There is some evidence that disabled children may have less access to universal services than other children. For example, there may be less health visiting for children receiving disability services (Gough, Li & Wroblewska, 1992). Both the universal and specialist services must be able and willing to recognise indicators of increased vulnerability, as well as signs that a disabled child is suffering harm as a result of the care he/she is or is not receiving at home or in other settings. Westcott & Jones (1999) identify three main factors that increase the vulnerability of disabled children: dependency, institutional care and communication.

Typically, disabled children are encouraged to be compliant and often are dependent on a large number of carers. In recent years attitudes encouraging a lack of recognition and attention to the abuse and neglect of disabled children have been energetically challenged (Tharinger, Horton & Millea, 1990; Marchant & Page, 1992;

Westcott, 1993; Morris, 1999) and there is now wide acceptance of their vulnerability. There remains, however, a long way to go in closing the gap between child protection services and services for disabled children (Oosterhoorn & Kendrick, 2001). Not least, there remains the considerable challenge of helping disabled children communicate about actual and potentially abusive situations. This can also be said to apply to all children who are socially excluded for any reason.

REACHING TROUBLED CHILDREN

Prevention of abuse and neglect must include seeking out distressed and disturbed children and young people who may already be both troubled and in trouble. Not only should we seek ways to support such vulnerable children in overcoming their current circumstances and difficulties, but we must also see them as potential future parents who may well need extra help if they are to parent safely and confidently. Whilst some activities of these vulnerable children, such as persistent offending, will be all too visible, others, such as prostitution, will be largely hidden from both the public and professionals.

The majority of these children and young people are likely to be hard to reach and often, by the time they come to attention, will have demonstrated a range of troubled and troubling behaviours. They may have a history of abuse and neglect (see Chapters 17 and 19) and a high proportion will have spent time during childhood in public care (Polnay and Ward, 2000). Many of these troubled children find themselves, deliberately or otherwise, outside the usual framework for the delivery of universal services. For example, they may have been excluded from school or stopped attending, making it difficult and time consuming for a school-based service (such as Connexions) to find them (see Chapter 16). Even when found, their attitude might make it impossible for them to make constructive use of the service. Many of these young people come from backgrounds that increase the risk of teenage and unplanned parenthood and are unlikely to access parent preparation programmes spontaneously. Some of the girls will even be reluctant to attend for routine antenatal care and may be engaged in behaviours such as substance abuse and smoking, which pose risks to the baby's health (see Chapter 4).

Runaways

Running away may be an early signal that a child is troubled. Because it is a common occurrence, the reason may not be sought and the significance for the individual child may not be immediately appreciated. Research carried out by the Children's Society in Leeds suggested that one in seven under 16 year-olds run away for at least a night and that approximately 2% of these young people run away 10 times or more from home or a care setting (Rees, 1993). Furthermore, 1% of these young people were recorded as having run away for the first time below the age of 8 years. Both in the UK and the USA, girls tend to leave home for longer periods than boys (Rees, 1993; Cairns & Cairns, 1994). Similarly, in the USA it is claimed that one out of every eight adolescents aged 12–18 run away at least once from home (Young et al., 1983). There is a high incidence of running away from residential care (Newman,

1989; Abrahams & Mungall, 1992), although these children have often begun their pattern of escape by initially running away from home (Rees, 1993).

It is claimed that three-quarters of adolescents running away are attempting to escape and "retreat" from conflict and violence in the home and/or significant problems at school, such as peer pressure and bullying (Nye, 1980; Straus, 1994; Stein, Rees & Frost, 1994). Other researchers claim that 40–50% of runaways are escaping from severe sexual and physical violence or emotional neglect (Adams & Gulotta, 1983). What is certain is that many of the children at risk living on the streets were previously at risk in the family home. As many as 78% of children in shelters report physical and/or sexual abuse as the primary reason for leaving home and running away (Farber et al., 1984). In other studies of adolescent runaways, 73% of girls and 38% of boys report being sexually abused (McCormack, Janus & Burgess, 1986) and 44% of runaways report being physically abused (Stiffman, 1989).

The vulnerability of this group of children and young people is emphasised by the use of the terms "endangered" runners (Roberts, 1982), "terrified" runners (Greene & Esselstyn, 1972), "victim" runners (Miller et al., 1980), or just "push-outs", "exiles", "castaways" and "throwaways" (Nye, 1980; Janus et al., 1987; White, 1989). However, it has been suggested that a significant minority of runaways are "social pleasure seekers", "explorers", or "manipulators" who, for no identifiable reason, place themselves at unnecessary risk of becoming victims and/or offenders of crime (Roberts, 1982; Lappin & Covelman, 1985). Nevertheless, the extent of distress felt by most runaways and the potential for further harmful experiences would indicate the need for a child and family assessment when a child runs away.

Straus (1994) claims that after 1 month, one in two runaway children resort to prostitution, stealing, drug dealing or other crime to support themselves. Pessimistically, she proposes that children who have spent more than 6 months on the street are nearly impossible to rescue by promoting interest in continuing education, looking for employment, working on family problems and giving up drugs. Such evidence reinforces the need to take a preventative approach to runaways by considering the underlying causes earlier rather then later.

When working with children already "on the street", consideration should be given to learning from experiences in the developing world, where street children are acknowledged as a major challenge for service providers (Scanlon et al., 1998).

SEXUAL EXPLOITATION AND PROSTITUTION

Research evidence has shown that those children who have grown up in adverse environments are most at risk of being targeted by individuals and organisations interested in physically and sexually exploiting children (see Chapter 12). Therefore, the prevention of child maltreatment to the under-5s, and early intervention with families whose older children run away from home, could have a massive knock-on effect on the prevention of children being sexually exploited (see Chapter 14). Evidence shows that children who have grown up in violent families and institutions are more likely to be sexually victimised and exploited, in later childhood and adolescence, than those who have had a caring family experience. This is referred to as "developmental victimology" (Finkelhor, 1995).

Runaways may be quickly drawn into prostitution (Straus, 1994). Alternatively, some may continue to live at home, while others may be living away from home in residential care or foster care. Absence from school because of either exclusion or truancy makes children especially vulnerable. A young person's vulnerability is recognised and targeted by those recruiting child prostitutes (Barnardo's, 1998). The 2nd World Congress on the Commercial Exploitation of Children in Yokohama (2001), highlighted the extent of the international trafficking of children for sexual purposes. Even within the UK, cases are emerging to indicate that children are being "brought" into this country as "unaccompanied" asylum-seeking minors before being passed on to work as prostitutes elsewhere.

Guidance issued in England and Wales (Department of Health et al., 2000) sees children involved in prostitution as primarily victims of abuse, whose needs should be assessed. Multi-agency prevention, protection and re-integration strategies are advocated. This should include facilitating the young person's access to health services and training health personnel (especially those in sexual health services) to the signs that a young person may be involved in prostitution. However, the majority of projects in the UK working directly with young people in prostitution have been set up by the voluntary sector, leaving many areas uncovered. It is to be hoped that the UK and Northern Ireland "National Plan for Safeguarding Children from Commercial Sexual Exploitation" (Department of Health et al., 2001), will provide the impetus needed for more universal and targeted services for this extremely vulnerable group of young people. It should be acknowledged that the National Plan also emphasises the need for widespread preventative action by all professionals working with children. This prevention includes support for parents and the willingness to listen to, and consult with, the young people themselves.

The need for action, both to prevent sexual exploitation and to provide therapeutic services for those already involved, has also been recognised at the European level. The Council of Europe's "Commitment and Plan of Action", presented in Yokohama, recognised "the importance of establishing services for children to prevent and protect against sexual exploitation and to ensure their recovery and re-integration". This was underpinned by the more general recommendation:

> "... urge each and every country to enhance or develop a comprehensive system of state-funded child protection services, consistent with Article 19 of the UNCRC, where every family at risk receives some health and social support. Those families at risk should receive targeted services in addition to universal support".

CHILDREN NOT LIVING WITH BIRTH PARENTS

The abuse and neglect of children living away from home has been well documented (Utting, 1991, 1997; Welsh Office, 2000). It is also acknowledged that children may be subjected to ongoing abuse in foster care (Hobbs, Hobbs & Wynne, 1999; see Chapter 5). A system should be in place to allow children and staff to report possible abuse. Allegations of abuse need to be swiftly and effectively investigated and therapeutic support offered rapidly to the children involved. The need for such an approach is now acknowledged (Department of Health, 2000b).

More pertinent to the issue of prevention is the recent concern over the poor outcomes for children "looked after" (the term introduced by the Children Act for children in public care). Such outcomes do not bode well for these young people's future parenting capacities. In part, they may due to the poverty (Bebbington & Miles, 1989) and abuse and neglect experienced in their families of origin. The picture is further complicated by the movement of children in and out of care and from one placement to another. During 1994–1998, each year almost one-fifth of the children in care moved through three or more placements in a year (Department of Health, 1999). Furthermore, children aged 14–15 years entering secure accommodation had an average of eight previous care placements (Falshaw & Browne, 1997). It has long been known that frequent placement changes result in long-term difficulties, especially for abused and neglected children (Lynch & Roberts 1982), which sometimes leads to antisocial and offending behaviour (Falshaw & Browne, 1997, 1999). Indeed, Chapter 19 outlines the special assessment and treatment needs of violent young offenders, who are often incarcerated for their emotional and behavioural problems.

At the time of the Acheson Inquiry into Inequalities in Health (Acheson, 1998), 30% of homeless people had been previously in care. Indeed, 75% of young people leaving care had no educational qualifications and one in seven young women leaving care was pregnant or already a mother. While in care these vulnerable children are 10 times as likely to be excluded from school than their peers, so also being denied services linked to school attendance.

In some English local authorities, the uptake of the annual "statutory" health assessment has been as low as 25% (Butler & Payne, 1997). Not only are outcomes poor for looked-after children, but the costs are high (Polnay, Glaser & Dewhurst, 1997). Official recognition of this disastrous state of affairs has led to a major government initiative under the "Quality Protects" programme to improve the standard of care offered to looked-after children (see Chapters 11 and 16). This has seen an unprecedented effort to consult with the young people themselves about how best to meet their needs. This, on its own, will not be enough; a significant shift in attitude and commitment by community and professionals to this often excluded group of young people will be required if a real difference is to be made to their lives (Polnay & Ward, 2000).

A related government initiative (see Chapter 11) is the recent adoption reform intended to both increase the number of adoptions and speed up the process for both children looked after and for prospective adopters (Department of Health, 2002a). Currently, about 40% of looked-after children have been in care for more than 3 years (Department of Health, 2000). Adoptions of older children are more vulnerable to breakdown (Howe, 1997). To succeed, the new proposals will require considerable investment in post-adoption support, which should include easy access to Child and Adolescent Mental Health Services.

Intercountry Adoption

Knowledge from comparative studies of national and intercountry adoptions is extremely urgent, given the evidence that Romanian orphans, experiencing intercountry adoption to the UK after 6 months of age, are more likely to suffer developmental problems. Rutter et al., (2001) concludes that early institutional privation (under 6 months) is associated with attachment disorder, inattention/ overactivity and quasi-autistic behaviour under 6 years of age. The earlier the child experiences a good adoptive family, the greater the chance of optimal psychological functioning and developmental recovery. Hence, there is a higher chance of problems in families who adopt children from other countries. This is sometimes related to cultural adjustment and/or to the previous experiences of the adopted child.

Rather than economically wealthy countries creating a market for children, where children in adversity and poverty are transposed across cultures and continents, these "First World" countries would be better financially supporting the development of national state-funded health and social services (including fostering and adoption) in economically disadvantaged countries. The ideal would be home visiting during early childhood to promote positive parenting (see Chapters 8, 9 and 10).

The real problem is that countries in transition do not have the same extent of community health and social services to support parents. Neither do these parents have available free legal representation to contest the fact that their child is being considered for adoption. Hence, some of the principles of the Hague Convention (1993) on intercountry adoption will be difficult to implement. Adequate legal, social and health-care provision are required to assess the chances of children in adversity being reunited with their natural families. Otherwise, some children may be placed for adoption because there are no adequate services to rehabilitate them with their own families. This would be against the principles of the UN Convention on the Rights of Child (1989).

Indeed, WHO (1999) estimated that 56% of children in Romanian residential facilities are there because of health problems, 41% due to socioeconomic problems in the family, and only 3% are true orphans with no family. Nevertheless, there are 78 international adoption agencies registered in Romania (the majority from USA). For the year 2000, there were 3035 intercountry adoptions, which represented 70% of all adoptions, with national adoptions being 1291 (30%) for the same period (Romanian Government, March 2001). This represents an intercountry adoption rate of 1 in 2000 Romanian children, at this time. If such a rate were to continue, it could have an effect on the future population demography of the country.

The long-term goal for all countries is to reduce the number of unwanted children, child neglect and child abandonment through the provision of adequate community health and social services to protect children within society. The promotion of foster and adoption services and national adoptions are essential to reduce the necessity of intercountry adoption as an alternative to childhood institutionalisation.

The principle of "what is in the best interest of the child" should govern all decisions about a child's placement, according to the UNCRC (United Nations Convention on the Rights of the Child, 1989). Obviously, one would not recommend that a child be adopted into an abusive and/or neglectful family. Likewise, one would not recommend a child to be adopted into a country with high violent/sexual crime rates, a lack of gun control, engaged in civil conflict or war. However, assessment of host families in intercountry adoption cases is often superficial and the assessment of the host country is often neglected.

Dangers of Marketing Children on the Internet

Examples of marketing children for adoption can readily be seen on the Internet, mainly from agencies based in USA. Most "shopping for children" websites provide pictures of children waiting for adoption, accompanied by short stories about them for selection purposes. Such images and stories are known to fuel the imagination and fantasies of sex offenders who target children (Elliott, Browne & Kilcoyne, 1995; see Chapter 20). The risk of "adoption services" being used by people with paedophile tendencies, to select pretty and vulnerable children, cannot be ignored and should not be underestimated. Restricting adoption only to couples would not solve the problem, as 48% of sex offenders are, or have been, married. One-third of sex offenders are in a parental role at the time they abuse the child (Elliott, Browne & Kilcoyne, 1995; see Chapter 18). In fact, the pictures and terminology used by some adoption websites (e.g. www.adoptanangel.com) would encourage the fantasies and attraction of sex offenders (apart from the child pornography available on the Internet). Internet websites which identify children are contravening their privacy and Article 16 of the UNCRC (1989). They are placing these disadvantaged children at risk of sexual abuse. Without professionally skilled comprehensive assessments of the prospective parents' mental health, parenting capacity and social and environmental circumstances, these "customers" might easily place adopted children in danger of physical and psychological harm.

Unaccompanied Asylum-Seeking Children

In the UK, there is a small (3349 in 1999) but increasing number of unaccompanied children seeking asylum each year. They are very vulnerable, many having experienced events outside the imagination of many professionals in Western countries. They may have unmet physical and mental health needs (Lynch & Cuningham, 2000) and may be suffering feelings of extreme loss in relation to their families. All under 18 year-old unaccompanied asylum seekers have the right to be looked after, to have somewhere to live and access to education and health services (Save the Children Fund, 1999). Children under 16 are likely to be placed in foster care or a residential establishment, but 16–18 year-olds are likely to find themselves placed in hostels or bed and breakfast accommodation with adults. This exposes them to the risks of exploitation and corruption. Many authorities do not offer this age group a full needs assessment (Audit Commission, 2000). This group of young people are one of the most socially excluded. How they fill their days must be a major challenge, as they can not work, they have very little money and most will not be in education. Additionally, some will only have been given leave to remain in the UK until their eighteenth birthday, when a decision will be made about their status. Fearing that their application to be recognised as a refugee will be refused, they may "disappear" before that birthday rather than face deportation, thereby joining the ranks of those who will not register themselves or their children with services (Lynch & Gough, 2001).

Private Fostering

Children placed in private foster homes are another group who can remain hidden from service providers. There are estimated to be 10 000 children privately fostered in the UK (Department of Health, 2001). The birth parent is usually the one responsible for choosing the placement, but their access to information may be limited, especially if the child is being sent to this country from abroad or the parents themselves have just arrived in the UK to study or work. There is a danger that the child will be placed with unsuitable or even abusive carers. Many of these placements will be cross-cultural. In theory, privately fostered children are protected by the Children Act (1989) and associated regulations, but this is dependant both on notification and local councils enforcing the required level of monitoring and supervision. Probably less than half of private fostering arrangements are officially known. It is the carer who has primary responsibility for notification, but the recent Department of Health publication (2001) encourages other professionals to notify local councils if they know of a child who is privately fostered and they think the council is unaware. The legislation excludes placement with a relative, but does not define what is meant by "relative". At least one Council leaflet implies that this means a close relative, such as aunt or grandmother. However, their use of the term "auntie" might well lead to some confusion in cultures where the term is applied to any close female friend of the family.

Kinship Care

In the USA, more is known about kinship care than in the UK. The US Department of Health and Human Services (2000) prepared a report to the Congress on Kinship Foster Care. Three per cent of children in the USA were living with relatives, of whom two-thirds were in the public arena. These carers received less services, support and supervision than unrelated foster carers. In the UK there has been a recent survey of grandparents raising children (Richards, 2001). Those caring for children following a family crisis, which for some included cases of abuse and neglect involving social services, faced particular difficulties and some of these children were exhibiting educational and behavioural difficulties. Many of the grandparents reported difficulties with their own children and between their children and grandchildren. There appeared to be little support from the statutory or voluntary sectors, and the respondents conveyed a sense that grandparents in a "parenting" role are not integrated into mainstream services. Services such as health visiting, Sure Start and Parentline need to ensure that foster parents, grandparents and other kinship carers are included in their remit.

REACHING CHILDREN OF TROUBLED PARENTS

Sometimes it is a troubled parent rather than the child who is the initial focus of professional attention. The needs of the children of offenders, mentally ill parents or those misusing drugs or alcohol may not be a priority for those treating adults. Sometimes services are not aware of the parent's predicament, and in many cases services that should be accessed by the parent on behalf of the child will be avoided. Links between child maltreatment, adult offending behaviour, mental illness and substance abuse are well established (Cleaver, Unell & Aldgate, 1999; see Chapters 2, 4); often the damaged suffered is emotional and without intervention is likely to be lifelong (see Chapter 15). Guidance on drug misusers as parents has been issued (Standing Conference on Drugs Abuse, 1997) and there is greater awareness among maternity staff facilitating the early identification of babies born to drug-using mothers. However, there is a need for more joint training in child protection to involve adult mental health professionals and those working with substance abusers.

A largely hidden group of children in need are those children who are primary carers for an adult, usually a parent who is physically or mentally ill. Early small-scale studies suggested that there are at least 10 000 young carers in the UK (O'Neil, 1988; Page, 1988). Later papers urge a qualitative rather than a quantitative approach, focusing on the impact on the child's health, psychosocial development and opportunities (Aldridge & Becker, 1993a; Jenkins & Wingate, 1994) The NHS and Community Care Act (1990) required assessment of carers needs but failed to address the subject of young carers. Today, if identified, these children and families should qualify for an assessment of their needs, as laid out in the Assessment Framework for Children in Need and their Families (Department of Health et al., 2000). Once again, this will often be dependent on professionals in education and community health responding appropriately to help such children and their families to access services. As Aldridge & Becker (1993b) state, "To neglect these children . . . is not simply a matter of oversight, but arguably an abuse of their rights, dignity and childhood".

As Chapter 19 points out, the link between domestic violence and child maltreatment is now accepted (e.g. Farmer & Owen, 1995; Browne & Hamilton, 1999; Eldeson, 1999) and the short- and long-term consequences of living in a violent household are well established (Browne & Herbert, 1997; Hall & Lynch, 1998; see Chapter 13). Less appreciated is the diminished access to services, including "universal" services, experienced by children living in refuges for woman fleeing domestic violence (Webb et al., 2001). Many of these children have unmet health and development needs. Without commitment to strategic planning of children's services that proactively seeks to include them, these children and others from marginalised families are in danger of remaining victims of the inverse care law (Tudor-Hart, 1971; Webb, 1998; Lynch & Gough, 2001). This applies to access to services and to preventative interventions as well as to treatment.

Groups whose needs must be specifically addressed include the homeless, travellers, and asylum-seeking, refugee and imprisoned families. Others may miss out on universal services merely because they are on the move, perhaps because of the nature of the parent's employment. Younger children are dependent on their parents to access services on their behalf. This is something parents overwhelmed by their own problems or without an understanding of how the system works will fail to do (see Chapter 7).

CONCLUDING STATEMENT

To hold the family members responsible for all forms of child abuse and neglect assumes that caregivers have complete control and overlooks the way society functions. Adverse environmental, political and societal factors may compromise parenting capacities and abilities in any setting. On the other hand, some families will fail to parent children as expected by the community and will not make use of available services. If we are to protect children effectively, we must resist any dichotomy of approach and always be open to exploring intra- and extrafamilial influences and solutions (Onyango & Lynch 2002).

Within the UK, recent reforms to the health and social care systems may facilitate inclusive services at the local level. Both the formation of Primary Care Trusts and the joint planning and delivery of children's health and social care services could provide opportunities to do this. This will only succeed, however, if the new structures understand and fullfil their public health obligations to the whole population. A "one size fits all" approach to children's service planning will not be sufficient. In any community the vulnerable children will be a diverse group and a range of flexible and imaginative services must be available if their needs are to be met. One exciting future prospect is the active involvement of children and young people in the development and provision of such services. Support from the Children's Task Force could mean that this will become a reality (Department of Health, 2002b).

REFERENCES

Abrahams, C. & Mungall, R. (1992). *Runaways: Exploring the Myths*. London: National Children's Home Action for Children.

Acheson, D. (1998). *Independent Inquiry into Inequalities in Health*. London: The Stationery Office.

Adams, G. R. & Gulotta, T. S. (1983). *Adolescent Life Experiences*. Monterey, CA: Brooks/Cole.

Aldridge, J. & Becker, S. (1993a). Children who care—inside the world of young carers. Loughborough University: Department of Social Science.

Aldridge, J. & Becker, S. (1993b). Punishing children for caring: the hidden cost of young carers. *Children and Society*, **7**: 376–387.

Audit Commission. (2000). *Another Country*. London: Audit Commission.

Barnardo's. (1998). *Whose Daughter Next? Children Abused through Prostitution*. London: Barnardo's.

Bebbington, A. & Miles, J. (1989). Children who enter local authority care. *British Journal of Social Work*, **19**: 349–368.

Browne, K. D., and Hamilton, C. E. (1999). Police recognition of the links between spouse abuse and child abuse. *Child Management*, **4**(2), 136–147.

Browne, K. D. & Herbert, M. (1997). *Preventing Family Violence*. Chichester: Wiley.

Butler, I. & Payne, H. (1997). The health of children looked after by the local authority. *Adoption and fostering*, **21**: 28–35.

Cairns, R. B. & Cairns, B. D. (1994). *Lifelines and Risks: Pathways of Youth in Our Time*. New York: Harvester Wheatsheaf.

Cleaver, H., Unell, I. & Aldgate, J. (1999). *Children's Needs—Parenting Capacity. The Impact of Parental Mental Illness, Problem Alcohol and Drug Use, and Domestic Violence on Children's Development*. London: Stationery Office.

Department of Health. (1999). *Children Looked After at 31 March 1994 to 1998, with Three or More Placements During the Year*. London: Department of Health.

Department of Health, Home Office, Department of Education and Employment, National Assembly for Wales. (2000). *Safeguarding Children Involved in Prostitution*. London: Department of Health.

Department of Health, Home Office, National Assembly for Wales, Scottish Executive, Northern Ireland Office. (2001). *National Plan for Safeguarding Children from Commercila Sexual Exploitation*. London: Department of Health.

Department of Health, Department for Education and Employment, Home Office. (2000). *Framework for the Assessment of Children in Need and Their Families*. London: Stationary Office.

Department of Health. (2000). *Adoption—a New Approach*. London: The Stationary Office (also on Adoption Website).

Department of Health. (2001). *Private Fostering: a Cause for Concern*. London: Department of Health (see also www.doh.gov.uk/scg/privatefostering).

Department of Health. (2002a). Adoption Website. www.Doh.gov.uk/adoption.

Department of Health. (2002b). Children's Task Force Website. www.Doh.gov.uk/childrenstaskforce.

Eldeson, J. L. (1999). The overlap between child maltreatment and woman battering. *Violence against Woman* **5**: 134–154.

Elliott, M., Browne, K. D. & Kilcoyne, J. (1995). Child sexual abuse prevention: what offenders tell us. *Child Abuse and Neglect: The International Journal*, **19**(5): 579–594.

Falshaw, L. & Browne, K. D. (1997). Adverse childhood experiences and violent acts of young people in secure accommodation. *Journal of Mental Health*, **6**: 443–455.

Falshaw, L. & Browne, K. D. (1999). A young man referred to specialist secure accommodation. *Child Abuse Review*, **8**: 419–432.

Farber, E. D., McCoard, W. D., Kinast, C. & Baum-Faulkner, D. (1984). Violence in families of adolescent runaways. *Child Abuse and Neglect*, **8**: 295–299.

Farmer, E & Owen M. (1995). *Child Protection Practice; Private Risks and Public Remedies*. London: HMSO.

Finkelhor, D. (1995). The victimisation of children: a developmental perspective. *American Journal of Orthopsychiatry*, **65**(2): 177–193.

Gough, D., Li, L. & Wroblewska, A. (1992). *Services for Children with a Motor Impairment and Their Families in Scotland*. Glasgow: Public Health Research Unit.

Government's Response to *Children's Safeguards Review*. (1998). London: The Stationery Office.

Government's Response to *Lost in Care (Waterhouse Inquiry)*. (2000). *Learning the Lessons*. London: The Stationery Office.

Greene, N. B. & Esselsteyn, T. C. (1972). The beyond control girl. *Juvenile Justice*, **23**: 13–19.

Hall, D. & Lynch, M. A. (1998). Violence begins at home. Domestic strife has lifelong effects on children. *British Medical Journal*, **316**: 1551.

Hobbs, G. F., Hobbs, C. J., & Wynne, J. M. (1999). Abuse of children in foster and residential care. *Child Abuse and Neglect*, **23**: 1239–1252.

Howe D. 1997. *Patterns of Adoption*. London: Blackwell Science.

Janus, M., McCormack, A., Burgess, A. W. & Hartman, C. (1987). *Adolescent Runaways: Causes and Consequences*. Lexington, MA: Lexington Books.

Jenkins, S. & Wingate, C. (1994). Who cares for young carers? *British Medical Journal*, **308**: 733–734.

Lappin, J. & Covelman, C. (1985). Adolescent runaways: a structural family therapy perspective. In Mirkin, M. and Koman, S. (eds), *Handbook of Adolescents and Family Therapy*. New York: Gardner.

Lau, A. (1991). Cultural and ethnic perspectives on significant harm: its assessment and treatment. In Adcock, M. and White, R. (eds), *Significant Harm*. Croydon: Significant Publications.

Lynch, M. A. & Cuningham, C. (2000). Understanding the needs of young asylum seekers *Archives of Disease of Childhood*, **83**: 384–387.

Lynch, M. A. & Gough, D. (2001). Reaching all children. *British Medical Journal*, **323**: 176–177.

Lynch, M. A. & Roberts, J. (1982). *Consequences of Child Abuse*. London: Academic Press.

McCormack, A., Janus, M. & Burgess, A. W. (1986). Runaway youths and sexual victimisation: gender differences in an adolescent runaway population. *Child Abuse and Neglect*, **10**: 387–395.

Marchant, R. & Page, M. (1992). *Bridging the Gap: Child Protection Work with Children with Multiple Disabilities*. London: NSPCC.

Miller, D., Miller, D., Hoffman, F. & Duggan, R. (1980). *Runaways—Illegal aliens in Their Own Land: Implications for Service*. New York: Praeger.

Morris, J. (1999). Disabled children, child protection systems and the Children Act 1989. *Child Abuse Review*, **8**: 91–108.

Newman, C. (1989). *Young Runaways: Findings from Britain's First Safe House*. London: The Children's Society.

Nye, F. (1980). A theoretical perspective on running away. *Journal of Family Issues*, **1**: 147–151.

O'Neil, A. (1988). *Young Carers: the Tameside Research*. Manchester: Tameside Metropolitan Borough Council.

Onyango, P. & Lynch, M. A. (2002). Avoiding a dichotomy when seeking to protect children: learning from experiences in Kenya and UK. Paper to be presented at the 14th International Congress on Child Abuse and Neglect. Denver: ISPCAN.

Oosterhoorn, R. & Kendrick, K. (2001). No sign of harm: issues for disabled children. communicating about abuse. *Child Abuse Review*, **10**: 243–253.

Page, R. (1988). *Report on the Initial Survey Investigating the Number of Young Carers in Sandwell Secondary Schools*. Sandwell: Sandwell Metropolitan Borough Council.

Polnay, L., Glaser, A. W. & Dewhurst T. (1997). Children in residential care; what cost? *Archives of Disease in Childhood*, **77**: 349–395.

Polnay, L. & Ward, H. (2000). Promoting the health of looked after children. *British Medical Journal*, **320**: 661–662.

Rees, G. (1993). *Hidden Truths: Young People's Experiences of Running Away*. London: The Children's Society.

Richards, A. (2001). *Second Time Around. A Survey of Grandparents Raising their Grandchildren*. London: Family Rights Group.

Roberts, A. R. (1982). Adolescent runaways in suburbia: a new typology. *Adolescence*, **17**: 387–396.

Romanian Government (2001). *Statistics Bulletin, March and May 2001*. Bucharest: National Authority for Child Protection and Adoption.

Rutter, M., Kreppner, J. & O'Connor, T. G. (2001). Specificity and heterogeneity in children's responses to profound institutional privation. *British Journal of Psychiatry*, **179**: 97–103.

Save the Children Fund. (1999). *Seeking Asylum in the UK*. London: Save the Children Fund.

Scanlon, T. J., Tomkins, A., Lynch, M. A. & Scanlon, F. (1998). Street children in Latin America. *British Medical Journal*, **316**: 1595–1600.

Standing Conference on Drugs Abuse. (1997). *Drug-using Parents: Policy Guidelines for Interagency Working*. London: Local Government Association.

Stein, M., Rees, G. & Frost, N. (1994). *Running the Risk: Young People on the Streets of Britain Today*. London: The Children's Society.

Stiffman, A. R. (1989). Physical and sexual abuse in runaway youths. *Child Abuse and Neglect*, **13**: 417–426.

Straus, M. B. (1994). *Violence in the Lives of Adolescents*. New York: Norton and Co.

Sullivan, P. M. & Knutson J. F. (1998). The association between child maltreatment and disabilities in a hospital based epidemiological study. *Child Abuse and Neglect*, **22**: 271–288.

Sullivan, P. M. & Knutson, J. F. (2000). Maltreatment and disabilities: a population-based epidemiological study. *Child Abuse and Neglect*, **24**: 1257–1273.

Tharinger, D., Horton, C. B. & Millea, S. (1990). Sexual abuse and exploitation of children and adults with mental retardation and other handicaps. *Child Abuse and Neglect*, **14**: 301–312.

Tudor Hart, J. (1971). The inverse care law. *Lancet*, **1**: 405–412.

United Nations (1989). *Convention on the Rights of the Child.* New York: United Nations.

Utting, W. (1991). *Children in the Public Care. A Review of Residential Child Care.* London: HMSO.

Utting, W. (1997). *People Like Us. the Report of the Review of the Safeguards for Children Living away from Home.* London: HMSO.

Webb, E. (1998). Children and the inverse care law. *British Medical Journal,* **316**: 1588–1591.

Webb, E., Shankman, J., Evans, M. R., & Brooks, R. (2001). The health of children in refuges for woman victims of domestic violence; cross sectional descriptive survey. *British Medical Journal,* **323**: 210–213.

Welsh Office. (2000). *Lost in Care (Waterhouse Inquiry).* London: The Stationery Office.

Westcott, H. L. (1993). *Abuse of Children and Adults with Disabilities.* London: NSPCC.

Westcott, H. L., & Jones, D. P. H. (1999). Annotation: the abuse of disabled children. *Journal of Child Psychology and Psychiatry,* **40**: 497–506.

White, J. L. (1989). *The Troubled Adolescent.* New York: Pergamon.

World Health Organization Regional Office for Europe. (1999). *Highlights on Health in Romania.* Copenhagen: WHO.

Young, R. L., Godfrey, W., Mathews, B. & Adams, G. R. (1983). Runaways: a review of negative consequences. *Family Relations,* **32**, 275–281.

Author Index

Index compiled by Linda English

Subject Index

accidents, 189
actuarial risk prediction, 304
adolescents
  runaways, 357–8
  victims at risk of sexual offending, 280,
    283–99
  young offenders, 328–32
adoption, 270, 274, 360–2
aetiology
  child factors, 99–100, 146, 221
  community and social support, 102
  developmental context, 97–100
  ecological analysis, 95–110, 220
  evolutionary context, 103–6
  immediate context, 100–1
  parental factors, 97–9, 146
  social and cultural context, 102–3
alcohol misuse, 49, 251–2, 319–20
anti-libidinal medication, 344, 348
antisocial behaviour, 168–9, 174, 328–32
anxiety management training, 209
anxious arousal, and sexual arousal, 118–19,
  120
assessment
  distinction from therapy, 240–1
  and domestic violence, 320, 323–4, 326–7
  and family therapy, 237, 240–1
  of outcomes, 193–6
  and physical maltreatment, 42–3, 45–6
  in prevention of cycle of abuse, 290–1
  of risk see risk assessment
  of sexually abused child, 82–3
  of traumatic impact, 206–8
Assessment Orders, 320
asylum-seeking children, unaccompanied,
  359, 362
attachment, 96, 169, 199
  assessment, 207
  and cycle of abuse, 98, 221–2, 228, 293

and emotional abuse and neglect, 252,
  260–1
home-based studies, 46
insecure, 204–5, 222
repair, 260–1, 293
and sexual offending, 345
attributions
  by child, 204
  by parents, 59, 224–5, 241
autonomy of child, 59, 223–4

battered women see domestic violence
behavioural family interventions, 149, 160
behavioural problems
  adolescent antisocial behaviour, 174,
    328–32
  early-onset antisocial behaviour, 168–9
  emotional abuse and neglect and, 62, 258
  management, 158, 328–32
  parental exaggeration, 100, 146, 224
  as risk factor, 100
  sexual abuse and, 82, 205–6
behavioural rehearsal, 349
behavioural therapy, 149, 160, 331, 340
Beyond Blame Study, 30–2
biological factors, 103–6, 221
boys, at risk of sexual offending, 280,
  283–99
broken families, 131

Campbell Collaboration, 195–6
care, children in
  and domestic violence, 320, 321, 328–32
  future challenges, 357–8, 360
  national variations, 269–70
  outcomes, 273–4, 292, 360
casework, 186
checklists see instruments
Child Abuse Potential Inventory, 327

Index compiled by Linda English